Strictly Structured VAX-BASIC

SECOND EDITION

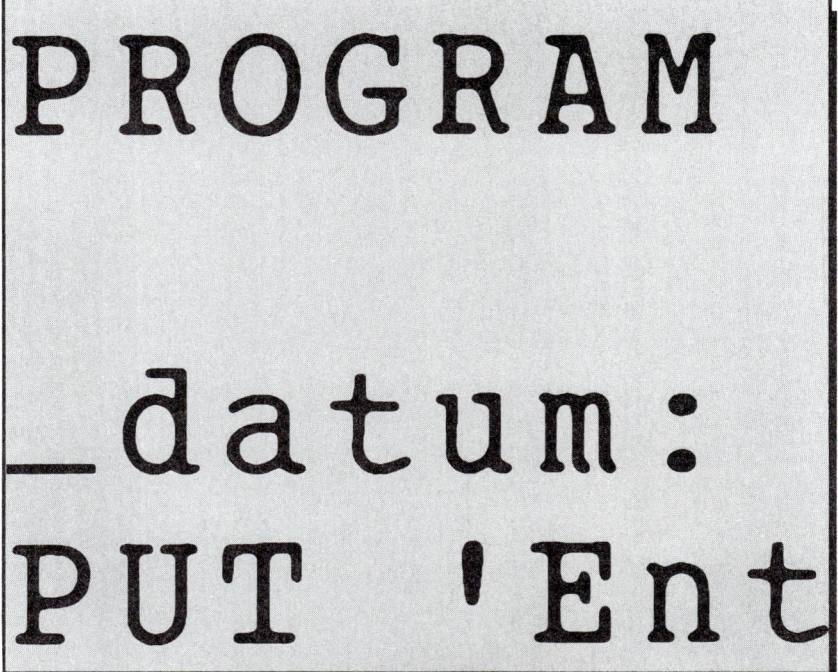

Eli Berlinger
Nassau Community College

WEST PUBLISHING COMPANY
St. Paul   New York   Los Angeles   San Francisco

PRODUCTION CREDITS

Cover art: Ilya Bolotowsky *Scarlet Diamond*, 1969 oil on canvas 48" × 48". Reprinted by permission of Albright-Knox art gallery; Buffalo, New York. Gift of Seymour H. Knox, 1969.
Copyediting: Lorretta Palagi
Composition: BI-COMP, Incorporated
Illustrations: Rolin Graphics
Text design: David Farr, *Imagesmythe Inc.*

COPYRIGHT © 1988 By WEST PUBLISHING COMPANY
50 W. Kellogg Boulevard
P.O. Box 64526
St. Paul, MN 55164-1003
All rights reserved
Printed in the United States of America

Library of Congress Cataloging-in-Publication Data

Berlinger, Eli.
   Strictly structured VAX-BASIC.
   Includes index.
  1. VAX computers—Programming. 2. BASIC (Computer program language) 3. Structured programming. I. Title.
QA76.8.V32B47 1988   005.2'45   87-34509
ISBN 0-314-64977-8

```
RUNNH
Enter a
Enter a
Enter a
```

Strictly Structured VAX-BASIC

To
Batya and David Productions
and
Lisa and Hagai Productions
and
All future productions

Contents

Preface xv

Overture | Programming Environment 1

ENVIRONMENTS 2
PROGRAMMING ENVIRONMENTS 3
THE VMS ENVIRONMENT 3
    Login 3
    Changing Your Password 4
    Logging Out 5
FILE MANAGEMENT IN VMS 5
    Getting a Directory Listing 5
    Deleting a File 6
    Renaming a File 7
    Purging Old Files 7
    Getting Help in VMS 8
    Changing to Basic 8
THE BASIC ENVIRONMENT 8
    Returning to VMS 9
    Creating a Program 9
    Retrieving an Old Program 10
    Saving a Program 10
    Renaming a Program 10
    Running a Program 11
    Listing a Program 11
    Deleting a Line 12
    Inserting a Line 12
    Getting Help in Basic 13
    Editing a Line 13
THE EDITOR ENVIRONMENT 14
    Leaving the Editor 14
    Getting Help in the Editor Environment 15
    Entering Change Mode 15
THE CHANGE MODE OF THE EDITOR 15
    Leaving the Change Mode 15
    Change Mode Features 15
    Getting Help in the Change Mode 16
SUMMARY 16

1 | Computers 19

1.1 BLOCK DIAGRAM OF A COMPUTER 20
1.2 INPUT DEVICES 20
1.3 OUTPUT DEVICES 21
1.4 THE ARITHMETIC LOGIC UNIT (ALU) 22
1.5 THE CONTROL UNIT 22
1.6 MEMORY 22
1.7 SYMBOLIC ADDRESSES 23
   Implicit and Explicit Declarations 23
   REAL or Floating Point Type 24
   INTEGER Type 25
   STRING Type 25
   DECIMAL Type 26
SUMMARY 27

ENRICHMENT TOPIC 1 | Additional Explicit Types 30

2 | Input/Output (I/O) 31

2.1 THE DECLARE STATEMENT 32
2.2 THE INPUT INSTRUCTION 32
2.3 THE PRINT INSTRUCTION 34
   Print Formatting 35
2.4 THE END STATEMENT 37
2.5 REMARKS AND COMMENTS 38
2.6 THE READ AND DATA STATEMENTS 40
SUMMARY 42

3 | Assignment Statements 45

3.1 ARITHMETIC OPERATIONS 46
3.2 HIERARCHY 46
3.3 PARENTHESES 46
3.4 ASSIGNMENT OPERATOR 47
3.5 SEQUENCES 48
3.6 MULTI-STATEMENT LINES 50
3.7 MULTI-LINE STATEMENTS 51
3.8 FLOW CHARTS (OPTIONAL TOPIC) 57
SUMMARY 59

4 | Program Design and Modularization—GOSUB 65

4.1 STRUCTURED PROGRAMMING 66
4.2 TOP-DOWN ANALYSIS (STEPWISE DECOMPOSITION) 66
4.3 MODULARITY 69
4.4 SUBROUTINES 70
   Labels 70

The GOSUB Statement 70
The RETURN Statement 71
General Form of GOSUB Subroutines 72
4.5 THE EXIT PROGRAM STATEMENT 73
4.6 FLOW CHARTS (OPTIONAL TOPIC) 82
SUMMARY 84

ENRICHMENT TOPIC

4 | VAX-BASIC Subprograms 89

ARGUMENTS AND PARAMETERS 89
Arguments 90
Parameters 90

5 | Loops 95

5.1 ENUMERATIVE LOOPS 96
5.2 SUMMING 98
5.3 CONTROLLED LOOPS 102
Comparison or Relational Operators 102
Logical or Boolean Operators 103
The WHILE Loop 104
Counting 105
The UNTIL Loop 108
5.4 THE RANDOM NUMBER GENERATOR 109
The RANDOMIZE Statement 109
Scaling the Random Number Generator 110
Shifting the Range of Random Numbers 110
Random Integers 111
5.5 PRIMING READ 116
5.6 FLOW CHARTS (OPTIONAL TOPIC) 121
SUMMARY 122

6 | Conditional Statements 129

6.1 IF-THEN-END-IF 130
6.2 IF-THEN-ELSE-IF 137
Nesting of IF-THEN-ELSE-IF 141
6.3 SELECT-CASE STATEMENT 150
6.4 MENUS AND MENU-DRIVEN SOFTWARE 152
6.5 FLOW CHARTS (OPTIONAL TOPIC) 156
SUMMARY 160

PROGRAMMING TOOL

A | Debugging 168

A.1 TEMPORARY PRINT STATEMENTS 169
Conditional Temporary PRINT Statements 170
A.2 STOP, CONTINUE, AND THE IMMEDIATE MODE 170
A.3 ⟨CONTROL⟩/C AND THE ERL VARIABLE 178
SUMMARY 179

7 One-Dimensional Arrays 185

7.1 ARRAYS 186
7.2 SUBSCRIPTS 186
7.3 DIMENSIONING ARRAYS WITH THE DECLARE STATEMENT 187
7.4 ASSIGNMENT STATEMENTS 188
7.5 READING VALUES INTO AN ARRAY 189
  Input Using Enumerative Loops 189
  Input Using Controlled Loops 189
7.6 PRINTING ARRAYS 191
7.7 CALCULATIONS USING LOOPS 191
7.8 SORTING ONE-DIMENSIONAL ARRAYS 195
  Sorting String Arrays 200
7.9 ASSOCIATED ARRAYS 201
SUMMARY 209

ENRICHMENT TOPIC

7 Variable Dimensioning and MAT Statements 216

VARIABLE DIMENSIONING 216
MAT STATEMENTS 216
  Input Using MAT INPUT 217
  The NUM Variable 217
  Input Using MAT READ 219
  Output Using MAT PRINT 220
  MAT Assignment Statements 222
ARRAYS AS ARGUMENTS 222

8 Terminal-Format Files 225

8.1 FILE TERMINOLOGY 226
8.2 THE OPEN STATEMENT 227
8.3 INPUT/OUTPUT WITH FILES 231
8.4 THE CLOSE STATEMENT 232
8.5 SETTING THE MARGINS 233
8.6 EXAMPLES 233
SUMMARY 244

ENRICHMENT TOPIC

8 MAT File Statement 250

PROGRAMMING TOOL

B Error Trapping 251

B.1 ERROR TRAPS—ON ERROR GO TO 252
B.2 SOME USEFUL BUILT-IN VARIABLES 252
  ERR Built-in Variable 253
  ERL Built-in Variable 253
  ERT$ Built-in Function 253
B.3 SEVERITY OF ERRORS 253

B.4 THE RESUME STATEMENT 254
   RESUME Without Line Number 254
   RESUME With Line Number 255
B.5 RETURNING ERRORS TO THE SYSTEM 255
B.6 EXAMPLES 255
   Trapping the End-Of-File Conditions 255
B.7 ERROR HANDLER CRITERIA 258

ENRICHMENT TOPIC B | **Error Trapping in Subprograms 259**
ON ERROR GO BACK 259
   The ERN$ Built-in Variable 259

9 | **String Processing 263**
9.1 THE LINPUT INSTRUCTION 264
9.2 COMBINING STRINGS—CONCATENATION 264
9.3 THE LENGTH FUNCTION—LEN 265
9.4 THE SEG$ FUNCTION 265
9.5 SEARCHING FOR A SUBSTRING—THE POS FUNCTION 266
9.6 EDITING STRINGS—THE EDIT$ FUNCTION 273
9.7 THE VAL FUNCTION 275
9.8 COMPARING STRINGS 277
SUMMARY 288

10 | **Two-Dimensional Arrays 295**
10.1 ROWS, COLUMNS, AND DIMENSIONING 296
10.2 READING A TWO-DIMENSIONAL ARRAY 297
   Entering Individual Elements 297
   Using a Nest of Loops 297
10.3 PRINTING ARRAYS 298
10.4 CALCULATING WITH ARRAYS 299
SUMMARY 306

ENRICHMENT TOPIC 10 | **More On Arrays 312**
VARIABLE DIMENSIONING 312
PASSING ARRAYS TO SUBPROGRAMS 312
ARRAYS OF HIGHER DIMENSIONS 313
MAT INSTRUCTIONS 313
   Using MAT INPUT and MAT READ 313
   MAT INPUT 314
   MAT INPUT # 315
   MAT LINPUT 315
   MAT LINPUT # 316
   MAT READ 316
NUM AND NUMZ BUILT-IN VARIABLES 316
USING MAT PRINT 317

11 | Print Using 319

11.1 THE PRINT USING INSTRUCTION 320
11.2 FORMATTING CHARACTERS 321
  Quotation Mark—' 321
  Left Justify—'L 321
  Right Justify—'R 322
  Center Justify—'C 323
  Extended Field—'E 323
  Numeric Field—# 324
  Decimal Point—. 325
  Comma—, 325
  Floating Dollar Sign—$$ 326
  Asterisk File—** 327
  Other Editing Characters 327
    MATCHING HEADS WITH DATA LINES 328
      Other Formats 330
    PRINT USING FOR TERMINAL-FORMAT FILES 330
    SUMMARY 330

12 | Relative Files 335

12.1 BASIC CONCEPTS OF RELATIVE FIELDS 336
12.2 DEFINING A PROGRAM BUFFER—THE MAP STATEMENT 336
  Defining String Length 337
12.3 OPENING A FILE—THE OPEN STATEMENT 338
12.4 READING RELATIVE FILES—THE GET STATEMENT 338
12.5 THE PUT STATEMENT 341
12.6 THE UPDATE STATEMENT 342
SUMMARY 349

13 | BASIC Built-in Functions 357

13.1 DEFINING THE BUILT-IN FUNCTION 358
  Quick Reference 358
13.2 MATHEMATICAL FUNCTIONS 359
13.3 PRINT FUNCTION 361
13.4 STRING FUNCTIONS 361
13.5 MATRIX FUNCTIONS 364
13.6 SYSTEM FUNCTIONS 365
13.6 PREDEFINED CONSTANTS 366
SUMMARY 374

14 | User-Defined Functions 377

14.1 ONE-LINE FUNCTIONS 378
14.2 ARGUMENTS AND PARAMETERS 379
14.3 USING GLOBAL VARIABLES 385

14.4 MULTI-LINE FUNCTIONS 388
  The DECLARE FUNCTION Statement 388
  Returning a Result from a MultiLine Function 389
14.5 RULES GOVERNING FUNCTIONS 392
  Function Name 392
  Parameters and Arguments 393
  Invoking a Function 394
14.6 SIDE EFFECTS 395
14.7 FLOW CHARTS 398
SUMMARY 399

ENRICHMENT TOPIC 14 | External Functions 406

DEFINING EXTERNAL FUNCTIONS 406
THE EXTERNAL STATEMENT 408
  Invoking an External Function 408
THE EXIT FUNCTION STATEMENT 410
  Error Trapping in External Functions 411

PROGRAMMING TOOL C | The GOTO 412

C.1 UNCONDITIONAL GOTO 413
C.2 CONDITIONAL GOTO 413
C.3 ARGUMENT AGAINST GOTOs 414
SUMMARY 415

A1 | Reserved Words 417

A2 | Error Messages 421

A3 | ASCII Codes 425

A4 | Solutions to Selected Exercises 429

Preface

This book is intended to be used in a first computer course for students with access to a VAX-11 computer. It can be used by students in all disciplines—those in computer and computer-related fields, those in scientific or engineering fields, those in technical fields, and those in the Arts. Exercises are given at many levels. Most require a minimal mathematics background, but some require a higher degree of mathematical sophistication.

The chapters are organized in a modular fashion. They may be taught in sequence as presented in the text, or they may be presented in a different order to suit the needs of the instructor. In addition, some chapters may be left out entirely; there is more material available than would normally be covered in one semester.

The textbook contains a number of Programming Tools. These contain relatively brief ancillary material which can be easily taught earlier or later than their placement in the text. They may even be omitted entirely, if desired. For example, Programming Tool A following chapter 6 teaches debugging techniques. However, these can be taught prior to chapter 6. Programming Tool B following chapter 8, on error trapping, may be taught in conjunction with chapter 8, Files, or it may be omitted entirely. It may also be presented earlier. It has been placed where it is to facilitate those who wish to trap the end-of-file condition instead of relying on a sentinel record.

Chapter 4 contains the essential concepts of structured programs, modularity, and style. This chapter is preceded by chapters on I/O and assignment statements. Therefore, by chapter 4, the student will already have written a number of programs. Some instructors may wish to teach this chapter before chapter 2; the modular style in which the text has been written will accommodate this and other variations.

Chapter 8 teaches the use of terminal files. In my classes, I frequently spend about 20 or 30 minutes as early as chapter 6 teaching students how to read a terminal-format file. All that is needed is the OPEN, INPUT, and CLOSE statements. I then create data files for my students to use as input to their programs. The students enjoy writing programs for which they do not have to create data themselves, and they get a feeling of accomplishment when they successfully access my file. This is particularly effective when a loop contains input instructions. A file I create can contain more data than students normally like to enter at the terminal. DATA statements are not as effective as data from a file. The students also get greater satisfaction.

The following chapters will generally be enough for a one-semester introductory course.

Overture
Chapters 1 through 6
Debugging
Chapter 7
Parts of chapter 8 (see above)
Chapters 9 and 10
Chapter 13

Some of these chapters could be left out and, perhaps, replaced by others. Two-dimensional arrays may not be required in all curricula, while inclusion of PRINT USING might be very important. These matters must be left to the individual instructor.

Some chapters also contain enrichment topics. These are entirely optional and the remaining chapters do not use the material contained in these sections (except in other enrichment topics sections). Included in these sections are features of VAX-BASIC that are not essential to the concept of programming, but which may be useful for the better student. Some of the subjects covered are additional data types, and external subprograms and functions.

There are four types of exercises at the end of each chapter. The first are general review questions that test the student's grasp of the elementary concepts contained in the chapter. Next, there are a number of syntax exercises. Their purpose is to make the student aware of the precise manner a statement should be written. They also point out some of the common errors students are prone to make.

The third and fourth categories of exercises are intertwined. They are the programming exercises. Many of these are multiple-part questions. All but the last part are short exercises, requiring the student to write statements or subroutines related to new material contained in the chapter. These can be assigned as homework problems.

The last part of each multi-part question, and all single-part questions, are complete programming projects. This last part is related to the material of the previous parts. However, the student must now include all instructions needed to run a program, including I/O, as well as material learned in previous chapters. These exercises are intended to be run on a VAX machine and submitted to the instructor for grading. In some cases, an exercise is begun in one chapter, and then increased in complexity as new material is added in succeeding chapters. Getting the student to write complete programs is an integral part of the learning process.

There are many people who are responsible for the production of this book. First is Pat Fitzgerald, who worked with me on the initial stages of the book. Next, there is the entire publishing team at West including Nancy Hill-Whilton, developmental editor; Tamborah Moore, production editor; and Lorretta Palagi, copy editor. They have been extremely supportive, and have been very effective in getting this book published in a timely manner. Then, there are the reviewers who worked with an early manuscript version. Some of them went well beyond their reviewing duties by making numerous comments, remarks, suggestions, and corrections. They were so useful that I have incorporated almost all of their suggestions in the final text. In fact, it was at the reviewers' request that one chapter and two

Programming Tools were added to the manuscript. I owe them all a great deal. They are:

Elizabeth A. Hope
Hillsborough Community College

Jan H. Bruell
University of Texas at Austin

Mary Allyn Webster
University of Florida

J. Nicholas Buehler
Merrimack College

Vivek Shah
Southwest Texas State University

Grace C. N. Yeung
California State University at Fresno

Kathryn L. Plunkett
University of Richmond

John M. Plunkett
University of Richmond

Edward Pudlo
DePaul University

Thanks are due also to Hofstra University in Hempstead, and to Mike Goldberg, manager of computer operations, for making their VAX-11 computer available to me. Without their assistance, none of the programs in this book would have been debugged—and none of them would have worked. Any errors now remaining in the programs must be blamed on Murphy. (If your name is Murphy, I did not mean you; it was the other Murphy.)

Of course, thanks are also due to my family for putting up with me during this production. My wife, especially, had to shoulder an extra burden preparing for our son David's wedding. This occasion took place right in the middle of final manuscript preparation and copy editing. She managed to deal with all the myriad of things that need dealing with at such a time, and did them very well. Thank you, Sandy.

And thank you all.

Strictly Structured VAX-BASIC

Overture: Programming Environment

Outline
Environments
Programming Environments
The VMS Environment
File Management in VMS
The Basic Environment
The Editor Environment
The Change Mode of the Editor
Summary

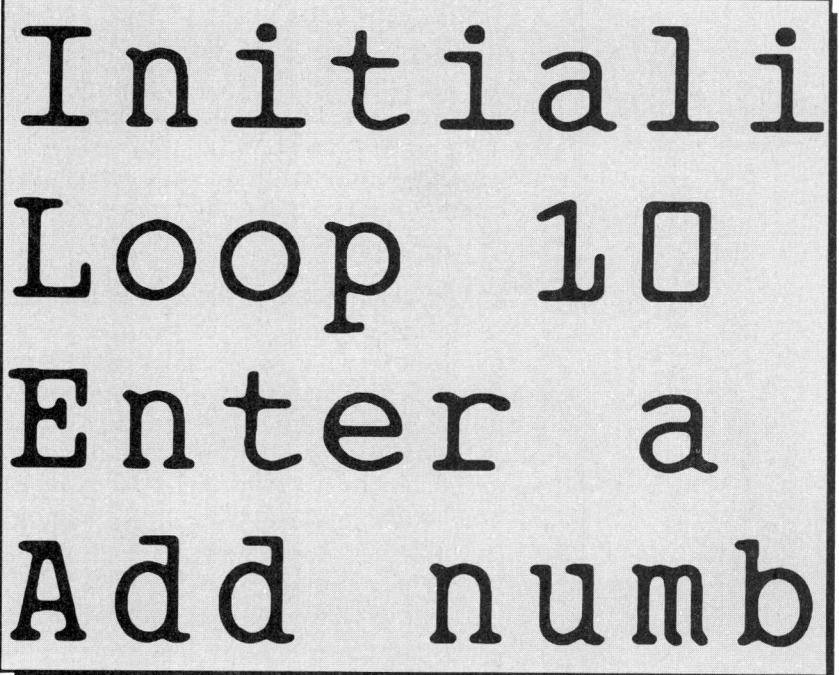

Introduction In this "overture," you will learn of the programming environment in which you will be working. You will learn the various commands that let you create, modify, and delete programs. This will prepare you for succeeding chapters that presuppose this knowledge.

ENVIRONMENTS

It is the year 2251. In a far-away galaxy, circling a medium-sized sun, is the Pleasure Planet. On it, in its main city of Kraxtl, is a huge building. Every floor of this building is devoted to games from around the galaxies. There is poker and blackjack from Earth, markel and praxle from Kryplor, frnkxtl and picxtge from Trxtken. A truly intergalactic hodgepodge.

When you enter the building, you see a tremendous lobby. All around you are screens showing the activity on the floors above. Above each screen is the name of the game being played. Next to each screen is a small book containing the rules of the game. You are at liberty to watch all the screens until you finally decide which game you would like to play.

You watch for a while and, being fairly conservative, you decide to play blackjack. From previous trips, you know that this game is played on the fourteenth floor. As you enter the elevator, you say to the robot elevator operator, "14, please."

The robot says, "I am not programmed to accept that response. Which game do you wish to play?"

"Now look, you miserable pile of tin. Take me to 14 before I turn you into a hunk of scrap metal," you respond.

"I am not programmed to accept that response. Which game do you wish to play?"

"BLACKJACK!" you bellow.

"Yes sir, that will be on the fourteenth floor. Have a nice day."

You wonder what the penalty is for murdering a robot, but content yourself with glaring ferociously. The robot says nothing.

You get off when the elevator stops and find yourself in a small lobby. Ahead of you is a long hallway with doors all along the corridor. Near the center of the lobby is a robot. At the left side of the lobby, along the wall, is a cashier's booth. With foreboding, you approach the robot. It speaks: "What will be the largest bet you are liable to place, sir?"

You answer: "Oh, about a sawbuck."

"I am not programmed to accept that response. What is your maximum bet?"

"Ten bucks, you Neanderthal numskull!"

"I am not programmed to accept that response. What is your maximum bet?"

"TEN DOLLARS, PEABRAIN!"

"Ten dollars. That will be room 7, down the hall to your left, sir. Please convert your money to chips at the cashier before you play. Have a nice day."

Room 7 is a brightly lit room. There are hundreds of people at various tables. The room is abuzz with activity. You sit down at a table. There is a robot dealing. "Which chip do you wish to bet, sir?"

"One dollar," you reply.

"I am not programmed to accept that response. Which chip do you wish to bet, sir?"

Giving up, you reply meekly, "A white chip." And the game progresses.

After a while, you begin to learn the responses the robot is willing to accept, and wind up having a very good time. In fact, after three hours of play, you are ahead $13 (3 white and 2 red chips), and decide to call it a night.

PROGRAMMING ENVIRONMENTS

What does the above have to do with programming? Each robot is in a different situation and will respond to a specific set of commands. It will not respond to words or commands that are not part of its vocabulary. The place the robot is in and the set of commands to which it will respond are called its *environment*. Each robot was in a different environment and was limited to responding only to the words for which it had been programmed.

So too with computers. As we shall see, we will be working in different environments within the VAX computer. Each environment has a different set of commands that will allow us to do different things. Using the wrong command in an environment will, at best, be ignored with a warning message. At worst, the environment will accept the command, but will interpret it differently from the way we intended. We will have to learn something about these environments before we can do anything useful on the machine (see Figure OV-1).

Figure OV-1 Environments

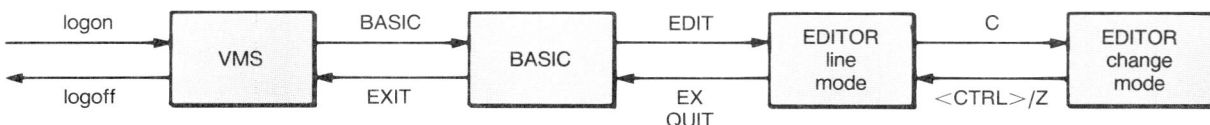

THE VMS ENVIRONMENT

NOTE! | The commands throughout this chapter are shown in upper case. However, either upper or lower case, or a combination of both, may be used. This is true for all environments—not only VMS.

Login

The process of getting connected to a computer is known as the **login**, or **logon**, procedure. You must first have a user ID (identification), and you must be given the password that lets you complete the login procedure.

Turn on the terminal. The switch is usually at the back or side of the CRT (cathode-ray tube) screen. After a short while, you will see the cursor. This will be an underline or a small rectangle. If you see nothing except the cursor, press the `<Return>` key. Eventually, you will see a prompt on the screen such as:

```
Username:
```

Enter your user ID and press `<Return>`. As you type, it is possible that you will not see the user ID appear at the screen. DON'T PANIC! The system is protecting your account by keeping others from looking over your shoulder and reading your ID. It is receiving everything you type, however. Just keep going.

After you have entered your user ID, the computer will prompt:

```
Password:
```

Type your password at the keyboard, then press <Return>. YOUR PASSWORD WILL NEVER BE ECHOED ON THE SCREEN. This is for your protection. You should never let others know your password, since this would give them access to all the files (data) you will be creating. It would be like giving someone a key to your house—an open invitation to disaster.

If you did something wrong, the computer will again ask for your user ID and password. If you have trouble a second time, ask for assistance from the lab personnel. That is why they are there.

If you do everything correctly, you will receive a welcome message, then see a dollar sign ($) followed by the cursor at the beginning of the last line on the screen. This is the prompt you will see whenever you are in the VMS (virtual memory system) environment. VMS is an operating system that acts as an **interface** (go-between) between you and the computer. (There are other operating systems used on the VAX-11, but VMS is the most popular, and is the one we will assume.)

In the VMS environment, there are various commands that let you manipulate the files in your account, let you change your password, and let you change to another environment. First let us learn how to change your password. You should do this the first time you log into your account. Initially, everyone probably has the same password. That affords no protection at all.

Changing Your Password

To change your password, type SET PASS and press the <Return> key. The prompt

```
Old password:
```

indicates that you should enter your old password. The computer wants to make sure this is your account and that some passer-by is not merely playing a trick on you. After you type in your old password, which will not appear on the screen, you will be prompted to type in a new one with the prompt

```
New password:
```

Type in the password that you wish to use the next time you log on. You will now be prompted to type it in again:

```
Verification:
```

That is to make sure that you really know what your password is, and have not made some typing error. If all goes well, you will see a message on the screen indicating that the password is changed, and the $ prompt will indicate that the computer is awaiting your next command.

NOTE! | **During the entire password-changing procedure, none of the passwords will be shown on the screen. However, all keystrokes you make will be received by the computer. Just type and have faith!**

Once you have changed your password, be sure to remember what it is! When you next log onto the computer, you will have to use it, instead of the original one.

You can change your password as often as you like. In most cases, once a month should be sufficient to protect your account. Change it more frequently if you have reason to believe someone may have seen it.

Logging Out

Disconnecting yourself from the computer is called *logging out* or *logging off*. When you see the $ prompt, type LOG at the terminal. You will receive a message that you have been disconnected. It is now safe to leave your terminal.

CAUTION! **ALWAYS BE SURE YOU HAVE LOGGED OUT BEFORE YOU LEAVE YOUR TERMINAL!**

FILE MANAGEMENT IN VMS

While you are in the VMS environment, you can perform various file management operations. You can look at a directory of the files in your account, you can delete files, you can rename files. You can also get rid of outdated versions of your files. This last will become very important to you as your account starts to fill up and you need room to save more files.

Getting a Directory Listing

Whenever you write a program (a list of instructions for the computer), which is what you will be doing in this course, you will save the program in what is called a **file.** Each program you save will have a different name. A listing of all file names is called a **directory listing.** Several different listing options are available.

Full directory listing: To get a listing of all files in your account, type

```
DIR
```

while you are in the VMS operating system environment. A listing of all your files will appear on the screen. Each file has the following format:

```
name.type;version
```

Example:

```
PROG1.BAS;1
```

Name is the name you give your file, in this case, `PROG1`. The name may be up to nine characters long.

Type is an extension to the name (maximum of three characters), a sort of last name for the file. In many cases, this extension tells what type of file it is. A BASIC file usually has the extension BAS, a FORTRAN file would have FTN or FOR, a data file (one that contains data that can be used by a program) usually has the file type DAT, while a text file that is meant to be read will usually have the file type DOC, for document.

Version is the version number of the file. Suppose that a file with the name `PROG1.BAS` already exists, and another file with the same name is now created. VMS saves *both* files. The older one is saved as version 1, and the newer as version 2. In a directory listing, both would appear, with different version numbers:

```
PROG1.BAS;2        PROG1.BAS;1
```

The newer version, with the higher version number, is listed first.

Partial directory listing: To get a listing of only certain files in your account, you can add a "mask" to the DIR instruction. You will then get a listing of only those files that fit the mask. For example,

```
DIR PROG1
```

will give you a listing of all files whose name is `PROG1`, including any extension and any version. Therefore, you might see a listing such as:

```
PROG1.BAS;3    PROG1.BAS;2    PROG1.BAS;1    PROG1.DAT;2
PROG1.DAT;1    PROG1.FTN;1
```

As another example, you could request a listing of all your BASIC files with the command

```
DIR *.BAS
```

A typical listing would be:

```
PROG1.BAS;3    PROG1.BAS;2    PROG1.BAS;1    PROG2.BAS;2
PROG2.BAS;1    PROG3.BAS;1
```

The asterisk, *, is called a **wild card.** It refers to all files with any given name. Similarly,

```
DIR PR*.*
```

lists every file whose name begins with the letters PR, and which has any extension.

Deleting a File

To delete a file, the DEL command can be used. This command can delete a single file, or the wild card, *, can be used to delete all files that match the given mask. The DEL command requires that all three parts of the name be specified, including name, type, and version. Examples are:

```
DEL PROG1.BAS;2
DEL PROG1.BAS;*
DEL PROG1.*;1
DEL PROG1.*;*
DEL PR*.BAS;*
```

The first example will cause the second version of `PROG1.BAS` to be deleted. The second example shows how to delete all versions of `PROG1.BAS`. The third example causes the first version of all files named `PROG1`, with any extension, to be deleted. The fourth example deletes all versions of files named `PROG1`, regardless of the extension. The fifth example causes all versions of all programs whose names begin with the letters `PR`, and whose extension is `BAS`, to be deleted.

CAUTION!   **Be careful when you use wild cards. Once a file has been deleted, it is irretrievably lost.**

Renaming a File

You can change the name of a file by using the RENAME command. The easiest way to use it is to type

```
RENAME
```

at the terminal. You will be prompted for the name of the file you wish to rename. You may include a version number; if you do not, the latest version will be renamed. After you enter the file to be renamed, you will be asked to supply the new name. After the file has been renamed, you can check the result by getting a directory listing.

Purging Old Files

After you have been working at the computer for a few days, you may find your account filling up with old versions of programs you no longer need. This can be serious, as you may have a limit on the number of files you can store in your account at any one time. Getting rid of old versions of a file is called **purging.** You may purge all files at one time, or a selected set of files. If you type

```
PURGE
```

then all files in your account are purged, and only the latest version of each file is kept. If you type

```
PURGE PROG1.BAS
```

then all versions of that program are deleted except the latest. If you type

```
PURGE PROG1
```

or

```
PURGE PROG1.*
```

then all files whose name is PROG1, whatever the extension, are purged, in each case retaining the latest version of each file.

After purging, a directory listing will show you the version number of each file that was retained.

Getting Help in VMS

You can get on-line help for any VMS command by typing `HELP`, either alone or followed by a command, when you see the $ VMS prompt. If you type `HELP` alone, then you will be given a list of topics for which help is available. After the list, you will see the prompt `Topic?`

If you type `HELP` followed by a command, such as `HELP DIR`, you will be given help for that command without first seeing the list of topics. You may also be given a list of subtopics for which help is available.

To get out of the help facility, keep pressing the `<Return>` key until the $ prompt appears.

Changing to BASIC

The VMS environment is like the lobby of the game building on the Pleasure Planet. From here, we can go to other environments: FORTRAN, COBOL, ASM, and others. We need the BASIC environment. To get there, type

```
BASIC
```

at the $ prompt. You will now be in a new environment. On the screen, you will see a message such as `BASIC 3.0` (this is the version of BASIC installed on your system), the word `Ready` followed on another line by the prompt `>`. This "greater than" symbol is the prompt you will see whenever the BASIC environment is ready to accept a command. Of course, the commands you may use must be valid in this environment. They are different from the commands you learned about in the VMS environment.

THE BASIC ENVIRONMENT

The BASIC environment allows you to create, modify, test, and debug programs. It also allows you to save programs as files in your account and to retrieve such programs.

Returning to VMS

Before we examine the BASIC environment, let us learn how to leave it. It is always good to plan our escape route. To leave the BASIC environment and return to the VMS environment, type:

EXIT

One of two things may happen. You might see the $ prompt again, telling you that you are back in VMS. Or, you could see a message stating that you have unsaved changes in your program. You are also told to type EXIT or CTRL/Z to exit. The > prompt tells you that you are still in BASIC. All of this means that you have made changes to the program on which you were working and have not saved these changes. You may save these changes (see the REPLACE instruction below). When you type EXIT again (or press the <Control> key while also pressing Z), you will leave BASIC.

Creating a Program

To create a program, you first clear from your working area, called **memory** by DEC (Digital Equipment Corporation), any program that may already be there, then give your new program a name. You do this with the NEW command. For example,

NEW PROG1

clears memory and names the program you are about to create PROG1. The name you choose may be up to nine characters long. You may not include an extension (type). (The NEW command will ignore any extension you supply and default to BAS. The OLD and REPLACE commands, explained below, let you change to another extension should you desire to do so.) If you type only NEW but do not supply a name, you will be prompted to supply one. If you do not, but simply press <Return>, then BASIC will call the program NONAME, as if you had typed NEW NONAME. You do not usually want to do this.

After you have cleared your working storage, or memory, and named your program, you may enter the program itself. For example, here is a simple program you may type for practice. You need not understand what it means or what it does, but type it just as it appears.

```
10  ! Program to print 10 numbers
20     DECLARE INTEGER I
30     FOR I = 1 TO 10
40        PRINT I;
50     NEXT I
60  END
```

This program is now in your working storage, but not saved in your account. If you were to log off, the program would be lost. You will learn how to save your program shortly.

Retrieving an Old Program

You may wish to work on a program you had saved previously. This program will be in a file in your account. To bring the program into your working storage, use the OLD command. For instance, the command

```
OLD PROG1
```

would retrieve the program `PROG1.BAS`, where `BAS` is the default extension. You can also supply an extension, as in `OLD PROG1.V2`. In that case, the extension you supply will be used.

If you type `OLD` without supplying a file name, you will be prompted to enter one.

Saving a Program

To save a program that is in your working storage, type

```
REPLACE
```

The program will be saved using the name you supplied in the NEW or OLD command. If the program was retrieved with OLD and an extension was supplied, then a new version of the program with this extension is created. If no extension was given, or if the program was created with NEW, then the extension BAS will be added by default. Therefore, if you started your session with `NEW PROG1`, the REPLACE command will create the file `PROG1.BAS` in your account. If you wish, you may supply your own extension:

```
REPLACE PROG1.V2
```

Each time you REPLACE a program with a given name, a new version is created in your account. The version number is shown in the message that appears at the terminal after you issue the command. To purge the old versions, you must leave BASIC and get back to the VMS environment.

Another command you can use to save a program is SAVE. This command always saves a program with the extension .BAS, even if you supplied another extension in the OLD command. The command is typed:

```
SAVE
```

Renaming a Program

It may happen that you forgot to type NEW when you started a new program. BASIC automatically names it `NONAME`. If you were to REPLACE the program, it would be saved as `NONAME.BAS`. This is undesirable.

CAUTION!  **DO NOT ISSUE THE NEW COMMAND AFTER YOU HAVE TYPED YOUR PROGRAM! The computer's memory will be cleared, and your program will be lost. You do not want to retype it, especially if it is a long program.**

You can rename the program in your working storage by using the RENAME command, and supplying a new program name. For example:

```
RENAME SALARIES
```

The program in memory will be renamed `SALARIES`. It is not saved, however. To save it, issue the REPLACE command.

Notice that the RENAME command in this environment is different from the RENAME command in the VMS environment. The command here only renames a program in memory; it does not affect the saved file in your account. The VMS command renames a file already saved in your account.

Running a Program

Running a program means causing the computer to execute, or carry out, the instructions in the program. The RUN command is used. After the program is in memory, because of the NEW or OLD commands, you may run it by typing

```
RUN
```

or

```
RUNNH
```

If you type `RUN`, then BASIC will print the name of the program, the date, and various other information before executing the program. If, instead, you type `RUNNH`, then this preliminary information will not be printed; the program will run immediately. (RUNNH stands for <u>RUN</u> with <u>N</u>o <u>H</u>eader.)

After either command, the program will execute. When it is finished, you will see `Ready` and the > prompt again, indicating that BASIC is awaiting your next command.

Listing a Program

After a program has been entered into memory, you may wish to look at it. The LIST command is used. It can be used several ways. Examples are:

```
LIST
LIST 20-40
LIST 20,40,50
LIST 10-30,40,60
```

In the first case, LIST, all lines in the program are listed. If the program is long, it may be more than one screen in length. To stop the listing, press the <Control> key while also pressing the S key. (We will call this <Ctrl>S in the future.) To restart the display press <Ctrl>Q. There may also be a <Scroll> key on your terminal. Press it once to stop the display. Press it again to restart it.

The second example, LIST 20-40, lists all lines from 20 to 40. This is called a **range of lines.** Several ranges may be specified as in LIST 10-40,120-170. All lines from line 10 to line 40, and all lines from line 120 to line 170 will output to the screen.

The third example, LIST 20,40,50, will list only the three lines stated. Lines 20, 40, and 50 will be shown.

The fourth example, LIST 10-30,40,60, illustrates how ranges and individual lines can be listed with one command. All lines from 10 to 30 will be listed, followed by lines 40 and 60.

The line numbers do not have to be in numerical sequence. The command LIST 90,40,50-80,10 works as you might expect it to. The lines are printed in the order specified.

Deleting a Line

Sometimes we find it necessary to delete a line from a program. This is easily accomplished. Type the line number followed by a <Return>. The line is deleted. For example, to delete line 60, which has the END statement, from the program you typed earlier, type 60<Return>. Now list the program; you will find it contains only lines 10 through 50:

```
10  ! Program to print 10 numbers
20    DECLARE INTEGER I
30    FOR I = 1 TO 10
40        PRINT I;
50    NEXT I
```

Inserting a Line

To insert a line in a program, type the line, including the line number. The line will be inserted into the program, ordered by line number. If we wish to insert a statement between lines 20 and 30, we could do so as follows:

```
25    PRINT 10 numbers are :''
```

A listing of the program now shows:

```
10  ! Program to print 10 numbers
20    DECLARE INTEGER I
25    PRINT "10 numbers are :"
30    FOR I = 1 TO 10
40        PRINT I;
50    NEXT I
```

You can see why we usually number our lines by tens.

Getting Help in BASIC

Help is available in the BASIC environment the same way that it is available in the VMS environment.

If you type HELP alone, you will get a list of topics for which help is available. It is a *long* list, because it includes every instruction available in BASIC.

To get help on a specific topic, type HELP followed by the topic. For instance, HELP PRINT will give you information on how to use the BASIC PRINT instruction. HELP EDIT will give you information on how to edit a line of your program.

To get out of the help facility, keep pressing the <Return> key until the > BASIC prompt appears.

Editing a Line

We will often have to edit a line to correct some typing error. There are two methods available. One method allows us to make small changes. The other is for major changes.

Minor editing: Small changes to a program can be accomplished with the EDIT command. Its format is:

```
EDIT line_number/search_string/replacement_string/
```

Suppose, for example, we wish to replace the semicolon in line 40 of the program above with a comma. We would type this:

```
EDIT 40/;/,/
```

To replace "numbers" in line 25 with "values", we type:

```
EDIT 25/numbers/values/
```

To delete something altogether, we can supply a null replacement string. To delete the colon in line 25, we type:

```
EDIT 25/://
```

To insert something into a line, we replace something there with itself plus what we wish to add. In line 40, we can insert "Number =" after PRINT by typing:

```
EDIT 40/PRINT /PRINT "Number ="/
```

In all of the above examples, a slash, /, was used as a separator. Any other character that is not in either the search or replacement string would do as well. The first character after the line number is taken as the separator. The last example could have been written as in the following examples:

```
EDIT 40#PRINT #PRINT "Number ="#
EDIT 40?PRINT ?PRINT "Number ="?
EDIT 40aPRINT aPRINT "Number ="a
```

In the last example, the lower case letter "a" was used as the separator as it does not appear elsewhere in the line; but a slash is usually used unless one of the strings contains a slash.

Major editing: To do substantial major editing that involves many changes, we need something more powerful than the above—an editor. An editor is again a new environment, with a new set of commands. To enter the editor, type

```
EDIT
```

with nothing else. You will leave BASIC and enter the editor environment.

THE EDITOR ENVIRONMENT

When you reach the editor, you will see a new prompt, the number symbol, #, instead of the > symbol. You therefore know that you are in a new environment.

The editor has two modes—the **line mode** and the **change mode.** Each is a separate environment with its own vocabulary. When you first enter the editor, you will be in the line mode. We are not really interested in the line mode and will shortly be passing through it into the change mode. (See Figure OV.1 on page 3). But first, let us learn how to get back to our BASIC environment.

Leaving the Editor

While we are in the editor, we will be making changes to our program. Eventually, we have to leave the editor and get back to BASIC. There are two ways to exit the editor—normal and panic.

Normal exit: The normal way to exit the editor is with the command EXIT or EX. When this command is typed in the line mode, you will be returned back to BASIC, and all the changes you have made to your program in the editor will be saved and reflected in your program. You can see the updated program by typing LIST.

NOTE! | **Changes you have made in the editor will only be reflected in the program you have in working memory. These changes will not be reflected in your file until you REPLACE the program from the BASIC environment.**

Panic exit: Sometimes, you do something really drastic and catastrophic while you are in the editor. You might, for instance, delete your entire program. What you would like to do is start over from the beginning. You can do so by typing QUIT to return to BASIC. The QUIT command will get you back to BASIC, but none of the changes you made to your program will be kept. Your program will be exactly as it was when you entered the editor. This gives you an opportunity to reenter the editor and try again.

Getting Help in the Editor Environment

While in the line mode of the editor, you can get on-line help just as you could in VMS and BASIC. At the # prompt, type HELP and you will see the list of items for which help is available. We will not be working in the line mode so most of this information is not relevant to us. You may be interested in learning how to use the KEYPAD while you are in the change mode of the editor, however, and here in the line mode is where you can learn that.

To leave the help facility, keep pressing the <Return> key until you get back to the # editor line mode prompt.

Entering Change Mode

You can enter the change mode from the line mode by typing the letter C followed by the <Return> key. It is in the change mode where you will be doing all your editing.

THE CHANGE MODE OF THE EDITOR

Leaving the Change Mode

As usual, we will start by introducing the command that lets us leave the change mode and return to the line mode. This is done by holding down the <Control> key and pressing the Z key. We call this the <Ctrl>Z combination. You know you are back in the line mode when you see the # prompt. From there you can return to BASIC.

Change Mode Features

When you enter the change mode, you will see the first 24 lines of your program. You will be able to move around your program to any point, allowing you to make changes anywhere. The following paragraphs describe the editing features available.

Moving the cursor: The cursor can be moved in change mode by using the four direction arrow keys ↑, ↓, ←, and →. To make corrections, the cursor must be positioned at the point where the correction is to be made.

Deleting characters: A character can be deleted by moving the cursor to the character following the one to be deleted, then pressing the <Delete> key. This key might have a picture of a large arrow pointing to the left on it. For example, suppose your file contains the word PRINMT, but it should be PRINT. Position the cursor, using the arrow keys, at the T in PRINMT.

Then press <Delete>. The M will disappear. As many characters as desired may be deleted in this manner.

Inserting characters: To insert characters into the file, move the cursor to the place where the insertion is to take place. Then type the characters to be inserted. **Use the keyboard only;** do not use the keypad at the right side of the terminal. If a number must be inserted, use only the numbers at the top of the keyboard. The keys on the keypad have been redefined to have different editing functions. As you use the editor, you will probably become familiar with them over a period of time. It is best for the beginner to leave these keys alone.

After you have made all the changes to your file as needed, leave the change mode and return to the line mode of the editor (<Ctrl>Z), leave the line mode and return back to BASIC (EX or QUIT). Once back in BASIC, you can LIST, REPLACE, RUN, and do all the functions mentioned earlier that are applicable in the BASIC environment.

Getting Help in the Change Mode

Help in the change mode is available mainly for the keypad. If you have not learned how to use the keypad, this help will not be of much use. To get help, press the <PF2> key above the keypad. You will get a layout of the keypad along with some other information. For additional help follow the directions on the screen. To get back to your work, follow the directions on the screen to exit the help facility.

SUMMARY | Here is a summary of commands used in the VMS environment:

SET PASS	Change the password
LOG	Logoff command
DIR	Directory listing of files in account
DEL	Delete file from account
RENAME	Rename a file in account
PURGE	Delete old versions of files from account
BASIC	Enter BASIC environment

Here is a summary of commands used in the BASIC environment.

EXIT	Return to VMS
NEW	Create new program
OLD	Retrieve old program from account
REPLACE	Save a program to account
RENAME	Rename program in memory
RUN,RUNNH	Run a program
LIST	List program in memory
EDIT	Edit a line, or enter editor environment

Here is a summary of commands used in the editor line mode

EXIT, EX	Normal exit to BASIC, save all changes
QUIT	Panic exit to BASIC, ignore all changes
C	Enter change mode of editor

Here is a summary of editor change mode concepts.

<Ctrl>Z	Return to line mode
↑, ↓, ←, →	Move the cursor
<Delete> key	Delete character to left of cursor
Keyboard keys	Insert characters at position of cursor
Keypad keys	Special functions

1 Computers

Outline

1.1 Block Diagram of a Computer
1.2 Input Devices
1.3 Output Devices
1.4 The Arithmetic/Logic Unit (ALU)
1.5 The Control Unit
1.6 Memory
1.7 Symbolic Addresses
    Implicit and Explicit Declarations
    REAL or Floating Point Type
    INTEGER Type
    STRING Type
    DECIMAL type
Summary
Review Questions
Enrichment Topics

```
Enter a
Add numb
End of l
Find ave
```

Introduction   The purpose of this book is to teach you to program a computer. A program is a sequence of instructions which, when executed by the computer, causes the computer to calculate a solution to a problem. Before we can program a computer, we must have a basic understanding of how a computer works.

1.1 BLOCK DIAGRAM OF A COMPUTER

All computers consist of five logical sections, as shown in Figure 1-1:

1. Input devices
2. Output devices
3. Memory
4. Arithmetic/logic unit (ALU)
5. Control unit.

**Figure 1-1
Block Diagram of a Computer**

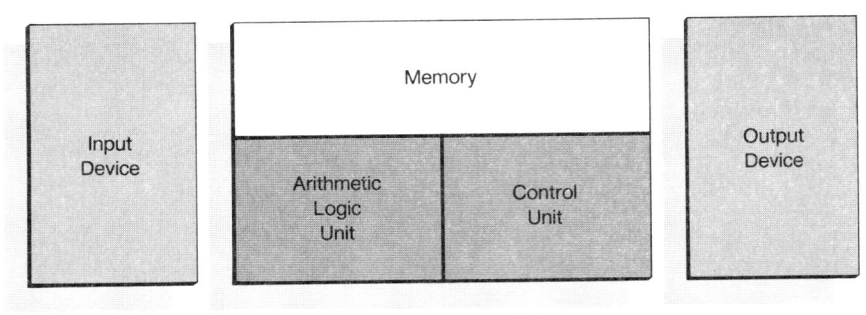

[Diagram: Input Device | Central Processing Unit (Memory, Arithmetic Logic Unit, Control Unit) | Output Device]

1.2 INPUT DEVICES

In computer terminology, the word "input" can be used in three different ways: as a noun, a verb, and an adjective. Input used as a noun refers to information that will be entered into the computer so that the computer can process it: "The computer needs input." Used as a verb, input refers to the process of getting data into the computer: "The computer input the data." The adjective form is a modifier: "The input device read the data." Therefore, the following strange sentence is perfectly valid in "computerese": "The input device was used to input the input."

Input devices allow data to be entered into the computer's memory. Among the many input devices in use are:

1. **Card readers,** which allow data to be entered by means of punched cards.
2. **Tape drives,** which allow data to be entered from previously prepared magnetic tapes. The tapes are similar to open reel tapes used for sound recording, but have digital information rather than music on them.
3. **Disk drives,** which allow information to be entered from magnetic discs. Small mini- and microcomputers use **floppy disks,** soft disks of magnetized material on which information has been recorded. Larger systems use **disk packs,** which are similar in appearance to a stack of records with space between them. The disks are magnetized on both surfaces (except for the outer disks), and read/write heads fit in the space between the disks to read and/or write information on the disk surface.
4. **Terminals,** which allow you to enter data into the computer directly. A terminal consists of two parts: a keyboard and a screen. Instead of a screen,

some terminals have printing devices similar to a typewriter. The keyboard of a computer terminal is the input device you will probably be using most of the time. Your terminal will be one of many attached to the same computer, and you, along with many others, will be interacting with the computer on a time-sharing basis. That is, the computer will share its time among its many users, but it will seem to each one that the computer is responding to him personally. This is known as an **interactive** or **time-sharing system.**

The keyboard is similar to that of a typewriter, with some exceptions. The exceptions are important to know but will not be discussed here, as they differ from one terminal to another. You will quickly learn your terminal's characteristics once you have used it for any length of time.

1.3 OUTPUT DEVICES

As was the case with the word "input," the word "output" can be used as a noun, verb, or adjective in computer jargon. So we could say (but probably should not say): "The computer output the output to the output device." The noun refers to the data that the computer has generated and is presenting to the user. The verb is what we say the computer is doing—it is outputting the data. The adjective is a modifier, as in "output device."

Output devices are devices to which the computer sends information. Some are:

1. **High-speed printers,** the most common device used for readable output. The data are printed on paper or on special forms. High-speed printers are available that can print thousands of lines per minute.
2. **Tape drives,** which we previously described as input devices. Just as a home tape recorder can both record and play back, a tape drive can act as both an input device and an output device. It records data output by a computer, which can later read the tape as input.
3. **Disc drives,** like tape drives, are output devices as well as input devices.
4. **Card punches** take output from the computer and record it by punching holes in computer cards. Punched cards are usually read by a card reader, thus providing input to a computer in a subsequent step.
5. **Terminals,** which are used for output as well as input. You will probably be using two types of terminals: a CRT and a *hard-copy terminal*.

A CRT (cathode-ray tube) looks like a television screen and allows you to receive output from the computer at your terminal. Since the output cannot be saved permanently when displayed on a CRT, this device is usually used when you are debugging a program. (Bugs are incorrect instructions that have been given to the computer, resulting in incorrect results.) The CRT is frequently combined with the keyboard into one unit. The hard-copy terminal also has a keyboard. Unlike the CRT, it uses paper (hard copy) and therefore generates a permanent record of the computer output. The printing is done by the computer when you direct it to output information. Information that you enter at the keyboard also appears on the hard copy.

A computer has three other sections: the memory, the arithmetic/logic unit, and the control unit. The arithmetic/logic unit and control unit, together, are called the **central processing unit** or **CPU.** All three are part of what is called the **mainframe** of the computer, which houses the CPU as well as various switches and indicators for the operator's use. See Figure 1.1, page 20.

1.4 THE ARITHMETIC/LOGIC UNIT (ALU)

The arithmetic/logic unit (ALU) is that part of the computer which performs the operations on data as required by the program. In addition to the usual operations of addition, subtraction, multiplication, and division, the ALU can also compare items of data to determine which is larger or smaller, or whether they are equal or not. Everything that the computer does to data is done in the ALU.

1.5 THE CONTROL UNIT

The control unit is like the supervisor on a difficult job. It interprets the instructions that have to be performed and sends out control signals to other parts of the computer so that the instructions may be executed (performed). It instructs the ALU to perform a particular operation if required, instructs the various input or output devices to enter or receive data, and determines which data are involved in the operation. It also determines which instruction is to be performed next from the list of instructions, or **program,** that has been given to the computer.

1.6 MEMORY

The memory section of the CPU is given special treatment here because an understanding of it is crucial to the programmer.

Memory in the computer can be compared to a stack of boxes, or cells (Figure 1-2). Each cell is called a **location** and has an **address.** The computer can access a particular location by its address.

Figure 1-2. Memory Locations

Each location can store one piece of data, which may be either a number or a **character string** (a sequence of alphabetic and punctuation characters).

1.7 SYMBOLIC ADDRESSES

The addresses used by the computer are difficult for programmers to remember. They are numerical and are usually expressed as hexadecimal (base 16) numbers. An example would be 2A53E6. How long do you think you would remember that you had stored someone's grade point average at that address? And what if you had many students? It is not easy to remember where a specific piece of information has been put if the amount of data is large.

Therefore, the computer lets us use more easily remembered symbolic addresses that consist of letters and numbers. These **symbolic addresses, symbolic names,** or **variables,** as they are called, are chosen for ease of recall. For example, we can use the symbolic address Grade_point_1 as the place where we store the grade point average of student 1. This is much easier than remembering we had stored it at address 2A53E6.

The symbolic names that can be used depend on the language the programmer is using. In addition, the specific name chosen often determines what type of data can be stored at the location assigned that name.

In VAX-BASIC, the type of datum that may be stored at a particular symbolic location can be established in two ways—by explicitly declaring the variable type, and by default, or implicit, declaration. Most programmers, and the authors of VAX-BASIC themselves, prefer the explicit method. Both methods will now be explained. The remainder of the book, however, will use the explicit method only.

Implicit and Explicit Declarations

In a certain town, warehouses are only allowed to contain one type of product. The specific product a warehouse may contain is determined in one of two ways. If the warehouse does not have a sign on the door, then the product it may contain is determined by its color: red warehouses contain food, yellow warehouses contain dry goods, green warehouses contain farm machinery, and so on. If the warehouse has a sign on the door, then the sign determines the product it contains regardless of the warehouse color. If the sign says "farm machinery," then farm machinery is stored there even if the warehouse is painted red. So, If there is no sign, then the color determines the contents *implicitly*, without need of any other information. If there is a sign, the sign determines the contents *explicitly*—the color does not matter.

Implicit comes from the word implied. The type of data that may be stored in an implicitly declared variable is determined by the name of the variable—specifically, by the suffix used at the end of the variable name. The suffix implies the type of datum. Nothing need be written to determine the type of data. The suffix is like the color on the warehouse—it determines what is inside without need of a sign.

In contrast to an implicitly declared variable, the type of data that can be stored in an explicitly declared variable is specifically stated in a DECLARE statement. The DECLARE statement is like the sign on the warehouse door—it overrides any suffix that might otherwise determine the nature of the contents.

We now proceed to discuss some of the basic types of data, and the variables that can store this data.

REAL or Floating Point Type

Implicit: A letter, followed by up to 30 additional letters, digits, underscores, or periods, specifies an address whose location can store a number which may or may not have a decimal point or fractional part, such as: 72.68, −15.7, −35, or 43. These are called **floating point numbers** or **real numbers.** The symbolic address that can store such a number is called a **floating point variable.** Examples are:

```
A, B, C, . . .
A1, B1, . . . A2, B2
Amount, TOTAL.1983, TAX, CLASS_2_AVG
Class_size, Sales_Total_Sept.1988, Area_of_circle
```

The first character must always be a letter, and no special characters, other than the period and underscore, may be used. The letters may be either upper or lower case. Periods and underscores are used to make the variable more easily read. Spaces or blanks are not permitted within a symbolic address. That is, we may not use the symbolic address `AVERAGE HEIGHT`; but we may use `AVERAGE_HEIGHT`, or `AVERAGE.HEIGHT`, or `average_height`. We may use lower case letters, or a combination of upper and lower case: `Average_Height`. Upper and lower case letters are treated equally. A maximum of 31 characters is permitted for the name of a variable, including the first character, which **must** be a letter.

As an example, the number 2.673 can be stored in the location whose symbolic name is A, while −2 can be stored in the location whose symbolic name is A1. Note that A and A1 refer to two different locations in memory. In fact, every symbolic name refers to a different location in memory.

Explicit: An explicitly declared real variable looks just like an implicitly declared one, except that we need the "sign on the warehouse door." This is done with the **DECLARE** statement. The "sign" has to state that the variable will contain a real, or floating point, value. The data-type REAL is used for this purpose. The DECLARE statement has the following form:

DECLARE REAL variable, variable, . . .

An example is:

DECLARE REAL Distance, Sales_1987, Area

A statement number is also required; we will learn about that in chapter 2. Each variable listed will be able to contain a single real value, which may contain a decimal fraction.

CAUTION! Certain combinations of characters have special significance to the computer. These are treated as reserved words and may not be used by the programmer as symbolic names. An example is the word REAL, which describes a variable type. Also, all system commands fall into this category (refer to Overture), as well as all built-in function names (refer to chapter 13). When in doubt about whether a specific name is permissible, be safe—don't use it! A reserved name can always be used safely, however, if an underscore or period is added to it. For example, the symbolic name, COUNT, cannot be used; it is a reserved word. But the name COUNT. (note the period) or COUNT_ (note the underscore) can be used, because they are not reserved.

INTEGER Type

Implicit: Any symbolic name followed by a percent symbol (%) implicitly denotes an address that can store integers (whole numbers) only. These are called **integer variables.** Examples are:

```
No._of_students%
ITEM_NUMBER%
Days.in.month%
```

An implicitly declared integer variable must start with a letter, may contain up to 29 additional letters, digits, underscores, or periods, and must end with a percent symbol. Therefore, the maximum length of an integer variable name is 31 characters, the same as for a real variable.

For example, B% is the symbolic address of a location that can store the number −17, while CLASS_SIZE% can store the number 25. An attempt to store 6.8 in integer variable A%, for instance, will cause the fraction to be lost. Only the 6 will be stored. The computer can process integers more quickly than floating point numbers, so it is often advantageous to use integer variables. Such variables may also require less memory than real variables.

Explicit: The explicit declaration of an integer variable is also made with a DECLARE statement, the same as for real variables. However, the data-type INTEGER is used. Because a "sign" is used in the declaration, the "warehouse color" is unimportant. That is, we no longer need a suffix to indicate that the variable is of integer type because we are explicitly stating that fact in the DECLARE statement. An example is:

DECLARE INTEGER Num_students, Item.number

Both variables are integer type and each can store one integer value. The value may be positive or negative, but may not contain a fractional part. Because of the explicit declaration, no % suffix is required or permitted.

STRING Type

Implicit: A symbolic name followed by a dollar sign ($) specifies a location that can store character data or character strings. For example, A$ can store the character string THE BOOK IS RED, while ADDRESS$ might store the character string 1157 MAIN STREET, ANYWHERE, USA. Examples of string variables are:

```
Name_$
Street_Address$
Part.number$
```

As was the case with integer variables, a string variable must begin with a letter, may be followed by as many as 29 additional letters, digits, underscores, or periods, but must be followed by a dollar sign (for implicit string declaration). Therefore, a total of 31 characters is permitted for a string variable.

Note that the implicitly declared variables A, A%, and A$ are symbolic names for three different locations in memory that store three different types of data.

Explicit: Again, the explicit declaration of a variable requires a DECLARE statement. To type string variables, the data-type required is STRING. An example of such a DECLARE statement is:

> **DECLARE STRING Last_name, Address, Description**

Again, as with previous explicit declarations, no suffix is required. The computer will know that the explicitly declared variables will contain strings because the DECLARE statement informs it (the sign on the barn door). The $ suffix is not required.

STRING-type variables can store strings up to 65535 characters in length in VAX-BASIC. These are considerably longer than the maximum string length of 255 characters in most other BASIC dialects.

DECIMAL Type (Explicit Only)

The DECIMAL type is peculiar to VAX-BASIC. There is no implicit declaration for it. This type allows storage of numbers in fixed-point form. The DECIMAL type allows specifying the number of digits and the number of decimal places. This contrasts to the REAL type, which has a floating decimal point. The DECIMAL type is very useful in financial situations where dollars and cents are required. If two dollars is divided by six, a REAL variable would store the value 0.333333; a DECIMAL variable can store the value 0.33. The data-type required is DECIMAL(s,d). The total number of digits, including those on both sides of the decimal point, is given by s; the number of digits after the decimal point is given by d. Consider the following example:

> **DECLARE DECIMAL(10,2) Price, Total, DECIMAL(8,2) Tax**

In this example, the two variables `Price` and `Total` can store numbers containing two decimal places and up to eight digits before the decimal point, a total of 10 digits. The variable `Tax` also will store numbers with two decimal places, but only six digits before the decimal point, a total of eight digits.

The maximum value for *s* in the DECIMAL declaration is 31. This gives 31-digit precision. A variable declared with DECIMAL(31,2) will be able to store a number that has 29 digits to the left of the decimal point, and two digits to its right. Such a number is larger than the gross national product of the United States or, for that matter, of the world.

NOTE! It is extremely important to understand that data are put into memory in locations that have names. To retrieve data from memory, we must remember the name of the location where it was put.

Let's reinforce this idea with an example. You have a summer job at a parts supply store. The parts are in bins and each bin has a symbolic name which is a combination of the aisle it is in and a sequence number. For instance, bin C27 is the twenty-seventh bin in aisle C. Each bin contains one type of part, such as a frammis, widget, or doo-dad. When an order comes in, the foreman writes the bin number that contains the required item on a piece of paper and hands it to you so that you can retrieve the part. The data correspond to the items, such as widgets; the symbolic addresses correspond to the bin numbers. An item is retrieved, not by specifying its name, but by specifying its location. If the foreman says, "bring me a widget," you will be unable to do so. If he says "bring me the part in bin E15," you will be successful since E15 is the address where widgets are stored.

In a similar manner, you will be unsuccessful if you tell the computer to store the number 2. But if you tell it, "Take the number two and store it in location A," you will succeed. Later, you will be able to say, "Print the number that is stored in location A" and it will print the number you stored there, two.

SUMMARY

1. A computer consists of five logical sections:
   a. Input devices
   b. Output devices
   c. Control unit
   d. Arithmetic/logic unit
   e. Memory.

2. Memory consists of locations to which we refer by means of symbolic names.

3. The data that can be stored in implicitly declared variables depend on the suffix attached to the variable name, according to the following rules.
   a. A letter, optionally followed by 0 to 30 additional letters, digits, underscores, or periods, is a symbolic name for a location that can store real numbers consisting of integer and fractional parts.
   b. A letter followed by 0 to 29 additional letters, digits, underscores, or periods, followed by a percent symbol (%) can store integer numbers only.
   c. The same combinations of characters followed by a dollar sign ($) can store character data.

4. Variables are explicitly declared with the DECLARE statement. The data that can be stored depends on the data-type used. The data-types discussed in this chapter are the following:

a. REAL is used to declare a real, or floating point, variable. A real value has a floating, or movable, decimal point.
b. INTEGER is used to declare an integer-type variable. Such a variable can store integers, or whole numbers, only.
c. DECIMAL(s,d) is used to declare a variable that can store a fixed point number. The s represents the total number of significant digits, and d is the number of decimal places after the decimal point. The number of places before the decimal point is the difference $s - d$.
d. STRING is used to declare a variable that can store string, or character, data. Such data cannot be (immediately) used for arithmetic.

REVIEW QUESTIONS

1. Name the five logical parts of a digital computer.
2. State the purpose of input devices. Name five input devices.
3. State the purpose of output devices. Name five output devices.
4. State the purpose of memory.
5. State the purpose of the ALU. What does ALU stand for?
6. State the purpose of the control unit.
7. Which sections of the computer make up the CPU? What does CPU stand for?
8. What is a symbolic address? What is another word for a symbolic address? What constitutes a legal symbolic address? (How many characters, etc.)
9. What are the three implicit types of symbolic addresses? What type of data can be stored in each type? How do the names used for the three types differ?
10. What is the difference between implicitly and explicitly declared variables? Specifically, what determines the type of value that can be stored?
11. What are the data-types used in the DECLARE statement? What is the purpose of each? How are the number of digits in a fixed-point variable declared?
12. Which of the following are legitimate symbolic addresses? For those that are not, state why they are not.
    a. SALES
    b. CUSTOMER.NAME
    c. CUSTOMER.NAME$
    d. NO.
    e. NO_%
    f. NO_$
    g. NO_&
    h. 42
    i. #2
    j. FIRST_NAME$
    k. OLD.SALES_TOTAL
    l. 1981.SALES.AMOUNT
    m. ACCOUNT.#
11. Assuming that the following are implicitly declared, which of the following locations, or variables, can store the number 42?
    a. A
    b. A%

c. A$
   d. Two of them (Which?)
   e. All of them
12. Assuming implicit declarations, which of the following locations, or variables, can store the number 42.6?
   a. A
   b. A%
   c. A$
   d. Two of them (Which?)
   e. All of them
13. Assuming implicit declarations, which of the following locations, or variables, can store the name ELI?
   a. A
   b. A%
   c. A$
   d. Two of them (Which?)
   e. All of them
14. What is the part of the computer that can add two numbers called?
15. What is the part of the computer where data are stored called?
16. What is the part of the computer that interprets instructions called?
17. What type of device is the keyboard of a terminal?
18. What type of device is CRT screen?

ENRICHMENT TOPICS 1

Additional Explicit Types

In this chapter, we learned of the data-types INTEGER, REAL, DECIMAL, and STRING. Some of these can be subdivided into additional categories. The range of values that these additional categories can store is specified in parentheses after the data-type.

INTEGER can be further subdivided into:

BYTE (−128 to 127)
WORD (−32768 to 32767)
LONG (−2147483648 to 2147483647)

The numbers in parentheses are the minimum and maximum values that can be accommodated by each type of variable.

REAL can be subdivided into:

SINGLE (6-digit precision)
DOUBLE (16-digit precision)
GFLOAT (15-digit precision, exponents from −308 to +308)
HFLOAT (33-digit precision, exponents from −4932 to +4932).

If the subdivision of the INTEGER or REAL type is not specified, then the system uses a default subdivision. The default varies from one installation to another.

In the following examples, statement numbers are required for the DECLARE statements. They will be discussed in the next chapter.

Example 1-1

```
DECLARE BYTE Var    ! INTEGER type, -127 to 128
DECLARE WORD Sum    ! INTEGERtype, -32768 to 32767
DECLARE LONG Z      ! INTEGER type, -2147483648 to 2147483647
DECLARE INTEGER I   ! INTEGERtype, system default precision
DECLARE SINGLE S    ! REAL type, 6 digits precision
DECLARE DOUBLE Dbl  ! REAL type, 16 digits precision
```

2 Input/Output (I/O)

Outline
2.1 The DECLARE Statement
2.2 The INPUT Instruction
2.3 The PRINT Instruction
　Print Formatting
　　Commas and Semicolons
　　The TAB Function
　　Suppressing Line Feeds
2.4 The END Statement
2.5 Remarks and Comments
2.6 The READ and DATA Statements
Summary
Review Questions
Syntax Exercises
Programming Exercises

Introduction We are now going to describe the instructions that allow us to enter data into the computer memory and to output data from memory. It is only when data are in memory that the computer can use them to produce the desired results. Symbolic names or variables are assigned values (data) with the assignment, INPUT, and READ statements. These values can be changed during execution of the program. Data and results may be printed using the PRINT instruction.

Assignment statements are discussed in chapter 3. This chapter discusses the INPUT, READ, DATA, PRINT, and END statements.

2.1 THE DECLARE STATEMENT

In chapter 1, we learned that the DECLARE statement is used to declare symbolic locations, or variables, explicitly. In this chapter, we begin using such variables. Therefore, we will spend a little additional time discussing the DECLARE statement.

The DECLARE statement has the following format:

sn DECLARE data-type variable, variable, . . .

where **sn** is a statement number and **data-type** is the type of data that will be stored in the variables that follow the data-type.

The statement number is an unsigned integer number in the range of 1 to 32767 (in some systems, the range could be 1 to 99999). We usually number our statements in increments of 10, and we always number them in the order we want them arranged in our program.

The data-type may correspond to any type of value that may be represented in the computer. We have discussed a number of these in chapter 1, namely REAL, INTEGER, DECIMAL, and STRING. Examples of DECLARE statements are:

```
10 DECLARE REAL X, Y, Z
20 DECLARE INTEGER NO.ITEMS, No_students, Year
30 DECLARE STRING Description, Address, Salesman
40 DECLARE DECIMAL(10,2) Sales, Salary, REAL Distance
```

The last example shows how one DECLARE statement can be used to include more than one data-type in a single DECLARE statement. The computer will recognize the data-type keywords; all variables following such a keyword will be of that type. Clearly, the keywords are reserved words that may not be used as variable names.

2.2 THE INPUT INSTRUCTION

The main instruction that allows you to enter data into memory from an external device is the INPUT instruction:

sn INPUT "prompt", list . . .

or

sn INPUT "prompt"; list . . .

where **sn** is a statement number as described above. In general, every statement must be preceded by a statement number. (In chapter 3, we will learn how one statement number can be used to precede several statements.) Statements are executed in numerical order. We usually number statements by tens so that we can later insert a forgotten statement into the program.

The **"prompt"** is an optional character string that will be printed at the terminal when the instruction is executed. It may be enclosed in either single or double quotes. Such a prompt is usually necessary so that we are reminded of the data that we are going to enter.

The **list** is a list of symbolic addresses or variables, separated by commas, where the data that we enter will be stored.

The prompt, if any, may be followed by either a comma or semicolon. If by a semicolon, then a question mark will appear immediately after the prompt when the prompt is output to the screen. If by a comma, then this question mark will appear at the beginning of the 14-column field that follows the prompt. So, if the prompt is 17 characters long, the next 14-column field would begin at column 29; that is where the question mark will appear. If there is no prompt, then a question mark will be printed in the first column available, usually column 1. (Note that one column is equal to one character.)

When the INPUT instruction is executed by the computer, the computer prints the prompt, if any, followed by a question mark, then waits until the required data have been typed. To be accepted by the computer, the data must always be followed by a carriage return (press <RETURN>). The data will then be stored and the computer will continue to process the remaining instructions of the program.

Example 2.1

```
10 INPUT "Enter 3 numbers"; A, B, C
```

This instruction prints the prompt `Enter 3 numbers?` at the terminal. The computer will wait until you type the three numbers, separated by commas, and press the <Return> key. The three numbers will be stored in locations A, B, and C in memory.

Example 2.2

```
10 DECLARE INTEGER NUMBER.1, NUMBER.2
50 INPUT "Enter 2 integers"; NUMBER.1, NUMBER.2
```

Instruction 50 prints the prompt `Enter 2 integers?` at the terminal, then waits until you type two integers separated by a comma, and press <Return>. The two integers will be stored in memory locations `NUMBER.1` and `NUMBER.2`. The prompt can be enclosed by either single or double quotes. (Do not use the symbolic address NUM, NUM$, NUM1$, or NUM2—they are reserved words. Adding a period or underscore after any of these names, as in NUM_, makes it a permissible symbolic name.)

Example 2.3

```
10 DECLARE STRING Name.
30 INPUT Name.
```

This instruction has no prompt. The computer prints a question mark, then waits quietly until you type a string and press <Return>. If the string (possibly a name) contains a comma, you must enclose it in quotes when you type it so that the computer treats it as a single string. Without the enclosing quotes, the comma is treated as a string separator. For example: 'COOL, JOE'. (NAME is a reserved word, so we added a period after it.)

In any of the above cases, the prompt could have been left out, as in the last example. LEAVING OUT THE PROMPT IS NOT A GOOD IDEA AND SHOULD BE AVOIDED! Without a prompt, nothing is printed at the terminal to assist you except a question mark. You will usually be left wondering what you were supposed to enter.

Example 2.4

```
10 DECLARE STRING Name., DECIMAL(8,2) Amount
20 INPUT "ENTER NAME AND AMOUNT "; Name., Amount
```

The prompt `ENTER NAME AND AMOUNT ?` is printed at the terminal, after which a name and an amount, separated by a comma, can be typed followed by a carriage return. The name is stored in `Name.`, and the amount in `Amount`. As before, since "Name" is a reserved word, a period was added to make it acceptable as a variable name.

NOTE! In all cases where more than one item is required, the values may be entered all on one line, separated by commas, or they may be entered one at a time on separate lines. If not enough data are entered on one line, the computer will print a question mark (?) on the next line as an indication that more data are needed. This will continue until the variables in the list have all been satisfied.

NOTE! If more data are entered than required, all excess values will be ignored. For example, if the instruction

```
30 INPUT "Enter three numbers"; No.1, No.2, No.3
```

is executing, and in response to the prompt, you type five numbers:

```
Enter three numbers? 10, 20, 30, 40, 50
```

then the numbers 40 and 50 will be ignored. The numbers 10, 20, and 30 will be stored in variables `No.1`, `No.2`, and `No.3`, respectively.

2.3 THE PRINT INSTRUCTION

Data from the computer's memory can be printed, or output, by means of the PRINT instruction, the general form of which is:

sn PRINT list

where **sn** is the statement number. For example:

```
50 PRINT "Name = "; Name., "Sales total is "; Sales
```

The list can consist of one or more variables, expressions, or constants. A variable is a symbolic name such as `A`, `B1`, or `Sales_total_1987`. An expression involves a calculation such as `A + B`. We will speak more of expressions in the next chapter. A constant is a numeric or string value such as 250, "ABC", or -5.7. Note that string constants must be enclosed in either single or double quotes.

Each item in the list of a PRINT statement must be separated from the others by a comma or semicolon. The difference between these will be made clear in the next section.

Print Formatting

Commas and Semicolons: Items in the list of a PRINT statement may be separated by either commas or semicolons. The choice of one or the other will determine the appearance of the output.

If a comma is used between items, then each value printed will begin in a new **field.** There are five such fields on one 72-character print line. Each is 14 columns wide, so fields begin in columns 1, 15, 29, 43, and 57. If the terminal is capable of 132-character lines, then there are four additional print zones starting at columns 71, 85, 99, and 113. Using a comma is like pressing the <Tab> key on a typewriter: the carriage moves to a specific position on the line. The comma causes the next data item to be printed at the start of a new field.

Using a semicolon between items in the output list will result in the printing of data in **packed format.** Numbers will be printed one after the other, using only a sufficient number of columns to print the number and allow for minimal spacing, usually one blank space. Specifically, the first column is used for the sign of the number. If the number is positive, then a blank appears in this position instead of a plus sign. The digits of the number follow this first position. Finally, a blank column follows the last digit to separate this number from the next item to be printed. Character strings will be printed in successive columns without any space between successive strings.

A mixture of commas and semicolons can be used to achieve a desired effect.

Example 2.5
```
10 INPUT "Enter 3 Numbers"; A,B,C
20 PRINT "A =";A, "B =";B, "C =";C
```

produces the following output at the terminal:

```
Enter 3 Numbers? 5,12,14
A = 5          B = 12         C = 14
```

The numbers 5, 12, and 14 were entered at the terminal in response to the prompt. Notice how the commas in the PRINT statement cause the next output to be printed in a new field, whereas the semicolon produces packed output.

If the prompt in the above example had been followed by a comma instead of a semicolon, then the question mark would have moved to a new field before accepting our input. The statements would have been:

```
10 INPUT "Enter 3 Numbers", A,B,C
20 PRINT "A =";A, "B =";B "C =";C
```

and the output when the statements are executed would be as follows:

```
Enter 3 Numbers          ? 5,-12,14
A = 5           B =-12           C = 14
```

The comma after the prompt causes the cursor to move to a new field, the one starting in column 29. Since the prompt ends in the second field, the cursor moves to the third and waits for the input.

The TAB Function: The TAB function allows the programmer to select the exact column at which the next printout is to occur. The syntax is:

TAB(N)

where **N** is the column number selected. **N** may be a real number, an integer, or a numeric variable, real or integer. For example, the statement:

```
50 PRINT TAB(10); X; TAB(40); Y
```

prints the value in X starting in column 11, and the value in Y starting in column 41. (If X and Y contain positive numbers, there will actually be a blank in these columns, with the first digit appearing in the following column. The minus sign of negative numbers will be in the columns stated above. Data stored in string variables will have their first characters printed in the above-mentioned columns.)

Perhaps you have noticed what appears to be a slight discrepancy: The TAB function seems to be off by one column. The reason is that the TAB function is "zero" based, while we tend to be "one" based. We number the 80 columns of our terminal from 1 to 80. The TAB function numbers them, instead, from 0 to 79. So TAB(0) really means column 1. You will quickly adjust to this.

NOTE! It is essential that a semicolon be used after a TAB function. If a comma is used instead, printout will occur at the field following the selected column number.

For example, here is how you should NOT use the TAB function:

```
100 PRINT TAB(5), X, TAB(10), Y
```

Because of `TAB(5)`, the computer goes to column 6 of the print line. However, notice that the TAB function is followed by a comma. Therefore, the first field will be skipped and the value of X will be printed at the start of the next field—in this case, the field starting in column 15. The variable X is followed by a comma also, so the computer moves to the start of the next, or third, field. The third field begins at column 29. Since the computer is already past column 11, the `TAB(10)` in the PRINT statement is ignored. Y is printed beginning in column 29.

Variables can be used as arguments of the TAB function. In the following example, assume that P contains the number 4, and Q contains the number 39.

```
30  PRINT TAB(P);10; TAB(P+10);20; TAB(Q);30; TAB(Q+20);40
```

The number 10 is printed in columns 5, 6, and 7, with column 5 being a blank where the minus sign would be if the number were negative. TAB(P+10) causes the computer to tab to column 15. The number 20 is printed in columns 15, 16, and 17. Because of TAB(Q), the next number, 30, is printed in columns 40, 41, and 42. Finally, 40 is printed in columns 60, 61, and 62.

By using the TAB function in the above manner, it is possible to produce some very sophisticated output.

The argument of the TAB function may be a real or integer variable. Thus, if the implicitly declared variables I and I% are both 10, I being real and I% being integer, either TAB(I) or TAB(I%) can be used to skip to column 10 (zero based).

Suppressing line feeds: After a PRINT statement has executed, further output from a succeeding PRINT statement is normally printed on a new line. Sometimes, it is necessary to have two PRINT statements produce their output on the same print line. We want one line to be used even though there are two PRINT statements. The first of the two PRINT statements must suppress the line feed. It is the line feed that causes a new line to be started. This line feed suppression is accomplished by terminating the first PRINT statement with a comma or semicolon.

Example 2.6
```
50   PRINT A,B,C,
60   PRINT 150
100  PRINT A,Y;Z;
110  PRINT 150
```

The comma or semicolon at the end of the PRINT statements on lines 50 and 100 suppresses the line feed and keeps the succeeding output on the same line. If a PRINT statement is terminated with a comma as in statement 50, then the first item of the next PRINT statement (the number 150 in statement 60) will be printed in a new field on the current line. If a PRINT statement ends in a semicolon, as in statement 100, the first item of the next PRINT statement (150 in statement 110) will immediately follow the previously printed item, in packed format. Remember that a positive number will always have a blank where the sign would be, and all numbers are followed by at least one blank.

2.4 THE END STATEMENT

Every BASIC program should have an END statement as its last instruction. This statement causes the computer to stop executing the program and serves as a signal to the interpreter that there are no more instructions. Therefore, END can only be used as the very last statement in a program. (The **interpreter** is the program that translates your program from BASIC into machine language, ready for execution.)

On some computers, the program will work without the END statement, but a diagnostic (error message) may be generated. The syntax for the END statement is:

sn END

where **sn** is the highest statement number in the program. Because 32767 is the highest statement number permitted on many systems, this number is frequently used for the END statement:

```
32767 END
```

If your system is capable of larger statement numbers, you may wish to adopt the largest permissible value for the END instruction.

It should be pointed out in passing that some dialects of BASIC will execute statements after an END statement, if control is somehow passed to those statements. Such dialects will allow you to have more than one END statement in a program. However, this is *not* the case with VAX-BASIC.

2.5 REMARKS AND COMMENTS

A well-written program has embedded comments that explain what the program is doing and how it is doing it. A relatively simple program can become an incomprehensible mess of mysterious gibberish in a very short time, even to the person who wrote it. In most programming environments, a program has to be maintained and modified for years, often not by the people who wrote it. Comments to explain how a program works are essential.

There are three ways of putting comments or remarks into a program. One way is the standard BASIC REM statement. Any statement beginning with the letters REM is treated by the computer as a remark. The statement is printed when a listing is obtained, but is ignored when the program is run. An example of such a statement is:

```
10 REM This is a remark
```

An exclamation point can be used instead of the keyword REM. We call the resulting statement a **comment** rather than a remark. The following statement is a comment:

```
10 ! This is a comment
```

Finally, we can put a comment at the end of a physical line before the carriage return, as illustrated by the statement:

```
50 PRINT X,Y,Z     ! Print 3 nos.
```

In general, a comment that explains a section of code consisting of several statements should be on its own physical line immediately above those statements:

2.5 REMARKS AND COMMENTS

```
100 ! comment
    statement
    statement
    ...
```

A comment that explains one particular statement should be placed at the end of that statement, assuming that it fits there:

```
100 statement    ! comment
```

or it should be placed on the following physical line if it does not fit on the same line:

```
100 very long statement
              ! comment
```

Physical and logical lines will be explained in the next chapter.

Example 2.7 | The following program inputs two numbers to the computer, and prints the numbers and their sum:

```
10 ! Example using I/O
20    DECLARE REAL A, B
30    INPUT "Enter two numbers"; A,B
40    PRINT "FIRST = ";A, "SECOND = ";B, "SUM = ";A+B
50    END
```

The following interaction is produced:

```
Enter two numbers? 6,10
FIRST =  6     SECOND =  10    SUM =  16
```

Another run of the same program would allow us to enter different numbers. For example:

```
Enter two numbers? -17.63, 8.42
FIRST = -17.63          SECOND =  8.42           SUM = -9.21
```

This time, the numbers use up so many columns that the output for each requires more than 14 columns, including the blank always put after a number. The next output must start at a new field boundary. The result is that the data must use five fields now, instead of the three used before.

Example 2.8 | This program illustrates line feed suppression. Four numbers are entered. The average of the first two numbers is found, then the average of the last two. Finally, the average of all four numbers is found.

```
10 REM Averages
20    DECLARE REAL A,B,C,D
30    INPUT "Enter 4 nos."; A, B, C, D
40    PRINT "First two are "; A; B, ! Note the comma
```

```
50    PRINT "Their average "; (A + B) / 2
60    PRINT "Last two are"; C; D, ! Again a comma
70    PRINT "Their average "; (C + D) / 2
80    PRINT     ! Skips a line
90    PRINT "The average of all is "; (A + B + C + D) / 4
32767 END
```

The following will appear at the terminal when the program is run:

```
Enter 4 nos.? 6,10,14,20
First two are   6   10          Their average    8
Last two are   14   20          Their average   17

The average of all is 12.5
```

Example 2.9 In this example, we will prompt the user to enter his first name, then his last name. The computer will then move to the right half of the screen, print the last name, a comma, a space, and finally, the first name.

```
10 ! Program to print a formatted name
20    DECLARE STRING First, Last
30 !
40 ! The input section
50    INPUT "Enter your first name "; First
60    INPUT "Enter your last name"; Last
70 !
80 ! The output section
90    PRINT TAB(40); Last; ", "; First
32767 END
```

A typical run of this program will produce the following interaction:

```
Enter your first name ? John
Enter your last name  ? Doe
                                        Doe, John
```

2.6 THE READ AND DATA STATEMENTS

Data that the program needs, and which are always the same for each run, can be put into a DATA statement and then made available for processing with a READ statement. The DATA statement establishes a "data pool" into which the program can dip to obtain the required information. The READ statement dips into the pool and always comes out with the first unused datum.

The syntax for these statements is:

sn READ list

and

sn DATA values

The DATA statement contains the values in the data pool. The READ statement reads these values.

Example 2.10

```
1000 READ A, B, C
      .
      .
      .
1100 DATA 18,26,40
```

When the READ statement executes, it goes to the DATA pool and obtains the first number, 18, which it stores in A. It obtains the second number, 26, and stores it in B, and the third number, 40, which it stores in C.

A program can have more than one DATA statement. All values in all of them form one data pool. The values are selected on a first-in, first-out basis.

CAUTION! A comment or remark may not be placed at the end of a DATA statement. Such a comment or remark would be treated as part of the DATA pool and would be read as data by a READ statement.

Example 2.11

```
10 DECLARE STRING A_string, B_string, C_string, D_string
20 DECLARE INTEGER A_integer, B_integer, C_integer, D_integer
100 DATA 'A',3,'B',8,'C'
110 DATA 10,'D',20
       .
       .
       .
500 READ A_string, A_integer
510 READ B_string, B_integer
520 READ C_string, C_integer, D_string, D_integer
```

The following assignments are made:

```
A_string = 'A'
A_integer = 3
B_string = 'B'
B_integer = 8
C_string = 'C'
C_integer = 10
D_string = 'D'
D_integer = 20
```

Although DATA statements may be placed anywhere in the program, it is good programming practice always to place them in a consistent location. Many programmers customarily place all DATA statements in one group at the end of the program while others place them at the beginning. The first method is recommended.

Example 2.12 DATA statements can be effectively used for supplying data to a program that will not change each time the program is run. A very good use of the

READ and DATA statements would be to have your program print identifying information about yourself at the top of the printout. This information could consist of your name, your teacher's name, your class, the program number, and its purpose.

In this example, we use READ and DATA statements to print the title of this book and the author's name. You should be able to easily modify the program to suit your specific requirements.

```
10  ! READ and DATA to print title and author of this textbook
20      DECLARE STRING Title, Author
30      READ Title, Author
40      PRINT TAB(10); "Title  : "; Title
50      PRINT TAB(10); "Author : "; Author
100     DATA "Strictly Structured VAX-BASIC"
110     DATA "Eli Berlinger"
32767 END
```

As an exercise, enter this program at your terminal and run it. Then change the DATA statements to include data about yourself and run it again.

SUMMARY

In this chapter, you learned how to enter data into the computer and how to have the computer output data.

1. The DECLARE statement is used to explicitly declare the variables used in a program and to give these variables their attributes. The attributes determine the type of data the variables can store. The syntax is:

sn DECLARE data-type variable, . . .

2. The data-types we have learned so far are REAL, INTEGER, DECIMAL, and STRING. They were discussed in detail in chapter 1.

3. The INPUT statement allows us to enter data into the computer from an external input device, such as the computer terminal. The syntax is:

sn INPUT "prompt"; list

4. The PRINT statement allows us to have the computer print calculated results. The syntax is:

sn PRINT list

5. The TAB function, used in a PRINT statement, allows output to begin in any selected column. (TAB is 0-based.) The syntax is:

TAB(column number)

It is used in a PRINT statement as follows:

sn PRINT TAB(col no.); item; TAB(col no.); item; ...

6. Commas can be used between elements of an output list to skip to a new field, and semicolons can be used to print in packed format.

7. Line feeds can be suppressed by terminating the PRINT statement with either a comma or a semicolon.

8. The REM statement, or an exclamation point, allows comments or remarks to be placed in a program.

9. The READ statement allows us to enter data into the computer from a data pool. The syntax is:

sn READ list

10. The DATA statement allows us to set up a data pool of values that may be read with a READ statement. The syntax is:

sn DATA values

REVIEW QUESTIONS

1. Explain the purpose of the DECLARE statement. What is the difference between implicitly and explicitly declared variables?
2. State the four data-types we have learned so far. When is each one used?
3. What is the purpose of an INPUT instruction? What is the purpose of a PRINT instruction?
4. What is the purpose of the prompt in an INPUT instruction?
5. What determines the number of items to be stored by an INPUT instruction? What determines the number of items to be printed by a PRINT instruction?
6. Explain the difference between the comma and the semicolon in a PRINT statement.
7. What is the purpose of the TAB function? How is it used?
8. What is meant by "line feed suppression"? How is it accomplished? Explain the difference between using the comma and using the semicolon to suppress the line feed.
9. What is the purpose of a remark or a comment? How are they different? Why are they necessary?
10. What is the END statement used for? Where is it put?
11. Explain the significance of statement numbers. How does the computer use them? Why do we usually number statements by tens?
12. What are the READ and DATA statements? What is the purpose of each?
13. How does the READ instruction differ from the INPUT instruction?

SYNTAX EXERCISES

Each of the following statements has a syntax error. Find it and correct it.

1. `INPUT "Enter 3 numbers"; A, B, C`
2. `INPUT "Enter a name, NAME_`
3. `INPUT 'Enter tax rate"; TAX_RATE`
4. `INPUT 'Enter sales': SALES`
5. `INPUT "Enter grade;" GRADE`

```
 6. PRINT "The result is:'; RESULT
 7. PRINT "The numbers are", No.1: No.2: No.3
 8. PRINT "First no."; FIRST, "Second no.": SECOND
 9. PRINT "Total sales;" TOTAL_SALES
10. PRINT 'Area of circle = '; AREA
11. PRINT TAB(10),First,TAB(20),Second,TAB(30),Third
```

PROGRAMMING EXERCISES

Write programs that will perform the requested activities. Include comments in the programs and identifying strings in the output. Use explicit declarations in all of your programs.

■ **1.** Enter three numbers. Print them in reverse order.

2. Enter a last name, and then a first name. Print the first name and then the last name, separated by a space.

3. Enter two numbers. Print both numbers, their sum, and the average of the two. Identify all output.

■ **4.** Enter a customer name and the price of a suit purchased by the customer. Print the customer's name, starting in column 10. On a new line, print the price of the suit starting in column 30. Each line should be identified—name or price—starting in column 1.

5. Enter the lengths of the three sides of a triangle. Print the lengths of the sides, identifying them as side 1, side 2, and side 3.

6. Enter the lengths of the sides of a rectangle, smaller side first. Print the sides, larger side first. The length of each side should be printed on a separate line, starting in column 20. Print the area of the rectangle on another line, starting in column 10. Use suitable identification for the output.

■ **7.** Write a program with three DATA statements, each containing a name in quotes and three numbers. Read each name and the three corresponding numbers. Print each name, the three numbers, and their average.

8. Write a program to read seven numbers from one DATA statement. Print the numbers starting in column 5, ten columns apart. Use columns 5, 15, 25, 35, 45, 55, 65.

9. Enter a name, street address, city, and zip code. Print the name starting in column 10. On the next line, print the street address starting in column 10. On the next line, print the city starting in column 10, and the zip code starting in column 30.

■ **10.** Print the alphabet on one line of output. HINT: Read the alphabet from DATA.

11. Print the first half of the alphabet on one line, starting in column 40, and the rest of the alphabet directly beneath the first half.

3 Assignment Statements

Outline
3.1 Arithmetic Operators
3.2 Hierarchy
3.3 Parentheses
3.4 Assignment Operator
3.5 Sequences
3.6 Multi-Statement Lines
3.7 Multi-Line Statements
3.8 Flow Charts
Summary
Review Questions
Syntax Exercises
Programming Exercises

Introduction In this chapter, you will learn how to perform a calculation and store the answer in memory. Recall that we performed some calculations in chapter 2 with PRINT statements. The results were printed but not stored in memory. Had they been needed again, it would have been necessary to recalculate them. With assignment statements, we can perform a calculation and then store the result for future use.

3.1 ARITHMETIC OPERATORS

There are five basic arithmetic operators available in BASIC.

+	Addition
−	Subtraction
*	Multiplication
/	Division
^, **	Exponentiation

The first two are self-explanatory.

Multiplication must be explicit in BASIC. That is, if the number stored in A is to be multiplied by the number stored in B, then you must write A*B. BASIC multiplication differs from mathematics in that multiplication is never assumed. AB will not produce the product of the numbers stored in A and B. In fact, AB is a symbolic address for a location in memory.

Division is indicated by the / symbol. A/B means divide the number stored in A by the number stored in B.

Exponentiation is the process of raising a value to a power. In mathematics, the expression 2^4 means multiply 2 by itself four times: 2*2*2*2=16. In BASIC, it is written 2^4 or 2**4. Similarly, A^4 means A*A*A*A.

3.2 HIERARCHY

When a series of operators appears, the operations are performed in a specified sequence. This sequence is called the **hierarchy** of operations.

Exponentiation (^) is performed first. If there are two or more exponentiations in a row, they are performed from right to left. That means that in evaluating the expression 2^3^4, 3 is first raised to the fourth power yielding 81 (3*3*3*3), then 2 is raised to the 81st power, yielding a *very* large 25-digit number (2*2*2* . . ., for 81 factors).

Multiplication (*) and division (/) are performed next, from left to right. Addition (+) and subtraction (−) are performed last, from left to right.

Example 3.1

```
2 + 3 * 4 ^ 2 / 5 - 6 * 7
2 + 3 * 16 / 5 - 6 * 7      4 squared = 16
    2 + 48 / 5 - 6 * 7      3 times 16 = 48
        2 + 9.6 - 6 * 7     48 divided by 5 = 9.6
            2 + 9.6 - 42    6 times 7 = 42
                11.6 - 42   2 plus 9.6 = 11.6
                   -30.4    11.6 minus 42 = -30.4
```

3.3 PARENTHESES

When operations are to be performed in an order different from that specified by the hierarchy of operations, parentheses must be used to indicate the desired sequence. The rules are similar to those used in mathematics.

As a rule, any expressions enclosed in parentheses are calculated first. Within parentheses, the hierarchy rules apply.

3.4 ASSIGNMENT OPERATOR

In addition, there may be several **levels** of parentheses in an expression. In that case, the expressions are evaluated from the innermost parentheses outward.

Example 3.2

```
3 * (2 + 7 * (8 + 9) * 2 - 4)
 3 * (2 + 7 * (17) * 2 - 4)      8 plus 9 = 17
  3 * (2 + 119 * 2 - 4)          7 times 17 = 119
   3 * (2 + 238 - 4)             119 times 2 = 238
    3 * (240 - 4)                2 plus 238 = 240
     3 * (236)                   240 minus 4 = 236
      708                        3 times 236 = 708
```

3.4 ASSIGNMENT OPERATOR

Now that we know how to perform a calculation, we need to be able to store the answer in memory so that the computer can use it for a succeeding calculation. This is done with an assignment statement. Its basic form is:

sn var = expression

where **sn** is a line number and **var** is a symbolic address or variable. The **expression** consists of variables and operators, and is calculated according to the rules discussed in the previous section. The result will be stored in location **var**.

Example 3.3

```
10   DECLARE INTEGER Amount, B, Result
20   DECLARE INTEGER No.of.Boys, No.of.Girls, Total.Number
30   Amount = 15
40   B = 30
50   Result = Amount * B + 5

100  No.of.Girls = 60
110  Total.Number = 150
120  No.of.Boys = Total.Number - No.of.Girls
```

First, at lines 30 and 40, the numbers 15 and 30 are stored in locations Amount and B, respectively. At line 50, these are then multiplied, yielding 450. The number 5 is added, for a total of 455. This result is stored in the variable Result.

At statement 100, a variable, No.of.Girls, is set to 60. Then at line 110, another variable, Total.Number, is set to 150. The calculation performed by statement 120 is then obvious because of the choice of variable names.

As we learned in chapter 1, a variable name can consist of a letter, followed optionally by an additional 29 letters, digits, underscores, or periods. Because of the flexibility provided by this naming convention, you should always choose variable names that are self-describing, as in statements 100 to 120 above. As programs get larger, the number of variables increases. A good choice of variable names is important to maintain control over a program, and to decrease the number of errors that the program contains.

The = symbol used in the above statements is not an equal sign in the mathematical sense, but is called the **assignment operator** in computing. It means that the expression on the right is to be stored in the location specified on the left. The two statements

```
A = B
```

and

```
B = A
```

are not the same and will not produce the same result. The first causes A to receive the value contained in B. The second causes B to receive the value contained in A.

For example, look at this program:

```
10 DECLARE INTEGER First.Number, Second.Number
20 First.Number = 100
30 Second.Number = 200
40 First.Number = Second.Number
```

Both locations, First.Number and Second.Number, will be 200 after line 40 has been executed. If line 40 had instead been:

```
40 Second.Number = First.Number
```

then both would have been 100.

NOTE! | **It is very important to understand this clearly. Many errors are directly attributable to a lack of understanding of which variable is assigned which value.**

A statement such as A + 10 = B is syntactically incorrect and will be rejected by BASIC as a syntax error. The variable that is assigned a value must be at the left side of an assignment statement. B = A + 10 will cause 10 to be added to the number stored in A, and the result to be stored in B.

3.5 SEQUENCES

A **sequence** is a type of program structure, consisting of a series of instructions executed one after the other. The first instruction of the sequence is performed, then the second, and so forth, until the last instruction of the sequence has been executed.

Example 3.4 | In the following program, we read a purchase price, calculate the tax, and compute the total of the price plus the tax. These values are then printed. The instructions that solve this problem form a sequence.

```
10 ! Read a price, calculate tax and total. Print results.
20    DECLARE DECIMAL(6,2) Price, Tax, Total
30    INPUT 'Enter the purchase price'; Price
40    Tax = .07 * Price        ! Calculate 7% tax
50    Total = Price + Tax      ! Calculate the total amount
60    PRINT 'Price :', Price
70    PRINT 'Tax   :', Tax
80    PRINT 'Total :', Total
90    END

runnh
Enter the purchase price? 199.95
Price : 199.95
Tax   : 14.00
Total : 213.95

Ready

>
```

Each instruction is executed, starting at the first and continuing until the last. Notice, for example, that statement 40 must be calculated prior to statement 50, or statement 50 would be adding an undefined Tax.

Example 3.5 As another example, here is a program that reads a name and address from DATA statements, and prints these to the output device.

```
10 ! Print a name and address
20    DECLARE STRING Name_, Address, City_state
30       READ Name_, Address, City_state
40       PRINT TAB(30); Name_
50       PRINT TAB(30); Address
60       PRINT TAB(30); City_state
70    ! Data statements
80       DATA "John Smith", "1234 Main Street"
90       DATA "Hometown, USA"
32767 END

runnh
                              John Smith
                              1234 Main Street
                              Hometown, USA

Ready

>
```

The executable statements in this program are lines 30, 40, 50, and 60. They are executed as a sequence. Line 20 is a DECLARE statement that provides information the computer needs, but is not considered executable. The DATA statements merely establish the data pool and are also not considered executable.

3.6 MULTI-STATEMENT LINES

This is a good place to learn a method of having more than one instruction for each line number. Such a line is called a **multi-statement line.**

VAX-BASIC assumes that a physical line that begins with a space or a <Tab> (press the <Tab> key) is a new instruction that will share the line number of the previous instruction. The computer assumes that every physical line is exactly one complete instruction. All the instructions on all physical lines that are part of one line number constitute what is called one **logical line.** The syntax of such a multi-statement logical line is:

```
sn       instruction    <Return>
<Tab>    instruction    <Return>
<Tab>    instruction    <Return>
            . . .
```

Instead of <Tab>, one or more spaces may be used. The logical line starts with a statement (or line) number and the first instruction (or a comment). The instruction is followed by a carriage return. If the next instruction is to be part of the same logical line, it must begin with a <Tab> or space, and is then followed by the instruction proper. This may continue for as many instruction lines as desired. VAX-BASIC knows that the logical line is ended when a new physical line begins with a line number in the first position of the line.

Example 3.6 Without multi-statement line:

```
10 INPUT X,Y
20 Z = X + Y
30 PRINT Z
40 END
```

Using multi-statement line:

```
10 INPUT X,Y
   Z = X + Y
   PRINT   Z
20 END
```

Example 3.7

```
10 ! Find average of five numbers
20     DECLARE REAL Grade_1, Grade_2, Grade_3, Grade_4, Grade_5, Sum, Avg
30     INPUT "Enter grades"; Grade_1, Grade_2, Grade_3, Grade_4, Grade_5
       Sum = Grade_1 + Grade_2 + Grade_3 + Grade_4 + Grade_5
                                            ! Add grades
       Avg = Sum / 5                        ! Find average
       PRINT Average of grades ="; Avg      ! Print average
32767 END                                   !
```

Each physical line of line 30 ends with a carriage return and the next instruction starts with at least one blank. Only one line number has been used for the four instructions of line 30. In addition, this example illustrates that each physical line may have its own comment.

> **NOTE!** While a comment, begun with an exclamation point, extends to the end of the physical line, a remark, begun with REM, extends to the end of the logical line; that is, up to the next statement number. Therefore, if REM is used, it must be the last item on a logical line.

3.7 MULTI-LINE STATEMENTS

Occasionally, we want a single statement to extend to more than one physical line. Frequently, a DECLARE statement will have to declare so many variables that not all will fit on one line. We could start a new DECLARE statement, but an alternative method may also prove useful.

The multi-statement line we considered earlier permits exactly one statement per physical line. For a single statement to span more than one physical line, a modification of the multi-statement line method is used. If a physical line ends with an ampersand, &, then VAX-BASIC assumes that the next physical line is a continuation of the previously begun statement. The syntax is:

```
sn start of statement           &
   continuation of statement &
   ...                          &
   continuation of statement &
   end of statement
```

The statement begins with a statement number. The first line, and each continuation line, ends with an ampersand. The last continuation line is ended with only a carriage return—no ampersand; this denotes the end of the statement. An example of a multi-line statement is:

```
10 DECLARE REAL      miles,         &
                     gallons,       &
                     mpg,           &
                                    &
           INTEGER   no.cars,       &
                     no.drivers,    &
                                    &
           STRING    make,          &
                     model
```

All of line 10 above is one long DECLARE statement. Three data-types are used to declare seven variables. Notice how a physical line containing only an ampersand at the end is used to separate parts of the multi-line statement for easier readability. Each line except the last ends with an ampersand.

In the above example, if each line had not been terminated with an ampersand before the <Return>, then BASIC would assume that the following physical line is a *new* statement. But this is not correct. Each physical line contains only a variable, or a type and a variable, and without the keyword DECLARE, these would have no meaning. It is the ampersand that tells the computer to treat all nine lines as a single DECLARE statement.

> **NOTE!** | **The ampersand must be immediately followed by the <Return>, with no intervening blanks.**

The next example illustrates multi-statement lines and the use of comments in multi-line statements. A comment ends at the end of the physical line. If the comment is actually longer, then the next physical line must have a new exclamation point.

Example 3.8 We wish to read a student's name and five test grades. Then we want the computer to calculate his test average. Finally, we want the student's name and average printed. The steps are:

>   Find student average:
>   Enter student name
>   Enter student grades
>   Calculate student average
>   Print name and average
>   Stop

If we follow this outline, which is an example of pseudocode (to be discussed in detail in chapter 4), we arrive at the following solution:

```
10  ! Find student average

20      DECLARE REAL GRADE1,GRADE2,GRADE3,GRADE4,GRADE5, &
                    SUM,                                 &
                                                         &
                DECIMAL(10,2) AVG,                       &
                                                         &
                STRING NAME.                             &

30      INPUT "Enter student name "; NAME.
        ! NAME is a reserved word in VAX-BASIC, so the period
        ! was added after the variable NAME

40      INPUT "Enter 5 grades "; GRADE1,GRADE2,GRADE3,GRADE4,GRADE5

50      ! Calculate sum of grades and average
        SUM = GRADE1 + GRADE2 + GRADE3 + GRADE4 + GRADE5
        AVG = SUM / 5

60      ! Output
        PRINT
        PRINT "Name   : ";NAME
        PRINT "Average: "; AVG

32767 END
```

```
runnh

Enter student name ? john smith
Enter 5 grades ? 87,92,83,71,80

Name    : john smith
Average:   82.6

Ready
```

Each logical line in the program above is followed by a blank line. Except for line 20, this is accomplished by pressing the <Tab> or space bar to make the computer think that a continuation line has begun, but this <Tab> or space is immediately followed by a carriage return, ending the line. As for line 20, there is an ampersand at the end of the last part of the DECLARE statement, which causes VAX-BASIC to treat the next line as part of the statement. The next line consists of a carriage return only, ending the statement.

Example 3.9 We have a number of coins and we would like a program that will determine their monetary value. The quantity of each denomination will be entered, and the total amount will be printed.

In pseudocode we have:

```
Find value of coins:
    Enter number of pennies
    Enter number of nickels
    Enter number of dimes
    Enter number of quarters
    Enter number of half dollars
    Enter number of dollars
    Calculate value of each denomination
    Add these values to get total
    Print total
Stop
```

The solution we arrive at is:

```
10  ! Calculate value of loose change

20      DECLARE INTEGER     No.Pennies, No.Nickels, No.Dimes,   &
                            No.Quarters, No.Halves, No.Dollars, &
                                                                &
                DECIMAL(6,2) Val.Pennies, Val.Nickels,          &
                             Val.Dimes, Val.Quarters,           &
                             Val.Halves, Val.Dollars,           &
                             Total.Value                        &

30  ! Enter number of coins
        INPUT 'Enter number of pennies '; No.Pennies
        INPUT 'Enter number of nickels '; No.Nickels
        INPUT 'Enter number of dimes   '; No.Dimes
        INPUT 'Enter number of quarters'; No.Quarters
```

54 | 3 ASSIGNMENT STATEMENTS

```
      INPUT 'Enter number of halves  '; No.Halves
      INPUT 'Enter number of dollars '; No.Dollars

40 !  Calculate value of each denomination
      Val.Pennies  = No.Pennies  * .01
      Val.Nickels  = No.Nickels  * .05
      Val.Dimes    = No.Dimes    * .10
      Val.Quarters = No.Quarters * .25
      Val.Halves   = No.Halves   * .50
      Val.Dollars  = No.Dollars  * 1.00

50 !  Calculate total amount
      Total.Value = Val.Pennies + Val.Nickels + Val.Dimes &
                  + Val.Quarters + Val.Halves + Val.Dollars &

60    PRINT 'Total value of coins is '; Total.Value

32767 END

runnh

Enter number of pennies  ? 13
Enter number of nickels  ? 6
Enter number of dimes    ? 3
Enter number of quarters ? 6
Enter number of halves   ? 1
Enter number of dollars  ? 8
Total value of coins is    10.73

Ready
```

Lines 20 and 50 above illustrate how one statement can be extended over two physical lines. You can see that an ampersand was required at the end of each physical line, because the next physical line was not a new statement; it was a continuation of the statement begun on the previous line. In line 20, we used this feature to get a blank line between parts of the DECLARE statement. The computer always assumes that the line following an ampersand and carriage return (&<Return>) is part of the same statement. When that combination ends the last part of an instruction, another physical line is needed to end the logical line. If that physical line contains a <Return> only, then a blank line appears in the listing. A new logical line can then be begun with a new line number.

Example 3.10 You invest $2500.00 in a bank account at a 8.25% yearly interest rate for two years. Interest is compounded once a year. Find and print the amount you will have in the bank after two years. The pseudocode is as follows:

> Compound interest:
>   Read the original principal and interest rate
>   Calculate the interest given at end of first year
>   Add first year interest to principal
>   Calculate the interest given at end of second year

> Add second year interest to principal
> Print resulting principal
> Stop

Notice that the second year's interest is calculated after the first year's interest is added to the bank balance. The program follows:

```
10  ! Compound interest program

20      DECLARE DECIMAL(8,2)    Principal, Interest,  &
                REAL            Int.rate              &

30  ! Read the original Principal and Interest rate
        READ Principal, Int.rate

40  ! Calculate first year's Interest
        Interest = Int.rate * Principal

    ! Add Interest to Principal
        Principal = Principal + Interest

50  ! Calculate second year's Interest
        Interest = Int.rate * Principal

    ! Add new Interest to Principal
        Principal = Principal + Interest

60  ! Output
        PRINT "Original balance is      "; 2500.00
        PRINT "Balance after two years is "; Principal

70      DATA 2500, .0825

32767 END
```

If you examine the above program closely, you will see how the compounding of interest works. The principal at line 50 is not the same as the principal at line 40. The first year's interest, which was calculated at line 40, was added to the original principal. The interest for the second year was calculated from this larger amount.

In the above program, keep in mind that the blank lines that separate statements are included by typing a space or <Tab> as the first character on the line and then pressing <Return>. The exception is line 20 where the ampersand at the end of the previous line makes VAX-BASIC assume that the logical line will be continued; the blank line is included simply by pressing <Return>.

Example 3.11 We will write a program that will calculate the hypotenuse of a right triangle, given the lengths of the other two sides. According to the Pythagorean theorem, the square of the hypotenuse is equal to the sum of the squares of the other two sides. If c is the hypotenuse, and a and b are the other two sides, then

3 ASSIGNMENT STATEMENTS

$$c^2 = a^2 + b^2$$

The hypotenuse can be found from this formula by taking the square root of both sides of the equation:

$$c = \sqrt{a^2 + b^2}$$

The square root can be found two ways. We can raise the radicand to the one-half power:

$$c = (a\hat{\,}2 + b\hat{\,}2)\hat{\,}0.5$$

or we can use a built-in function supplied by BASIC that can find square roots. This is the SQR function. Whatever we want the square root of, we put that into parentheses following the name of the function, SQR:

$$c = SQR\ (a\hat{\,}2 + b\hat{\,}2)$$

We will adopt the second method so as to learn how to use this function:

```
10  ! Find length of hypotenuse
20      DECLARE REAL Side_1, Side_2, Hypotenuse
30  ! Input section
        INPUT "Enter sides of triangle "; Side_1, Side_2
40  ! Calculation section
        Hypotenuse = SQR (Side_1^2 + Side_2^2)
50  ! Output section
        PRINT TAB(40); "Sides are    "; Side_1; "and"; Side_2
        PRINT TAB(40); "Hypotenuse is"; Hypotenuse
32767 END
```

In line 40, the parentheses contain a calculation. This calculation is performed before the square root is taken. We could also have performed the calculation in a previous statement, and then taken the square root of the result. Line 40 would then have been as follows:

```
40      ! Calculation section
        Sum_of_squares = Side_1^2 + Side_2^2
        Hypotenuse = SQR (Sum_of_squares)
```

The variable Sum_of_squares should be DECLAREd as REAL. A typical run of this program would produce the following:

```
runnh
Enter sides of triangle? 3,4
                                        Sides are    3 and 4
                                        Hypotenuse is 5
```

Another run might be:

```
runnh
Enter sides of triangle? 2.5,3.5

                             Sides are    2.5 and 3.5
                             Hypotenuse is 4.301163
```

3.8 FLOW CHARTS (optional topic)

A **flow chart** is a pictorial representation of a program's logic. Many programmers use flow charts to help them plan a program. Flow charts are frequently required as part of the documentation supplied with a delivered program. Where very large programs are involved, a flow chart is almost a necessity for comprehension of the intricacies of program design.

The flow chart is a diagram consisting of connected symbols (see Fig. 3-1). Each symbol's shape depends on the type of operation it represents. In this section, we introduce three shapes: the ellipse, which is used to designate the beginning or end of the program; the parallelogram, which is used for input and output instructions; and the rectangle, which is used for assignment instructions. As new program structures are added in future chapters, the appropriate flowchart symbols will be introduced.

The flow chart begins at the top with an ellipse containing the word START. It ends at the bottom with another ellipse labeled STOP. These ellipses are called the flow chart **terminators.** A flow chart can have only one START terminator, and, if the program is well written, it will have only one STOP terminator. In fact, in a structured program, there may be only one place where the program may STOP.

If the program has an input or output instruction, then that instruction appears inside a parallelogram on a flow chart. If the program has several input instructions in a row, or several output instructions in a row, then all of these input instructions or output instructions can be put into one paral-

Figure 3-1.
Flow Chart Symbols

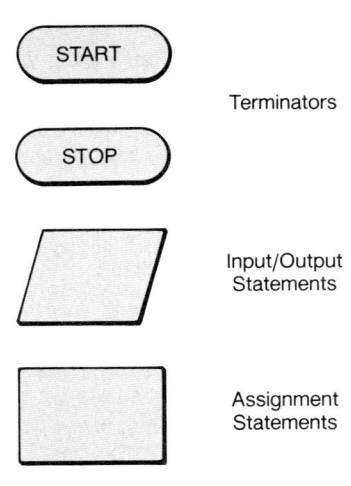

58 3 ASSIGNMENT STATEMENTS

lelogram. We do not, however, put both input and output instructions into the same parallelogram symbol.

Assignment statements in your program appear inside rectangles on the flow chart. Where the program has more than one assignment statement in a row (a sequence), all of them can be put into one rectangle. However, it is usual practice for only those statements that are closely related to be put into the same rectangle. If a program has a long sequence of assignment statements, these can usually be separated into groups of three, four, or five statements, each with a specific purpose. Each group is then placed in its own rectangle.

The symbols described above are connected with lines known as **flow lines** that indicate the direction in which the flow chart should be read. Normally, this would be from the top of the flow chart to the bottom. Occasionally, the direction is different from the norm and arrowheads are placed at the ends of the flow lines to indicate the direction of flow.

Here are some examples of programs and their flow charts.

Example 3.12 Figure 3-2 is the flow chart for the following program:

```
10 DECLARE INTEGER A, B, C, D
20     A = 10
30     B = 20
40     C = A * B + 5
50     D = C - A + 2 * B
60     PRINT A,B,C,D
32767 END
```

Figure 3-2.
Simple Flow Chart

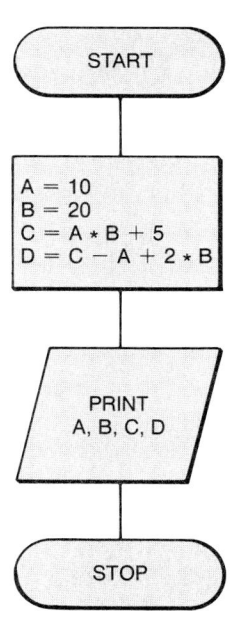

Example 3.13 | Figure 3-3 is the flow chart for the following program:

```
10 ! Read a Price, calculate Tax and Total. Print results.
20   DECLARE DECIMAL(10,2) Price, Tax, New.bal
30   INPUT 'Enter the purchase price'; Price
40   Tax = .08 * Price     ! Calculate 8% Tax
50   New.bal = Price + Tax ! Calculate the new balance
60   PRINT 'Price :', Price
70   PRINT 'Tax   :', Tax
80   PRINT 'Total :', New.bal
32767 END
```

Figure 3-3.
Flow Chart with Input and Output Statements

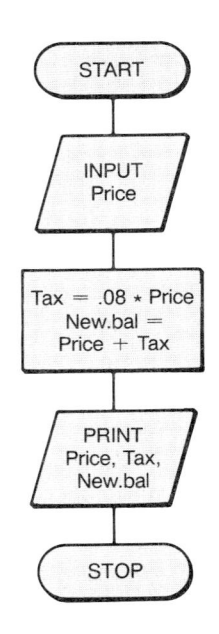

SUMMARY

Assignment statements are used to perform calculations and to store the results in memory. Arithmetic operators, used to perform arithmetic operations, are executed according to a set hierarchy. A logical line contains one or more physical lines. A physical line can contain one statement and a statement can extend over more than one line. A flow chart is a diagram of a program's logic.

Here, briefly, is a review of these topics.

1. Assignment statements:

sn variable = expression

Example: 120   A = B + C

2. Operators:

+ Addition
− Subtraction
* Multiplication
/ Division
^, ** Exponentiation

3. *Hierarchy of operators:*

^, ** Highest priority, execute right to left
*, / Next highest priority, execute left to right
+, − Lowest priority, execute left to right

4. *Logical lines:* These begin with a statement number and contain one or more physical lines. A logical line may be continued on a new physical line in one of two ways: One way is to end a physical line with an ampersand followed immediately by a carriage return; the next physical line is assumed to be a continuation of the statement on the previous line. The other way is to begin a physical line with a space or <Tab>; the new line is assumed to be a new statement on a new physical line of the current logical line. This method requires that exactly one statement be on each physical line.

5. *Physical lines:* These physically occupy one line of a CRT screen or other output device. See item 4 for more information on creating physical lines.

6. *Multi-statement lines:* These are logical lines that contain more than one statement, with each statement beginning on a new physical line.

7. *Multi-line statements:* These are statements that extend over more than one physical line. The method of ending a physical line with an ampersand is required. The statement ends when a physical line is not terminated with an ampersand.

8. *Flow charts:* Flow charts are composed of symbols connected by lines. Each symbol has a specific meaning.

REVIEW QUESTIONS

1. What is the purpose of an assignment statement? What is the syntax of an assignment statement?

2. In mathematics, addition is said to be commutative because A+B yields the same result as B+A. Does the assignment operator, =, have the commutative property? Explain. Specifically, what is the difference, if any, between the BASIC statements A=B and B=A?

3. What is meant by the **hierarchy** of operations? What is the hierarchy of the five operations discussed in this chapter?

4. What is the purpose of parentheses in an expression?

5. What is a multi-statement line? How many statement numbers are used for a multi-statement line?

6. What is a logical line? What is a physical line? How is a physical line ended? How is a logical line ended? How many statement numbers are used for a logical line?

7. Why would you use a multi-statement logical line instead of letting each statement have its own statement number?

8. What is the SQR function used for? How is it used?

9. What is a flow chart? Why is it used?

10. Which flow chart symbol is used for an assignment statement? Which is used for an input instruction? Which for an output instruction? What are the symbols used at the beginning and end of a flow chart called? What shape do they have? What is a flow line?

SYNTAX EXERCISES | The following statements all contain one or more syntax errors. Find and correct them.

1. `Total = A + B + C +`
2. `TAX = Tax_rate times Price`
3. `Price + Tax = Total`
4. `Total = Principal + Interest`
     `      = Principal + Rate * Principal`
5. `1987_Interest = Rate * 1987_Principal`
6. `Averages = A + B + C divided by 3`
7. `Area := Length * Width`
8. `Test_avg = (Test_1 + Test_2 + Test_3 / 3`
9. `Test-sum = Test.1 + Test.2 + Test.3 + Test.4`
10. `Card = "Ace of spades'`
11. `10_spot = "10 of Hearts"`
12. `Message = Stop!`
13. `100 Sum_of_numbers = First_number + Second_number`
          `+ Third_number + Fourth_number + Fifth_number`
14. `100 PRINT "The five student's grades are "; GRADE_1; GRADE_2;`
          `GRADE_3; GRADE_4; GRADE_5`
15. `100 INPUT "Enter 2 numbers :"; A, B`
    `SUM = A + B`
    `PRINT "Sum ="; SUM`

PROGRAMMING EXERCISES | Write programs or program segments that will carry out the requested activities. All output should contain strings that identify the output values. No value should be printed without being identified.

■ **1.** Enter the lengths of the three sides of a triangle. Find the length of the perimeter. Print the lengths of the three sides on one line, and the length of the perimeter on the next.

2. Enter the length of a side of a square. Print the length of a side and the area of the square.

3. Enter a customer name and the price of a suit. Read the sales tax rate from DATA. Calculate the tax on the suit and the total cost. Print the customer's name starting in column 10 of a line. On the next line, print the price of the suit, starting in column 30. On the line after that, print the tax, also starting in column 30. On the last line, print the total cost, starting in column 50. Each line should be suitably identified as name, price, tax, or total, starting in column 1 of the appropriate line.

■ **4.** Enter four numbers from the terminal. Find the average of the first two numbers, the average of the last two numbers, and the average of all four. Print the first two numbers and their average on one line, suitably identified. Print the second two numbers and their average on another line, again suitably identified. Print and identify the combined average on a third line.

5. Enter a salesman's name and the amounts of five of his sales. Find the total of the sales. Now figure a 10% commission. Print the salesman's name, his total sales, and his commission, all of them suitably identified.

6. Read two numbers into two integer variables, INT_A and INT_B. Divide INT_A by INT_B to get INT_C. Print INT_C (with a comment). Now read the same two numbers into the real variables REAL_A and REAL_B. Divide REAL_A by REAL_B to get REAL_C. Print REAL_C (also with a comment). Use the DATA statement:

```
100 DATA 8,3,8,3
```

Why are the answers different?

7. Write a program that will accept as input four integers, X, A, B, and C, and compute the value of Y using the formula $y = ax^2 + bx + c$. Print the x and y values.

8. Write a program that can solve the quadratic equation

$$ax^2 + bx + c = 0$$

The program will allow you to enter the coefficients of the equation, calculate the two solutions, and then print the coefficients and the solutions. Square roots can be obtained by raising to the one-half power, or by using a built-in function called SQR: To find the square root of A, use SQR(A). The formulas for the two roots are:

$$X_1 = \frac{-b + \sqrt{b^2 - 4ac}}{2a}$$

and

$$X_2 = \frac{-b - \sqrt{b^2 - 4ac}}{2a}$$

9. A man dies, leaving a widow and three children. In his will, he leaves 25% of his estate to his firstborn child, 25% of the remainder to his second child, 25% of the remainder after that to his third child, and the residue of the estate to his wife.

   a. Write the statements that calculate the amount bequeathed to each child and the amount left to the widow. The amount of the estate should be stored in the variable Estate.

   b. Write a program that lets you enter the amount of the estate and then calculates how much is left to the wife and to each child. The program should then print the amount left to each, suitably identified.

10. Given a rectangle whose length is in the variable Length, and whose width is in the variable Width:

   a. Write a statement that will find the length of the perimeter. The perimeter is the boundary of the rectangle.

b. If the area of a rectangle is 200 square feet, then it can be subdivided into eight pieces, each of 25 square feet, because 200 / 25 = 8. Given the Length and Width of a rectangle, write statements that find the area of the rectangle, and the number of pieces the rectangle may be divided into, such that each piece is 25 square feet.

c. A farmer has a rectangular piece of land and needs a program to help him calculate two quantities. The program will let him enter the length and width of his field. It will then calculate the amount of fence he needs to surround the property, and will also calculate the number of plots of 40000 square feet each into which the field can be divided. Finally, the program will print these calculations.

11. A company has three salesmen. The owner would like to know what percentage of the total sales each salesman accounts for. Read in each salesman's name and sales amount, then print his name, amount of sales, and percent of total sales. Use the following data statements:

DATA JIM JONES, 5000
DATA JILL JOHNSON, 7000
DATA SAM SMITH, 500

HINT: Use three different name variables and three different sales variables.

12. A bank account has a balance of $3500 at the beginning of an interest period. During this period, the following transactions take place:

Deposits of $246.50, $97.62, 325.00, and $123.87 are made.
Withdrawals of $62.50, $200.00, and $400.00 are made.
Interest at 1.625% on the balance is added at the end of the period.

a. If the deposits are in Deposit_1, Deposit_2, Deposit_3, and Deposit_4, and the withdrawals are in Withdraw_1, Withdraw_2, and Withdraw_3, write the statements that calculate the interest and the new balance.

b. Write a program that reads the data, calculates the new balance, and prints all results. All necessary values, such as deposits, withdrawals, and interest rate, are to be read from DATA statements. Print the original balance, the interest, the total deposits, the total withdrawals, and the new balance.

c. Same as part b, but data are to be entered with INPUT instructions.

13. You have a charge account at a department store. At the beginning of January, you receive a statement indicating a balance of $672.84 due on your account. You make a partial payment of $100.00. Because you did not pay the full amount, the store charges you a penalty of 1.85% of the unpaid amount, which will appear on your February bill. In addition, you charge purchases in January of $34.99, $87.95, and $62.99 on which you have to pay tax of 8.25%.

a. Write the statements that will calculate the penalty you are charged and the new balance. Assume that all needed data are in suitably named variables.

b. Write a program to calculate and print your February bill. The bill should show the January balance, the payment you made, the penalty charged on the unpaid balance, the purchases you made, the tax on each purchase, and the new balance. All information may be read from DATA statements, or you may use INPUT instructions with suitable prompts.

14. A doctor tells the nurse to administer intravenously a certain volume of solution to a patient in a specified period of time. For instance, 500 milliliters over a period of 12 hours. The nurse must calculate the number of drops per minute necessary to achieve the desired goal.

a. Write the statements that will convert milliliters per hour to drops per minute. (Note: 1 drop = .065 milliliters.)

b. Write a program to help the nurse. Input to the program will be the number of milliliters of fluid to administer and the number of hours in which to do it. The program should first calculate the number of milliliters per hour, then the number of milliliters per minute, and finally the number of drops per minute. The printout should show the drops per minute required for the nurse to carry out the doctor's instructions.

15. Use READ, DATA, and PRINT statements to print your name in bold headlines as in the following example:

```
         JJ     OOO      EEEEE
         JJ    OOOOO     EEEEE
         JJ    OO OO     EE
         JJ    OO OO     EE
         JJ    OO OO     EEEEE
         JJ    OO OO     EEEEE
         JJ    OO OO     EE
      JJ JJ    OO OO     EE
      JJJJJ    OOOOO     EEEEE
       JJJ      OOO      EEEEE
```

4 Program Design and Modularization—GOSUB

Outline

4.1 Structured Programming
4.2 Top-Down Analysis (Stepwise Decomposition)
4.3 Modularity
4.4 Subroutines
    Labels
    The GOSUB Statement
    The RETURN Statement
    General Form of GOSUB Subroutines
4.5 The EXIT PROGRAM Statement
4.6 Flow Charts
Summary
Review Questions
Syntax Exercises
Programming Exercises
Enrichment Topics
    VAX-BASIC Subprograms
    Arguments and Parameters

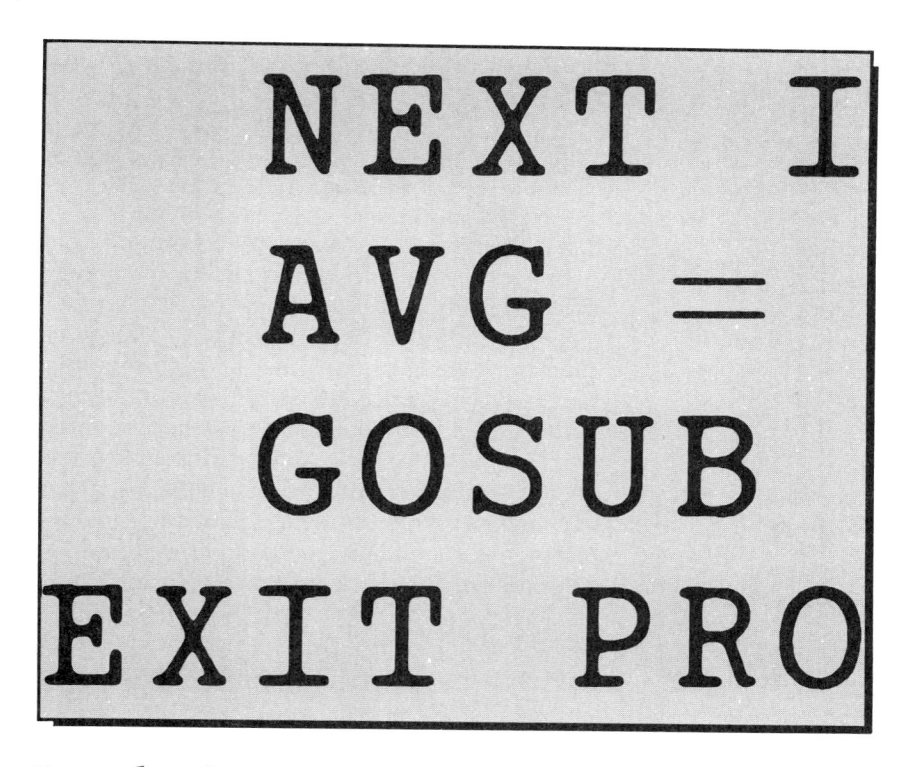

Introduction   This is an extremely important chapter. In it, you will learn how to design a program properly, and how to code it properly. You should read and study it carefully. At the same time, it is possible that some of the material may not make sense to you if you are a beginning programmer. But as you begin to write more advanced programs, you are urged to reread this chapter occasionally because the material in it will become increasingly valuable as you gain more experience.

4.1 STRUCTURED PROGRAMMING

In the early days of programming, computers had very small memories and were very slow. A good program was one that worked, used little space, and was optimized to take as little time as possible. Today, memories are large and present few constraints on the program. Time is also not a factor in most cases because of the high speeds at which today's computers operate. These factors have made the older methods of programming obsolete, except at the very lowest level of the machine, known as the microprogramming level.

A good program today is one that is clearly written, easily comprehended, easily debugged (corrected for errors), easily maintained, and easily modified. To meet these requirements, the concept of a **structured program** has arisen. A structured program has the following property:

> The program is divided into segments, or **modules.** Within each module, each statement can be reached only from the statement above it, and each statement, when it has executed, will pass control only to the statement below it.

In a structured program, you always know how you arrived at a particular instruction, and you always know where you are going after that instruction is completed. Each statement affects only a limited section of the program. If a statement must be modified for any reason, the effect of this change will be limited to a small section of the program, and there will be no widespread side effects. In an unstructured program, side effects can produce errors that can be notoriously difficult to track down and correct. In the early days of programming, expensive programs were often trashed because they had become unmanageable due to the interlocking nature of their statements. A change in a single statement could produce a plethora of problems throughout the entire program.

4.2 TOP-DOWN ANALYSIS (STEPWISE DECOMPOSITION)

One of the most important techniques used in designing structured programs is the **top-down approach** to program analysis, also called **stepwise decomposition.**

In the top-down approach, the problem to be solved is considered to be the top or highest level. This level is then divided into smaller steps that constitute the next level. If any of these steps requires further refinement, it is divided into even smaller steps, yielding additional levels. Eventually, the problem is sufficiently decomposed so that it can be coded in the target language; in our case, VAX-BASIC. The process is commonly referred to as stepwise decomposition, or decomposition for short.

The analysis at each level is done using statements called *pseudocode*. Unlike code that is written in a "foreign" language such as BASIC, pseudocode is written in English. Because we can usually think better in our native tongue than in a foreign language, we always use pseudocode to develop and refine the logic of our programs.

In the decomposition of a program into levels, higher levels are assigned lower level numbers. For example, the highest level, level 0, might always be:

   Solve the problem

But this statement does not provide any detail. We could go on to the next level, level 1:

   Solve the problem:
     Read data
     Calculate results
     Print results
   Stop

As you can see, level 1 has more detail than level 0, but there is still too much information missing to allow us to code the program. We could go on to level 2 by refining one or more of the three level 1 statements. For example, the second statement of level 1, "Calculate results," could be refined as follows:

   Calculate results:
     Add all numbers
     Divide by the number of numbers
     Store average
   Return

Notice that we did not write "Stop" at the end of this level 2 decomposition; that is because the program does not stop there. Instead, we wrote "Return." This means we will return to level 1 of the program to continue with the next level 1 instruction. Only the end of level 1 will have a "Stop." The meaning of the statements "Stop" and "Return" will be made clearer later in this chapter.

It is important to understand that each level of the top-down program is self-sufficient. The logic at each level should be completely evident and comprehensible. The details may be hidden, as they are expanded at a lower level, but the logic is there. If levels 2 and below are thrown away, level 1 should be understandable all by itself. Similarly, if everything below level 2 is thrown out, each of the level 2 decompositions should be logically correct.

If the decomposition at any level does not make sense when examined as an isolated unit, then the decomposition is considered faulty. The program has not been analyzed correctly, and the probability is strong that debugging and maintaining the program will be difficult even though the program is structured.

The following shows an incorrect decomposition of a problem. The solution may work, and even give correct results, but someone trying to understand just the first level will be wondering: "Is there any output from this program?"

Level 1:
    Solve the problem:
        Read the data
        Calculate the average
    Stop

Level 2:
    Calculate the average:
        Add the numbers
        Divide by the number of numbers
        Store average
        Print average
    Return

There will be output because level 2 has the statement "Print average." Unfortunately, this does not help someone reading level 1; in level 1, it appears as if the program stops after the calculations have been completed. It is also confusing to someone reading level 2. What, after all, does "Print average" have to do with "Calculate the average"?

Programming Tip: Read each level of your pseudocode as if no other level existed. If each level makes sense when treated this way, then you have a good decomposition.

As an example, consider the problem of throwing a party. Level 0 is:

Throw a party

Level 1 might be:

Throw a party:
  Invite guests
  Provide food
  Have party
  Clean up
Stop

At level 2, we would have decompositions of each of the level 1 statements:

Invite guests:
  Get personal telephone book
  Make up guest list
  Send invitations
Return to next step at previous level

Provide food:
  Make menu
  Cook food
  Serve food
Return to next step at previous level

We could go on with more level 2 decompositions, but let us move on to one of the level 3 decompositions:

```
Make menu:
   Select aperitif
   Select soup
   Select salad
   Select entree
   Select dessert
   Select after-dinner wine
Return to next step at previous level
```

And so on, step after step, level after level. Note carefully that each stage of the decomposition is a complete solution in and of itself of one step at the previous level. This self-sufficiency means each step at each level can be comprehended without referring to any other step. This is the hallmark of a program that has been properly decomposed.

4.3 MODULARITY

One method of making a program easy to write, debug, and maintain is to write it using **modules.** Each pseudocode statement at one level of decomposition that is further developed at the next level becomes a module. Such modules are called **subroutines** or **functions,** depending on how many values they calculate and how they are coded.

To explain modules, consider a chef using a cookbook to prepare a meal. To prepare Thanksgiving dinner, the chef does not look under "Thanksgiving." Instead, he (or she) decomposes the problem into different courses and looks under sections labeled "Soups," "Salads," "Appetizers," "Main courses," "Desserts," and so on. These are the level 1 modules.

Each category could be further divided into lower levels. For instance, "Main courses" might be subdivided into "Meats," "Fowl," and "Seafood." These would be level 2. "Meats" might be subdivided into "Beef," "Veal," Lamb," and so on, for level 3. At the lowest level, you will finally find a recipe for a particular dish.

Each of the levels described above could be considered a module. "Soups" is a module; so are "Salads" and "Main courses." Each of them, in turn, contains submodules.

In the following pseudocode,

```
Solve the problem:
   Read the data
   Calculate the results
   Print the results
Stop
```

we consider the program to consist of three modules: "Read the data," "Calculate the results," and "Print the results." As we will see, these modules can be written as self-contained independent units that are controlled by a module at a higher level.

A module, then, is a group of statements that is more or less self-contained, and that performs a specific, well-defined function. A module should have one purpose, and this should be stated in a comment at the beginning of the module. If the module's purpose cannot be described simply, it usually means that the decomposition of the problem is faulty. Either the module is doing too much, or it is doing only part of a job.

4.4 SUBROUTINES

One type of module that can be used to write BASIC programs is a subroutine. A subroutine may use any amount of data to calculate any number of results. Based on the discussion above, a subroutine should have one clearly defined purpose. First, some preliminaries.

Labels

A label is an identifier consisting of 1 to 31 letters, digits, periods, or underscores, but whose first character is a letter. In that respect, a label is like a variable; however, a label is not used to store anything. Instead, it is used as a reference point in a program.

A label may not begin in the first column of a new line because only statement numbers may begin in the first column. It may be placed anywhere in a logical line, but must precede any statement or comment on a physical line. The label is followed by a colon. Some examples of labels are:

```
100 Add_grades: Sum = Grade.1 + Grade.2
200 Find_avg:
        Sum = grade1 + grade2 + grade3
        Avg = Sum / 3
300 ! Read grades, find average, print result
    Read_grades:
        INPUT "Enter 3 grades "; grade_1, grade_2, grade_3
    Find_sum:
        Sum = grade_1 + grade_2 + grade_3
    Average:
        Avg = Sum / 3
    Output:
        PRINT "Average = "; Avg
```

At the moment, it may appear that there is no difference between using a comment and using a label; but there is a very important distinction—a label may be referred to by another statement in a different part of the program; a comment may not. The use of such labels will become apparent shortly.

The GOSUB Statement

One way of achieving program modularity is with the GOSUB statement and subroutines. The syntax of a GOSUB statement is:

sn GOSUB label

where **label** is the label of the statement where the subroutine begins. The GOSUB statement may be on a line by itself, in which case it requires a statement number such as:

```
100 GOSUB Find_avg
```

or it may be part of a multi-statement line, such as:

```
100   INPUT X, Y, Z
      GOSUB Find_avg
      PRINT Avg
```

When the GOSUB statement is executed, control passes to the label specified in the GOSUB statement. Notice that the label reference in the GOSUB statement does not have a colon. The colon is used only where the identifier is actually used as a label. In the above examples, control would pass to the subroutine whose first statement has the label `Find_avg:`. After returning from that subroutine, the statement following the GOSUB statement would execute. In this example, `PRINT Avg`. See Figure 4-1.

Figure 4-1
Invoking a Subroutine and Returning

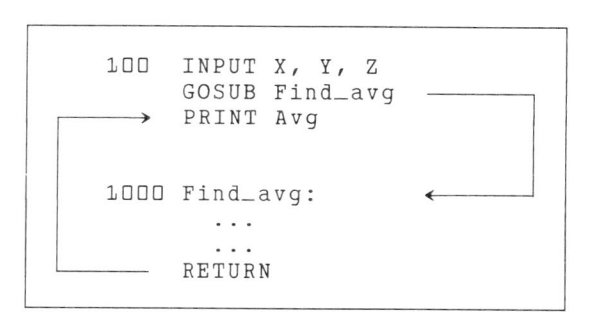

```
100   INPUT X, Y, Z
      GOSUB Find_avg
      PRINT Avg

1000  Find_avg:
      ...
      ...
      RETURN
```

Most dialects of BASIC require that a statement number be used in a GOSUB statement, instead of a label. This would be the statement number of the first statement in the subroutine. VAX-BASIC permits this usage also. For example, suppose that your subroutine begins at line 500. You can invoke the subroutine with the statement:

```
100 GOSUB 500
```

But the method that uses a label is preferred to the method that uses a line number because a label is much more descriptive of the purpose of the subroutine; hence, the program is much easier to comprehend and maintain. In addition, if the statement numbers in the program are changed for any reason, the reference to a label will remain valid, while the reference to a statement number may no longer be correct. Since a label is better than a line number, this textbook will only use labels in GOSUB statements.

The RETURN Statement

The last statement of the GOSUB subroutine must be the RETURN statement. It returns control to the statement following the GOSUB statement that invoked the subroutine. If line 30 contains `GOSUB Enter_data`, and the next statement is at line 40, then when the subroutine at the label `Enter_data` ends by executing its RETURN statement, statement 40 is executed.

The syntax of the RETURN statement is:

sn RETURN

For example:

```
1550 RETURN
```

The RETURN statement can be part of a multi-statement line, but this is not good programming practice. The RETURN statement should *always* be on a line by itself at the end of the subroutine. Structured programming requires that there be only one RETURN statement in a subroutine. Every section of code has one way in and one way out, and the way out of a subroutine is the RETURN statement.

To repeat, IN A STRUCTURED PROGRAM, THERE IS ONLY ONE RETURN STATEMENT IN EACH SUBROUTINE, AND THE ONLY WAY TO LEAVE THE SUBROUTINE IS THROUGH THIS STATEMENT.

General Form of GOSUB Subroutines

The general form of the GOSUB statement and its corresponding subroutine is:

```
sn1  GOSUB label            ! Invoke the subroutine
                              . . .
                              . . .
sn2  label:                 ! Start of subroutine
                              . . .
        subroutine statements
                    . . .
sn3  RETURN
                            ! End of subroutine
```

Example 4.1

```
30 GOSUB Routine       ! Invoke the subroutine
         . . .
100 EXIT PROGRAM

1000 Routine:          ! Start of subroutine
              . . .
        subroutine statements
                  . . .
1100 RETURN            ! End of subroutine
```

Notice that no colon is used after the label in the GOSUB statement. The colon is used only where the identifier actually acts as the label; in this case, line 1000.

Statement 30 above could be changed to:

```
30 GOSUB 1000        ! Invoke the routine
```

This method of using the statement number is less desirable than that of using the label.

Figure 4-2 shows the order in which statements are executed when subroutines are used.

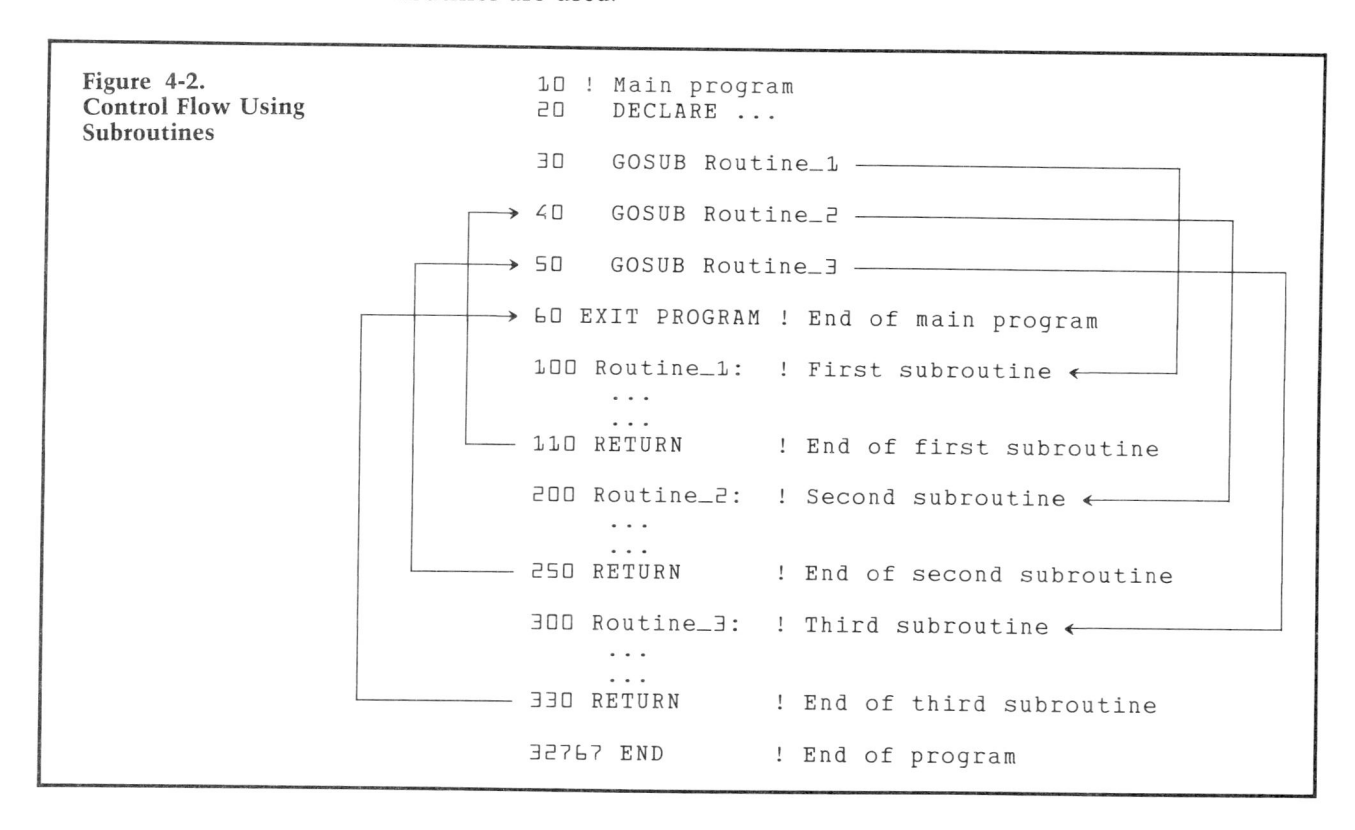

Figure 4-2.
Control Flow Using Subroutines

```
10  ! Main program
20     DECLARE ...
30     GOSUB Routine_1
40     GOSUB Routine_2
50     GOSUB Routine_3
60  EXIT PROGRAM ! End of main program
100 Routine_1:   ! First subroutine
    ...
    ...
110 RETURN       ! End of first subroutine
200 Routine_2:   ! Second subroutine
    ...
    ...
250 RETURN       ! End of second subroutine
300 Routine_3:   ! Third subroutine
    ...
    ...
330 RETURN       ! End of third subroutine
32767 END        ! End of program
```

4.5 THE EXIT PROGRAM STATEMENT

You will recall that, at the end of the first level of decomposition, we had a "Stop" pseudocode instruction. Each statement at level 1 invokes a subroutine. Level 1 is called the **main program.** It is written first, using the lowest line numbers.

After the main program, we have all of our subroutines. But we want the subroutines to execute only when they are invoked by a GOSUB statement. Therefore, we need some way of stopping program execution after the last statement of the main program has been executed. We use the EXIT PROGRAM instruction for this purpose, as illustrated in Example 4.1. After this instruction executes, you will see the message `Ready`, and be back in the BASIC environment.

Example 4.2 | A worker has put in his regular hours and some additional overtime hours. Overtime is paid at one and one-half times his regular rate of pay. We have to write a program that will calculate his salary. Input to the program is the employee's name, employee number, his regular rate of pay, his regular hours worked, and the number of overtime hours worked. The program has to calculate his salary, then print his name, employee number, and salary.

The first level of pseudocode looks like this:

> Payroll program:
>   Enter employee data
>   Calculate employee salary
>   Print employee results
> Stop

There are no details yet, but we can already write the main program for this problem:

```
10 ! Payroll program
20     (reserved for DECLARE statement)
30     GOSUB Enter_data        ! Enter employee data
40     GOSUB Calculate_salary  ! Calculate employee salary
50     GOSUB Print_results     ! Print employee results
60  EXIT PROGRAM
```

Notice that every GOSUB statement has a comment. This reinforces the self-documenting feature of the subroutine labels. Also notice the indenting. Each of the statements in a module is indented with respect to the first and last statements of the module. This indentation improves program readability.

As you read the comments in the main program, you can see that the program above is a complete solution to the problem. In contrast, suppose that printing of the output were to be done in the module that calculates the salaries. The main program would then look like this:

```
10 ! Payroll program
20     (reserved for DECLARE statement)
30     GOSUB Enter_data        ! Read employee data
40     GOSUB Calculate_salary  ! Calculate employee salary
50  EXIT PROGRAM
```

Can you see that this program is incomplete? There is something missing! Where does the program provide for output? It is clear that proper decomposition requires that the printout procedure be part of this level 1 main program and not be deferred to the subroutine that calculates the salary.

Let us go on to level 2. Each of the three statements at level 1 requires refinement, as follows:

> Enter employee data:
>   Enter employee name
>   Enter employee number
>   Enter base rate of pay
>   Enter regular hours
>   Enter overtime hours
> Return

Calcuate employee salary:
  Calculate regular pay
  Calculate overtime pay
  Calculate total pay
Return

Print employee results:
  Print employee number
  Print employee name
  Print employee salary
Return

The logic for each of these statements is simple enough to put into code without the need for further decomposition. Since the employee's name, number, and base pay do not change very frequently, only when a new contract is signed, these will be read from data statements. The hours worked, on the other hand, may change every week; this will be input from the terminal with an INPUT instruction. The subroutines begin at lines 100, 200, and 300, and appear below:

```
100    Read_data:           ! Enter employee data
110      READ Employee.Name
         READ Employee.No.
         READ Base.Pay
120      PRINT "Employee : "; Employee.Name    ! This is a prompt
         INPUT "Enter regular hours worked "; Reg.Hrs
         INPUT "Enter overtime hours worked"; Ovt.Hrs
130    RETURN

200    Calculate_salary:  ! Calculate employee salary
210      Reg.Pay = Base.Pay * Reg.Hrs            ! Regular pay
         Ovt.Pay = Base.Pay * Ovt.Hrs * 1.5      ! Overtime pay
         Salary = Reg.Pay + Ovt.Pay              ! Total salary
220    RETURN

300    Print_data:        ! Print employee results
310      PRINT
         PRINT Employee.No.
         PRINT Employee.Name
         PRINT 'Total employee salary = '; Salary
         PRINT
320    RETURN
```

Each of the subroutines begins with its label and a comment describing its purpose. This comment is generally the same as the comment attached to the GOSUB statement that invoked the subroutine.

Figure 4-3 shows what the complete program looks like, after we have put all the pieces together. Line 60 is where the program ends. Without line 60, the computer would try to execute the statements beginning at line 100 after it had executed line 50. Those statements, beginning at line 100, are a subroutine, however. When the RETURN statement at line 130 is reached, an error would occur, because there would be no statement to return to. A

Figure 4-3.
Payroll Program

```
10  ! Payroll program
20      DECLARE STRING         Employee.Name, Employee.No., &
                REAL           Reg.Hrs, Ovt.Hrs, &
                DECIMAL(8,2)   Base.Pay, Reg.Pay, Ovt.Pay, &
                               Salary
30      GOSUB Read_data        ! Read employee data
40      GOSUB Calculate_salary ! Calculate employee salary
50      GOSUB Print_data       ! Print employee results
60    EXIT PROGRAM

100   Read_data:         ! Enter employee data
110     READ Employee.Name
        READ Employee.No.
        READ Base.Pay
120     PRINT "Employee : "; Employee.Name
        INPUT "Enter regular hours worked "; Reg.Hrs
        INPUT "Enter overtime hours worked"; Ovt.Hrs
130   RETURN

200   Calculate_salary:  ! Calculate employee salary
210     Reg.Pay = Base.Pay * Reg.Hrs             ! Regular pay
        Ovt.Pay = Base.Pay * Ovt.Hrs * 1.5       ! Overtime pay
        Salary = Reg.Pay + Ovt.Pay               ! Total salary
220   RETURN

300   Print_data:        ! Print employee results
310     PRINT
        PRINT TAB(25); Employee.No.
        PRINT TAB(25); Employee.Name
        PRINT TAB(25); 'Total employee salary = '; Salary
        PRINT
320   RETURN

1000 ! DATA statements
1010     DATA "John Smith", 123-45-6789, 12.49

32767 END


runnh

Employee : John Smith
Enter regular hours worked ? 40
Enter overtime hours worked? 3.6
                        123-45-6789
                        John Smith
                        Total employee salary = 567.05
```

subroutine must be executed only after being invoked by a GOSUB statement.

Be aware that the blank lines in the above program actually contain a typed space. If you refer to the discussion on logical lines in chapter 3, you will recall that this is how a physical line becomes part of the current logical line.

Look at each of the modules in Fig. 4-3, including the main program, and see how the logic of each one can be understood without reference to any other. The program as a whole has been created out of pieces. By decomposing a problem, we can always reduce it from one complicated problem to many simple ones. It is generally much easier to program many simple problems than one hard one.

Example 4.3 A customer has a charge account at a department store. On the last day of each month, he receives a statement showing the balance owed on the account. During the following month, the customer makes a payment toward the balance due (possibly a partial payment) and also makes some purchases.

We want to write a program that can prepare the statement for the following month. Input to the program will be the previous month's balance, the payment made during the month, and five purchases made during the month. The new balance will be calculated by subtracting the payment from the previous balance, then adding all of the five purchases to the result. For now, we will ignore the interest due on any unpaid balance (admittedly this is unrealistic). The first-level decomposition is:

    Charge account program:
      Enter data
      Calculate new balance
      Print new account statement
    Stop

Continuing with our decomposition, we have level 2:

    Enter data:
      Enter name
      Enter previous balance
      Enter payment
      Enter five purchases
    Return

    Calculate new balance:
      Subtract payment from previous balance (unpaid balance)
      Add all purchases
      Add sum of purchases to unpaid balance (new balance)
    Return

    Print new account statement:
      Print name
      Print previous balance
      Print payment
      Print sum of purchases
      Print new balance
    Return

We now write the code for each module and put them together for our program, as shown in Figure 4-4.

78 | 4 PROGRAM DESIGN AND MODULARIZATION—GOSUB

Figure 4-4.
Charge Account Program

```
10  ! Charge account program
20      DECLARE STRING         Name., &
                DECIMAL(7,2)   Purch.1, Purch.2, Purch.3, &
                               Purch.4, Purch.5, &
                DECIMAL(8,2)   Old_Balance, Payment, New_Balance, &
                               Sum_of_Purchases, Unpaid_Balance
30      GOSUB Read_data          ! Enter data
40      GOSUB Find_new_balance   ! Calculate new balance
50      GOSUB Print_statement    ! Print new account statement
60      EXIT PROGRAM

100 Read_data:                   ! Enter data
110     INPUT 'Enter name'; Name.
120     INPUT 'Enter previous balance'; Old_Balance
130     INPUT 'Enter payment'; Payment
140     INPUT 'Enter the five purchases'; &
               Purch.1, Purch.2, Purch.3, Purch.4, Purch.5
150 RETURN

200 Find_new_balance:            ! Calculate new balance
210     Unpaid_Balance = Old_Balance - Payment
220     Sum_of_Purchases = Purch.1 + Purch.2 + Purch.3 &
               + Purch.4 + Purch.5
230     New_Balance = Unpaid_Balance + Sum_of_Purchases
240 RETURN

300 Print_statement:             ! Print new account statement
310     PRINT
320     PRINT Name.
330     PRINT 'Old balance       '; Old_Balance
340     PRINT 'Payment           '; Payment
350     PRINT 'Sum of purchases  '; Sum_of_Purchases
360     PRINT
370     PRINT 'New balance       '; New_Balance
380     PRINT
390 RETURN

32767 END

runnh

Enter name? Mike Macho
Enter previous balance? 645.78
Enter payment? 300
Enter the five purchases? 23.95,78.98,13.69,0,0

Mike Macho
Old balance         645.78
Payment             300.00
Sum of purchases    116.62

New balance         462.40
```

In Figure 4-4, note that 32767 has again been used as the number of the END statement. This statement number is the maximum permitted in VAX-BASIC and a number of other BASIC dialects. Therefore, it is safe to use it as the last statement number of the program.

Example 4.4 This next example illustrates how a subroutine can be invoked more than once from different places in a program. It also has a subroutine invoking other subroutines.

We have three salesmen. Each salesman receives a salary equal to $200.00 plus 5% of his monthly sales. A program is needed to calculate and print each salesman's salary. Input to the program will be the salesmen's names and their sales totals. Output will be their names, their sales, and their salaries.

In this program, we have to do the same thing three times, once for each salesman. There are two ways this can be handled, and these two methods lead to two different solutions.

One method has the following first-level pseudocode:

```
Salesmen's salaries:
   Process first salesman
   Process second salesman
   Process third salesman
Stop
```

The alternative generates this first-level pseudocode:

```
Salesman's salaries:
   Read data for all salesmen
   Calculate salaries for all salesmen
   Print output for all salesmen
Stop
```

These two first-level decompositions generate different programs. It is not clear at this point which will be the better solution. Such a situation is very common in programming. Frequently, a programmer faced with such a choice must try both methods to determine which program is better. The better program is the one that is clearer and more easily comprehended by a person who did not write the program.

We will continue with the first method presented above, because it allows us to illustrate something new: one subroutine invoking another.

The main program thus far will be coded as follows:

```
10 ! Salesmen's salaries
20     (reserved for DECLARE statement)
30     GOSUB Process_salesman        ! Process first salesman
40     GOSUB Process_salesman        ! Process second salesman
50     GOSUB Process_salesman        ! Process third salesman
60  EXIT PROGRAM
```

This main program calls the same subroutine three times because all three salesmen require identical processing. Instead of repeating the same statements three times, once for each salesman, we write a subroutine that does all that is necessary to process one salesman, and then invoke that subroutine three times, once for each salesman. Let us work on that subroutine. It will be at level 2.

> Process a salesman:
>   Read data for salesman
>   Calculate salary for salesman
>   Print output for salesman
> Return

We can code the subroutine this way:

```
1000    Process_salesman:               ! Process a salesman
1010      GOSUB Enter_data              ! Enter salesman's data
1020      SALARY = 200.00 + 0.05 * SALES
1030      GOSUB Print_data              ! Print salesman's data
1040    RETURN
```

Notice how this one subroutine has one definable purpose even though it is used for input, processing, and output. In this case, the purpose is to process one salesman. Recall that in a proper decomposition of a problem, every module must have this characteristic of uniqueness of purpose.

The subroutine at line 1000 calls other subroutines from lines 1010 and 1030. These subroutines will be at the third level of pseudocode. Their logic follows:

> Enter salesman's data:
>   Enter salesman's name
>   Enter salesman's sales
> Return
>
> Print salesman's data:
>   Print salesman's name
>   Print salesman's sales
>   Print salesman's salary
> Return

The salary calculation is only one line of code, so we will not need a subroutine for it. The input and output subroutines are straightforward. Their code appears in the final program (Fig. 4-5).
Again, notice how the top-down decomposition process allowed us to concentrate on the overall solution to the problem before we had to get into the details. At each step, we went only one level deeper into the logic. This is very important! If you try to work in a linear fashion, from the beginning to the end, without a decomposition into modules, it is very easy to lose sight of what you are doing at any one moment.

The brain can only keep track of approximately seven things at one time.[1] (Try going to the store to shop for 15 items without a shopping list.)

---

1. The Magical Number Seven, Plus or Minus Two: Some Limits on Our Capacity for Processing Information", G. A. Miller, Psychological Review 63:81-97.

Figure 4-5.
Salesmen's Salaries

```
10  ! Salesmen's salaries
20      DECLARE STRING          NAME., &
                DECIMAL(10,2)   SALES, &
                DECIMAL(8,2)    SALARY
30      GOSUB Process_salesman      ! Process first salesman
40      GOSUB Process_salesman      ! Process second salesman
50      GOSUB Process_salesman      ! Process third salesman
60   EXIT PROGRAM                   ! End of program

1000 Process_salesman:               ! Process a salesman
1010    GOSUB Enter_data             ! Enter salesman's data
1020    SALARY = 200.00 + 0.05 * SALES
1030    GOSUB Print_data             ! Print salesman's data
1040 RETURN

1100 Enter_data:                     ! Enter salesman's data
1110    INPUT "Enter salesman's name"; NAME.
1120    INPUT "Enter salesman's sales"; SALES
1130 RETURN
1200 Print_data:                     ! Print salesman's data
1210    PRINT TAB(40); NAME.
1220    PRINT TAB(40); 'Sales  : '; SALES
1230    PRINT TAB(40); 'Salary : '; SALARY
1240 RETURN

32767 END


runnh
Enter salesman's name? Nancy Notting
Enter salesman's sales? 9400
                                        Nancy Notting
                                        Sales  :  9400
                                        Salary :   670

Enter salesman's name? Bruce Bolling
Enter salesman's sales? 8700
                                        Bruce Bolling
                                        Sales  :  8700
                                        Salary :   635

Enter salesman's name? Ruth Ryan
Enter salesman's sales? 10200
                                        Ruth Ryan
                                        Sales  : 10200
                                        Salary :   710
```

Therefore, the level you are currently working at can only be decomposed into about seven statements or modules. If any one of your modules starts getting much longer than that, your decomposition is probably inadequate. Think in bigger chunks! Combine many steps into one larger step. The decomposition of that larger step will then yield the smaller ones at the next level.

NOTE! It should be pointed out that many experienced programmers would have incorporated the `Input_data` and `Print_data` subroutines into `Process_salesman`. This is not a good idea. According to a programming concept called data abstraction, **all input and output functions should be performed by subroutines that are separate from all other calculations.** (The concept of data abstraction is greatly simplified here from its true meaning in computer science. Technically, the concept defined here is I/O abstraction.) When this rule is observed, the rest of the program is concerned only with the calculations, and not at all with the details of input and output. If, at some future time, the program must be modified in such a way that the form or type of input must be changed, only the subroutine dealing with the input must be reworked. Nothing else in the program need be affected. A similar remark is applicable if the output must be changed.

In Example 4.4 (Figure 4-5), the data were entered from the terminal. Suppose the input had to come from DATA statements instead. If the INPUT statements had been included in `Process_salesman`, we would have to change that subroutine to reflect the change in the form of input. This subroutine also calculates salary, and presumably it would also print the results.

Now, it is virtually a law of nature that if you change something that works, it won't work anymore. While changing the input instructions in our subroutine, we may inadvertently cause something else to go wrong. Merely to change the form of input may require us to debug the entire module!

However, if we leave the subroutines `Enter_data` and `Print_data` as separate modules, and don't incorporate them into subroutine `Process_salesman`, **then changing the form of input can affect only the subroutine `Enter_data`. `Process_salesman` will not be affected at all;** it has data abstraction incorporated into its design.

Similarly, if we are not satisfied with the appearance of the output, we need only modify `Print_data`. **This change will not affect any other part of the program.**

You should come back to this idea of data abstraction after you have gained some experience in writing lengthier and more difficult programs.

4.6 FLOW CHARTS (optional topic)

Because modules are independently written, self-contained units, each module has its own flow chart.

Only the main program has START and STOP in the terminators of its flow chart. The terminator at the beginning of a subroutine flow chart contains the name, or label, of the subroutine. The terminator at the end of a subroutine contains the word RETURN.

When a module (the main program is considered a module) contains a GOSUB statement, that statement is contained in a rectangular box with a double bar at each end (Fig. 4-6).

In addition to the GOSUB statement itself, a comment to explain the purpose of the invoked subroutine should also be included to expand on the purpose of the subroutine. This comment can be put into the same box as the GOSUB statement, or it can be put into a special symbol that is used to include comments on a flow chart. This symbol is called an **annotation symbol**.

Figure 4-6.
GOSUB Flow Chart Symbol

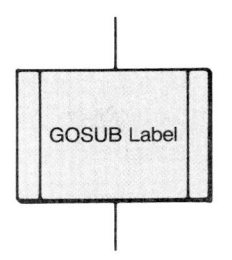

An annotation symbol (Fig. 4-7) is an open, three-sided box, connected to a flow line of a flow chart by a dotted line. The annotation is put into the open box.

Figure 4-7.
Annotation Symbol

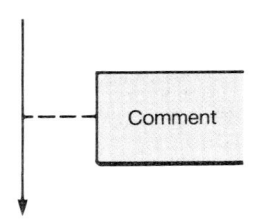

Figure 4-8.
Sample Program with Module Flow Charts

```
10  ! Salesmen's salaries
20      DECLARE STRING          Name., &
                DECIMAL(10,2)   Sales, &
                DECIMAL(8,2)    Salary
30      GOSUB Process_Salesman      ! Process first Salesman
40      GOSUB Process_Salesman      ! Process second Salesman
50      GOSUB Process_Salesman      ! Process third Salesman
60      EXIT PROGRAM                ! End of program

1000 Process_Salesman:              ! Process a Salesman
1010    GOSUB Enter_data            ! Enter Salesman's data
1020    Salary = 200.00 + 0.05 * Sales
1030    GOSUB Print_data            ! Print Salesman's data
1040 RETURN

1100 Enter_data:                    ! Enter Salesman's data
1110    INPUT Enter Salesman's name '';  Name.
1120    INPUT Enter Salesman's Sales''; Sales
1130 RETURN

1200 Print_data:                    ! Print Salesman's data
1210    PRINT TAB(40); Name.
1220    PRINT TAB(40); 'Sales  : '; Sales
1230    PRINT TAB(40); 'Salary : '; Salary
1240 RETURN

32767 END
```

Figure 4-8. (*Cont.*)

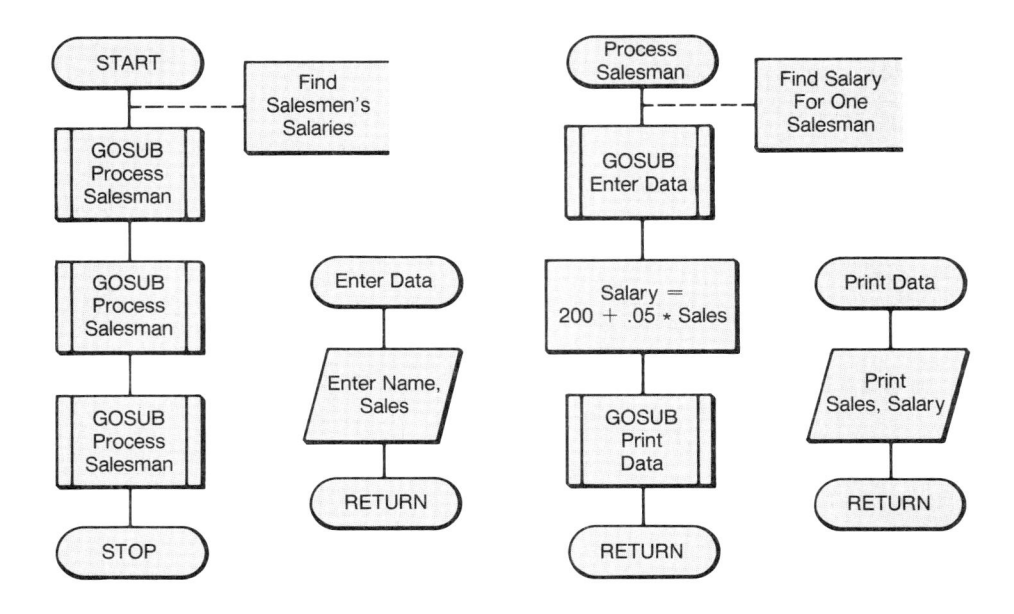

An annotation should always be placed at the beginning of a flow chart to explain the purpose of the program or subroutine.

To illustrate the use of flow charting when subroutines are used, we will flow chart one of the problems we did earlier in this chapter. The program is reproduced in Figure 4-8, followed by the flow charts for all the modules.

Notice how the annotations are used on the flow charts. The purpose of a module would not be easily discerned without them.

SUMMARY

In this chapter, you learned a number of techniques that make programs easier to write, debug, and maintain.

1. Structured programming: A technique in which each statement of every module can be reached only in one way, and each statement goes only to one other statement.

2. Top-down analysis: A method of analyzing a problem by gradually decomposing it into smaller and smaller pieces. The problem at one level becomes one or more simpler problems at the next level. Decomposition continues until a level is reached where the problem is trivial.

3. Modules: Modules are sections of code that are self-contained. A module must be invoked in order for it to execute. A module generally has one specific purpose and contains a limited number of statements. The number of statements in a module should normally be less than 10.

4. GOSUB: The GOSUB statement is used to invoke, or call, a subroutine. The syntax for the GOSUB statement is:

    GOSUB label

where **label** is the label of a subroutine. A less desirable alternative is:

    GOSUB sn

where **sn** is the statement number of the first statement of the subroutine.

5. *RETURN:* The RETURN statement is placed at the end of a subroutine. It causes control to revert to the module that invoked the subroutine.

6. *Main program:* The main program is the embodiment of the level 1 decomposition of the program. It calls all the subroutines at level 2.

7. *Data abstraction:* A method of programming by which all modules, except those directly concerned with input/output (I/O), are written to be independent of the form of the I/O (more accurately known as *I/O abstraction*).

8. Each module in a program has its own flow chart. A GOSUB statement is put into a rectangular box with a double bar at each end. The terminator at the top of a module flow chart contains the label of the module. The terminator at the bottom of a module flow chart contains the word RETURN. An annotation symbol (an open, three-sided box) can be used to put comments called annotations on a flow chart.

REVIEW QUESTIONS

1. What is meant by structured programming?
2. What is meant by top-down program decomposition?
3. What is meant by modularity?
4. What is a subroutine? How is a subroutine written in BASIC? What is the advantage of using subroutines?
5. How is a subroutine invoked in BASIC? How do you return from a subroutine?
6. There are two ways the statements in a subroutine can be reached: a right way and a wrong way. State these two methods. How do you avoid the wrong way?
7. What flow chart symbol is used for a GOSUB statement? How is a subroutine flow charted?

SYNTAX EXERCISES

The following statements or program segments contain various syntax errors. Find and correct them.

```
 1. 50 GOSUB Fin_results:
 2. 50 GOSUB Find Average;
 3. 50 GOSUB Get_data
 4. 50 GOSOB Print_result
 5. 1000 Get_data            ! Input routine
 6. 1000 Print_data          ! Output routine
 7. 1000 Find_grade            Determine student grade
 8. 1000 Calculate_bill     ! Calculate customer bill
 9. 1050 RETURN                 to main program
10. 1050 ! RETURN
11. 1050    RETURN            to invoking procedure
12. 1000 Find average:       Find average of 3 nos.
    1010    SUM = A + B + C
    1020    AVG = SUM/3
    1030 END
13. 20 DECLARE REAL A, B, C, INTEGER I, J, K,
          STRING STR_1, STR_2, STR_3
```

14. `20 DECLARE REAL INPUT`
15. `20 DCLARE INTEGER I, J, K, REAL SUM, AVG`
16. `20 DECLARE Grade_1, Grade_2, Grade_3`

PROGRAMMING EXERCISES

Most of these exercises were first encountered in chapter 3. They are to be programmed here using subroutines.

Write programs or subroutines that will carry out the requested activities. Separate subroutines should be used for input, calculations, and output. The main program should invoke these subroutines. All output should contain strings that identify the output values; no value should be printed without being identified.

■ **1.** Enter the lengths of the three sides of a triangle. Find the perimeter. Print the lengths of the sides on one line, and the perimeter on the next.

2. Enter the length of the side of a square. Find the perimeter and the area of the square. Print the length of the side, the perimeter, and the area of the square on separate lines.

3a. Write a subroutine that calculates the tax (4%) and total price of an item when the sale price is given.

3b. Write a program to perform the following: Enter a customer name and the price of a camera. Calculate the tax on the camera at 4%, and the total cost. Print the customer's name starting in column 10 of a line. On the next line, print the price of the camera starting in column 30. On the line after that, print the tax, also starting in column 30. On the last line, print the total cost, starting in column 50. Each line should be suitably identified as name, price, tax, or total, starting in column 1 of the appropriate line.

■ **4a.** Given four numbers, write a subroutine that calculates the average of the first two numbers, the average of the last two numbers, and the average of all four numbers.

4b. Enter four numbers from the terminal. Find the average of the first two numbers, the average of the last two numbers, and the average of all four. Print the first two numbers and their average on one line, suitably identified. Print the second two numbers and their average on another line, suitably identified. Print the combined average on a third line, again suitably identified. Write the program.

5a. Given five sales, write a subroutine that calculates the salesman's commission and salary. The commission is 10% of total sales, and the salary is $200 plus the commission.

5b. Enter a salesman's name and five sales he has made. Find the total of the sales. Figure a 10% commission on his sales. Now calculate his salary, which is $200.00 plus his commission. Print the salesman's name, his total sales, his commission, and his salary, all of them suitably identified. Write the program.

6. Three students each take five tests. Enter the students' names and test grades. For each student, find that student's average. Also find the class average of all three students combined. Print each student's name, his five test grades, and his average, all on one line. Then skip a line and print the class average. The output should make use of the TAB function to space all the values for a neat appearance. HINT: Invoke the same subroutine three times.

7. Write a program that will input four integers, X, A, B, and C, and compute the value of Y using the formula

$$y = ax^2 + bx + c.$$

Print the x and y values.

8. Write a program that can solve a quadratic equation. The program will allow you to enter the coefficients of the equation, calculate the two solutions, then print the coefficients and the solutions. Square roots can be obtained by raising to the one-half power, or by using a built-in function called SQR—to find the square root of A, use SQR(A).

9. A man dies, leaving a widow and three children. In his will, he leaves 25% of his estate to his firstborn child, 25% of the remainder to his second child, 25% of the remainder after that to his third child, and the residue of his estate to his wife.

    a. Write a subroutine that calculates the amount left to each child, and the amount left to the wife, given the value of the estate.

    b. Write a program that lets you enter the amount of the estate, then calculates how much is left to the wife and to each child. The program should then print the amount left to each.

10a. Write a subroutine that calculates the perimeter of a rectangle, given the length and width.

10b. A farmer has a rectangular piece of land and needs a program to help him calculate two quantities. The program will let him enter the length and width of his field. It will then calculate the amount of fence he needs to surround the property, and will also calculate the number of plots of 40,000 square feet each into which the field can be divided. Finally, the program will print the amount of fence, and the number of plots into which his land can be divided.

11. A company has three salesmen. The owner would like to know what percentage of the total sales each salesman has accounted for. The program will read each salesman's name and sales amount, then print his name, amount of sales, and percent of total sales. Use the following data statements:

    DATA JIM JONES,5000
    DATA JILL JOHNSON,7000
    DATA SAM SMITH,500

HINT: Use three different variables to store the names and three to store the sales.

12. A bank account has a balance of $3500 at the beginning of an interest period. During this period, the following transactions take place:

    Deposits of $246.50, $97.62, 325.00, and $123.87 are made.
    Withdrawals of $62.50, $200.00, and $400.00 are made.
    Interest at 1.625% is added at the end of the period.

■ **a.** Write a subroutine that calculates the new balance. Assume that deposits are in the variables Deposit_1, Deposit_2, and so on, and that withdrawals are in variables Withdraw_1, Withdraw_2, and so on.
b. Write a program to calculate the new balance. All necessary values, such as deposits, withdrawals, and interest rate, are to be read from DATA statements. Print the original balance, the interest, total deposits, total withdrawals, and the new balance.
c. Same as part b, but data is to be entered with INPUT instructions.

13. You have a charge account at a department store. At the beginning of January, you receive a statement indicating a balance of $672.84 which you owe on your account. You make a partial payment of $100.00. Because you did not pay the full amount, the store charges you a penalty of 1.85% of the unpaid balance, which will appear on your February bill. In addition, you make purchases in January of $34.99, $87.95, and $62.99. You have to pay sales tax of 7% on these purchases, and you charge it all to your account.

a. Write a subroutine to calculate the penalty and the new balance. You may assume that all values have been read into suitable variables.
b. Write a program to calculate and print your February bill. The bill should show the January balance, the payment you made, the penalty charged on the unpaid balance, the purchases you made, the tax on each purchase, and the new balance. All information may be read from DATA statements, or you may use INPUT instructions with suitable prompts.

14. A student works at a used car lot to earn tuition for college. He earns 5% of the sale price for each car he sells. The price of the cars depends on their age: $8000.00 for one-year-old cars, $6000.00 for two-year-old cars, and $5000.00 for three-year-old cars. (After three years, the cars fall apart.)

Write a program that lets you enter the number of units of each type of car the student sold. The program then calculates the commission he earned from each category of car, and the total commission for all the cars. Output is to consist of the number of cars sold in each category, the commission earned in each category, and the total commission.

ENRICHMENT TOPICS 4

VAX-BASIC Subprograms

In addition to GOSUB subroutines, modules called **subprograms** can be used to modularize a program in VAX-BASIC. These subprograms have the advantage of permitting arguments to be passed to the subprogram so that the subprogram can manipulate data contained in different variables whenever it is invoked.

These subprograms are called **external modules** because they are placed after the END statement of the user's main program, and are, therefore, external to the main program. These modules, even though they are after the main program's END statement, will be executed when they are properly invoked. The invoking procedure is described below.

Alternatively, subprograms can be kept in separate files in the user's or system's account, allowing the user to build a library of modules that can be included with any program. Modules kept in a file separate from the main program must be linked with the main program in a separate step before the program can be run. This linking procedure will not be explained here. If you wish to use such subprograms, see your instructor or system manager for details, or refer to the DEC VAX-BASIC programming guide.

ARGUMENTS AND PARAMETERS

To use subprograms, it is necessary that you learn about **arguments** and **parameters.** These are explained in detail in chapter 14. A brief account is included here.

Metaphorically speaking, there is a factory in Moline that produces air-to-ground fernortens for the army. Everything required to produce them comes into the plant. One of the parts required is a right-angled frammis, for which only the raw materials come into the plant. The assembly of the frammis is subcontracted to a firm in Dry Gulch. The raw materials are sent from the factory in Moline to the firm in Dry Gulch. After assembly, the finished product is sent back from Dry Gulch to Moline.

The materials that the factory in Moline sends to the assembly plant in Dry Gulch are comparable to what are called **arguments** in computer terminology. The materials returned from Dry Gulch are comparable to **parameters.** The analogy is not an exact one, and will be made clearer below.

When a main program (or even a subprogram) invokes an external subprogram, data that the subprogram needs must be passed to it from the invoking program. Results must be passed from the subprogram back to the invoking program. This data transfer takes place via the **argument and parameter lists.**

Arguments

Arguments are variables that exist in the invoking procedure. They are sent to the subprogram by placing them in parentheses after the subprogram name in the statement that invokes the subprogram.

The subprogram is invoked by a CALL statement, as follows:

  sn CALL sub-name (arguments)

where **sub-name** is the name of the subprogram. It can consist of one to 31 characters in VAX-BASIC. For example,

```
50 CALL Find_sum (No.1, No.2, No.3, Sum)
```

would invoke the subroutine `Find_sum`, and send to it the current values stored in the variables `No.1`, `No.2`, `No.3`, and `Sum`.

NOTE! | **Not all arguments that are sent to a subprogram have to have legitimate values. Only those that will be *used* by the subprogram must be predefined. The others can be defined in the subprogram and be returned as calculated results.**
There may be from 0 to 31 arguments in a CALL statement in VAX-BASIC. Zero arguments would mean that no data are sent to the subprogram, and no data are returned from it. You would invoke such a subprogram if, for example, you wanted to print the same identifying information at the top of every program you write, such as your name and identification number.

Parameters

Parameters are variables that are known in the subprogram. Each parameter is matched with an argument in the CALL statement of the invoking procedure. There must be exactly as many parameters as there are arguments. Furthermore, the data-type of each parameter must be the same as that of its corresponding argument.

Parameters are defined by putting them in parentheses following the subprogram name in the statement that defines the subprogram.

A subprogram has the following syntax:

  sn1 SUB sub-name (parameter list)
      ...
      ...
  sn2 END SUB

where **sub-name** is the name of the subprogram. It can consist of one to 31 characters in VAX-BASIC.

The parameter list has the form

data-type variable, . . .

similar to a DECLARE statement, but containing individually typed variables. An example of a subprogram is shown below:

```
10000 SUB Find_sum (INTEGER A, INTEGER B, INTEGER C,  INTEGER Sum)
10010   Sum = A + B + C
10020 END SUB
```

This subprogram would be invoked by the CALL statement shown earlier, CALL Find_sum (No.1, No.2, No.3, Sum). There are four arguments (No.1, No.2, No.3, and Sum) and four parameters (A, B, C, and Sum). All of them are INTEGER type. When the subprogram is invoked, each argument is sent to its corresponding parameter. The subprogram calculates a value for Sum using the values sent to it in the parameters A, B, and C. When END SUB executes, all parameters are sent back to their corresponding arguments.

All variables used in a subprogram are local to the subprogram; there are no global variables (except those deliberately specified in a COMMON statement, not discussed in this textbook). All variables that the subprogram requires must be sent to it through the argument list and received through the parameter list.

A subprogram will have a DECLARE statement to declare all variables it uses that are not in the parameter list. These variables may have the same name as variables in the main program, but they are not the same entities. The computer treats them as different locations.

In the above example, the first three arguments are named different from the parameters, while the fourth is named the same as the parameter. The names are completely local. Arguments and parameters are matched by position, not name. If every A in the subprogram were replaced with X, every B with Y, and every C with Z, then everything would work just as before.

Example 4.5   Here is a program written using an external subroutine. The main program inputs two values into variables A and B. These are sent to the subprogram, in addition to two other, undefined variables, ADD and MULT. The subprogram will interchange the values of A and B. It will also find their sum and product, returning these to ADD and MULT. For illustrative purposes, the parameters of the subprogram have been given names different from those of the main program.

```
10 ! Program using external subprogram
   ! Two numbers are entered
   ! Numbers are interchanged, added, and multiplied
20    DECLARE REAL A, B, ADD, MULT
30    INPUT "Enter two different numbers "; A, B
40    CALL CALC (A, B, ADD, MULT)
50    PRINT TAB(35); "Numbers are"; A; "and"; B
60    PRINT TAB(35); "Sum is"; ADD, "Product is"; MULT
70    END
```

```
1000    SUB CALC (REAL X, REAL Y, REAL SUM, REAL PRODUCT)
1010    ! This subprogram will receive two arguments,
        ! interchange their values,
        ! and find their sum and product
1020        DECLARE REAL TEMP
1030      ! Find sum and product
            SUM = X + Y
            PRODUCT = X * Y
1040      ! Interchange the values in X and Y
            TEMP = X
            X = Y
            Y = TEMP
1050    END SUB
```

The subprogram is invoked by the statement:

```
40    CALL CALC (A, B, ADD, MULT)
```

When the CALL statement above executes, A and B have already been assigned values, because the subprogram will use these values. ADD and MULT need not have values before the CALL executes.

When the CALL is executed, the values in A and B are sent to the subprogram and are called X and Y there, respectively. The subprogram assigns values to the variables SUM and PRODUCT. This results in ADD and MULT being assigned those values. The subprogram interchanges the values of X and Y. When we return to the calling program as a result of reaching the END SUB statement, the values in the corresponding arguments, A and B, take on the new, interchanged, values of X and Y, respectively. Therefore, the values in A and B will have been interchanged. The DECLARE statement in the subprogram is used to declare the local variable TEMP.

Requirements for subprograms are as follows:

1. The subprogram name can be up to 31 characters in VAX-BASIC.
2. Arguments and parameters must agree in number and type.
3. The subprogram is invoked with a CALL statement, which also contains the argument list.
4. The subprogram must begin with the SUB statement. It must end with the END SUB or SUBEND statement. END SUB must be two words and is the preferred ending; SUBEND is one word.
5. Values returned from a subprogram are returned via the argument and parameter lists. If the subprogram modifies any parameter, then the corresponding argument must be a variable; it cannot be a constant.
6. All variables in a subprogram are local to the subprogram. (The only exceptions would be those put into a COMMON statement, not described here.) Otherwise, there are no global variables in a subprogram.
7. A subprogram executes only when it is invoked. If a subprogram is encountered without having been invoked, control passes to the statement following the END SUB statement.

A subprogram can be written and stored under its own filename in the user's account. It can then be used by any program that requires that subprogram. Therefore, a user or a group can build a library of frequently used subprograms and include them in any program where they are required. The mechanism for doing this, linking, is not described here. Refer to the DEC BASIC Reference Manual for your machine, or your instructor will describe the procedure.

There are a number of other features applicable to subprograms. For information, see the DEC BASIC Reference Manual.

5 Loops

Outline

5.1 Enumerative LOOPS
5.2 Summing
5.3 Controlled Loops
  Comparison or
    Relational Operators
  Logical or Boolean
    Operators
  The WHILE Loop
  Counting
  The UNTIL Loop
5.4 The Random Number
    Generator
  The RANDOMIZE
    Statement
  Scaling the Random
    Number Generator
  Shifting the Range of
    Random Numbers
  Random Integers
5.5 Priming Read
5.6 Flow Charts
Summary
Review Questions
Syntax Exercises
Programming Exercises

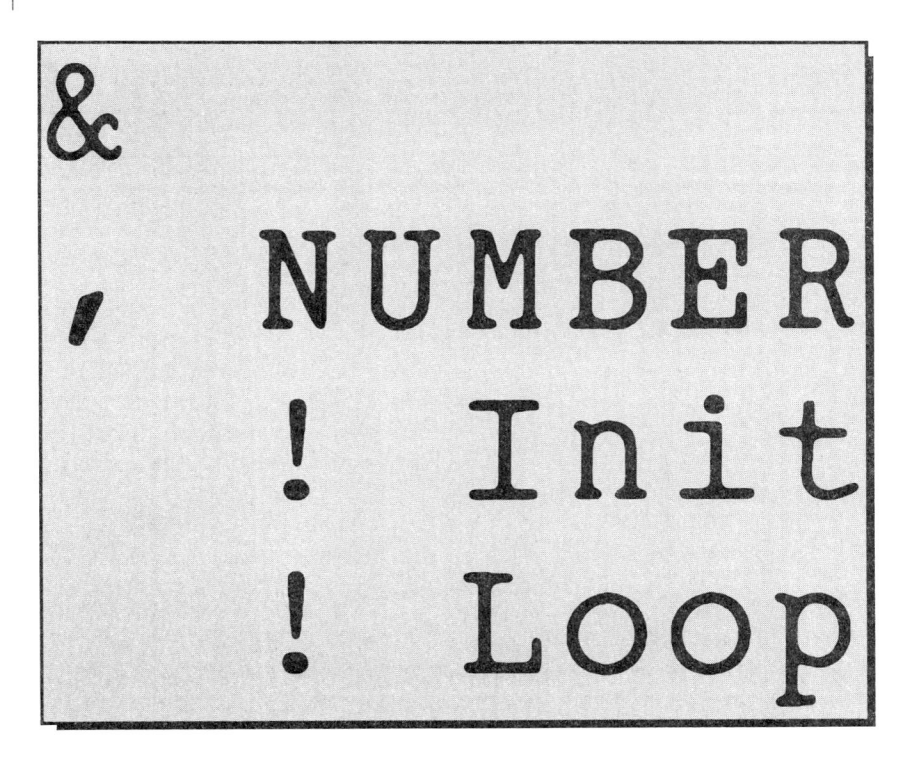

Introduction In this chapter you will learn how the computer can be directed to execute a sequence of instructions more than once. This is one of the most powerful capabilities of a computer and serves to differentiate it from a calculator.

We will discuss two types of loops: **enumerative** and **controlled.**

An enumerative loop is one that executes the loop a fixed number of times. It might be 10 times, or 100, or more.

A controlled loop is one that executes as long as a certain condition exists. When the condition changes, loop execution ends, and we say that the loop has terminated.

5.1 ENUMERATIVE LOOPS

An enumerative loop is a structure in which a given sequence of instructions is executed a fixed number of times. When an enumerative loop begins, a counter called the **loop variable** is set at a number called the **initial value.** Each time the loop is executed, the counter is changed by a certain amount, called the **increment** or **step.** The loop executes repeatedly until the counter passes a specific value known as the **final value.** All statements in the loop are executed while the loop remains **active.**

The syntax for an enumerative loop is:

>   sn1 FOR var = init TO final [STEP incr]
>   loop statements
>   sn2 NEXT var

where

>   **var**   = an integer or real variable
>   **init**   = the initial value assigned to **var**
>   **final**   = the final value the variable **var** may reach
>   **incr**   = the amount by which **var** changes each time the loop executes
>   **sn1, sn2** = statement numbers.

Note that **STEP incr** is optional, as indicated by the brackets. If omitted, the default value is +1. The increment can be either positive or negative, thus allowing the loop variable to increase or decrease. The increment can be either a whole number or a number containing a decimal fraction.

The loop begins with the FOR statement and ends with the NEXT statement.

Example 5.1 Here is a loop that will print the numbers from 1 to 100. Each line of output will have five numbers, because a comma is used at the end of the PRINT statement. (You may recall that this causes suppression of the line feed after printing a number.) Each number is printed at the start of a new field on the same line as the previous number. After five numbers have been printed on a line, that line is filled and a new line is automatically begun.

The complete program is:

```
10  ! Print the numbers from 1 to 100
20      DECLARE INTEGER   I
30      FOR I = 1 TO 100
40        PRINT I,
50      NEXT I
32767 END
```

The program could also have been written in various ways using multi-statement lines. Here is one of them:

```
10  ! Print the numbers from 1 to 100
20      DECLARE INTEGER   I
30      FOR I = 1 TO 100
          PRINT I,
        NEXT I
32767 END
```

```
RUNNH
 1              2              3              4              5
 6              7              8              9             10
11             12             13             14             15
16             17             18             19             20
21             22             23             24             25
26             27             28             29             30
31             32             33             34             35
36             37             38             39             40
41             42             43             44             45
46             47             48             49             50
51             52             53             54             55
56             57             58             59             60
61             62             63             64             65
66             67             68             69             70
71             72             73             74             75
76             77             78             79             80
81             82             83             84             85
86             87             88             89             90
91             92             93             94             95
96             97             98             99            100
```

If you try to run this program, but your output does not look like this, and appears to run in diagonals, then the margins on your terminal have not been defined. The computer does not realize that your screen is only 80 characters wide; it thinks that it is one long infinite line. So, every 14 columns, the width of one field, it prints another number. But when column 80 is reached, the *screen* knows it is at the end of the line and simply directs succeeding output to a new line. The result is the staggered output you see.

To set the margin for your terminal, you can include the following statement in the program:

```
25    MARGIN 80
```

This statement sets the margin for you terminal at 80 columns. The output should then appear as above. If you wish to reset the margin to its previous, default value, you can add the statement

```
32760 MARGIN 0
```

at the end of your program. This statement will reset the margin to the value it had when you logged on the computer.

The FOR statement in line 30 is the beginning of the loop. The variable I is the loop counter. Its first value is 1. Each time the loop is executed, I is increased by 1 (the default), until it attains its final value of 100.

The only statement in the loop is the PRINT statement. When it executes, the current value of the loop counter, I, is printed. The statement, NEXT I, signifies the end of the loop. The loop variable, I, is incremented each time NEXT I is encountered, and the result is then compared to 100. If the result is not greater than 100, the statement (or statements, if there are more than one) in the loop is executed again.

After the loop has been executed with I equal to 100, I becomes 101. Because 101 is greater than the final value of 100, the loop ends and, in this case, the END statement is reached, ending execution of the program. (Incidentally, after the loop ends, the computer resets I to its final value of 100.)

Example 5.2 We will repeat the program described in Example 5.1, except that the numbers will be printed in reverse order. To accomplish this, we will set a loop variable N to 100 and cause it to decrement by specifying a negative increment:

```
10  ! Print numbers from 100 down to 1
20      DECLARE INTEGER    N
30      FOR N = 100 TO 1 STEP -1
          PRINT N,
        NEXT N
32767 END
```

Each time the loop executes, N is decreased by 1 because of the negative STEP in the FOR statement. The loop executes for the last time when N is equal to 1.

Example 5.3 This time, we will print only the even numbers between 1 and 100 to illustrate a different STEP value. By this time, the program should be self-explanatory.

```
10  ! Print even numbers from 1 to 100
20      DECLARE INTEGER    J
30      FOR J = 2 TO 100 STEP 2
          PRINT J,
        NEXT J
32767 END
```

```
RUNNH
 2       4       6       8      10
12      14      16      18      20
22      24      26      28      30
32      34      36      38      40
42      44      46      48      50
52      54      56      58      60
62      64      66      68      70
72      74      76      78      80
82      84      86      88      90
92      94      96      98     100
```

If the output on your screen is not as shown above, set the margins for your terminal as explained in Example 5.1.

5.2 SUMMING

One common application of a loop is called **summing,** in which we add a list of numbers by forming a running total. Each number is added to the previous total to form the new sum. A location in memory—say, TOTAL—is initially set to 0. Then each successive number is added to the amount in that location. If location X contains the number and TOTAL contains the sum, then the summing instruction is TOTAL = TOTAL + X. That is, the number in X is added to the number in TOTAL, and the result replaces the previous value in location TOTAL.

The instruction TOTAL = TOTAL + X is a summing instruction, where TOTAL is called the **accumulator.** Notice that this statement makes little sense in mathematics. In computing, however, it is very meaningful. The assignment operator, =, is not a statement that the left side is equal to the right side. Instead, it causes the value calculated on the right side of the expression to be stored in the variable specified on the left side.

Initialization: When a summing instruction is used, a new value is added to a previous sum, and the result becomes the new sum. What happens the first time the summing instruction executes and the computer tries to add the first value to the previous sum? There must be a previous sum to add the new value to. If it some unknown value (called *garbage* in computer jargon), then the result is unpredictable. "Garbage in, garbage out," or "GIGO," for short. So before the first value can be added to the sum, we must **initialize** the sum to a known, desirable value. In most cases, this initial sum will be 0. In general:

> Whenever an accumulator (variable used in summing) is used, it is necessary to initialize the accumulator. A variable is an accumulator if it appears on both sides of an assignment statement. Such a variable, therefore, must be initialized.

Failure to adhere to this dictum can cause irksome errors that are difficult to locate.

Example 5.4   We will enter 10 numbers from the terminal and find their average. In pseudocode we have the following:

```
Average 10 numbers:
   Initialize the sum to 0
   Loop 10 times
      Input a number
      Add number to sum
   End of loop
   Find average
   Print average
Stop
```

The coded solution is shown in Figure 5-1.

Input and output have been accomplished by subroutines, in accordance with the data abstraction concept mentioned in chapter 4.

Example 5.5   This program will add all even numbers from 1000 to 2000. In pseudocode:

```
Add even numbers between 1000 and 2000:
   Initialize sum
   Loop from 1000 to 2000 by two's
      Add loop counter to sum
   End of loop
   Print sum
Stop
```

```
Figure 5-1.
Sample Program with
Enumerative Loop
10  ! Average of 10 numbers
20       DECLARE INTEGER    I, &
                    REAL         SUM, NUMBER, AVG
30       SUM = 0                  ! Initialize the sum
40       FOR I = 1 TO 10          ! Loop 10 times
50          GOSUB Enter_datum    ! Enter a number
60          SUM = SUM + NUMBER   ! Add number to sum
70       NEXT I                   ! End of loop
80       AVG = SUM / 10           ! Find average
90       GOSUB Print_answer       ! Print result
100  EXIT PROGRAM                 ! End main program

500  Enter_datum:                 ! Enter a number
510     INPUT 'Enter a number'; NUMBER
520  RETURN


700  Print_answer:                ! Print result
710     PRINT 'The average of all the numbers is'; AVG
720  RETURN

32767 END

RUNNH
Enter a number? 45
Enter a number? 62
Enter a number? 8
Enter a number? 98
Enter a number? 62
Enter a number? 59
Enter a number? 56
Enter a number? 21
Enter a number? 37
Enter a number? 36
The average of all the numbers is 48.4
```

The coded solution to the program in Example 5.5:

```
10  ! Sum of even nos. from 1000 to 2000
20      DECLARE INTEGER   X, SUM
30      SUM = 0                           ! Initialize sum to zero
40      FOR X = 1000 TO 2000 STEP 2 ! X is the no. to add
50         SUM = SUM + X                  ! Form the sum
60      NEXT X
70      PRINT 'Sum of even numbers from 1000 to 2000 ='; SUM
80      END
```

Notice that we are using the loop variable for two purposes: as a counter for the loop, and as the number to be added. Even though the loop counter goes from 1000 to 2000, the loop will execute only 501 times. This is because we are incrementing the counter by 2 each time we execute the loop.

We did not use a subroutine for the output this time, because only the one PRINT statement is involved. Most programmers would not bother to write a module for such a simple purpose. If we want to "pretty up" the output by including one or more headings or other special formats, then we should write a subroutine for the output.

Example 5.6

In this example, we let the initial and final values of the loop counter be read in as variables. Therefore, the range of the loop counter may be different each time the program is run.

The program will ask us to enter two integers. It will then print all integers between those two numbers. The program is quite simple:

```
10  ! Print a range of integers
20     DECLARE INTEGER I, Init, Final
30     INPUT "Enter Initial and final loop values"; Init, Final
40     FOR I = Init TO Final
           PRINT I,
       NEXT I
32767 END
```

Any nonreserved variable names could have been used instead of Init and Final. These were chosen because they are descriptive. Incidentally, Initial is a reserved word and could not be used as a variable; hence, we used Init. But Initial_ (with the underscore) or Initial. (with the period) could have been used instead of Init.

Example 5.7

We will do one more example of an enumerative loop before we learn about controlled loops. In this example, we have three students who each took three tests. The teacher wants a program that will read each student's name and three grades, find the average, and then print the student's name and average.

The main program has the following logic:

    Student grades:
      Print headings
      For each of three students
        Process student
      Next student
    Stop

    Process student:
      Read name and grades
      Find average
      Print name and average
    Return

Data will be read from DATA statements. The code follows:

```
10  ! Program to calculate student average
20     DECLARE DECIMAL(4,1) Grade_1, Grade_2, Grade_3, Average, &
                            Sum, &
            STRING Name_, &
            INTEGER Student
```

```
 30    GOSUB Headings                    ! Print headings
 40    FOR Student = 1 TO 3
           GOSUB Process_student         ! Process one student
       NEXT Student
 50 EXIT PROGRAM

1000 Process_student:                    ! Process one student
1010     READ Name_, Grade_1, Grade_2, Grade_3
1020     Sum = Grade_1 + Grade_2 + Grade_3
         Average = Sum / 3
1030     PRINT Name_; TAB(30); Average
1040 RETURN

1100 Headings:                           ! Print headings
1110     PRINT
         PRINT "Name"; TAB(30); "Average"
         PRINT "----"; TAB(30); "-------"   ! Underline headings
         PRINT
1120 RETURN

10000 ! DATA Statements
10010    DATA Pat, 86,92,81
10020    DATA Nancy, 96,89,91
10030    DATA Eli, 98,95,96

32767 END
```

5.3 CONTROLLED LOOPS

We will now discuss loops that depend on the satisfaction of a condition rather than on a fixed number of iterations. First, it is necessary to explain the concept of **logical expressions.**

Comparison or Relational Operators

Comparison or **relational operators** are used to form conditions or logical expressions. There are six of these operators:

$<$ is less than
$>$ is greater than
$<=$ is less than or equal to
$>=$ is greater than or equal to
$=$ is equal to
$<>$ is not equal to

Examples of logical expressions are:

$A > B$
$X = 0$
$Y >= 10$
$A - 2 * B = B - 2 * A$
$250 <> Q1 + Q2$
$I + J = 100$

A logical expression always has a value of either true or false. This is known as its **truth value.** For example, the expression A < 10 is true if the number in A is 5, but false if it is 10.

Notice that when the = sign is used as a comparison operator its meaning is different from its meaning as an assignment operator. The comparison operator is more like the equality symbol of mathematics. The expression I + J = 100 is true if the sum of I and J is equal to 100, false otherwise.

Logical or Boolean Operators

In addition to the six comparison operators, there are three **logical** or **Boolean** operators, which are used to combine logical expressions. They are:

NOT
AND
OR

Examples of logical expressions using logical operators are:

A > B AND C > D
A + B < C OR D = 50
NOT A < B
(A + B > C OR D < E) AND C − D <> 10
NOT (A > B AND B < C)

When AND is used in a logical expression, both halves of the expression must be true if the entire expression is to be true. In the first example above, A must be greater than B, *and* C must be greater than D for the compound expression to be true. If either of these conditions is false, or if both are false, then the compound expression is false as well.

When OR is used in a logical expression, only one half of the expression need be true for the compound expression to be true. In the second example above, it is required only that A + B be less than C, *or* that D be equal to 50. Both conditions are not necessary. If both are true, however, then the expression is also true. Of course, if both are false, then the compound expression is false.

The third example illustrates the use of NOT. The word NOT, if used, must *precede* a logical expression. NOT A < B means the opposite of A < B. That is, if A is less than B, then the expression NOT A < B is false. If A is greater than or equal to B, then NOT A < B is true. It is incorrect to write A NOT < B. If NOT is used, it must always *precede* a logical expression. Its effect is to reverse the truth value of the expression.

It is very important to realize that the logical operators can only combine logical expressions. For example, A > B AND < C is incorrect. The correct expression would be A > B AND A < C. The phrase < C in the first case is not a complete logical expression, as it has no truth value, but A < C is a complete logical expression.

Hierarchy of operators: Just as the arithmetic operators have a hierarchy, so do the relational and Boolean operators. The complete order of precedence, from highest to lowest, is shown below:

```
^, **
*, /
+, −
>, <, >=, <=, =, <>
NOT
AND
OR
```

For example:

A + B > C OR D < E AND C − D <> 10

The expression is treated as if parentheses had been placed as follows:

[(A + B) > C] OR {(D < E) AND [(C − D) <> 10]}

If the sum of A and B is greater than C, the expression will be true. Or, if D is less than E and, also, the difference of C − D is not equal to 10, then the expression will also be true. The OR separates the two parts of the condition and causes the expression to be true if either side is true.

If necessary, parentheses can be used to change the order of operations. When parentheses are used, the expressions in the parentheses are always evaluated first, as explained in chapter 3. For example:

(A + B > C OR D < E) AND C − D <> 10

Note the parentheses in this example. It is now the word AND that separates the two parts of the expression. For the expression to be true, the difference of C − D must not be equal to 10, and at the same time, either the sum of A and B must be greater than C, or D must be less than E.

The WHILE Loop

One type of controlled loop is the WHILE loop. A condition (logical expression) is given, and the loop executes repeatedly as long as the condition remains true. When the condition becomes false, the loop terminates. The syntax is:

sn1 WHILE logical expression
...
...
sn2 NEXT

For example:

```
100    WHILE X > 0
         . . .
         . . .
200    NEXT
```

All statements in the loop, between the WHILE and NEXT statements, will be executed repeatedly until X is no longer greater than 0.

Example 5.8 We want to write a program that will read numbers and sum them, and continue this process until the sum exceeds 200. Then it is to print the sum. In pseudocode we have:

   Sum numbers until the sum exceeds 200:
      Initialize the sum to 0
      Loop while sum <= 200
         Enter number
         Add number to sum
      End of loop
      Print sum
   Stop

The coded solution is:

```
10 ! Sum numbers until sum exceeds 200
20     DECLARE REAL      Number, Sum
30     SUM = 0                  ! Initialize sum
40     WHILE Sum <= 200
50        INPUT 'Enter No. '; Number
60        Sum = Sum + Number  ! Add it to sum
70     NEXT                    ! Repeat
80     PRINT 'Sum ='; Sum      ! Print answer
90  END
RUNNH
Enter No. ? 48
Enter No. ? 36
Enter No. ? 71
Enter No. ? 54
Sum = 209
```

Line 50 accepts a number typed from the keyboard, and line 60 adds this number to the sum. Both of these statements are then repeated over and over again as long as the sum remains less than 200. The loop then terminates, and the PRINT statement at line 80 executes. As you can see from the output shown, the sum was less than 200 prior to adding the last number, 54; it became greater than 200 once this number was included.

Here, as in the previous example, we did not use subroutines for the I/O because only one simple statement was involved. For any output other than this simple case, a subroutine should certainly be used to gain the advantages of I/O abstraction.

Counting

Counting is similar to summing except that, instead of adding data to the sum, we increase the sum by a specific amount (usually 1) each time around the loop. As with summing, the variable used to do the counting must be initialized to an appropriate value (usually 0) since it is an accumulator.

Example 5.9 This is a modification of the previous program. In addition to adding numbers until the sum exceeds 200, we will also count the number of numbers added. This step adds a counting operation to the summing we already had. We will print both the sum and the count.

In pseudocode, the solution looks like this:

> Add and count numbers:
>   Initialize sum and count to 0
>   Loop while the sum <= 200
>   Enter number
>   Add number to sum
>   Add 1 to count of numbers
>   End of loop
>   Print the sum of numbers and the count
> Stop

Figure 5-2.
Sample Program with WHILE Loop

The coded solution is shown in Figure 5-2. A new feature is introduced in line 30. For the first time, we have put two separate statements on one

```
10  ! Summing and counting with WHILE

20      DECLARE REAL      X, SUM, COUNT.

30      SUM = 0 \ COUNT. = 0          ! Initialize sum and count

40      WHILE SUM <= 200
50         INPUT 'Enter no.'; X       ! Enter datum
60         SUM = SUM + X              ! Add no. to sum
70         COUNT. = COUNT. + 1        ! Add to count of nos.
80      NEXT                          ! Repeat

90      GOSUB Printout                ! Print sum and count

100    EXIT PROGRAM

200 Printout:                         ! Print sum and count
210    ! Heading
         PRINT
         PRINT 'Result of adding numbers until sum exceeded 200'
         PRINT
220      PRINT TAB(20); 'Sum of numbers    = '; SUM
         PRINT TAB(20); 'Number of numbers = '; COUNT.
230 RETURN

32767 END

runnh
Enter no.? 52
Enter no.? 64
Enter no.? 37
Enter no.? 94

Result of adding numbers until sum exceeded 200

                    Sum of numbers    =  247
                    Number of numbers =  4
```

physical line. This requires that we separate the two statements in some way. The backslash serves the purpose. We will use this technique only when two or more statements are very closely related and perform similar functions. In this case, both statements are initializations; thus they are closely related and have a similar purpose. Notice that the backslash used to separate statements is not the same as the slash used as a division symbol.

The variable COUNT is a reserved word in VAX-BASIC, so a period was added to make it COUNT., which is not reserved. The counting instruction is at line 70. Notice that a specific number, in this case 1, is added to the COUNT. variable. In line 60, the summing instruction, the datum that was read in is added to the summing variable SUM.

Example 5.10 We would like to find the length of time necessary for one dollar to grow to one million dollars at 10 percent interest compounded once a year. To solve this problem, we begin with an amount of one dollar. A loop is used in which the interest for one year is calculated and added to the principal, yielding the new amount.

In pseudocode we have the following:

> Compound interest:
>   Initialize principal to one dollar
>   Initialize number of years to 0
>   Loop while principal < $1,000,000
>   Calculate interest (10% of principal)
>   Add interest to principal
>   Add 1 to number of years
>   End of loop
>   Print number of years
> Stop

The coded solution is as follows.

```
10    ! Becoming a millionaire

20        DECLARE DECIMAL(9,2)    PRINCIPAL, INTEREST, &
                  INTEGER          YEARS &

30        PRINCIPAL = 1.00                   ! Initial Principal = $1.00
          YEARS = 0                          ! Initial Years = 0

40        WHILE PRINCIPAL < 1000000
             INTEREST = .10 * PRINCIPAL      ! Interest = 10% of principal
             PRINCIPAL = PRINCIPAL + INTEREST ! Add interest to principal
             YEARS = YEARS + 1               ! Add 1 to number of years
          NEXT

50        PRINT "Initial amount = $1.00"
          PRINT "Interest rate  =    10%"
          PRINT "No. of yrs. to become millionaire = "; YEARS

32767 END
```

The WHILE loop is at statement 40. The three statements between WHILE and NEXT are executed as long as the amount in PRINCIPAL remains less than $1,000,000. Please notice that the number, one million, must be written without the dollar sign or commas. A number in BASIC may not include these symbols.

You may be interested to learn the time required is only about 145 years. The program is easily modified to allow for different initial amounts and interest rates. For example, a subroutine could be used that would allow you to enter various initial amounts and interest rates. The program would then print the length of time required to reach one million dollars from your initial amount, at the entered interest rate.

Incidentally, `INT` is a reserved word and could not have been used as a variable name to store the interest. We could have used a modified version such as `INT.` or `INT_`, as we did previously for `COUNT`.

The UNTIL Loop

Loop control with the UNTIL statement is similar to that with the WHILE statement, except that the conditions used with these two types of loops have opposite effects. The names of the WHILE and UNTIL statements are descriptive of their functions:

> The condition used with the WHILE statement allows the loop to continue. As long as the condition remains true, the loop continues to execute.

> The condition used with the UNTIL statement causes termination of the loop. As long as the condition is false, the loop continues to execute. When the condition becomes true, the loop terminates.

Thus, the following two statements could be used interchangeably to start a loop:

```
WHILE X < 100
UNTIL X >= 100
```

Note that the opposite of < is >=. The opposite of <= would be >.

Many languages make a further distinction between WHILE and UNTIL. In those languages, the UNTIL loop is always executed at least once, regardless of the truth value of the condition. The WHILE loop, on the other hand, might not execute at all if the condition is initially false. In such languages, the WHILE test is made at the top of the loop but the UNTIL test is made at the bottom of the loop. In VAX-BASIC and many other BASICs that have both the WHILE and the UNTIL, the test in both cases is made at the top of the loop. Therefore, they are interchangeable.

Example 5.11 | The problem in Example 5.10 can be solved using an UNTIL loop. All that is required is that statement 30 be replaced with:

```
40 UNTIL PRIN >= 1000000
```

The rest of the program remains unchanged.

5.4 THE RANDOM NUMBER GENERATOR (optional topic)

Many problems require the computer to generate unpredictable numbers. That is what the random number generator does. Such unpredictable numbers are very useful in simulating real-life situations—getting the computer to "toss a coin," for example.

The random number generator is a built-in function that is invoked with the name RND. To store a random number into location NUMBER at line 100, we would use the following instruction:

```
100 NUMBER = RND
```

where RND is the name of the BASIC random number generator. Each time it is used in a program, it returns a different number. The number is always a six-place decimal fraction whose value is between 0.000000 and 0.999999.

The following program will print 10 different numbers:

```
10   ! Print 10 random numbers
20     DECLARE REAL Number, INTEGER I
30     FOR I = 1 TO 10
           Number = RND
           PRINT Number
       NEXT I
32767 END
```

It is useful to think of the random number generator as a machine that produces an unending series of numbers. Each time it is used, it returns the next number of the series. But because the numbers are all jumbled, we never know which number will come next.

The RANDOMIZE Statement

We have just learned that the RND function produces a series of numbers that we can think of as random. However, the random number generator is merely a program with a fixed set of instructions. As such, it produces the same series of numbers each time it is used. A program using the random number generator therefore produces the same results each time it is run. We need some way of making the random number generator produce truly unpredictable values, or what we generally think of as random numbers. That is what the RANDOMIZE or RANDOM statement does.

NOTE! Some machines constantly randomize their random number generator. On such machines, the RANDOMIZE statement discussed in this section is not required and is sometimes not permitted.

The RANDOMIZE statement causes the RND function to start somewhere in the middle of the series rather than at the beginning. This is called **seeding** the random number generator. On some machines, the starting point is determined by the system time (the number of milliseconds since midnight). If a program containing the random number generator also has the RANDOMIZE statement, and if this program is run twice on such a machine, more than a millisecond apart, then the random number generator will produce two different sequences of numbers. Other machines use a different scheme to randomize their generators.

The RANDOMIZE statement is used as follows:

10 RANDOMIZE

or

10 RANDOM

CAUTION! The RANDOMIZE statement should execute only once in a program. It must *never* be placed in a loop, or its entire purpose will be negated.

NOTE! Many programmers who use the random number generator leave out the RANDOMIZE statement until their program is completely debugged. That way, they get the same results each time the program is executed, which aids them in debugging it. After they are reasonably certain that there are no more errors in the program, they insert the RANDOMIZE statement at the beginning of their program. From then on, the program always gives different results.

Scaling the Random Number Generator

The random number generator always returns a value between 0.000000 and 0.999999. (Trailing zeros are generally dropped if the value is printed. In other words, the number 0.807000 is printed 0.807.) In most applications, we require numbers in a different range. We get them by **scaling** the random number generator.

The expression 10 * RND represents numbers between 0.00000 and 9.99999 because the number returned by RND has been multiplied by 10. Therefore, instead of decimal fractions between 0 and 1, we now have decimal fractions between 0 and (nearly) 10. Similarly, 100 * RND would return numbers between 0.0000 and 99.9999. 50 * RND would return numbers between 0.0000 and 49.9999. Multiplying the RND function by a number causes the range of numbers returned to be "stretched" by the multiplier. N * RND returns numbers in the range 0 through 0.999999N, or essentially 0 through N.

Shifting the Range of Random Numbers

The previous section showed how to get random numbers with any specified range width, but the range always began at zero. This section explains how to get any starting and ending points desired, by adding or subtracting a number to a given range.

Example 5.12 We have previously seen that 100 * RND gives random numbers in the range 0.0000 to 99.9999. If we use instead 100 * RND − 50, then each

5.4 THE RANDOM NUMBER GENERATOR (OPTIONAL TOPIC)

number will be reduced by 50. Therefore, the numbers we get will be between −50.0000 and 49.9999. Notice that the range of numbers is still 100, but the beginning and ending points of the range have been shifted.

Example 5.13 We want random numbers in the range 200.000 through 799.999. There is a difference of 600 between the largest and smallest numbers, so we must multiply the RND function by 600. This gives us numbers between 0.000 and 599.999. Then we must move the zero up to 200 by adding 200. The random numbers we require can therefore be obtained by using the formula 600 * RND + 200.

In general, to get random numbers in the range from A to "almost" B, use the expression (B − A) * RND + A.

Random Integers

Many applications require random integers instead of the random real numbers we have been discussing. They are easily obtained. We use the INT function to truncate the real number, as shown in the following examples.

Example 5.14 To obtain random integers in the range 1 to 100, we proceed as follows:

100 * RND	0.00000 to 99.9999
100 * RND + 1	1.00000 to 100.9999
INT(100 * RND + 1)	1 to 100

The last step uses the INT function to drop the fractional part of the random number.

Example 5.15 We want random integers in the range 200 through 800. This is a little tricky, because it looks as if there is a difference of 600 between the smallest and largest numbers, but there are actually 601 integers in the range when both the 200 and the 800 are counted. We proceed as follows:

601 * RND	0.0000 to 600.999
601 * RND + 200	200.0000 to 800.999
INT(601 * RND + 200)	200 to 800

Example 5.16 Here is a program that will print 100 random integers at the terminal, five integers per line. The integers will be in the range of 50 to 100. There are 51 integers in this range, so the RND function will be multiplied by 51. The program appears below.

```
10 ! 100 random integers in the range 50 to 100
20     DECLARE INTEGER Number, I
30     RANDOMIZE                      ! Randomize the RND generator
40     FOR I = 1 TO 100
           Number = INT(51*RND + 50)
           PRINT Number,              ! Comma to suppress line feed
       NEXT I
50     END
```

Because of the RANDOMIZE statement, the program will print a different set of 100 numbers each time it is run.

> **NOTE!** If you run this program and the numbers are staggered diagonally down the screen, it means the margins for your terminal are not set. Add the statement
>
> ```
> 25    MARGIN 80
> ```
>
> to the program to set the margin at 80 columns.

Example 5.17 This program can be used to give a student drill in arithmetic. The computer will generate two random double-digit integers and then ask the user to add them. If the result is correct, the program ends. If not, the program prompts the user for a correct answer. Here is the pseudocode:

    Arithmetic drill:
      Randomize the RND function
      Generate two double-digit integers
      Add them to get correct answer
      Print problem for student
      Get student answer
      WHILE student answer <> correct answer
        Print message for student
        Let student try again
      End of loop
      Print message that answer is correct
    Stop

The WHILE loop will execute only if the answer given by the student is incorrect. If the student gets the answer right the first time, then the loop does not execute at all. Once the student gives the correct answer, processing continues after the loop, where a message of success is given to the student.

Before you proceed, review the pseudocode and be sure you understand the logic of the program thus far. Here is the resulting main program:

```
10  ! Program for arithmetic drill, 2-digit nos.

20       RANDOM                   ! Randomize RND function

30       DECLARE INTEGER          First_no., Second_no., &
                                  Student_ans., Correct_ans. &

40       GOSUB Make_problem       ! Generate two random integers

50       Correct_ans. = First_no. + Second_no.
                                  ! Calculate correct answer

60       GOSUB Print_problem      ! Print the problem

70       GOSUB Get_answer         ! Get student's answer
```

```
 80      WHILE Student_ans. <> Correct_ans.
            GOSUB Get_again       ! Let student try again
         NEXT

 90      GOSUB Wrapup ! Congratulate student for correct answer
100   EXIT PROGRAM
```

This is a fairly complex problem, but you can see that by thinking in large chunks and not getting involved with details at this point, we have already obtained the overall solution.

It may not be clear how the numbers are generated, so we will go through this program slowly. In the range 10 through 99, there are 90 integers. Since we need a width of 90, we use 90 * RND. This gives us numbers from 0.0000 to 89.9999. Then we add 10 to get numbers from 10.0000 to 99.9999. Finally, we take the integer part of these numbers to get the two-digit integers in the range 10 through 99.

The pseudocode for the subroutine `Make_problem`, which generates two random integers, is:

> Generate two random integers, 10 to 99:
>   For each number
>   Multiply RND by 90
>   Add 10
>   Take integer part
>   Return

The code for this subroutine is:

```
1000 Make_problem:   ! Generate two random integers, 10 to 99
1010    First_no. = INT(90 * RND + 10)
        Second_no. = INT(90 * RND + 10)
1020 RETURN
```

We will print the numbers for the student to add in the form of an ordinary arithmetic problem. The numbers will be one above the other, and a line will be drawn under the second number. The problem will appear in the middle of the screen, starting at column 35. It will look like this:

```
                                    57
                                  + 45
                                  ----
```

As you can see, the second number will have a plus sign (+) written in front of it, as specified in the code:

```
1100 Print_problem:           ! Print the problem
1110    PRINT ! Blank line for appearance
        PRINT TAB(35); First_no.
        PRINT TAB(34); '+'; Second_no.
        PRINT TAB(34); '----'
1120 RETURN
```

The subroutine `Get_answer` merely gets the student's answer to the problem. To make the problem look nice when the program is run, we first move the cursor to the problem on the screen. When the student types his answer, it will appear directly under the problem he is solving. To do this, we use the TAB function in a PRINT statement, suppress the line feed, and follow up with the INPUT instruction. The code appears as follows:

```
1200 Get_answer:            ! Get student's answer
1210     PRINT TAB(33);     ! Move cursor to problem on screen
1220     INPUT Student_ans.
1230     PRINT              ! Skip a line for appearance
1240 RETURN
```

Subroutine `Wrapup` is merely a PRINT statement, as shown in Figure 5-3.

Subroutine `Get_again` must print a message telling the student that his answer is incorrect. It must also reprint the problem and allow him to enter a new answer. The pseudocode is:

> Let student try again:
>   Print message
>   Reprint problem
>   Get answer
> Return

The corresponding subroutine is:

```
1500 Get_again:                     ! Let student try again
1510     PRINT 'Your answer is incorrect. Please try again.'
         PRINT
1520     GOSUB Print_problem  ! Print the problem
1530     GOSUB Get_answer     ! Get students answer
1540 RETURN
```

As you can see, this subroutine uses the previously written routines for printing the problem and getting the student's answer. Not only is the logic of our program cleaner, but we have been saved the necessity of rewriting the same code.

It is important to understand what has been accomplished here. A difficult problem was decomposed into a large number of smaller ones. Each of the smaller problems was analyzed and coded separately. At any one time, we had only one small problem to handle. This is the power of top-down decomposition and modularity.

We will now put the pieces together in Figure 5-3 to show you what the program will look like as a complete entity.

If the program is run twice, then two different numbers will be generated by the random number generator because of the RANDOM statement at line 20. Without RANDOM, the same problem would be presented each time the program was run.

Figure 5-3.
Arithmetic Drill Program

```
10  ! Program for arithmetic drill, 2-digit nos.

20      RANDOM                  ! Randomize RND function

30      DECLARE INTEGER         First_no., Second_no., &
                                Student_ans., Correct_ans. &

40      GOSUB Make_problem      ! Generate two random integers

50      Correct_ans. = First_no. + Second_no.
                                ! Calculate correct answer

60      GOSUB Print_problem     ! Print the problem

70      GOSUB Get_answer        ! Get student's answer

80      WHILE Student_ans. <> Correct_ans.
           GOSUB Get_again      ! Let student try again
        NEXT

90      GOSUB Wrapup ! Congratulate student for correct answer

100  EXIT PROGRAM

1000 Make_problem:  ! Generate two random integers, 10 to 99
1010     First_no. = INT (90 * RND + 10)
         Second_no. = INT (90 * RND + 10)
1020 RETURN

1100 Print_problem:            ! Print the problem
1110   PRINT ! Blank line for appearance
       PRINT TAB(35); First_no.
       PRINT TAB(34); '+'; Second_no.
       PRINT TAB(34); '----'
1120 RETURN

1200 Get_answer:       ! Get student's answer
1210     PRINT TAB(33); ! Move cursor to problem on screen
1220     INPUT Student_ans.
1230     PRINT          ! Skip a line for appearance
1240 RETURN

1300 Wrapup:           ! Print congratulations
1310   PRINT 'Congratulations! Your answer is correct'
       PRINT
1320 RETURN

1500 Get_again:        ! Let student try again
1510     PRINT 'Your answer is incorrect. Please try again.'
         PRINT
1520     GOSUB Print_problem   ! Print the problem
1530     GOSUB Get_answer      ! Get student's answer
1540 RETURN

32767 END
```

Figure 5-3. (*Cont.*)

```
runnh
              68
         +    91
              ----
         ?  145
```

Your answer is incorrect. Please try again.

```
              68
         +    91
              ----
         ?  159
```

Congratulations! Your answer is correct

Instead of ending the program when the correct answer is given, it is also possible to have the program present a new problem for the user to solve. This would require that statements 40 through 90 be made into a subroutine that would be invoked from an outer loop. That problem will be left as an exercise.

5.5 PRIMING READ

In many cases, the data that we are reading determine whether we wish to continue the loop or terminate it. Generally, this type of loop requires two INPUT instructions: one before the loop and one at the very end of the loop. The one before the loop is called the **priming read.**

Recall that the loop condition for a WHILE or UNTIL statement is tested at the top of the loop, before the loop is even entered. The condition depends on data, so there must be data before the test is made. The priming read gets the initial datum for this first test. Once the loop is entered, this datum is processed, and an instruction at the end of the loop reads the next datum. The condition is then tested with the new datum. This sequence of events will be clarified by the following examples.

Example 5.18 We want to enter some numbers at the terminal and find their average. The amount of data may be different each time the program is run. To indicate where the numbers end, we enter −999 as the last number. The number −999 is an example of a data flag, or **sentinel**—a number that is used as a signal, but which is not really part of the data itself. Because a number with a lot of nines is used so frequently for this type of sentinel, the process is often referred to as "the rule of 9's." The sentinel is not included in the average.

In pseudocode we have:

```
Average of numbers to sentinel:
   Initialize sum and count of numbers
   Enter first number
```

```
                         Loop UNTIL number = sentinel
                            Add number to sum
                            Add 1 to count of numbers
                            Enter another number
                         End of loop
                         Average = sum / count of numbers
                         Print average
                       Stop
```

Figure 5-4.
Sample Priming Read
Program with a Sentinel

The final program is shown in Figure 5-4.

```
10  ! Average of any number of numbers.

20      DECLARE REAL    Number, Sum, Avg, &
                INTEGER     Count. &

30      Sum = 0                         ! Initialize sum
        Count. = 0                      ! Initialize count

40      INPUT 'Enter number         '; Number
                                        ! Priming read because loop
                                        ! condition depends on input
50      UNTIL Number = -999             ! Test for sentinel
            Sum = Sum + Number          ! Add number
            Count. = Count. + 1         ! Count number
            INPUT 'Enter number, -999 to end'; Number
                                        ! Enter next no.
        NEXT                            ! End of loop

60      Avg = Sum /Count.               ! Divide sum by no. of nos.

70      PRINT TAB(25); 'Average of'; COUNT.; 'numbers is'; Avg
80  END

runnh
Enter number               ? 67
Enter number, -999 to end  ? 87
Enter number, -999 to end  ? 94
Enter number, -999 to end  ? 32
Enter number, -999 to end  ? 18
Enter number, -999 to end  ? 77
Enter number, -999 to end  ? -999
                        Average of 6 numbers is 62.5
```

In this program, we used the variable COUNT. to count the numbers. The variable COUNT is a reserved word and cannot be a user-defined variable. Therefore, we added a period after the symbolic name to alter its form so that we could use it for our own purposes.

Example 5.19 | We are going to enter a number of records that represent charges at a department store. Each record consists of a name, an account number, and five prices, representing the costs of purchased items. The prices must be added to get a total purchase price. Then 8% sales tax must be added and the total cost, including tax, must be found.

Output will consist of the name, the account number, the cost of each item, the total cost without tax, the tax, and the total cost including tax.

Records are to be processed until a sentinel record with the name XXXX is read. The account number and purchases for this sentinel record are immaterial and may be zeros.

There are several ways to do this problem. Because our loop depends on a sentinel, the name XXXX, we require a priming read. The name in this last record is the only information that will be used, however, so we have a choice. Our priming read could consist of the entire first record, including name, account number, and five purchases; or the priming read might consist only of the name, while the remaining data could be read inside the loop. Let us pseudocode both versions for comparison.

Pseudocode, version 1:

Customer bill:
   Enter record (name, account number, five purchases)
   Loop UNTIL name = XXXX
     Do calculations
     Print results
     Enter next record
   End of loop
Stop

Pseudocode, version 2:

Customer bill:
   Enter name (only)
   Loop UNTIL name = XXXX
     Enter rest of record
     Do calculations
     Print results
     Enter next name
   End of loop
Stop

From a user's viewpoint, the major difference between these two methods is in the contents of the last record.

Version 1 requires that all data for the sentinel record be supplied: name, account number, and five purchases. As only the name is used in the loop test, the remaining data are extraneous and are ignored even though they must be entered. If we were obtaining our data from a file on a disk, this is the method we would use; a disk does not mind supplying extra data.

On the other hand, version 2 requires entering only the name, XXXX, for the sentinel record. The other data, the account number and five purchases, are not needed. We will be entering our data from the terminal via an INPUT statement. Because the second method requires less from the user, and is therefore more "user-friendly," we will code the second method:

```
10  ! Prepare customer bill
    ! Each record is read in three parts:
    !    1) The name
    !    2) Acct. no.
    !    3) 5 purchases
    ! Last record is the sentinel XXXX

20     (Reserved for DECLARE statement)

30     INPUT "Enter name "; NAME.      ! Priming input
       UNTIL NAME. = 'XXXX'
           GOSUB Read_rec              ! Read rest of record
           GOSUB Prepare_bill          ! Do calculations
           GOSUB Print_bill            ! Print results
           INPUT "Enter name "; NAME.
       NEXT

50  EXIT PROGRAM
```

The subroutine for entering the data consists of a few INPUT statements, as shown in Figure 5-5.

The subroutine to do the calculations uses the following logic:

Do calculations:
    Add all the purchases
    Compute the tax
    Compute the total
Return

Each of these steps is a single statement. The code appears in Figure 5-5.

The output routine in pseudocode is:

Print results:
    Print account number and name
    Print purchases (column 40)
    Print total purchases (column 55)
    Print tax (column 55)
    Print total (column 70)
Return

These will be coded with various PRINT statements and will involve various formats to improve the output appearance. The final program is coded as in Figure 5-5.

To make the program even a little more user friendly, the WHILE condition has been written to allow the sentinel to be entered in either upper or lower case letters. Of course, if someone decides to enter XxXx, or any other combination of both lower and upper case X's, that would not be recognized as a sentinel.

Enter this program at your terminal and run it. Remember to enter XXXX or xxxx when you receive the name prompt to terminate program execution.

Figure 5-5.
Billing Program

```
10   ! Prepare customer bill
     ! Each record is read in three parts:
     !    1) The name
     !    2) Acct. no.
     !    3) 5 purchases
     ! Last record is the sentinel XXXX

20      DECLARE STRING        NAME., ACCT_NO., &
                DECIMAL(7,2)  PUR.1, PUR.2, PUR.3, PUR.4, PUR.5, &
                DECIMAL(9,2)  PURCHASES, TOTAL, TAX &

30      INPUT "Enter name "; NAME.      ! Priming input

40      UNTIL NAME. = 'XXXX' OR NAME. = 'xxxx'
            GOSUB Read_rec              ! Read rest of record
            GOSUB Prepare_bill          ! Do calculations
            GOSUB Print_bill            ! Print results
            INPUT "Enter name, XXXX to end "; NAME.
        NEXT

50 EXIT PROGRAM

500 Read_rec:        ! Read rest of record (except name)
510      INPUT 'Account number'; ACCT_NO.
520      INPUT 'Enter the five purchases'; &
              PUR.1, PUR.2, PUR.3, PUR.4, PUR.5
530 RETURN

1000 Prepare_bill:  ! Do calculations
1010     PURCHASES = PUR.1 + PUR.2 + PUR.3 + PUR.4 + PUR.5
1020     TAX = 0.08 * PURCHASES ! 8% tax
1030     TOTAL = PURCHASES + TAX
1040 RETURN

1500 Print_bill:     ! Print results
1510     PRINT
         PRINT TAB(30); 'Customer Receipt'
         PRINT
1520     PRINT ACCT_NO.; TAB(15); NAME.
         PRINT
1530     PRINT 'Purchase 1'; TAB(40); PUR.1
         PRINT 'Purchase 2'; TAB(40); PUR.2
         PRINT 'Purchase 3'; TAB(40); PUR.3
         PRINT 'Purchase 4'; TAB(40); PUR.4
         PRINT 'Purchase 5'; TAB(40); PUR.5
         PRINT
1540     PRINT 'Total purchases'; TAB(55); PURCHASES
         PRINT
1550     PRINT 'Tax'; TAB(55); TAX
         PRINT
1560     PRINT 'Total'; TAB(70); TOTAL
1570 RETURN

32767 END
```

5.6 FLOW CHARTS (optional topic)

A loop is a new control structure, so we need a flow chart symbol (Fig. 5-6a) to represent it.

The loop control information is put into the symbol, which is reached by a flow line from above. The body of the loop is placed below the symbol, connected to the symbol by a flow line. At the end of the loop body, a flow line goes upward and enters the loop symbol from the left side. This constitutes the loop. A flow line leaves the loop symbol from the point at the right, and travels down past the loop body, to the next section of the program (see Fig. 5-6b).

Figure 5-6a.
Flow Chart Symbol for Loop

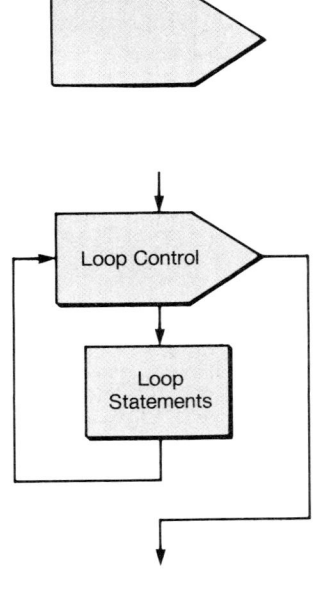

Figure 5-6b.
Loop Structure Flow Chart

Example 5.20 Here is a subroutine with a flow chart (Fig. 5-7) that illustrates the loop symbol.

Figure 5-7.
Subroutine and Flow Chart

```
500 Add_numbers:            ! Add numbers until sentinel
510     COUNT. = 0 \ SUM = 0
520     INPUT 'Enter no.'; X ! priming input
        UNTIL X = -999
            COUNT. = COUNT. + 1
            SUM = SUM + X
            INPUT 'Enter no. (-999 to end)'; X
        NEXT
        ! COUNT. has number of numbers, excluding sentinel
530     RETURN
```

Figure 5-7. (continued)

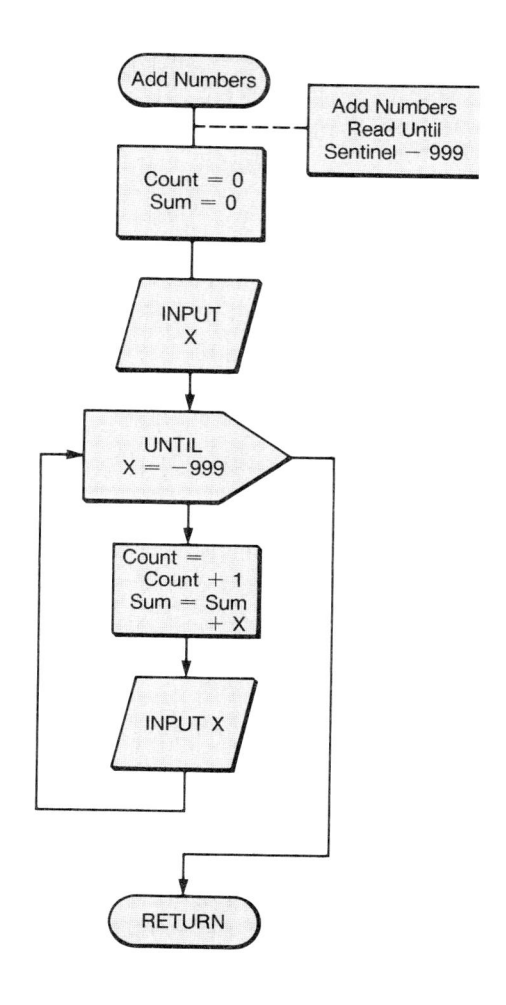

```
          Add Numbers
              │
              │- - - Add Numbers
              │      Read Until
              │      Sentinel - 999
         ┌─────────┐
         │ Count=0 │
         │ Sum = 0 │
         └─────────┘
              │
           ┌─────┐
           │INPUT│
           │  X  │
           └─────┘
              │
     ┌──► ┌──────────┐
     │    │  UNTIL   │──┐
     │    │ X = -999 │  │
     │    └──────────┘  │
     │         │        │
     │    ┌─────────┐   │
     │    │ Count = │   │
     │    │Count + 1│   │
     │    │Sum = Sum│   │
     │    │   + X   │   │
     │    └─────────┘   │
     │         │        │
     │    ┌─────────┐   │
     │    │ INPUT X │   │
     │    └─────────┘   │
     │         │        │
     └─────────┘        │
                        │
                   ┌────────┐
                   │ RETURN │
                   └────────┘
```

SUMMARY | This chapter introduced several types of loop control statements.

1. *The enumerative loop:* In the following examples, loop variable I will take on the values 0, 2, 4, 6, 8, and 10, and X will take on the values 10, 5, and 0:

    FOR I = 0 TO 10 STEP 2
      statements
    NEXT I

    FOR X = 10 TO 0 STEP -5
      statements
    NEXT X

2. *The controlled loop:*

    WHILE X < 0
      statements
    NEXT

```
        UNTIL A = B or A = C
          statements
        NEXT
```

   3. *Summing and counting,* which involves the following steps:
   a. Initialize the accumulator
   b. In the loop, have a statement that updates the accumulator in the following form:

   accumulator = accumulator + (item to be summed)

   4. The *random number generator,* RND, and the randomizing statement, RANDOM or RANDOMIZE:
   a. To get random numbers in the interval 0 <= number < range use range * RND
   b. To get random numbers in the range low <= number < high use (high − low) * RND + low
   c. To get random integers in the range low <= integer <= high, inclusive, use INT((high − low + 1) * RND + low)
   Note that this formula will generate integers from low to high, inclusive.
   d. RANDOMIZE uses the system time to seed the random number generator. It should execute only once per program run.

   5. This chapter also taught how more than one statement can be put on one physical line. To do this, the statements are separated by a backslash, \. Only relatively minor, closely related statements should be handled this way. An example:

```
50 SUM = 0 \ COUNT. = 0 \ No._of_Nos. = 0
```

REVIEW QUESTIONS

1. What is the purpose of a loop?
2. What is the difference between an enumerative loop and a controlled loop? When would you use each?
3. How does a loop differ from a sequence?
4. What are the symbols used to represent comparison operators? What do they stand for?
5. What are the logical operators? What do they stand for? Under which conditions will statements using logical operators be true, and under what conditions will they be false?
6. What are the differences between the WHILE loop and the UNTIL loop?
7. How does the computer know when it is at the end of a loop? How do the ends of enumerative and controlled loops differ?
8. If a loop is to be executed 250 times, what type of loop would you use? What are the statements that begin and end the loop?
9. If a loop is to be executed until the sum of a quantity reaches 250, what type of loop would you use? What are the first and last statements of this loop?
10. What is summing? What is counting? How do summing and counting differ?
11. When is it necessary to initialize a variable?

12. What is a priming read? Why is it used? What is the consequence of not using a priming read when one is indicated?
13. What is a sentinel? Why is it used? What is the "rule of 9's?"

SYNTAX EXERCISES

The following statements have one or more commonly made errors. Find and correct them.

```
 1. 100 FOR 1 TO 10
 2. 100 FOR 100 TO 200
 3. 100 FOR I = 100 TO 1
 4. 100 FOR K = 80 TO 20
 5. 100 FOR M = 100 TO 1 BY -1
 6. 100 FOR J = 0 TO 10 BY 2
 7. 100 FOR No. = 1 TO 10
        SUM + No. = SUM
    NEXT No.
 8. 100 FOR No. = 1 to 10
        SUM = SUM + No.
    NEXT No
 9. 100 FOR I = 1 TO 10
10. 100 WHYLE A > B
11. 100 WHILE X LESS THAN 100
12. 100 WHILE A > B AND C
13. 100 WHILE A > B & C < D
14. 100 WHILE A OR B < 10
15. 100 WHILE A + B + C EQUALS 100
16. 100 WHILE A - B
17. 1000 WHILE A > 0
         SUM = SUM + A
     NEXT A
18. 1000 WHILE A + B <> 100
         INPUT A,B
         A + B = SUM
     NEXT
19. 1000 WHILE X < 100
         INPUT "Enter 2 no."; A, B
         SUM = A + B
         PRINT SUM
     NEXT
```

PROGRAMMING EXERCISES

Write programs to solve the following problems. Subroutines should be used to decompose the problems into logical units. Input and output should always be performed by separate modules.

1. Make a table of numbers from 1 to 10, their squares, and their cubes. Each row of output will have the number in the first field of the line, the square in the second field, and the cube in the third. Put headings at the top of the table that label the columns.

2. Make a table of squares and square roots of numbers from 1 to 100.

3. Put 25 numbers into DATA statements. Write a loop that will find the average of the 25 numbers. Print the average, with suitable identification.

4a. A group of DATA statements each has five numbers. The last DATA statement contains five zeros. Write a loop that will read the five numbers in each DATA statement, find their sum, and print the sum. The loop is to end when the last DATA record has been read.

4b. Make up a few DATA statements, each with a name and five sales. The last one will have the word DONE instead of a name, and five zeros instead of the sales. (This is the sentinel record, which is not to be processed.) Each salesman's salary is $200.00 plus 15% of his total sales. Calculate this salary; then print the salesman's name, his total sales, and his salary. This output should all be on one line. Repeat for all salesmen.

When this has been done, skip a line and print the total sales and the total salary paid to all salesmen. Use suitable headings. (You might want to use the TAB function in this program.)

5a. A bank gives 5% interest on the amount in a savings account. The interest is put into the account and begins to earn interest. Write a loop that calculates the interest and new balance in the account every year for 20 years. Assume that the amount in the account is in a variable called `Principal`.

5b. A bank account has a balance of $1000.00. Each year, interest is credited at the rate of 6%. Write a program that prints the old balance, interest credited, and new balance every year for 20 years. The output should have appropriate column headings. The interest rate should be read from a DATA statement so that it can be changed easily. The original balance should be entered from the terminal.

6. Modify problem 5 to allow semiannual compounding. Repeat for quarterly compounding.

7. Write a program that will allow you to input two integers, and will then print the sum of all the integers in the range defined by the two entered values.

8. Modify problem 7 so that three numbers are entered at the terminal. The first is the starting value and the second is the ending value, as before. The third number represents the step interval to be used in selecting integers to be added.

For example, if the input is 5,14,3, the sum will be 38 (5 + 8 + 11 + 14 = 38). Notice that the third integer, 3, is the step interval between successive integers in this list.

9. Write a program to determine the number of years it would take to double your money in a bank account. Input the original balance in the account and the interest rate. Assume yearly compounding.

10. Modify problem 9 for semiannual compounding and for quarterly compounding.

11. Write a program that determines how many successive integers (1, 2, 3, and so on) must be added before the sum exceeds 250. Print the number of integers and the sum.

12. Write a program that generates 25 random numbers, prints each one, and finally prints their average.

13. The computer can simulate the rolling of a pair of dice by selecting two random integers from 1 to 6. The sum of the two integers represents the total of the pair of dice.

a. Write a subroutine that simulates the rolling of a pair of dice by getting two random integers in the range of 1 to 6, and adding these to get the sum showing on the pair of dice.

b. Write a loop that keeps rolling a pair of dice, and counts the number of times it is necessary to roll them until the sum on the dice is seven.

c. Write a program that will have the computer roll a pair of dice until a 7 is obtained. Print the number of rolls required. Run the program several times and compare the results to the value that is theoretically expected: six rolls to obtain one 7.

14. Write a program that will perform the experiment of problem 13 one-hundred times. Print the number of rolls required to get each 7. Also, find the total number of rolls and the ratio of 7's rolled to the total number of rolls. Print this ratio. Run the program and compare the result to the theoretical ratio, 0.16666 (= 1/6).

15. This problem is for students who have some statistical background. In problem 14, find the arithmetic mean number of rolls required to get a 7, and the standard deviation of the sample. The theoretical values are:

Mean = 6
S.D. = 5.4772 (= $\sqrt{30}$)

16. A rabbit hutch initially has two bunnies, a male and a female. In six months, the female has eight babies. In another six months, half of the resulting 10 bunnies (the five females) have eight bunnies each. This trend continues, so that every six months, half the bunnies in the hutch have eight babies each.

a. Write a loop that starts with two rabbits, calculates the number of bunnies produced every six months, adds them to the total number of rabbits, and adds one half year to the total number of years. The loop should end when 100,000 rabbits exist.

b. Write a program that prints the number of bunnies in the hutch every six months, together with the number of years, until the number of bunnies reaches one million. Ignore factors that might limit population growth (such as wolves).

17. Write a program that computes an amortization table. Input to the program will be the amount of a loan (car, home, or other), the yearly interest rate, and the monthly payment.

For each month, the computer will calculate the interest due that month (at 1/12 the yearly interest rate); subtract that interest from the payment to get what is called the **amortization** (reduction of principal); and then subtract the amortization from the balance to get the new balance on the loan.

The computer will print the payment number, the interest, the amortization, and the new balance for each month until the balance is less than the payment. For the final month, the interest will be calculated, the amortization will be the balance, and the new balance will be zero.

18. The number e is a mathematically important number, like pi. It can be calculated from the following formula:

$$e = \frac{1}{1!} + \frac{1}{2!} + \frac{1}{3!} + \frac{1}{4!} + \cdots$$

Each denominator is a factorial; in other words, n! is the product of all numbers from 1 to n. Theoretically, the calculation involves an infinite number of terms, but a good approximation can be obtained by using only a few terms.

  a. Write a subroutine that can calculate a N! given the number N.
  b. Write a loop that can calculate the sum of the first five terms of the series for e. It may make use of the subroutine of problem 18a.
  c. Write a program that calculates e by using the first five terms of the sequence. Print the value of e obtained.

19. You work for a baseball team, and the manager wants you to write a program for him that will use as input each player's name, times at bat, number of singles, number of doubles, number of triples, and number of home runs. The output should be the name, batting average, and slugging percentage of each player. The batting average is calculated by taking the total number of hits (singles, doubles, triples, and home runs) and dividing by the number of times at bat. The slugging percentage is calculated by taking the number of singles, plus two times the number of doubles, plus three times the number of triples, plus four times the number of home runs, and dividing that total by the number of times at bat:

$$\frac{(\text{no. singles}) + 2(\text{no. doubles}) + 3(\text{no. troubles}) + 4(\text{no. home runs})}{\text{no. of times at bat}}$$

Use "EOF" as the end of file sentinel, and when it is read, print the number of players, team batting average, and team slugging percentage.

20. This program can be used as an arithmetic drill. Have the computer select two random integers between 100 and 999. These numbers should be printed by the computer in the form of an addition problem, with one number under the other as in (Fig. 5-3). The person using the program must find the sum and type it as input to your program. If the sum is correct, inform the student and have the computer make up a new problem. If not, print a message to the user, reprint the problem, and let the user keep trying until the answer is correct.

6 Conditional Statements

Outline
6.1 IF-THEN-END IF
6.2 IF-THEN-ELSE-END IF
   Nesting of IF-THEN-ELSE
6.3 SELECT-CASE STATEMENT
6.4 Menus and Menu-Driven Software
6.5 Flow Charts
Summary
Review Questions
Syntax Exercises
Programming Exercises

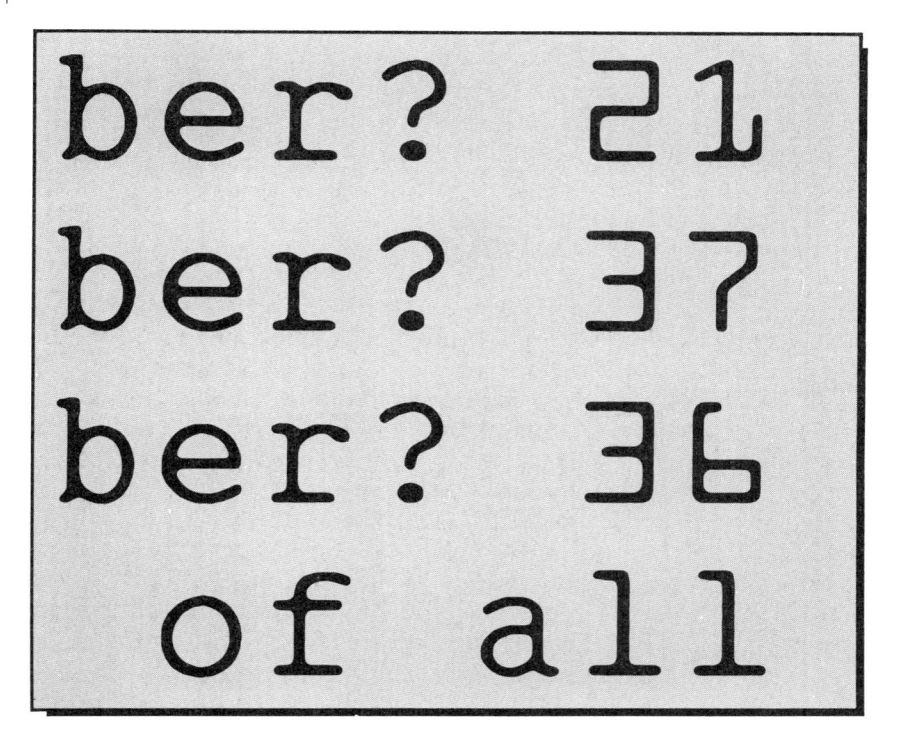

```
ber? 21
ber? 37
ber? 36
of all
```

Introduction   In computing, we often have to await the outcome of one calculation before we know what calculations should be performed next. Conceivably, we could print the first result, look at it, and then select an appropriate follow-up routine. But that would be too time consuming—in today's high-technology world, we need to be able to make decisions quickly, so we need some means of getting the computer involved in this decision-making process.

So far, we have not discussed how the computer can be instructed to "make decisions"; that is, choose among alternative statements to execute. That is the topic of this chapter.

6.1 IF-THEN-END IF

Frequently, we do not know the outcome of a calculation in advance; yet, the result of this calculation may determine what we wish to do next. A conditional statement will examine a logical expression and, depending on the result, select from among a number of alternative courses of action.

One type of conditional statement is the IF-THEN-END IF structure. The IF-THEN-END IF structure allows execution of a statement or group of statements if a certain condition is true, and skipping of those statements if the condition is false. Its syntax is:

    sn IF condition THEN statement END IF

or

    sn IF condition
       THEN
          statement
           ...
           ...
       END IF

where

    sn = a statement number (optional)
    condition = a logical expression
    statement = a BASIC statement

The keywords END IF are optional, but it is strongly recommended that they always be used. Many errors can be avoided by doing so.

If the condition is true, then the statement or statements following the keyword THEN are executed normally.

If the condition is false, then all statements following the keyword THEN, up to the keywords END IF, are skipped. If END IF is not present, then all statements up to the next line number are skipped.

The IF-THEN statement is different from other BASIC constructs; the IF clause may be on one physical line, and the THEN on another. The END IF that ends the entire statement may be on some later line. Even though the statement is spread out over more than one line, no ampersand is needed for the continuation lines (as is the case, for instance, with a DECLARE statement spread over more than one line).

NOTE! The entire IF-THEN-END IF structure must be on *one logical line.* This line may have as many physical lines as required, however.

Example 6.1

```
100 IF X < 0 THEN X = X + 1 END IF

200 IF A + B = C
    THEN A = A + 1
         B = B + 1
         PRINT C
    END IF
```

In both examples, if the condition is true, all statements following the word THEN are executed. If the condition is false, the computer skips these statements and continues execution after the END IF.

Example 6.2

```
100 IF X < 0 THEN X = X + 1

200 IF A + B = C
       THEN A = A + 1
            B = B + 1
            PRINT C
```

Example 6.2 is like Example 6.1 except that the END IF clause is omitted. Because of its absence, all statements up to the next line number are skipped when the condition is false.

Example 6.3

We wish to enter 10 numbers into the computer and add all of those that are greater than zero. The logic is:

> Sum of positive numbers:
>   Initialize sum to zero
>   Loop from 1 to 10
>   Enter number
>   If number > 0 then add number to sum
>   End of loop
>   Print sum
> Stop

The program can be written as shown in Figure 6-1a or 6-1b. The program shown in Figure 6-1c looks similar *but does not work!* Program (b), which uses the END IF, is the preferred method. Examples in this book will always end a conditional statement with END IF.

The third program, program (c), will not work because the first time a nonpositive number is encountered, control passes to the next logical line, statement 40, which is outside the loop. The loop does not execute again, so no additional numbers are read or processed.

In the case shown in figure 6-1c, VAX-BASIC will protect you from the error. Because there is no END IF statement, the NEXT statement ends up within the THEN clause. But putting a NEXT statement within a THEN clause will be flagged as an error by VAX-BASIC. For most other statements, there is no way for the computer to know that the statement was not meant to be in the range of the THEN. The statement will simply not execute, and there will be no warning that something is wrong. Consider:

```
100 IF X < 0
       THEN PRINT "Number is negative, enter new value"
            INPUT "Enter value"; X
       Sum = Sum + X
110 etc.
```

The indenting suggests that the summing instruction should always be done, and that only the PRINT and INPUT instructions are part of the THEN clause. Unfortunately, that is not how the statement will be inter-

Figure 6-1.
Two Right Ways and a Wrong Way to Add a Series of Positive Numbers.

(a) A right way

```
10 ! Sum of positive numbers
20    DECLARE REAL        NUMBER, SUM, &
             INTEGER      I
30    SUM = 0   ! Initialize sum
      FOR I = 1 TO 10
         INPUT 'Enter positive or negative number'; NUMBER
         IF NUMBER > 0 THEN SUM = SUM + NUMBER
40    NEXT I
50    PRINT 'Sum of positive numbers is'; SUM
60    END
```

(b) A better right way

```
10 ! Sum of positive numbers
20    DECLARE REAL        NUMBER, SUM, &
             INTEGER      I
30    SUM = 0   ! Initialize sum
      FOR I = 1 TO 10
         INPUT 'Enter positive or negative number'; NUMBER
         IF NUMBER > 0 THEN SUM = SUM + NUMBER # END IF
      NEXT I
40    PRINT 'Sum of positive numbers is'; SUM
50    END
```

(c) A wrong way

```
10 ! Sum of positive numbers, ERROR IN PROGRAM
20    DECLARE REAL        NUMBER, SUM, &
             INTEGER      I
30    SUM = 0   ! Initialize sum
      FOR I = 1 TO 10
         INPUT 'Enter positive or negative number'; NUMBER
         IF NUMBER > 0 THEN SUM = SUM + NUMBER
      NEXT I
40    PRINT 'Sum of positive numbers is'; SUM
50    END
```

preted. If the condition is false, everything up to line 110, the next statement number, will be skipped, *including the summing instruction*. The statement should have been written with an END IF to end the conditional structure:

```
100 IF X < 0
       THEN PRINT "Number is negative, enter new value"
            INPUT "Enter value"; X
```

```
        END IF
        Sum = Sum + X
110 etc.
```

Now the statement will work as desired.

To repeat, **ALWAYS TERMINATE A CONDITIONAL STATEMENT WITH END IF.**

Of course, every statement in this program (counting the entire IF-THEN-END IF as one statement) can have its own statement number. The program will be less efficient, however, and run more slowly.

The point has already been made twice but is so important that it will be made a third time:

FOR THE IF-THEN, IF THE CONDITION IS FALSE, CONTROL PASSES TO THE INSTRUCTION FOLLOWING **END IF**—IF THERE IS AN **END IF**. WHEN NO **END IF** IS PRESENT, CONTROL PASSES TO THE NEXT STATEMENT NUMBER.

Example 6.4 | Enter 10 numbers, and find the average of all positive numbers entered and the average of all negative numbers entered. Here is the pseudocode:

```
Average of positive and negative numbers:
  Initialize sums and counts
  Loop (10 times)
    Enter a number
    Process the number
  End of loop
  Find the averages
  Print results
Stop
```

For "Process the number" we have:

```
Process the number:
  If the number is positive then
    Add number to positive sum and
    Add 1 to positive count
  End if
  If number is negative then
    Add number to negative sum and
    Add 1 to negative count
  End if
Return
```

Notice that our logic ignores any zeros that are entered. They affect neither the positive count nor the negative count.

At the step called "Find the averages," we have to be careful. In arithmetic, division by zero is not permitted. If our program attempts such a division, an error will occur: program execution will be terminated and no

134 | 6 CONDITIONAL STATEMENTS

results will be printed. To keep this from happening, we test each count before dividing. If the positive or negative count is zero, we know that there are none of that type of number, and we do not attempt to find the average.

The pseudocode for finding averages is as follows:

```
Find the averages:
    If count of positive numbers > 0 then
        find positive average
    End if
    If count of negative numbers > 0 then
        find negative average
    End if
Return
```

Figure 6-2.
Program to Calculate and Print the Average of All Positive Numbers Entered and of All Negative Numbers Entered

In the output routine, we do not wish to print an average unless it exists. Again, we test the counts and print the average only if the count is positive. The coded solution appears in Figure 6-2.

```
10   ! Average of positive and negative numbers
20         DECLARE REAL    SUM_POS, SUM_NEG, AVG_POS, AVG_NEG, &
                           NO., &
                   INTEGER NUM_POS, NUM_NEG
30         GOSUB Initialize     ! Initialize sums and counts
40   ! Do it for 10 numbers
           FOR I = 1 TO 10
               INPUT 'Enter positive or negative number'; NO.
               GOSUB Process_no.   ! Process the number
           NEXT I
50         GOSUB Find_avgs       ! Find the averages
60         GOSUB Print_avgs      ! Print averages
70      EXIT PROGRAM

1000 Initialize:                ! Initialize sums and counts
1010     SUM_POS = 0
         SUM_NEG = 0
1020     NUM_POS = 0
         NUM_NEG = 0
1030 RETURN

1500 Process_no.:               ! Process the number
1510  ! Process positive number
         IF NO. > 0 THEN
             SUM_POS = SUM_POS + NO.
             NUM_POS = NUM_POS + 1
         END IF
1520  ! Process negative number
         IF NO. < 0 THEN
             SUM_NEG = SUM_NEG + NO.
             NUM_NEG = NUM_NEG + 1
         END IF
1530 RETURN
```

Figure 6-2. (*Cont.*)

```
2000 Find_avgs:                  ! Find averages
2010   ! Find average of positive numbers, if any
       IF NUM_POS > 0
       THEN AVG_POS = SUM_POS / NUM_POS
       END IF
2020   ! Find average of negative numbers, if any
       IF NUM_NEG > 0
       THEN AVG_NEG = SUM_NEG / NUM_NEG
       END IF
2030 RETURN

2500 Print_avgs:                 ! Print Averages
2510   ! Print positive average, if any
       IF NUM_POS > 0
       THEN PRINT TAB(25); 'Average of positive numbers = '; AVG_POS
       END IF
2520   ! Print negative average, if any
       IF NUM_NEG > 0
       THEN PRINT TAB(25); 'Average of negative numbers = '; AVG_NEG
       END IF
2530 RETURN
32767 END
```

Notice the conditional statements in the three subroutines starting at lines 1500, 2000, and 2500.

Example 6.5 In a particular class, each student takes five tests. The students' names and test marks are in DATA statements. Following the last student's name and grades is a sentinel record, which contains the word END and no grades.

A program needs to be written that will print each student's name, test average, and letter grade. The letter grade will be A, B, C, D, or F, depending on the test average. The sentinel record is not to be processed; there is no one whose name is END. The logic is:

    Class grading problem:
      Read a name (priming read)
      Loop UNTIL name = "END" or "end"
        Read five test grades
        Find average of test grades
        Find letter grade
        Print student data
        Read next name
      End of loop
    Stop

Notice that the condition tests for both an upper and lower case sentinel. The program will be more user-friendly if we do not impose a restriction on capitalization. (We do not concern ourselves with combinations of upper and lower case letters.)

136 | 6 CONDITIONAL STATEMENTS

Figure 6-3.
Class Grading Program

```
10  ! Class grading problem
20     ! Calculate test average and letter grade
       ! for an undetermined number of students

30        DECLARE STRING    NAME., GRADE, &
                   INTEGER  TEST1, TEST2, TEST3, TEST4, TEST5, &
                   DECIMAL(4,1)  AVG &

40        READ NAME.              ! Priming read for name
50        UNTIL NAME. = "END"
60        ! Read test grades
             READ TEST1, TEST2, TEST3, TEST4, TEST5
70        ! Find average
             AVG = (TEST1 + TEST2 + TEST3 + TEST4 + TEST5) / 5
80           GOSUB Letter_grade   ! Assign letter grade
90           GOSUB Print_data     ! Print student data
100          READ NAME.           ! Next name
110       NEXT

120   EXIT PROGRAM

1000 Letter_grade:               ! Find letter grade
1010     IF AVG >= 90 THEN GRADE = 'A' END IF
1020     IF AVG >= 80 AND AVG < 90 THEN GRADE = 'B' END IF
1030     IF AVG >= 70 AND AVG < 80 THEN GRADE = 'C' END IF
1040     IF AVG >= 60 AND AVG < 70 THEN GRADE = 'D' END IF
1050     IF AVG < 60 THEN GRADE = 'F' END IF
1060 RETURN

1500 Print_data:                 ! Print student data
1510     PRINT NAME.; TAB(40); AVG; TAB(55); GRADE
         PRINT
1520 RETURN

2000 ! DATA statements
2010    DATA John Smith,75,82,78,75,83
2020    DATA Jane Doe,92,97,94,88,92
2030    DATA Montague Smythe-Jones III,90,85,87,91,83
2040    DATA END

32767 END

RUNNH
John Smith                    81.6    B
Jane Doe                      78.6    C
Montague Smythe-Jones III     94.4    A
```

This pseudocode is simple enough, but it contains one pseudo-statement that could use some elaboration. Let us expand the statement "Find letter grade":

Find letter grade:
   If test average >= 90 then grade = "A"
   If test average >= 80 and < 90 then grade = "B"
   If test average >= 70 and < 80 then grade = "C"
   If test average >= 60 and < 70 then grade = "D"
   If test average <60 then grade = "F"
Return

The code for this subroutine is show below.

```
1000 Letter_grade:              ! Find letter grade
1010     IF AVG >= 90 THEN GRADE = 'A' END IF
1020     IF AVG >= 80 AND AVG < 90 THEN GRADE = 'B' END IF
1030     IF AVG >= 70 AND AVG < 80 THEN GRADE = 'C' END IF
1040     IF AVG >= 60 AND AVG < 70 THEN GRADE = 'D' END IF
1050     IF AVG < 60 THEN GRADE = 'F' END IF
1060 RETURN
```

As you can see, finding the letter grade will require five conditional statements. In three of these statements, the conditions are compound logical expressions.

Now we can finally write the code for the solution (Fig. 6-3). A few DATA statements have been included at the end of the program. The number of such statements is virtually unlimited, and can be as many as required for the class in question. The sentinel record is the final DATA statement.

Note that in the program of Figure 6-3 all IF statements could have been put on one line number, as shown below. *This would not be true if END IF had not been used.*

```
1010     IF AVG >= 90 THEN GRADE = 'A' END IF
         IF AVG >= 80 AND AVG < 90 THEN GRADE = 'B' END IF
         IF AVG >= 70 AND AVG < 80 THEN GRADE = 'C' END IF
         IF AVG >= 60 AND AVG < 70 THEN GRADE = 'D' END IF
         IF AVG < 60 THEN GRADE = 'F' END IF
```

6.2 IF-THEN-ELSE-END IF

The IF-THEN-ELSE-END IF structure includes two alternative paths that the computer can take, depending on the truth value of a condition. The syntax of the IF-THEN-ELSE structure is:

sn IF Condition THEN statement ELSE statement END IF

or

>   sn IF condition
>   THEN
>   statement
>   . . .
>   ELSE
>   statement
>   . . .
>   END IF

where

> sn   = a statement number
> condition = a logical expression
> statement = a BASIC statement

The END IF is again optional, but is strongly recommended. If it is not present, then the ELSE clause ends at the next statement number. If it is present, the ELSE clause ends at the END IF.

The entire IF-THEN-ELSE-END IF structure must be on the same logical line. If the condition is true, then the statements following the THEN keyword, up to the ELSE keyword, are executed and those after the ELSE keyword, up to the END IF (or the next statement number), are not. If the condition is false, then the statements following the ELSE keyword are executed and those between THEN and ELSE are not.

NOTE! **If the THEN and ELSE clauses contain only one statement each, then the conditional may be written on one line as follows:**

> sn IF condition THEN statement ELSE statement END IF

For example:

```
100 IF X > 0 THEN S1 = S1 + X ELSE S1 = S1 - X
```

If X is positive, its value is added to S1; if negative, its value is subtracted from S1. Therefore, S1 will always increase, because subtracting a negative number has the same effect as adding a positive one.

To repeat, **all statements of the IF-THEN-ELSE structure must be on the same logical line,** although not necessarily on the same physical line. The IF-THEN-ELSE structure ends at the END IF if there is one, of at the next statement number if there is not.

Example 6.6 We will input 10 numbers, some positive, some negative, but none are zero. Using the IF-THEN-ELSE-END IF, we will find the average of the positive numbers and the average of the negative numbers.

This problem is similar to Example 6.4. The pseudocode is:

```
Positive and negative averages:
   Initialize sums and counts
   Loop 10 times
      Input number
      Process number
   End of loop
   Find averages
   Print averages
Stop
```

The only difference between this problem and Example 6.4 is in the subroutine to process the numbers. Here is the pseudocode:

```
Process the number:
   If number is positive then
      Add number to positive sum
      Add 1 to positive count
   Else
      Add number to negative sum
      Add 1 to negative count
   End if
Return
```

The subroutine for this is as follows:

```
1500 ! Process_no.:
1510     IF NO. > 0
         THEN ! Positive number
               SUM.POS = SUM.POS + NO.
               NUM.POS = NUM.POS + 1
         ELSE ! Negative number
               SUM.NEG = SUM.NEG + NO.
               NUM.NEG = NUM.NEG + 1
         END IF
1520     RETURN
```

Figure 6-4.
Program to Compute and Print Averages

For convenience, Figure 6-4 presents the code for the entire program. Notice the use of IF-THEN-ELSE-END IF in subroutine 2500—the print routine—in addition to its use in subroutine 1500.

```
10 ! Average of positive and negative numbers

20      DECLARE REAL  NO., SUM.POS, SUM.NEG, AVG.POS, AVG.NEG, &
              INTEGER NUM.POS, NUM.NEG &

30      GOSUB Initialize    ! Initialize sums and counts
```

140 6 CONDITIONAL STATEMENTS

Figure 6-4. (*Cont.*)

```
40      ! Do it for 10 numbers
        FOR I = 1 TO 10
           INPUT 'Enter positive or negative number'; NO.
           GOSUB Process_no.   ! Process the number
        NEXT I

50      GOSUB Find_avgs        ! Find the averages
60      GOSUB Print_avgs       ! Print averages

70    EXIT PROGRAM

1000 Initialize:               ! Initialize sums and counts
1010    SUM.POS = 0 \ SUM.NEG = 0
1020    NUM.POS = 0 \ NUM.NEG = 0
1030 RETURN

1500 Process_no.:              ! Process the number
1510    IF NO. > 0
        THEN ! Positive number
           SUM.POS = SUM.POS + NO.
           NUM.POS = NUM.POS + 1
        ELSE ! Negative number
           SUM.NEG = SUM.NEG + NO.
           NUM.NEG = NUM.NEG + 1
        END IF
1520 RETURN

2000 Find_avgs:                ! Find averages
2010    ! Find average of positive numbers, if any
        IF NUM.POS > 0
        THEN AVG.POS = SUM.POS / NUM.POS
        END IF
2020    ! Find average of negative numbers, if any
        IF NUM.NEG > 0
        THEN AVG.NEG = SUM.NEG / NUM.NEG
        END IF
2030 RETURN

2500 Print_avgs:               ! Print Averages
2510    ! Print positive average, if any
        IF NUM.POS > 0
        THEN PRINT TAB(25); 'Average of positive numbers = '; AVG.POS
        ELSE PRINT TAB(25); 'No positive numbers'
        END IF
2520    ! Print negative average, if any
        IF NUM.NEG > 0
        THEN PRINT TAB(25); 'Average of negative numbers = '; AVG.NEG
        ELSE PRINT TAB(25); 'No negative numbers'
        END IF
2530 RETURN
32767 END
```

Nesting of IF-THEN-ELSE

The IF-THEN-ELSE-END IF structure can be nested, so that either the THEN clause or the ELSE clause contains another conditional instruction. Such a structure is useful in simplifying the conditions required for subsequent tests. The most useful of these nested structures is the one in which the ELSE clause contains a new IF structure. Consider the following:

```
IF condition-1 THEN statement-1
   ELSE IF condition-2 THEN statement-2
      ELSE IF condition-3 THEN statement-3
         ELSE statement-4
         END IF
   END IF
END IF
```

For example:

```
120   IF Height < 5 THEN Size = "Short"
      ELSE IF Height < 6 THEN Size = "Medium"
         ELSE IF Height < 6.5 THEN Size = "Tall"
            ELSE Size = "Very Tall"
            END IF
         END IF
      END IF
```

Condition-2 will be tested only if condition-1 has already failed. Similarly, by the time condition-3 is tested, it will already be known that condition-1 and condition-2 are both false. Statement-4 will be executed only if all previous conditions are false. The first true condition will cause its corresponding statements to be executed. The computer will then skip to the statement following all the END IF's (or to the next statement number) even if another (later) condition is true.

The nested IF-THEN-ELSE-END IF is used very frequently, and to conserve space on the line, we will adopt a variation of the above format, as follows:

```
IF condition-1 THEN statement-1
ELSE IF condition-2 THEN statement-2
ELSE IF condition-3 THEN statement-3
ELSE statement-4
END IF   END IF   END IF
```

For example:

```
120   IF Height < 5            THEN Size = "Short"
      ELSE IF Height < 6       THEN Size = "Medium"
      ELSE IF Height < 6.5     THEN Size = "Tall"
      ELSE                          Size = "Very Tall"
      END IF   END IF   END IF
```

This form sacrifices the indenting, but is still very readable. Its meaning is also very clear; it reads almost as if it were in everyday English instead of code. There is one END IF clause for each IF in the expression, and they have all been put together on one line.

We will go one step further. The multiple END IF clauses are only required if a statement follows the nest of conditionals on the same logical line. If we move such a statement, and all succeeding ones to a new logical line, we can reduce the multiple END IF's to a single END IF. We are relying on the rule that a conditional statement must all be on one logical line, and terminates at the end of that line. Therefore, *when only one END IF is used to close a nest of IF-THEN-ELSE statements, we must put any succeeding statements on a new line with a new statement number.* The format then becomes:

```
sn1    IF condition-1 THEN statement-1
       ELSE IF condition-2 THEN statement-2
       ELSE IF condition-3 THEN statement-3
       ELSE statement-4
       END IF
sn2    next statements
```

For example:

```
120    IF Height < 5          THEN Size = "Short"
       ELSE IF Height < 6     THEN Size = "Medium"
       ELSE IF Height < 6.5   THEN Size = "Tall"
       ELSE                        Size = "Very tall"
       END IF
130 ! Next statement
```

In general, we will always put a nest of conditional statements on its own logical line anyway, so this should cause no undue hardship.

Example 6.7 Earlier in this chapter (Example 6.5), we did a problem in which we assigned letter grades. Figure 6-5 shows a simpler solution using a nest of IF-THEN-ELSE statements. The nest is in subroutine Letter_grade at line 1000.

The change is in subroutine Letter_grade. If any condition is false, the computer proceeds to the next ELSE IF. At each IF statement, it is known that all previous conditions are false. If any condition is true, then the corresponding statement is executed, after which the computer proceeds to the next statement number or END IF, skipping all the remaining statements in the nest of conditionals.

For illustrative purposes, we included an END IF for each IF in line 1010. As per our previous discussion, this line could have been written using only one END IF, as follows:

```
1010       IF AVG >= 90 THEN GRADE = 'A'
           ELSE IF AVG >= 80 THEN GRADE = 'B'
           ELSE IF AVG >= 70 THEN GRADE = 'C'
           ELSE IF AVG >= 60 THEN GRADE = 'D'
           ELSE GRADE = 'F'
           END IF
1020 RETURN
```

6.2 IF-THEN-ELSE-END IF | **143**

Figure 6-5.
Class Grading Program

```
10  ! Class grading problem
20     ! Calculate test average and letter grade
       ! for an undetermined number of students

30        DECLARE STRING   NAME., GRADE, &
                  INTEGER   TEST1, TEST2, TEST3, TEST4, TEST5, &
                  DECIMAL(4,1)   AVG &

40        READ NAME.              ! Priming read for name
50        UNTIL NAME. = "END"
60        ! Read test grades
             READ TEST1, TEST2, TEST3, TEST4, TEST5
70        ! Find average
             AVG = (TEST1 + TEST2 + TEST3 + TEST4 + TEST5) / 5
80           GOSUB Letter_grade   ! Assign letter grade
90           GOSUB Print_data     ! Print student data
100          READ NAME.           ! Next name
110       NEXT
120  EXIT PROGRAM

1000 Letter_grade:                ! Find letter grade
1010    IF AVG >= 90 THEN GRADE = 'A'
        ELSE IF AVG >= 80 THEN GRADE = 'B'
        ELSE IF AVG >= 70 THEN GRADE = 'C'
        ELSE IF AVG >= 60 THEN GRADE = 'D'
        ELSE GRADE = 'F'
        END IF   END IF   END IF   END IF
1060 RETURN

1500 Print_data:                  ! Print student data
1510    PRINT NAME.; TAB(40); AVG; TAB(55); GRADE
        PRINT
1520 RETURN

2000 ! DATA statements
2010    DATA John Smith,75,82,78,85,88
2020    DATA Jane Doe,92,87,54,78,82
2030    DATA Montague Smythe-Jones III,100,95,97,91,89
2040    DATA END

32767 END
```

No statements can follow the IF-THEN-ELSE nest on the same logical line if this is done.

Example 6.8 | Let's play craps. Here are the rules, simplified, and ignoring the betting aspect:

You roll a pair of dice. If the total is 7 or 11, then you are an immediate winner. If it is 2, 3, or 12, then you are an immediate loser. Anything else is called your "point." You keep throwing the dice until you get your point again, in which case you win, or until you roll a 7, in which case you lose.

The computer will handle the rolling of the dice. Output will consist of an appropriate message informing you whether you won or lost. Here is the pseudocode:

> Crap shoot:
>   Roll a pair of dice
>   Find out if you won or lost
>   Print the result
>   Stop

The main program will be as follows:

```
10  ! Crap shooting
20      RANDOMIZE
30      (Reserved for DECLARE statement)
40      GOSUB Roll_dice          ! Roll the dice
50      GOSUB Determine_result   ! Find out if win or lose
60      GOSUB Print_result       ! Print result
70  EXIT PROGRAM
```

When you first read the instructions for this problem, you may have thought it was a very difficult problem, yet see how easily we have already solved the overall problem. The magic of top-down decomposition!

Rolling the pair of dice involves getting two random integers between 1 and 6, and adding them. Incidentally, this is not the same as getting one random number between 1 and 12. If you generate a random number between 1 and 12, all 12 numbers are equally likely to occur. With two dice, however, you will roll a 7 far more often than a 12. Many combinations of two dice add up to 7 (1 and 6, 2 and 5, and so on), but only one combination adds up to 12 (6 and 6). This subroutine for rolling the dice poses no difficulty.

Let us work on the next step, Determine_result:

> Find out if you won or lost:
>   If 7 or 11, you won
>   Else if 2, 3, or 12, you lost
>   Else process point
>   Return

The code for this subroutine is:

```
2000 Determine_result:                   ! Find out if win or lose
2010    IF DICE = 7 OR DICE = 11 THEN RESULT = 'WIN'
        ELSE IF DICE = 2 OR DICE = 3 OR DICE = 12
             THEN RESULT = 'LOSE'
             ELSE GOSUB Process_point   ! Process point
        END IF
2020 RETURN
```

Again, you must be aware that only one END IF has been used in line 2010; therefore, a new line number is *essential* for the next statement, in this case, the RETURN statement.

Now the subroutine that processes the point:

```
Process point:
   Save the point
   Roll the dice
   UNTIL seven or point is rolled
      Roll the dice
   End of loop
   If point shows you won, else you lost
Return
```

Notice that we roll the dice before the loop and again inside the loop. Without the first roll, we could not get into the loop, because the dice would already show the point. Instead of rolling the dice to get a new value, we could have set the value to zero. In fact, any code that guarantees that the dice are different from the point, prior to reaching the loop, would be sufficient. This subroutine is coded as follows:

```
2100 Process_point:              ! Process point
2110    POINT = DICE             ! Save the point
2120    GOSUB Roll_dice          ! Roll the dice
        UNTIL DICE = 7 OR DICE = POINT
           GOSUB Roll_dice       ! Roll the dice
        NEXT
2130    IF DICE = POINT          ! Why did we leave loop?
        THEN RESULT = 'WIN'      ! Rolled point
        ELSE RESULT = 'LOSE'     ! Rolled seven
        END IF
2140 RETURN
```

The output routine tests the value of RESULT and prints an appropriate message. The complete program is shown in Figure 6-6. Notice the use of the nested IF-THEN-ELSE structures in the program. They simplify the conditions considerably.

Notice, also, the different ways of writing the conditional statements on one or more physical lines.

Example 6.9 | We will write a program whose input will be a number of records, each consisting of a student name, three grades, and the final exam grade. For each student, the program is to calculate the average, counting the final twice. The average is to determine whether the student receives a PASS or FAIL in the course; PASS if the average is at least 70, FAIL otherwise.

The program is to print the student's name, average, and PASS or FAIL. In addition, the program is to find the number of students and the class average. The last record contains the sentinel EOF. When the sentinel is entered, the program will print the total number of students and the class average.

146 | 6 CONDITIONAL STATEMENTS

Figure 6-6.
Crap Shooting Program

```
10  ! Crap shooting
20      RANDOMIZE
30      DECLARE STRING    RESULT, &
                INTEGER   DIE.1, DIE.2, DICE, POINT &

40      GOSUB Roll_dice          ! Roll the dice
50      GOSUB Determine_result   ! Find out if win or lose
60      GOSUB Print_result       ! Print result
70      EXIT PROGRAM

1000 Roll_dice:                  ! Roll the dice
1010    DIE.1 = INT(6 * RND + 1)
        DIE.2 = INT(6 * RND + 1)
        DICE = DIE.1 + DIE.2
1020    PRINT "Dice show"; DICE  ! Keep user informed
1030 RETURN

2000 Determine_result:                    ! Find out if win or lose
2010    IF DICE = 7 OR DICE = 11 THEN RESULT = 'WIN'
        ELSE IF DICE = 2 OR DICE = 3 OR DICE = 12
            THEN RESULT = 'LOSE'
            ELSE GOSUB Process_point  ! Process point
        END IF
2020    RETURN

2100 Process_point:              ! Process point
2110    POINT = DICE             ! Save the point
2120    GOSUB Roll_dice          ! Roll the dice
        UNTIL DICE = 7 OR DICE = POINT
            GOSUB Roll_dice      ! Roll the dice
        NEXT
2130    IF DICE = POINT          ! Why did we leave loop?
        THEN RESULT = 'WIN'      ! Rolled point
        ELSE RESULT = 'LOSE'     ! Rolled seven
        END IF
2140 RETURN

3000 Print_result:               ! Print results
3010    IF POINT = 0 THEN PRINT TAB(20); 'Dice show '; DICE
        ELSE PRINT TAB(20); 'Point = '; POINT, 'Dice show '; DICE
        END IF
3020    IF RESULT = 'WIN'
        THEN PRINT TAB(20); 'You win. Take the money'
        ELSE PRINT TAB(20); 'You lose. Come again anytime.'
        END IF
3030    PRINT
3040 RETURN

32767 END
```

Solution in pseudocode:

```
PASS-FAIL grading:
   Print headings
   Initialize sums for class statistics
   Enter first name (priming read)
   Loop UNTIL name = "EOF"
      Find student average
      Assign PASS or FAIL
      Print student record
      Accumulate class statistics
      Enter next name
   End of loop
   Calculate class average
   Print class statistics
Stop
```

The pseudocode leads to the following code:

```
10  ! Student pass-fail program
20     (Reserved for DECLARE statement)
30     GOSUB Print_headings   ! Print headings
40     GOSUB Initialize       ! Initialize for class statistics
50     INPUT 'Enter name'; NAME.
       UNTIL NAME. = 'EOF'
          GOSUB Enter_tests   ! Enter student tests
          GOSUB Find_avg      ! Find student average
          GOSUB Pass_fail     ! Assign PASS or FAIL
          GOSUB Print_rec     ! Print student record
          GOSUB Class_stats   ! Accumulate for class statistics
          INPUT 'Enter name (EOF to end)'; NAME.
       NEXT
60     CLASS.AVG = CLASS.SUM / CLASS.COUNT
70     GOSUB Print_stats      ! Print class statistics
80  EXIT PROGRAM
```

Assigning the PASS or FAIL grade uses an IF-THEN-ELSE-END IF statement:

```
1400 Pass_fail:                   ! Assign PASS or FAIL
1410    IF AVG >= 70 THEN GRADE = 'PASS'
        ELSE GRADE = 'FAIL'
        END IF
1420 RETURN
```

The program uses a multi-statement physical line—more than one statement on one physical line. We do this by separating the statements with a backslash. You will see this used in Fig. 6-7 in lines 1110 and 2010. As was stated in chapter 5, we do this only for relatively minor, closely related statements. The complete program appears in Figure 6-7.

148 6 CONDITIONAL STATEMENTS

Figure 6-7.
Student Pass/Fail Program

```
10   ! Student pass-fail program

20         DECLARE STRING     NAME., GRADE, &
                   INTEGER    TEST_1, TEST_2, TEST_3, FINAL, &
                              SUM, CLASS.SUM, CLASS.COUNT, &
                   DECIMAL(4,1) AVG, CLASS.AVG

30         GOSUB Print_headings   ! Print headings
40         GOSUB Initialize       ! Initialize for class statistics

50         INPUT 'Enter name (EOF to end)'; NAME.
           UNTIL NAME. = 'EOF' OR NAME. = 'eof'
             GOSUB Enter_tests    ! Enter student tests
             GOSUB Find_avg       ! Find student average
             GOSUB Pass_fail      ! Assign PASS or FAIL
             GOSUB Print_rec      ! Print student record
             GOSUB Class_stats    ! Accumulate for class statistics
             INPUT 'Enter name (EOF to end)'; NAME.
           NEXT

60         CLASS.AVG = CLASS.SUM / CLASS.COUNT

70         GOSUB Print_stats      ! Print class statistics

80     EXIT PROGRAM

1000 Print_headings:              ! Print headings
1010    PRINT TAB(40); 'Class grades, pass - fail'
        PRINT
1020    PRINT 'Name'; TAB(35); 'Tests'; TAB(50); 'Final'; &
              TAB(65); 'Grade'
        PRINT
1030 RETURN

1100 Initialize:                  ! Initialize for class statistics
1110    CLASS.SUM = 0 \ CLASS.COUNT = 0
1120 RETURN

1200 Enter_tests:                 ! Enter student tests
1210    INPUT 'Enter three tests'; TEST_1, TEST_2, TEST_3
        INPUT 'Enter the final'; FINAL
1220 RETURN

1300 Find_avg:                    ! Find student average
1310    SUM = 0
        SUM = TEST_1 + TEST_2 + TEST_3 &
              + 2 * FINAL          ! Final counts twice
1320    AVG = SUM / 5
1330 RETURN
1400 Pass_fail:                   ! Assign PASS or FAIL
```

Figure 6-7. (*Cont.*)

```
1410     IF AVG >= 70 THEN GRADE = 'PASS'
         ELSE GRADE = 'FAIL'
         END IF
1420 RETURN

1500 Print_rec:               ! Print student record
1510     PRINT
1520     PRINT NAME.; TAB(30); TEST_1; TAB(35); TEST_2; &
               TAB(40); TEST_3; TAB(50); FINAL; TAB(65); GRADE
1530     PRINT
1540 RETURN

1600 Class_stats:             ! Accumulate for class statistics
1610     CLASS.SUM = CLASS.SUM + AVG
         CLASS.COUNT = CLASS.COUNT + 1
1620 RETURN

2000 Print_stats:             ! Print class statistics
2010     PRINT \ PRINT
2020     PRINT 'Number of students is '; CLASS.COUNT
         PRINT 'Class average is      '; CLASS.AVG
         PRINT
2030 RETURN

32767 END


RUNNH
Name                          Tests            Final        Grade
Enter name (EOF to end)? JOHN
Enter three tests? 56,78,92
Enter the final? 81

JOHN                          56   78   92     81           PASS

Enter name (EOF to end)? MARSHA
Enter three tests? 87,89,92
Enter the final? 94

MARSHA                        87   89   92     94           PASS

Enter name (EOF to end)? DOPEY
Enter three tests? 12
?24
?18
Enter the final? 21

DOPEY                         12   24   18     21           FAIL

Enter name (EOF to end)? EOF

Number of students is  3
Class average is       62.6667
```

6.3 SELECT-CASE STATEMENT

VAX-BASIC has another structure that can be used to select among different alternatives. This can be used in place of, and is an improvement to, the nested IF-THEN-ELSE structure. It is called a SELECT block, or SELECT-CASE statement. It has the following syntax:

```
SELECT expression
   CASE test
      statement(s)
   CASE test
      statement(s)
   ...
   [CASE ELSE
      statement(s)]
END SELECT
```

where

expression = a numerical or string expression
test = a value or range of values against which the expression is compared.

An example is:

```
SELECT A + B
    CASE < 0
        PRINT "Sum of A and B is less than 0"
    CASE = 1
        PRINT "Sum of A and B is 1"
    CASE 2
        PRINT "Sum of A and B is 2"
    CASE 3, 4, 5, 6
        PRINT "Sum of A and B is 3, 4, 5, or 6"
    CASE 50 TO 100
        PRINT "Sum of A and B is between 50 and 100"
    CASE 10,15,25 TO 50
        PRINT "Sum is 10, 15, or between 25 and 50"
    CASE ELSE
        PRINT "Sum of A and B is something else"
END SELECT
```

As you can see from the above example, there are a number of different types of tests that may be used in the CASE block. Here is a list of possibilities:

1. A relational test may be used, such as in the first and second CASE blocks. The expression in the SELECT statement is tested against this test. If it is true, then the statements in that CASE block are executed. If not, they are skipped. The expression in the SELECT becomes the left side of the relational test, while the right side of the CASE clause supplies the right side of the test. In the first CASE above, the complete boolean expression is therefore A + B < 0. If this is true, the PRINT statement is executed, otherwise the next CASE test is tried.

2. One or more values may be given without a relational operator, as in the third and fourth CASE statements above. There is then an implied relational = operator, and if necessary, a series of logical OR operators. In the third CASE statement, the complete boolean expression is A + B = 2. In the fourth, it is:

A + B = 3 OR A + B = 4 OR A + B = 5 OR A + B = 6

If the test in the third CASE is true, its PRINT statement is executed; if not, the fourth CASE is tested. If the expression matches any of those in the fourth CASE, its PRINT statement is executed; otherwise the fifth CASE test is made.

3. A range of values can be tested against the SELECT expression. The first value is stated, followed by the word TO, and the last value. If the expression is between these values, the corresponding statement block is executed. In the fifth CASE above, if A + B is between 50 and 100, inclusive, then the PRINT statement in the CASE block is executed. If A + B is not in this range, then the next CASE test is made.

4. A combination of the above can be used, as in the sixth CASE example. If the expression has any of the values 10, 15, or anything between 25 and 50, inclusive, then the corresponding statements will be executed.

Whenever the test in a CASE statement is true, the corresponding statements are executed, and the program continues with the first statement after the END SELECT statement. When the test is false, the next CASE test is made.

Notice that the test of a CASE is made only if the previous test failed, or if it is in the first CASE block. Values in two CASE tests may overlap. If both tests are true, only the statements in the first CASE are executed because the second CASE containing the overlap would never get tested.

If all tests in all CASE blocks fail, then the statements in the CASE ELSE block are executed, *if* it is present. This is an optional block. If all tests fail and there is no CASE ELSE, then the program resumes with the first statement after END SELECT.

There may be more than one statement in each CASE block and each statement in a SELECT block may have its own statement number, if desired.

The expression in the SELECT statement may be a string expression. For example:

```
SELECT TRANSACTION_TYPE   ! TRANSACTION_TYPE is STRING
  CASE "deposit"
    GOSUB Make_deposit
    GOSUB Print_receipt
```

```
            CASE "withdrawal"
               GOSUB Make_withdrawal
               GOSUB Print_receipt
            CASE "interest"
               GOSUB Credit_interest
               GOSUB Print_receipt
            CASE ELSE
               PRINT "Error in transaction type"
         END SELECT
```

Notice that IF-THEN-ELSE could be used instead of SELECT, but when it is applicable, SELECT-CASE is often simpler to use.

Example 6.10 Earlier in this chapter, we did a problem in which we assigned letter grades. At first we used the IF-THEN construction (Example 6.5), then the IF-THEN-ELSE construction (Example 6.7). For comparison, we now present the applicable subroutine using the SELECT-CASE construction.

The IF-THEN-ELSE version was as follows:

```
1010      IF AVG >= 90 THEN GRADE = 'A'
          ELSE IF AVG >= 80 THEN GRADE = 'B'
          ELSE IF AVG >= 70 THEN GRADE = 'C'
          ELSE IF AVG >= 60 THEN GRADE = 'D'
          ELSE GRADE = 'F'
```

The SELECT-CASE version is presented below:

```
1010      SELECT AVG
             CASE >= 90
                GRADE = 'A'
             CASE >= 80
                GRADE = 'B'
             CASE >= 70
                GRADE = 'C'
             CASE >= 60
                GRADE = 'D'
             CASE ELSE
                GRADE = 'F'
          END SELECT
```

6.4 MENUS AND MENU-DRIVEN SOFTWARE

When you go to a fine restaurant, you are given a menu—a list of choices from which to make a selection. After telling the waiter you want appetizer "C", you are asked to make a selection from the salad menu, then the soup, entree, and dessert menus. Each selection you make results in the selected item being served.

A computer menu is also a list of choices from which you make a selection. Each choice you select will cause a different subroutine to be executed. After the appropriate subroutine has finished its activity, the menu is reprinted, allowing you to make another choice.

6.4 MENUS AND MENU-DRIVEN SOFTWARE

Menu-driven software has the following logic:

Menu-driven software:
    Loop while not done
        Print menu
        Make selection
        Invoke chosen subroutine
    End of loop
Stop

Example 6.11 In this example, we use a menu to tell the computer to print random numbers in various ranges. The program does not have much practicality, but it does illustrate the concept of menu-driven software.

The pseudocode for the main program is as given previously. Each subroutine is very simple, so we will proceed directly to the program shown in Figure 6-8a. The INVOKE routine has been written using the SELECT-CASE statement. The IF-THEN-ELSE statement can be used instead. That variation is shown in Fig. 6-8b.

Figure 6-8a.
Sample Program Showing the Concept of Menu-Driven Software

```
10  ! Random numbers in selected ranges

20      RANDOMIZE
30      DECLARE STRING    DONE, JUNK, &
                INTEGER   MIN.CHOICE, MAX.CHOICE, SELECTION, &
                REAL      NUMBER

40      DONE = 'NO'
        WHILE DONE <> 'YES'
          GOSUB Print_menu    ! Print the menu
          GOSUB Choose        ! Make selection
          GOSUB Invoke        ! Invoke proper subroutine
        NEXT
50   EXIT PROGRAM

500 Print_menu:               ! Print the menu
510   PRINT \ PRINT \ PRINT
520   PRINT '1. Print number from 101 to 200'
      PRINT '2. Print number from 201 to 300'
      PRINT '3. Print number from 301 to 400'
      PRINT '4. Print number from 401 to 500'
      PRINT '0. End program'
530   MIN.CHOICE = 0 \ MAX.CHOICE = 4
    ! Used by 'make selection' routine
530 RETURN

600 Choose:                   ! Make selection
610   PRINT \ INPUT 'Make selection'; SELECTION
620   WHILE SELECTION < MIN.CHOICE OR SELECTION > MAX.CHOICE
          PRINT
          PRINT 'Selection out of range'
          INPUT 'Make selection'; SELECTION
      NEXT
```

Figure 6-8a. (*Cont.*)

```
 630 RETURN
 700 Invoke:                      ! Invoke proper subroutine
 710    SELECT SELECTION
              CASE 1
                    GOSUB Sub_100    ! 101 to 200
              CASE 2
                    GOSUB Sub_200    ! 201 to 300
              CASE 3
                    GOSUB Sub_300    ! 301 to 400
              CASE 4
                    GOSUB Sub_400    ! 401 to 500
              CASE 0
                    GOSUB Finish     ! Finish up
        END SELECT
 720 RETURN

 800 Output:                       ! Output routine
 810    PRINT \ PRINT
 820    PRINT TAB(40); 'The number is'; NUMBER
        PRINT
        INPUT 'Press <Return> when ready'; JUNK
 830 RETURN

1000 Sub_100:                      ! Random number 101 to 200
1010    NUMBER = INT ( 100 * RND + 101 )
1020    GOSUB Output               ! Output NUMBER
1030 RETURN

1500 Sub_200:                      ! Random number 201 to 300
1510    NUMBER = INT ( 100 * RND + 201 )
1520    GOSUB Output               ! Output NUMBER
1530 RETURN

2000 Sub_300:                      ! Random number 301 to 400
2010    NUMBER = INT ( 100 * RND + 301 )
2020    GOSUB Output               ! Output NUMBER
2030 RETURN

2500 Sub_400:                      ! Random number 401 to 500
2510    NUMBER = INT ( 100 * RND + 401 )
2520    GOSUB Output               ! Output NUMBER
2530 RETURN

10000 Finish:                      ! Finish-up routine
10010    DONE = 'YES' ! To stop main program
10020    PRINT \ PRINT
10030    PRINT 'End of program. Have a nice day.'
         PRINT
10040 RETURN

32767 END
```

**Figure 6-8b.
The Invoke Subroutine
Rewritten Using
IF-THEN-ELSE**

```
700 Invoke:                       ! Invoke proper subroutine
710    IF SELECTION = 1 THEN GOSUB Sub_100      ! 101 to 200
       ELSE IF SELECTION = 2 THEN GOSUB Sub_200  ! 201 to 300
       ELSE IF SELECTION = 3 THEN GOSUB Sub_300  ! 301 to 400
       ELSE IF SELECTION = 4 THEN GOSUB Sub_400  ! 401 to 500
       ELSE IF SELECTION = 0 THEN GOSUB Finish   ! Finish up
720 RETURN
```

The instruction

```
INPUT 'Press <Return> when ready'; JUNK
```

makes the computer wait for a response from the user and gives the user an opportunity to examine the output before the menu is printed again. This could be very important since the menu might push the output off the top of the screen.

Notice how the input routine checks the entered selection for validity. Variables MIN.CHOICE and MAX.CHOICE are used in this routine for ease in adding additional choices to the menu. By changing the values of these variables when another choice is added, the input routine will still check for the proper range of entries.

The output for a typical run of this program is shown in Figure 6-9.

**Figure 6-9.
Output from the
Menu-Driven Software
Program**

```
RUNNH

1. Print number from 101 to 200
2. Print number from 201 to 300
3. Print number from 301 to 400
4. Print number from 401 to 500
0. End program

Make selection? 1

                                        The number is 172

Press <Return> when ready?

1. Print number from 101 to 200
2. Print number from 201 to 300
3. Print number from 301 to 400
4. Print number from 401 to 500
0. End program

Make selection? 3

                                        The number is 331
```

156 | 6 CONDITIONAL STATEMENTS

Figure 6-9. (*Cont.*)

```
              Press <Return> when ready?

              1. Print number from 101 to 200
              2. Print number from 201 to 300
              3. Print number from 301 to 400
              4. Print number from 401 to 500
              0. End program

              Make selection? 6

              Selection out of range
              Make selection? 4

                                       The number is 437

              Press <Return> when ready?

              1. Print number from 101 to 200
              2. Print number from 201 to 300
              3. Print number from 301 to 400
              4. Print number from 401 to 500
              0. End program

              Make selection? 0

              End of program. Have a nice day.
```

6.5 FLOW CHARTS (optional topic)

In this chapter, we have introduced new control structures and so we need new flow chart symbols. The symbol to be used for the IF-THEN and IF-THEN-ELSE statements is the diamond (Fig. 6-10a).

Figure 6-10a.
Branching Flow Chart Symbol

Figure 6-10b.
IF-THEN Structure Chart

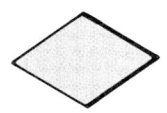

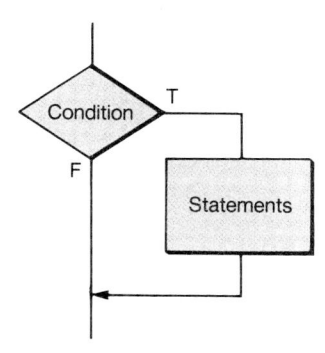

Figure 6-10c.
IF-THEN-ELSE Structure Flow Chart

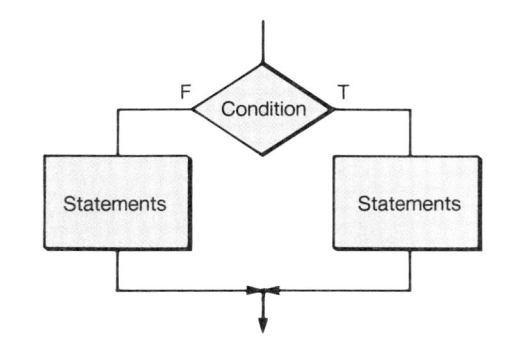

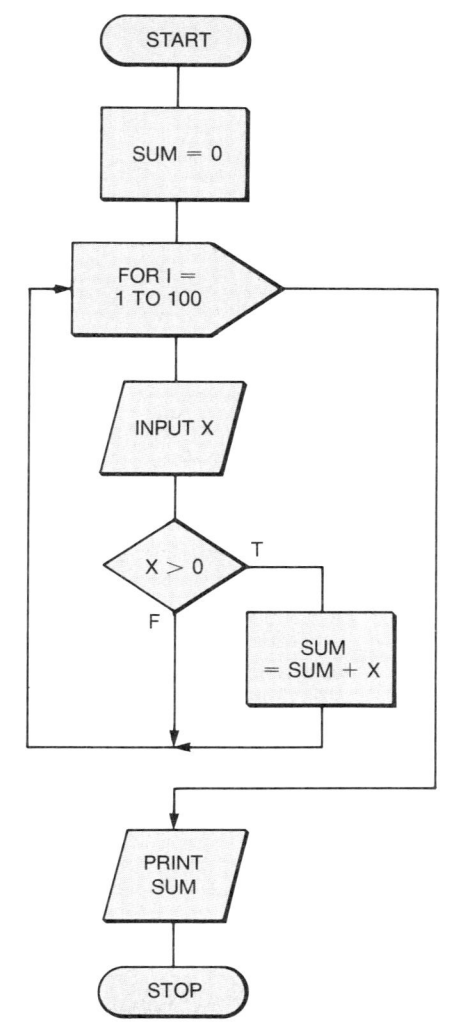

Figure 6-11.
Sample Program and Flow Chart Showing IF-THEN Structure

```
10  ! Enter 100 numbers, add the positive numbers
20      DECLARE INTEGER   I, REAL X, SUM
30      SUM. = 0             ! Initialize sum
40      FOR I = 1 TO 100
            INPUT X
            IF X > 0 THEN SUM = SUM + X    END IF
        NEXT I
50      PRINT SUM.
60      END
```

Figure 6-12.
Sample Subroutine and Flow Chart Showing Two IF-THEN Structures

```
1400 Pass_fail:                    ! Assign PASS or FAIL
1410    IF AVG >= 70 THEN GRADE = 'PASS'    END IF
1420    IF AVG < 70 THEN GRADE = 'FAIL'     END IF
1420 RETURN
```

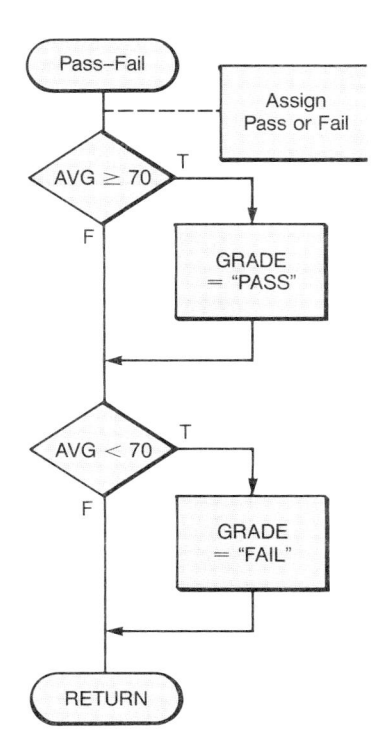

The symbol is entered by a flow line from above to the uppermost point of the diamond. The condition being tested is printed inside the diamond symbol. Two flow lines, marked T and F, emanate from the symbol. The one labeled T usually comes from the right-most point of the diamond and is the branch taken when the condition is true. The other one, labeled F, exits either from the left-most or lowest point of the diamond and is the branch taken if the condition is false. An example appears in Figure 6-11.

Figure 6-12 is a subroutine and flow chart with two conditional statements.

Figure 6-13 is a subroutine and flow chart containing an IF-THEN-ELSE structure.

As you can see in Figure 6-13, the IF-THEN-ELSE structure is flow charted using one branching symbol with one of the two alternative paths emanating from each side. The IF-THEN structure is usually flow charted

Figure 6-13.
Subroutine and Flow Chart Showing IF-THEN-ELSE Structure

```
1400 Pass_fail:                    ! Assign PASS or FAIL
1410    IF AVG >=70 THEN GRADE = 'PASS'
         ELSE GRADE = 'FAIL'
         END IF
1420 RETURN
```

Figure 6-13. (*Cont.*)

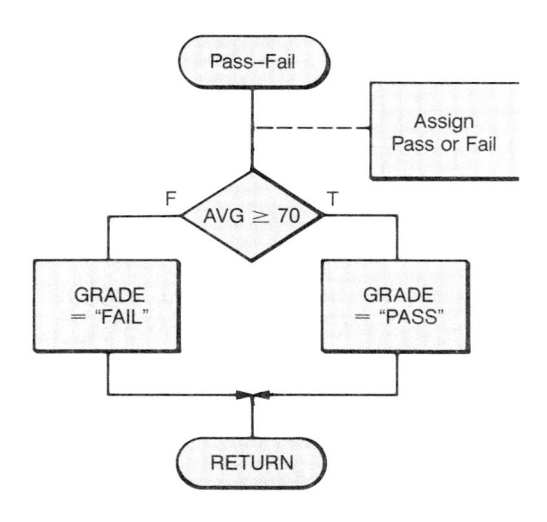

Figure 6-14.
SELECT-CASE flow chart symbol

Figure 6-15.
Subroutine and Flow Chart Showing SELECT-CASE Structure

with the T branch coming from the right side of the diamond, and the F branch exiting at the bottom.

The symbol for the SELECT-CASE structure is not standard. We will use the symbol as shown in Figure 6-14.

An example of a subroutine using SELECT-CASE, and its corresponding flow chart, is shown in Figure 6-15.

```
700 Invoke:                     ! Invoke proper subroutine
710    SELECT SELECTION
          CASE 1
             GOSUB Sub_100       ! 101 to 200
          CASE 2
             GOSUB Sub_200       ! 201 to 300
          CASE 3
             GOSUB Sub_300       ! 301 to 400
          CASE 4
             GOSUB Sub_400       ! 401 to 500
          CASE 0
             GOSUB Finish        ! Finish up
       END SELECT
720 RETURN
```

Figure 6-15. (*Cont.*)

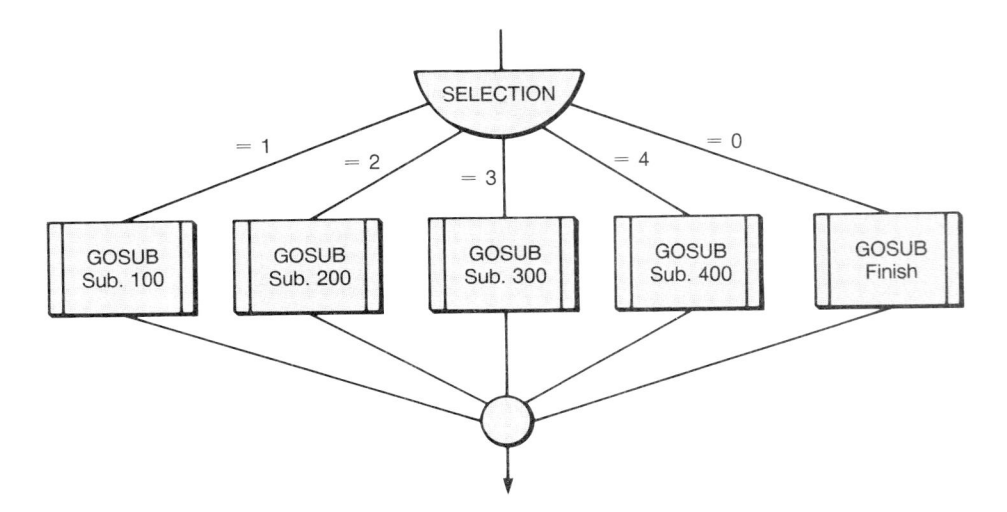

SUMMARY

Three types of selection instructions can be used to have the computer make decisions. They are the IF-THEN structure, the IF-THEN-ELSE structure, and the SELECT-CASE structure.

Statements following an IF-THEN or IF-THEN-ELSE structure that are not part of the structure must follow the END IF clause, or be in a new logical line with a new statement number. All statements that are part of the IF-THEN or IF-THEN-ELSE structure must be on the same logical line.

1. The syntax of the IF statements is:

IF condition THEN statements END IF

and

IF condition THEN statements ELSE statements END IF

2. The syntax of the SELECT-CASE structure is:

SELECT expression
  CASE test
    statement(s)
    ...
  [CASE ELSE
    statement(s)]
END SELECT

The test may be the second part of a simple boolean expression, such as: >100, or a list of one or more values separated by commas, such as: "a","e","i","o","u", or a range of values such as: 0 TO 100 or "A" TO "Z". It may also be a combination of these. Each statement may have its own statement number. Test values may overlap, but only the first CASE whose test is true will be executed.

REVIEW QUESTIONS

1. What is a conditional statement and when is it used?
2. What is the difference between an IF-THEN and an IF-THEN-ELSE structure. When would you use each?
3. What is the syntax of the IF-THEN structure?
4. What is the syntax of the IF-THEN-ELSE structure?
5. In an IF-THEN statement, how does the computer know when the THEN clause is ended?
6. In an IF-THEN-ELSE statement, how does the computer know when the THEN clause is ended? How does it know when the ELSE clause is ended?
7. In an IF-THEN statement, if the condition is false, which statement is executed next? Answer the question for an IF-THEN-ELSE statement.
8. What is the syntax of the SELECT-CASE statement?
9. What kinds of tests are available in the CASE clause?
10. Which statements are executed when the conditions of two CASE clauses are both true?
11. When are the statements in a CASE ELSE executed? What happens if there is no CASE ELSE?

SYNTAX EXERCISES

The following statements contain various syntax errors. Find and correct them.

```
1.  100 IF X > 0 PRINT X
2.  100 IF A <> B INPUT A, B
3.  100 IF A OR B < 5 THEN
            INPUT "Enter name A"; A
            INPUT "Enter name B"; B
        END IF
4.  100 IF A + B <= 10
            INPUT A, B
5.  100 IF A = 10 OR 20 OR 30
            THEN PRINT "Failing grade - no hope"
6.  100 IF A > 60 AND <= 100
            THEN PRINT "Passing grade"
7.  100 IF A = 0 & B = 0 INPUT "Enter A & B"; A, B
8.  100 IF A + B < 0 PRINT "Sum = "; A + B END IF
9.  100 IF A*B >= 0 THEN
            PRINT A, B
            INPUT "Enter numbers"; A, B
    110 ELSE
            PRINT "Product is negative"
        END IF
10. 100 IF A^2 + B^2 = C^2 THEN
            PRINT "Right triangle"
    110 ELSE
            PRINT "Not right triangle"
    120 END IF
```

```
11. 100 IF Salary < 200
        THEN Tax = 0
        END
12. 100 IF Salary < 200 THEN Tax = 0
        ELSE Tax = .15 * (Salary - 200)
        END
13. 100 SELECT Salary
            CASE 0 TO 200
                Tax = 0
            CASE > 200
                Tax = .10 * (Salary - 200)
        END CASE
14. 100 SELECT Salary
            CASE Salary < 200
                Tax = 0
            CASE Salary >= 200
                Tax = .10 * (Salary - 200)
        END SELECT
15. 100 SELECT
            CASE < 200
                Tax = 0
            CASE >= 200
                Tax = .10 * (Salary - 200)
        END
16. 100 SELECT
            CASE < 200
                Tax = 0
            CASE < 1000
                Tax = .10 * (Salary - 200)
            ELSE
                Tax = 80 + .20 * (Salary - 1000)
        END
```

PROGRAMMING EXERCISES

Write programs or subroutines, as directed, to solve the following problems. Be sure to identify all output.

■ **1.** Here is a little number game you can write for someone else to play. Have the computer make up a random integer between 0 and 100. Ask the person running the program to guess what the number is. If he guesses too low, print a message such as "TOO LOW. GUESS AGAIN." If he guesses too high, print the message "TOO HIGH. GUESS AGAIN." If he guesses correctly, tell him so, and also print the number of guesses it took.

2. Enter numbers from the terminal. If a number is negative, ignore it. If it is greater than 100, print "NUMBER TOO LARGE." If it is any other number except 0, count it and sum it. Continue until a 0 is entered; then print the sum, the count, and the average.

3. Enter numbers from the terminal or from DATA statements. Find the smallest of these numbers and the largest. Print these two values. (Use −9999 as a sentinel to get out of the loop.)

4. A student takes five tests.
   a. Write a subroutine that finds the lowest grade, given five grades.
   b. Write a subroutine that finds the average of five grades, dropping the smallest.
   c. Write a program that lets you enter a name and five grades from the terminal. The program should find the average, dropping the lowest grade. Find the student's letter grade, as in Example 6.5 or 6.7. Print the student's name, his average, and his letter grade. HINT: Use a variable called Low_grade to keep track of the lowest grade.

5. Repeat the logic of problem 4, allowing for as many students as there are in the class. After the last student, a sentinel record containing the name STOP will be entered to end the program.

6. Enter the numerical test grades for 35 students, either from the terminal or from DATA statements. Count the number of students who received A's, the number who received B's, and so on. Print the counts, identifying them with the grades they represent (see Example 6.5 or 6.7).

7. A bank needs a program to calculate statements for its charge card customers. The program first asks for the customer's name and address, the previous month's closing balance, the payment made to the account that month, and the total of all purchases made that month. First, the program subtracts the payment made during the month from the previous balance. If the difference is positive, meaning that only a partial payment was made, then a finance charge of 1.5% is calculated on the unpaid balance. The new balance is calculated by adding the unpaid balance, the finance charge (if any), and the purchases made during the month.
   a. Write a subroutine that will calculate the finance charge, if any, and the new balance, given the old balance, the payment, and the total purchases.
   b. Write and run the complete program. Output should consist of the customer's name and address, the previous balance, the finance charge (if any), the purchases, and the new balance. The output should be arranged neatly, in a form one might expect on a bank statement.

8. The following table describes the way a company pays its salesmen.

CODE	SALESMAN TYPE	SALARY	COMMISSION
1	TRAINEE SALESMAN	$150.00	5% OF SALES
2	JUNIOR SALESMAN	$200.00	7% OF SALES
3	SALESMAN	$350.00	12% OF SALES
4	SENIOR SALESMAN	$450.00	15% OF SALES

Data for the program consists of records, each containing three data items: a name, the salesman's code, and his sales. Using the following DATA statements, write a program that will print each salesman's name, type (not code), salary, commission, and total pay (salary plus commission). When EOF is read, print the number of salesmen, total salaries, total commissions, and total pay. (You may add additional DATA statements as desired.)

DATA Sally Smith, 3, 245.54
DATA Mike Jones, 1, 212.66

```
DATA Eli Berlinger, 4, 1234.32
DATA Lucy Cardin, 2, 2343.21
DATA EOF, 0, 0
```

9. Same as problem 8, but when EOF is read, print the number of salesmen, total salaries, total commissions, and total pay for each type of salesman. You will have to make up additional DATA statements so that there will be more than one salesman of each type.

10. This program can be used for arithmetic drill. Have the computer select two random integers between 100 and 999. These numbers should be printed by the computer in the form of an addition problem, with one number under the other. The person using the program must find the sum and type it as input to your program. If the sum is correct, inform the user and have the computer make up a new problem. If not, print a message to the user, reprint the problem, and let the user try twice more. If the answer is still incorrect after three attempts, print the correct answer for the user. After each problem, ask the user if he wishes to stop or continue. If he wishes to stop, print a sign-off message. If he wishes to continue, present him with a new problem. Note: This problem is an extension of problem 20 in chapter 5.

■ **11.** The solution to the equation ax + b = 0 is given by x = −b/a. Write a program that allows you to enter the coefficients a and b, then prints the coefficients and the solution. The program is to continue until the coefficients entered are both zero. Caution: If you enter a 0 for coefficient a and a nonzero value for coefficient b, then there is no solution ("division by zero" is not possible) and the output should state that fact.

12. The quadratic equation $ax^2 + bx + c = 0$ has two solutions, given by the expressions,

$$x_1 = \frac{-b + \sqrt{b^2 - 4ac}}{2a}$$

and

$$x_2 = \frac{-b - \sqrt{b^2 - 4ac}}{2a}$$

The quantity $b^2 - 4ac$ is called the **discriminant.** If it is 0, then there are two equal real solutions. If it is positive, then there are two unequal real solutions. If it is negative, then there are two imaginary or complex solutions.

    a. Write a subroutine that determines the nature of the solutions—real and equal, real and unequal, or imaginary—given the coefficients a, b, and c.

    b. Write a program that reads the coefficients of several equations from the DATA statements given below. If the discriminant of an equation is negative, print a message stating that the roots are complex. If it is not negative, find the roots and print them. The DATA statements are:

```
DATA 2,11,−4
DATA 3,5,2
```

```
DATA 1,-5,6
DATA 5,-2,4
DATA -5,-2,4
DATA 0,0,0
```

You may add as many additional equations as you wish. However, make certain that the first coefficient is not 0, or you will get a "division by zero" error when the program attempts to find the solution. Your program could check for this possibility and print an appropriate message.

13. Example 6.8 was a program that simulated a game of craps. Write a program that plays craps as follows: You start with $100. Each time you play, you bet $10. If you win, you get your bet plus another $10. If you lose, then you lose your bet, of course. You play 100 times or until you are out of money. At the end, have the computer print the number of times you played, and the amount of money you have left. HINT: Use Example 6.8 as a subroutine.

14. A credit card company charges interest to its cardholders. The rate of interest depends on the amount owed:

Amount Owed	Interest Rate
0.01 to 100.00	2% of amount owed
100.01 to 1000.00	$2.00 plus 1.5% on amount over 100.00
Over 1000.00	$15.50 plus 1% on amount over 1000.00

■ **a.** Write a subroutine that will calculate the interest charge, if any, and the new balance, given the amount owed.

b. Write a program that will allow you to enter a customer's name, address, and amount owed. The program will calculate the interest to be charged. It will then print a statement with the customer's name, address, amount owed, interest charged, and new balance (amount owed plus interest).

15. Same as problem 4b, but the program should repeat for additional customers until a sentinel of END is entered as the customer name.

16. This problem illustrates a technique known as the **Monte Carlo simulation method**. We will use it to get an estimate for π.

Suppose we have a square whose sides have a length of two units. The area will be four square units. Consider a circle inscribed in the square. The circle has a diameter of two units, hence a radius of one unit. The area of the circle is π times the radius squared, or simply π. The ratio of the area of the circle to the area of the square is $\pi/4$.

Assume that this square with its inscribed circle is hung on the wall as a dart board. An unskilled person throwing darts at the diagram will find darts hitting everywhere at random. Some will be in the circle; some in the square, but not in the circle; others will miss the target altogether. Because of the randomness, the number hitting in the circle will be proportional to the area of the circle, while those landing in the square, including the circle, will be proportional to the area of the square. If we divide the number of darts falling inside the circle by the number falling inside the square (including the circle), the result should be close to $\pi/4$, or one-quarter the value of π. Four times that number will be π, approximately.

Area (circle) = π
Area (square) = 4

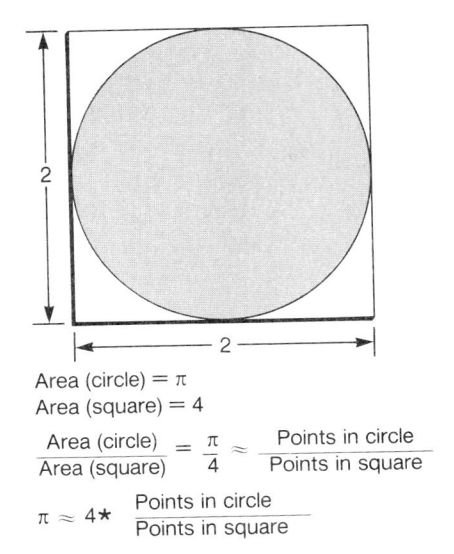

$$\frac{\text{Area (circle)}}{\text{Area (square)}} = \frac{\pi}{4} \approx \frac{\text{Points in circle}}{\text{Points in square}}$$

$$\pi \approx 4 * \frac{\text{Points in circle}}{\text{Points in square}}$$

To use this method with a computer, assume that the circle has its center at the origin, has a radius of 1, and has the square circumscribed around it. The computer can get two random numbers between -1 and $+1$, representing the x and y coordinates of a point in the square. The resulting point represents a dart landing in the square, and is counted as such. To find whether the point is also in the circle, we need only find its distance from the origin with the distance formula $d = \sqrt{x^2 + y^2}$. If the distance is less than 1, then the point is in the circle. If not, then it is in the square but not in the circle.

a. Write a subroutine that simulates the throwing of darts at the square by generating two numbers between -1 and 1.

b. Write a subroutine that simulates the throwing of 100 darts at the square, and counts the number of darts that fall within the inscribed circle.

c. Write a program that uses the Monte Carlo method to estimate π as explained above. Run the program with 500 points. Print the estimated value of π. Note! Do not use PI as a variable; it is a reserved word.

17. Repeat problem 16c with runs of 100 points, 200 points, and so on, until a run with 1000 points has been made. For each run, print the number of points and the estimate obtained.

18. Write a menu-driven program that can perform decimal/metric conversions. Conversions performed should be between centimeters and inches, meters and feet, and kilometers and miles. Each of the six choices should allow an amount to be entered, then print the equivalent amount in the other system of measure. A seventh choice will end the program. Note: 1 inch = 2.54 centimeters, 1 foot = 0.3048 meters, 1 mile = 1.6093 kilometers.

19. Write a menu-driven program that can perform decimal/metric conversions. Conversions performed should be between ounces and grams, pounds and kilograms, and gallons and liters. Each of the six choices should allow an amount to be entered, then print the equivalent amount in the other system of measure. A seventh choice will end the program. Note: 1 ounce = 28.35 grams, 1 pound = 0.4536 kilograms, 1 gallon = 3.7854 liters.

20. Write a menu-driven program that allows all conversions mentioned in problems 18 and 19. The menu should be presented in two columns with the first six choices in the first column and the second six in the second column. The last choice, which ends the program, should be under these 12 choices, midway between the two columns. For example, if the first six choices are printed starting in column 20, and the next six in column 40, the last choice should start under these in column 30.

21. A bank needs a program to handle savings accounts. Initially, the original balance in an account will be entered at the terminal, and the interest rate given on deposits will be read from DATA. The rest of the program will be menu-driven. Choices will be: make a deposit, make a withdrawal, credit interest, or end the program. The amount of a deposit or withdrawal will be entered at the terminal. After each transaction, the program should print the balance before the transaction, the type of transaction (deposit, withdrawal, or interest), the amount of the transaction, and the new balance after the transaction. When the "end program" choice is selected, the final balance should be printed before terminating the program.

A Programming Tool: Debugging

Contents
A.1 Temporary PRINT Statements
Conditional Temporary PRINT Statements
A.2 STOP, CONTinue, and the Immediate Mode
A.3 <Control>/C and the ERL Variable
Summary
Review Questions
Programming Exercises

```
83648 to
default
precisio
precisi
```

Introduction By now, you have written a number of programs. One thing you may have noticed is that your programs usually contain some errors the first time you try to run them. Perhaps you think this happens because you are a beginner. You will be pleased to learn, then, that even the most experienced programmers write inadvertent errors, called **bugs,**[1] into their programs. In fact, the more experienced the programmer and the more complex the program, the more difficult the job of debugging.

A number of techniques can be used to make the job of debugging more efficient and less frustrating. Some of these techniques will be discussed in this chapter.

---

[1] The story is told that one day in the early days of computing, circa 1955, when much of the computer's innards consisted of relays, a computer malfunctioned. Many hours, possibly days, were spent tracking down the problem. Suddenly, a technician discovered the remains of a small moth caught between the contacts of a relay. When he removed the hapless creature, the computer functioned normally again. Hence, to this day, someone who fixes a computer is "getting the bugs out."

A.1 TEMPORARY PRINT STATEMENTS

An important aspect of the debugging process is to know what is going on in the program. Therefore, an experienced programmer inserts a large number of PRINT statements in his program to print the values of significant variables. He can follow the action of his program by looking at these values and comparing them to expected values. If a variable has the wrong value, then he knows approximately where the error has occurred.

Each PRINT statement used for debugging should include some identifying remark so that the programmer knows which PRINT statement caused the specific output. Typically, the programmer might print the line number followed by a list of variables. Or, he might print a sequence number (1, 2, 3, etc.), followed by a list of variables.

Once the program is fully debugged, the temporary PRINT statements are easily removed. If, for instance, all the debugging PRINT statements have line numbers ending with a 4 (14, 24, 34, etc.), they can be deleted easily.

CAUTION! **Extreme care must be taken when a debugging statement is put into a loop, because the statement will execute each time around the loop! If the loop has a large repetition factor, the amount of output could become so large as to be useless.**

Example A.1 Suppose we want the sum of all numbers from 1 to 10,000. We might write the following program to solve this problem:

```
10      SUM = 0
20      FOR I1 = 1 TO 10000
            SUM = SUM + II
        NEXT I1
30      PRINT 'Sum = '; SUM
32767 END
```

When we run this program, however, it does not work. We get an answer of 0. Perhaps you can see why. If not, we might put in a debugging PRINT statement as follows:

```
10      SUM = 0
20      FOR I1 = 1 TO 10000
            SUM = SUM + II
24          PRINT SUM, II
        NEXT I1
30      PRINT 'Sum = '; SUM
32767 END
```

We now begin to get reams and reams of output—10,000 lines, in fact, because the PRINT statement will execute 10,000 times! Each line of output contains two zeros. We quickly abort the program. (To abort the program, press the <Break> key, if there is one. If there is not, hold down the <Control> key and press C.)

170 PROGRAMMING TOOL: DEBUGGING

Even though we interrupt the output, the error should now be apparent. The first zero on each line is the current sum. The second is the number we are adding to the sum, II. Why is II always 0? The answer is clear now that we are directed to it: The loop counter is the variable I1, while the number we are adding is the variable II. II should be I1:

```
10      SUM = 0
20      FOR I1 = 1 TO 10000
           SUM = SUM + I1
24         PRINT SUM, I1
        NEXT I1
30      PRINT 'Sum = '; SUM
32767 END
```

The program is now working, but again it is producing reams of output. The output is correct, however. We abort the program again, and remove the debugging PRINT statement, run the program again, and get the correct result: Sum = .50005E 8, which is the exponential form of the integer 50005000.

Notice that we would not want to let the program continue to the end with the debugging statement in the loop. The program would take too long to run. But what if there were statements after the loop that we wanted to check? Could we speed up the loop? The answer is yes. Here is how:

Conditional Temporary PRINT Statements

Instead of putting an unconditional PRINT statement in the loop, we could use a conditional one that would print only every twentieth, or fiftieth, or hundredth time around the loop. Our previous program, with such a debugging statement, would look like this:

```
10      SUM = 0
14      K = 0                          ! For debugging purposes
20      FOR I = 1 TO 10000
           SUM = SUM + I
24         K = K + 1 \ IF K = 50 THEN PRINT SUM, I \ K = 0   END IF
                                   ! Print when I is multiple of 50
28      NEXT I
30      PRINT 'Sum = '; SUM
32767 END
```

The PRINT statement will print only every fiftieth time around the loop, when K = 50. On a CRT terminal, that will not take too long. Once the program is debugged, statements 14 and 24 can be removed (Type 14<Return> and 24<Return>).

A.2 STOP, CONTINUE, AND THE IMMEDIATE MODE

An extremely useful debugging tool is the STOP statement, together with immediate mode statements. The STOP statement has the form:

sn STOP

For example, if the statement `86 STOP` is inserted into the program, then the program will stop execution when it reaches line 86 and the following messages will appear at the terminal:

```
%BAS-I-STO, Stop
-BAS-I-FROLINMOD, from line 86 in module EX06

Ready
```

These messages tell you that a STOP instruction was encountered in line 86 of program EX06. (The name of the module, of course, depends on the name of the program.) If the STOP was in a subroutine, a complete traceback will be given from the routine back to the main program. A program can have many STOP statements, which cause the program to interrupt whenever it reaches any one of them.

To continue execution after a STOP statement has interrupted a program, the programmer can enter `CONT` at the terminal. Execution will continue from the point where the STOP occurred until the next STOP is encountered, or until the program reaches the END or EXIT PROGRAM statement.

Once a program has been interrupted by a STOP statement, what can we do with it? Here is where the **immediate mode** comes in. An immediate mode statement looks just like a program statement (also called a **deferred execution statement**), except that it does not have a line number and must begin in column 1. When such a statement is entered, it is executed immediately instead of being saved for later execution.

For instance, if we type `30 PRINT "ANS = ";A` this instruction is inserted into the program at line 30. When the program is run, the statement is executed when line 30 is reached. But suppose we type

```
PRINT "ANS = ";A
```

without a line number or leading space. This is an immediate mode statement, and it is executed as soon as we press <Return>. We immediately see `ANS = value` printed at the terminal, where `value` is the number stored in `A`.

As another example, if we type `A = 100`, without a line number, then the value in `A` is immediately set to 100.

To use these techniques for debugging, we proceed as follows:

1. We insert STOP instructions at key places in the program where we want to check the values of certain variables.
2. When we receive the message indicating that a STOP has been reached, we print the variables in the immediate mode to check their values.
3. If the values are as they should be, we type `CONT` to allow execution to proceed to the next STOP statement, where we repeat step 2. Otherwise, we perform step 4.
4. If the values are not as they should be, we can either list the program and check the logic to find the error immediately, or we can fix the values in the immediate mode and CONTinue the program to check the remaining logic. Later, we can fix the section of code that caused the error.

172 PROGRAMMING TOOL: DEBUGGING

> **NOTE!** If you change the program while you are STOP'ed, you will be unable to CONTinue. The error message `CAN'T CONTINUE` will appear if you attempt to do so. You can CONTinue only if the program is unchanged. Even if you change the value of some variables, using assignment statements in immediate mode, you will be able to CONTinue execution as long as the program is unchanged.

Example A.2

This example will illustrate an error commonly made by students when summing is involved. We use this error to illustrate the debugging techniques under discussion.

We will write a program that will calculate the growth of a population each year for a specified number of years. The program will let us enter the initial population, the yearly growth rate, and the number of years for which the growth is to be calculated. For each year, the program will print the population at the beginning of the year, the growth in the population during that year, and the population at the end of the year.

We might come up with the following pseudocode:

```
Population growth:
   Print headings
   Enter original population, growth rate, number of years
   Loop from 1 to number of years
      Calculate growth and new population
      Print old population, growth, and new population
   Next year
   Stop
```

The code, with appropriate subroutines, would then be as shown in Figure A-1.

This program is *not* correct; it contains a logical error. In addition, other errors may occur when the program is run due to programming oversight. We will examine these problems as they occur. Let's attempt to run the program.

In the following dialogue, our responses are underlined and the computer's are not. We will enter an original population of 5000, a growth rate of 2 percent, and a period of 5 years.

```
RUNNH

Year            Old Pop.        Growth          New Pop.

Enter original population? 5000
Enter yearly growth rate? 2
Enter number of years? 5
 1              5000            10000           15000
 2              5000            10000           15000
 3              5000            10000           15000
 4              5000            10000           15000
 5              5000            10000           15000

Ready
```

Figure A-1.
Program Containing Bugs,
to Calculate Population
Growth

```
10  ! Population growth projection
20       DECLARE INTEGER   YEAR, NO.OF.YRS, OLD.POPULATION, &
                           GROWTH, NEW.POPULATION, &
                 REAL      GROWTH.RATE
30       GOSUB Headings          ! Print headings
40       GOSUB Input_rtn         ! Enter original population,
                                 ! growth rate, and number of years
50       FOR YEAR = 1 TO NO.OF.YRS
            GOSUB Calculate      ! Calculate growth, new population
            GOSUB Print_rtn      ! Print yearly results
         NEXT YEAR
60    EXIT PROGRAM

500   Headings:                  ! Print headings
510      PRINT \ PRINT
520      PRINT 'Year', 'Old Pop.', 'Growth', 'New Pop.'
         PRINT
530   RETURN

1000  Input_rtn:                 ! Enter population, growth rate,
                                 ! number of years
1010     INPUT 'Enter original population'; OLD.POPULATION
         INPUT 'Enter yearly growth rate'; GROWTH.RATE
         INPUT 'Enter number of years'; NO.OF.YRS
1020  RETURN

1500  Calculate:                 ! Calculate growth and new population
1510     GROWTH = GROWTH.RATE * OLD.POPULATION
         NEW.POPULATION = GROWTH + OLD.POPULATION
1520  RETURN

2000  Print_rtn:                 ! Print old population, growth,
                                 ! and new population
2010     PRINT YEAR, OLD.POPULATION, GROWTH, NEW.POPULATION
2020  RETURN

32767 END
```

A number of things are wrong with this program. First, the headings are in the wrong place; they should be after the input. We can easily fix that by invoking the input routine before the routine that prints the headings. The main program will then be:

```
10  ! Population growth projection
20       DECLARE INTEGER   YEAR, NO.OF.YRS, OLD.POPULATION, &
                           GROWTH, NEW.POPULATION, &
                 REAL      GROWTH.RATE
```

174 | PROGRAMMING TOOL: DEBUGGING

```
30         GOSUB Input_rtn        ! Enter original population,
                                  ! growth rate, and number of years
40         GOSUB Headings         ! Print headings
50         FOR YEAR = 1 TO NO.OF.YRS
              GOSUB Calculate     ! Calculate growth, new population
              GOSUB Print_rtn     ! Print yearly results
           NEXT YEAR
60     EXIT PROGRAM
```

Notice how easily we were able to accomplish this correction, because we used subroutines. If you use the editor, you do not even have to move the statements themselves; you need only change line number 30 to 40, and vice versa. When you exit the editor, BASIC will reorder the statements according to their line numbers.

Another problem is that the growth is 10000 on a population of 5000. That is not 2 percent but 200 percent. Finally, the same results are printed for each year. To determine what is wrong, let us put a STOP instruction in subroutine Calculate where the calculations take place. The subroutine will then be as follows:

```
1500 Calculate:              ! Calculate growth and new population
1510    GROWTH = GROWTH.RATE * OLD.POPULATION
        NEW.POPULATION = GROWTH + OLD.POPULATION
1514 STOP     ! For debugging purposes
1520 RETURN
```

We try running the program again. Because of the STOP instruction, the program stops after each year's growth and new population are calculated but before they are printed. We will use the immediate mode to check variables that can help us determine what is wrong. Here is our interaction with the computer:

```
RUN
Enter original population? 1000
Enter yearly growth rate? 2
Enter number of years? 5

Year           Old Pop.       Growth         New Pop.

%BAS-I-STO, Stop
-BAS-I-FROLINMOD, from line 1514 in module POP

Ready

PRINT OLD.POPULATION, GROWTH.RATE, GROWTH, NEW.POPULATION
   5000         2          10000        15000
```

We can see the growth rate problem immediately: it should be 2 percent, but instead it is 2, which is 200 percent. Clearly, we must divide the yearly percentage rate by 100 to get 0.02, the decimal equivalent of 2 percent. A convenient place to do this is in the input routine. After we enter the yearly percentage rate, we can divide it by 100 to get the growth rate required for our calculations. The input routine will now be:

```
1000 Input_rtn:               ! Enter population, growth rate,
                              ! number of years
1010     INPUT 'Enter original population'; OLD.POPULATION
         INPUT 'Enter yearly percentage growth rate'; YEARLY.RATE
            GROWTH.RATE = YEARLY.RATE / 100
         INPUT 'Enter number of years'; NO.OF.YRS
1020 RETURN
```

Notice the new variable that we introduced in the INPUT instruction for the growth rate, and the change in the prompt. We run the program again, getting this output:

```
RUN
Enter original population? 5000
Enter yearly growth rate? 2
Enter number of years? 5

Year              Old Pop.        Growth         New Pop.

%BAS-I-STO, Stop
-BAS-I-FROLINMOD, from line 1514 in module POP

Ready

PRINT  OLD.POPULATION,  GROWTH.RATE,  GROWTH,  NEW.POPULATION
 5000              .02             100           5100
Ready
```

The program now seems to be correct, because all values are as they should be. We let the program continue by typing CONT, and the interaction continues as follows:

```
CONT
 1              5000            100            5100

%BAS-I-STO, Stop
-BAS-I-FROLINMOD, from line 1514 in module POP

Ready

PRINT OLD.POPULATION, GROWTH, NEW.POPULATION
 5000           100           5100

Ready
```

There is still a problem. At the end of the first year, the new population was 5100. That should have become the old population for the second year. But the old population is still at 5000. This problem can be corrected in a number of ways. For example, we could add the statement

```
 2015    OLD.POPULATION = NEW.POPULATION
```

in the print routine. This is not a good idea, however, because the program would be difficult to understand, even though it would work.

A better idea would be to modify the calculation routine. The pseudocode would be:

> Calculate growth and new population:
>   Let old population (this year) be new population (last year)
>   Calculate new growth (this year)
>   Calculate new population (this year)
> Return

This changes subroutine 1500 to the following:

```
1500 Calculate:            ! Calculate growth and new population
1510    OLD.POPULATION = NEW.POPULATION
        GROWTH = GROWTH.RATE * OLD.POPULATION
        NEW.POPULATION = GROWTH + OLD.POPULATION
1514 STOP       ! For debugging purposes
1520 RETURN
```

We try to run the program again.

```
RUN

Enter original population? 5000
Enter yearly growth rate? 2
Enter number of years? 5

%BAS-I-STO, Stop
-BAS-I-FROLINMOD, from line 1514 in module POP

Ready

PRINT OLD.POPULATION, GROWTH, NEW.POPULATION
 0              0              0
```

Now what is happening? This is certainly not correct! Why is the old population zero? Looking back at the changes we recently made, we concentrate our attention on the statement:

```
OLD.POPULATION = NEW.POPULATION
```

Apparently, NEW.POPULATION was 0, therefore OLD.POPULATION also becomes 0. Examining the input routine, we see why. The original population is put into OLD.POPULATION, and then the calculation routine replaces it with NEW.POPULATION. Let us, therefore, read the original population into NEW.POPULATION instead. The revised input routine is as follows:

```
1000 Input_rtn:             ! Enter population, growth rate,
                            ! number of years
```

```
1010      INPUT 'Enter original population'; NEW.POPULATION
          INPUT 'Enter yearly growth rate'; YEARLY.RATE
              GROWTH.RATE = YEARLY.RATE / 100
          INPUT 'Enter number of years'; NO.OF.YRS
1020 RETURN
```

The entire program, as it now stands, is shown in Figure A-2.

We have removed statement 1514, which was the STOP instruction we inserted for debugging. The program now seems correct. A sample run appears in Figure A-3.

Figure A-2.
Debugged Version of Program to Calculate Population Growth

```
10  ! Population growth projection
20       DECLARE  INTEGER   YEAR, NO.OF.YRS, OLD.POPULATION, &
                            GROWTH, NEW.POPULATION, &
                   REAL     GROWTH.RATE, YEARLY.RATE
30       GOSUB Input_rtn      ! Enter original population,
40       GOSUB Headings       ! Print headings
                              ! growth rate, and number of years
50       FOR YEAR = 1 TO NO.OF.YRS
             GOSUB Calculate   ! Calculate growth, new population
             GOSUB Print_rtn   ! Print yearly results
         NEXT YEAR
60    EXIT PROGRAM

500  Headings:                ! Print headings
510      PRINT \ PRINT
520      PRINT 'Year', 'Old Pop.', 'Growth', 'New Pop.'
         PRINT
530  RETURN

1000 Input_rtn:                ! Enter population, growth rate,
                               ! number of years
1010     INPUT 'Enter original population'; NEW.POPULATION
         INPUT 'Enter percent growth rate'; YEARLY.RATE
              GROWTH.RATE = YEARLY.RATE / 100
         INPUT 'Enter number of years    '; NO.OF.YRS
1020 RETURN

1500 Calculate:           ! Calculate growth and new population
1510     OLD.POPULATION = NEW.POPULATION
         GROWTH = GROWTH.RATE * OLD.POPULATION
         NEW.POPULATION = GROWTH + OLD.POPULATION
1520 RETURN
2000 Print_rtn:                ! Print old population, growth,
                               ! and new population
2010     PRINT YEAR, OLD.POPULATION, GROWTH, NEW.POPULATION
2020 RETURN

32767 END
```

Figure A-3.
Sample Run of the Program to Calculate Population Growth

```
RUN
Enter original population? 5000
Enter percentage growth rate? 2
Enter number of years? 5

Year          Old Pop.         Growth          New Pop.

 1             5000             100             5100
 2             5100             102             5202
 3             5202             104             5306
 4             5306             106             5412
 5             5412             108             5520
```

A.3   <Control>/C AND THE ERL VARIABLE

A common bug is the endless loop. Consider, for example, the following loop:

```
10    SUM = 0
      UNTIL SUM = 100
        SUM = SUM + 1/3
      NEXT
```

It might seem that this loop will execute exactly 300 times and then end. In fact, the loop will never end because the representation of the number one-third is not exact. Dividing 1 by 3 yields the repeating decimal 0.3333 . . . , which the computer stores as the finite decimal 0.333333. When three of these are added, the result is 0.999999, not 1. Adding 300 of them yields 99.9999, not 100. Since the loop continues until the SUM is 100, and this never happens, the loop goes on "forever."

If a program contains several loops and it is apparent that an infinite loop exists, how can we determine in which loop the program is stuck? This information can be obtained by aborting the program and determining which statement was executing at the time.

To abort a program, type <Control>/C (hold the <Control> button and press C), or press the <Break> key if there is one.

To find the statement being executed at the time a program was aborted, type PRINT ERL in the immediate mode. ERL is a built-in variable that contains the statement number the computer was executing when an error occurred. Because the computer considers an abort as an error condition, ERL will contain the statement number of the statement that was interrupted. If, for instance, we were to run a program containing the endless loop just discussed, and after some time we were to abort it with <Control>/C, then the immediate mode statement PRINT ERL would print 10 at the terminal. This would tell us that line 10 was executing at the time of the abort.

After a <Control>/C abort, the program can be told to continue executing from the point where it was interrupted. This is done with the CONT immediate mode instruction, just as if the program had been stopped with a STOP. We would not continue execution of the infinite loop example, but the facility is useful for checking the progress of a program with a long loop. Consider the following loop:

```
100    FOR I = 1 TO 10000
           .
           .
       NEXT I
```

If the loop contains a large number of statements, it will take a long time to execute, and we might wonder if the program is working. After all, there could be an infinite loop somewhere else. We can abort the program with <Control>/C and then type the immediate mode statement PRINT ERL,I, which will print both the line number and the loop counter. If the line number is 100, then we know we are in the above loop. The value of I will then tell us the number of iterations already completed. For instance, the output might be

```
100            2379
```

We would know that the loop was executing, that it has already finished 2378 iterations, and that it was performing iteration number 2379 when we aborted it. If everything seems normal, we can type CONT and the program will continue executing. We can perform such an abort as often as we want.

SUMMARY

In this chapter, you learned a number of techniques that can be used to debug a program.

1. Insert PRINT statements in your program at strategic points to print the current values of significant variables. If you know what the values should be, then you can isolate the problem area.

2. Use STOP instructions at strategic points in the program to halt execution. Immediate mode statements can then be used to print significant values and to change the values of those variables if desired. The program can be told to continue execution by typing the CONT instruction in the immediate mode.

Immediate mode instructions look like deferred mode instructions but have no line numbers and must begin in column 1. Examples are:

```
PRINT VAL1, VAL2, VAL3
X = 20
IF Y > 0 THEN PRINT Y
```

3. Abort a program with a <Control>/C. The ERL variable can then be used to determine which statement was interrupted. Other immediate mode statements can also be used to obtain additional information concerning the state of the program. Execution can be resumed by typing CONT.

REVIEW QUESTIONS

1. What is meant by "debugging"? Do all programs require debugging? Where did the expression "get the bugs out" probably originate?

2. How are temporary PRINT statements used as a debugging tool? How do they help in the debugging process?

3. What are immediate mode statements? How do they help in the process of debugging a program? What distinguishes an immediate mode statement from a delayed execution statement?

4. How are STOP and CONT used as debugging tools? What is the difference between typing `RUN` and typing `CONT` after a STOP instruction has halted execution?

5. How many STOP instructions can a program have while it is being debugged?

6. From a user's viewpoint, what is the difference between using temporary PRINT statements within a program and using immediate mode PRINT instructions after execution has been interrupted with a STOP instruction? What are some advantages and disadvantages of each?

7. What information does the ERL built-in variable provide? In what situation would you use this variable? How would you use it?

PROGRAMMING EXERCISES

1. Write a program that will let you enter two numbers and print their product. Instead of using INPUT, use a STOP instead. When the program reaches the STOP, use the immediate mode to assign the values to the variables directly. Then continue execution with CONT.

2. Type the following program into your computer and run it. Abort it with a <Control>/C at various times. Print the line number where the abort occurred, as well as the values of all of the loop variables. Then allow the program to continue until it terminates normally.

NOTE! | **The program may "crash" because of an error related to INTEGER typing. If it does, determine what is wrong, and find a way around it.**

```
10 ! Find mean, variance, standard deviation of integers
20    DECLARE INTEGER    I, J, A, B, &
             REAL        MEAN, VAR, STDEV
30       ! Find sum of numbers
         A = 0
         FOR I = 1 TO 10000
            A = A + I
         NEXT I
40       ! Find sum of squares
         B = 0
         FOR J = 1 TO 10000
            B = B + J^2
         NEXT J
50       MEAN = A/10000
         VAR = (B - A^2 / 10000)/10000
         STDEV = SQR (VAR)
60       PRINT Mean =, MEAN
         PRINT Variance =, VAR
         PRINT St. Dev. =, STDEV
70    END
```

The program calculates the mean, variance, and standard deviation of the successive integers from 1 to 10000.

3. Here is a program that is supposed to find the sum of the numbers from 1 to 10, then from 1 to 9, and so on down to the sum from 1 to 1. It contains several errors. Use the techniques learned in this chapter to debug the program.

```
10  ! Program to find sums of various ranges of integers
20      DECLARE INTEGER   I, SUM
30      FOR I = 10 TO 1 BY 1
40         GOSUB Find_sum        ! Find sum
50         GOSUB Print_sum       ! Print sum
60      NEXT I
70   EXIT PROGRAM

1000 Find_sum:                   ! Find sum
1010     FOR I = 1 TO NO.
            SUM = SUM + I
         NEXT I
1020 RETURN

1500 Print_sum:                  ! Print sum
1510     PRINT 'Sum of numbers from 1 to'; I; 'is'; SUM.
1520 RETURN

32767 END
```

4. Here is a program that is supposed to find the number of years it takes a population to double if the rate of increase in the population is 3% per year. The program contains several errors. Use the techniques learned in this chapter to debug the program.

```
10  ! Time to double a population
20     DECLARE INTEGER POPULATION, GROWTH, NO.OF.YEARS, GROWTH.RATE
30        GOSUB Calculate     ! Calculate number of years
40        GOSUB Print_rtn     ! Print number of years
50     EXIT PROGRAM

1000 Calculate:                ! Calculate number of years to
                               ! double population
1010    GOSUB Initialize       ! Initializations
1020    UNTIL POPULATION = 2 * POPULATION
           GROWTH = GROWTH.RATE * POPULATION
           POPULATION = GROWTH + POPULATION
        NEXT
1030 RETURN

1100 Initialize:               ! Initializations
1100    NO.OF.YEARS = 0
        READ GROWTH.RATE
1120 RETURN

2000 Print_rtn:                ! Print number of years required
2010    PRINT NO.YEARS; 'required to double population'
2020 RETURN
```

```
10000 DATA 3%

32767 END
```

5. Here is a menu-driven program with errors. Use various debugging techniques to find the errors.

```
10  ! Checking account management
20      DECLARE STRING Open_bal, Balance, &
                INTEGER Selection, Check, Deposit, Debit, Credit, &
                DECIMAL (8,2) Total_deposits, Total_checks
30          WHILE Selection <> 0
                GOSUB Print_menu
                GOSJB Make_selection
                GOSUB Execute_routine
            END
40          GOSUB Print_routine
50      EXIT PROGRAM

1000 Print_menu:
1010        PRINT "1. Enter opening balance"
            PRINT "2. Subtract checks"
            PRINT "3. Add deposits"
            PRINT "4. Other debits"
            PRINT "5. Other credits"
            PRINT "0. Print totals and exit"
            PRINT
1020 RETURN

1100 Make selection:
1110        INPUT "Enter selection "; Selection
1120 RETURN

1200 Execute_routine:
1210        SELECT Selection
                CASE 1 GOSUB Open_balance
                CASE 2 GOSUB Subtract_checks
                CASE 3
                    Add_deposits
                CASE 4
                    GOSUB Other debits
                CASE 5
                    GOSUB Other_credits
                CASE ELSE
                    PRINT \ PRINT "Selection out of range"
                    PRINT
            END CASE
1220 RETURN

2000 Open_balance:
2010        PRINT
            INPUT "Enter opening balance"; Open_bal
            PRINT
```

```
2020      Total_deposits = 0 \ Total_checks = 0
          Total_credits = 0 \ Total_debits = 0
2030 RETURN

2100 Subtract_checks:
2110      WHILE Check <> 0
              INPUT "Enter check, 0 to end"; Check
              Total_checks = Total_checks + Check
              Balance = Balance - Check
          NEXT
2120 RETURN

2200 Add_deposits:
2210      INPUT "Enter deposit, 0 to end"; Deposit
          WHILE Deposit = 0
              Tot_deposits = Total_deposits + Deposit
              INPUT "Enter deposit, 0 to end"; Deposit
              Balance = Balance - Deposit
          NEXT
2220 RETURN

2300 Other_debits:
2310      INPUT "Enter debit, 0 to end"; Debit
          WHILE Debit <> 0
              Total_debits = Total_debits + Debit
              Balance = Balance - Debit
              INPUT "Enter debit, 0 to end"; Debit
          NEXT
2330 RETURN
2400 Add_credits:
2410      INPUT Enter credit, 0 to end''; Credit
          WHILE Credit = 0
              Total_credits = Total_credits + Credit
              INPUT "Enter credit, 0 to end"; Credit
              Balance = Balance + Credit
          NEXT
2420 RETURN

2500 Print_routine:
2510      PRINT \ PRINT
          PRINT "Opening balance      : "; Open balance
          PRINT
          PRINT "Total checks         : "; Total_checks
          PRINT "Total deposits       : "; Total_deposits
          PRINT "Total other credits  : "; Total_debits
          PRINT "Total other debits   : "; Total_credits
          PRINT
          PRINT "Closing balance      : "; Balance
2520 RETURN

32767 END
```

7 One-Dimensional Arrays

Outline

7.1 Arrays
7.2 Subscripts
7.3 Dimensioning Arrays with the DECLARE Statement
7.4 Assignment Statements
7.5 Reading Values Into an Array
    Input Using Enumerative Loops
    Input Using Controlled Loops
7.6 Printing Arrays
7.7 Calculations Using Loops
7.8 Sorting One-Dimensional Arrays
    Sorting String Arrays
7.9 Associated Arrays
Summary
Review Questions
Syntax Exercises
Programming Exercises
Enrichment Topics
    Variable Dimensioning
    MAT Statements
        Input using MAT INPUT
        The NUM Variable
        Input Using MAT READ
        Output Using MAT PRINT
        MAT Assignment Statements
    Arrays As Arguments

Introduction The variables we have discussed previously have one memory location for each symbolic name. That is, variable X is a specific location that can contain exactly one number. Such variables are called **scalars** or **simple variables.** In contrast to a scalar, an **array** is a block of memory locations that is given one symbolic name. It is capable of storing hundreds, or even thousands, of numbers or strings called **elements.** One-dimensional arrays will be discussed in this chapter.

7.1 ARRAYS

An array is a block of contiguous storage locations in memory. The entire block is given one name, called the **array name.** Each separate location of the array is called an **element** of the array.

An array, conceptually, may be considered a linear arrangement of its elements. This is called a **one-dimensional array.** But it may also be a rectangular array, arranged in rows and columns. This is called a **two-dimensional array.** Or, it can be regarded as a box, with rows, columns, and planes going back—a **three-dimensional array.** And there may be even more than three dimensions, although such arrays are difficult to visualize. This chapter deals only with one-dimensional arrays.

Figure 7-1 represents a one-dimensional array, X, that contains eight elements. It is a one-dimensional array because its elements are grouped in a single column. They could also be represented as a single row.

**Figure 7-1.
One-Dimensional Array with Eight Elements**

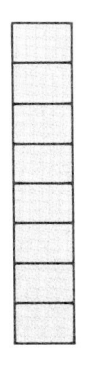

7.2 SUBSCRIPTS

Because we now have many memory locations with only one symbolic name, we need a method of referring to the individual locations within the array. This is done by using a **subscript** with the array name.

A subscript is a number in parentheses following the array name which indicates the ordinal position of the array element from the beginning of the array. For instance, A(5) is how we would refer[1] to the fifth element of array A.

Subscripts are integers whose numbering begins with 0. Thus, an array of nine elements has subscripts ranging from 0 through 8, a total of nine locations (see Fig. 7-2). The actual number of storage locations in an array is equal to the highest numbered subscript plus 1.

The numbers in the parentheses in Figure 7-2 are the ordinal positions of the elements. The element X(0) is frequently called the **"zero'th" element.** The subsequent elements are X(1), X(2), etc.

It is extremely important to understand the meaning of a subscript. The subscript is the position of the element in the array; it has **nothing** to do

---

[1] In mathematics, this element is written A_5. It is not possible to write actual subscripts in BASIC or other languages; hence, the method of parentheses is required.

Figure 7-2.
One-Dimensional Array with Nine Elements—X(0) Through X(8)

```
X(0)
X(1)
X(2)
X(3)
X(4)
X(5)
X(6)
X(7)
X(8)
```

with what is stored in that position. Consider a row of cubbyholes on a wall. If the cubbyholes are considered as elements of an array, then the cubbyhole number is the subscript. If we put $200 into the fifth cubbyhole, then the subscript is 5, while the element is 200; thus, X(5) = 200.

It should be noted that, in BASIC, we usually do not use X(0). Frequently, this element is used to store information about the array rather than actual data. For instance, the number of elements assigned values might be stored in X(0) and the first data value in X(1). This is called a **one-based array.** There are, however, numerous applications in which the zero'th element *is* used as a data value. Such an array is called a **zero-based array.**

Unless we have a specific reason to do otherwise, we will ignore X(0) and work with one-based arrays. For example, if the array shown in Figure 7-2 were treated as a one-based array, it would be said to contain only eight elements.

The rest of this chapter will deal with one-based arrays and we will refer to an array whose subscripts go from 0 to 8 as an eight-element array, even though it has nine locations. This is standard terminology for one-based arrays.

7.3 DIMENSIONING ARRAYS WITH THE DECLARE STATEMENT

Whenever an array is used, it must be **dimensioned.** Dimensioning informs the computer of the size of the array and allows it to reserve sufficient storage in memory for all of the elements. In VAX-BASIC, the DECLARE statement is used for this purpose, in addition to its other function of data-typing.[2] The size of the array specified in the DECLARE statement does not include the zero'th element; BASIC always assumes one-based arrays for dimensioning purposes.

The syntax of the DECLARE statement when used for dimensioning is:

sn DECLARE data-type array-name (dimension), . . .

---
[2] Another statement can be used for dimensioning when implicit typing is used—the DIM statement. As we prefer to use explicit typing only, the DIM statement will not be introduced. (But see the enrichment section at the end of this chapter for variable dimensioning.)

Example 7.1

```
10 DECLARE REAL    Height(100), &
           INTEGER No.of.students(10), &
           STRING  Names(50)
```

In this example, `Height` is a real array of 100 elements, `No.of.students` is an integer array of 10 elements, and `Names` is a string array of 50 elements.

In general, the rules governing the names of array variables are identical to those of simple variables (or scalars). Implicit typing can be used, but this will limit the number of elements permitted in the array to 10. Explicit typing with the DECLARE statement is preferred and will be used for all examples. In no event may a scalar and an array have the same name.

7.4 ASSIGNMENT STATEMENTS

We can assign values to array elements just as we assign values to simple variables. For example, the statements in Example 7.2 would assign values as indicated in Figure 7-3.

Example 7.2

```
10   X(1) = 20   \ X(2) = 14   \ X(3) = -5
20   X(4) = 13   \ X(5) = -12  \ X(6) = 17
```

Figure 7-3.
Sample Array of Six Elements

X(0)	0 (Not used in one-based array)
X(1)	20
X(2)	14
X(3)	−5
X(4)	13
X(5)	−12
X(6)	17

Notice again that the value stored in an array element has absolutely no connection to the value of the subscript. The subscript merely indicates where the number is located relative to the beginning of the array. The statement

```
X(5) = -12
```

means that the number −12 has been stored as the fifth element of the array X as in Figure 7-3.

Although X(0) was not assigned a value in Example 7.2, it is shown in Figure 7-3 as having a value of zero. Generally, when a program is run, BASIC initializes all elements of a numeric array to zero by default. You should never rely on this however; you should explicitly perform any initializations that are critical to your program.

7.5 READING VALUES INTO AN ARRAY

Data can be stored into an array by means of INPUT or READ instructions. For example,

```
100 INPUT 'Enter 5 integers'; A(1),A(2),A(3),A(4),A(5)
```

causes five integers typed in at the keyboard to be stored into the first five elements of array A [ignoring A(0)]. The numbers to be stored are the numbers you type when the prompt appears on the terminal screen.

The second example stores three numbers into the real array called DAT. The numbers will come from one or more DATA statements included in the program:

```
200 READ DAT(1), DAT(2), DAT(3)
```

Input Using Enumerative Loops

One of the most powerful features of an array is the fact that the subscript can be a variable. This feature permits the use of loops for the processing of arrays.

Example 7.3 A program segment follows that will enter 10 numbers typed at the terminal into array Y. We assume that the array has been properly dimensioned with a DECLARE statement earlier in the program.

```
100 FOR I = 1 TO 10
       INPUT 'Enter number'; Y(I)
    NEXT I
```

The loop counter, I, is used as the subscript of the array. When the loop counter is 1, the value is stored into Y(1), and when it is 2 the value is stored into Y(2). When I is 10, the last value is stored into Y(10).

When using a loop such as the one above to enter values into an array, you must enter the data one value at a time followed by a <Return>. If you try entering several values at one time, only the first will be used; the others will be ignored. For the above loop, you will be required to enter a number followed by a <Return> ten times.

Input Using Controlled Loops

Frequently, we know that an array will be used to store the data for a program, but we do not know the number of elements needed. In such a case, a sentinel can be used to signal when the last datum has been entered.

Example 7.4 A teacher needs a program that uses an array to store the names of students in his class. The number of students varies from one section to the other and from semester to semester. The array must be dimensioned so that it is large enough to hold all the students in the largest conceivable class. When enter-

7 ONE-DIMENSIONAL ARRAYS

ing the names, the teacher can use a sentinel to signal the program when there are no more names. In pseudocode, we have the following:

> Read elements, up to sentinel:
>   Read first name (priming read)
>   Loop until name is sentinel
>   Store name into array
>   Read next name
>   End of loop
>   Save number of names read in a variable
> End of input routine

The following code is written as a subroutine. Notice that the subroutine saves the number of elements actually stored in the array in the variable NO.OF.ELEMENTS, so that the rest of the program will know how many data were stored in the array. We assume that the array was dimensioned in the main program.

```
1000 Input_rtn:     ! Enter elements into array, until sentinel
1010     SUBSCRIPT = 0
         INPUT 'Enter name, XXX to end'; NAME_
         WHILE NAME_ <> 'XXX'
            SUBSCRIPT = SUBSCRIPT + 1
            NAMES(SUBSCRIPT) = NAME_
            INPUT 'Enter name, XXX to end'; NAME_
         NEXT
1020     NO.OF.ELEMENTS = SUBSCRIPT
1030 RETURN
```

The names are first read into a simple variable called NAME_. If the data value is not the sentinel, then the subscript is increased by one, and the name is stored into the array at the position of the subscript: NAMES(SUBSCRIPT). After the sentinel is read, the subscript points to the last value read. This subscript is stored into the variable NO.OF.ELEMENTS, where it can be used by the rest of the program.

Another way to write this routine without using the scalar variable NAME_ is shown in the following routine.

```
1000 Input_rtn:     ! Enter elements into array, until sentinel
1010     SUBSCRIPT = 1
         INPUT 'Enter name, XXX to end'; NAMES(SUBSCRIPT)
         WHILE NAMES(SUBSCRIPT) <> 'XXX'
            SUBSCRIPT = SUBSCRIPT + 1
            INPUT 'Enter name, XXX to end'; NAMES(SUBSCRIPT)
         NEXT
1020     NO.OF.ELEMENTS = SUBSCRIPT - 1
1030 RETURN
```

Notice that SUBSCRIPT is initialized to 1. The names are read directly into the array, even the sentinel. Because the sentinel is in the array, and we do not want it to be treated as data, the value of NO.OF.ELEMENTS is set to one less than the final subscript. This does not remove the sentinel, but the rest of the program can use `NO.OF.ELEMENTS` to avoid processing it.

7.6 PRINTING ARRAYS

Arrays can be printed using loops. To print the first 50 elements of array C, we can use the following program segment:

```
100    FOR I = 1 TO 50
           PRINT C(I),
       NEXT I
```

Because a comma was used after the PRINT instruction, five numbers will be printed on each line of the output.[3] If we wanted to print only every second number in the array, we could add a STEP to the loop:

```
100    FOR I = 1 TO 50 STEP 2
           PRINT C(I),
       NEXT I
```

The elements C(1), C(3), C(5), and so on will be printed, up to C(49).

If the data had been read in with a sentinel, and if the number of elements had been stored in a variable called `NO.OF.ELEMENTS`, then these elements could be printed using a loop such as the following:

```
200    FOR I = 1 TO NO.OF.ELEMENTS
           PRINT NAMES(I)
       NEXT I
```

This technique can be used with any array, of course. It is not restricted to string arrays only.

7.7 CALCULATIONS USING LOOPS

In general, calculations involving arrays require loops. The loop counter is often used as the subscript to select the element to be used in the calculation.

Example 7.5 Find the average of 100 numbers that have previously been stored in array B:

```
100 Find_avg:  ! Find the avg of the 100 elements of array B
110     SUM = 0
        FOR I = 1 TO 100
            SUM = SUM + B(I)
        NEXT I
120     AVG = SUM / 100
130 RETURN
```

---

[3] Remember to set your terminal's margins if they are not set. The statement to use is `MARGIN 80` inserted somewhere near the top of your program.

As you can see, the loop allows us to calculate the sum of all 100 elements with little effort. Without the loop, we would have to find the sum by using a statement such as:

```
200 SUM = B(1) + B(2) + B(3) + B(4) + B(5) + &
          B(6) + B(7) + B(8) + B(9) + etc.
```

Not only does this approach lack a certain elegance, it is quite impractical for 100 numbers. The loop simplifies the problem greatly.

Example 7.6

We will write a program that will let you enter the cost of the 10 most recently sold homes in your town. The program will then calculate the average price of these homes and print the result. In pseudocode, we have the following program:

> Find average home sale price:
>   Read price of 10 homes
>   Calculate average price
>   Print average price
> Stop

The input and calculate routines will both use loops. The code appears in Figure 7-4.

Figure 7-4.
Program to Calculate Average Home Sale Price

```
10 ! Program to calculate average home sale price, 10 homes
20    DECLARE DECIMAL(10,2) Price(10), Sum_prices, Avg_price, &
              INTEGER      Home
30        GOSUB Enter_home_prices
40        GOSUB Find_avg_price
50        GOSUB Print_avg_price
60 EXIT PROGRAM

1000 Enter_home_prices:
1010     FOR Home = 1 TO 10
             INPUT "Enter price of home"; Price(Home)
         NEXT Home
1020 RETURN

1100 Find_avg_price:              ! Find average price of a home
1110     Sum_prices = 0
         FOR Home = 1 TO 10
             Sum_prices = Sum_prices + Price(Home)
         NEXT Home
1120     Avg_price = Sum_prices / 10
1130 RETURN

1200 Print_avg_price:
1210     PRINT \ PRINT
         PRINT "Average price of 10 homes is"; Avg_price
         PRINT \ PRINT
1220 RETURN

32767 END
```

Example 7.7 | Our program will read 25 numbers from DATA statements into an array, then find the two smallest numbers and print them.

To solve this problem, we have to keep track of two numbers: the smallest and the next-to-smallest. Let these variables be called SMALLEST and NEXT_SMALLEST, respectively.

The logic will be as follows:

Array search program:
  Read the values into an array, NUMBER
  Find the two smallest numbers
  Print the numbers
Stop

Find the two smallest numbers:
  Initialize SMALLEST and NEXT_SMALLEST to first element
  Loop from the second element to the twenty-fifth

    If the element is less than SMALLEST,
      then NEXT_SMALLEST becomes old SMALLEST
        and the element becomes the new SMALLEST

    If the element is between SMALLEST and NEXT_SMALLEST
      then the new NEXT_SMALLEST becomes the element
  End of loop
  Return

From the pseudocode, you can understand the logic involved. If the element being tested is the smallest so far, then the previous smallest is made the current next-smallest, and the element itself becomes the new smallest number. If the element being tested lies between the smallest and current next-smallest, then we make it the new next-smallest.

The coded solution, including the necessary input/output routines, appears in Figure 7-5.

It would be easy to make a subtle error in this program that could be very difficult to find. Let us look at some of the code involved:

```
1530      IF NUMBER(I) <= SMALLEST
          THEN NEXT_SMALLEST = SMALLEST
               SMALLEST = NUMBER(I)
          END IF
1540      IF NUMBER(I) > SMALLEST AND NUMBER(I) < NEXT_SMALLEST
          THEN NEXT_SMALLEST = NUMBER(I)
          END IF
```

The intention is that only one of the conditions in these two statements should be true, and that is exactly the case. But we could have easily written the conditions slightly differently, as follows:

```
1530      IF NUMBER(I) < SMALLEST
          THEN NEXT_SMALLEST = SMALLEST
               SMALLEST = NUMBER(I)
          END IF
1540      IF NUMBER(I) >= SMALLEST AND NUMBER(I) < NEXT_SMALLEST
          THEN NEXT_SMALLEST = NUMBER(I)
          END IF
```

194 | 7 ONE-DIMENSIONAL ARRAYS

Figure 7-5.
Program to Read Values Into an Array and Find the Two Smallest

```
10  ! Array search program

20      DECLARE INTEGER   NUMBER(25), I, SMALLEST, NEXT_SMALLEST

30      GOSUB Input_rtn          ! Read the numbers into the array
40      GOSUB Find_2_smallest    ! Find the two smallest numbers
50      GOSUB Print_2_smallest   ! Print the two smallest numbers

60   EXIT PROGRAM

1000 Input_rtn:                  ! Read the numbers into the array
1010    FOR I = 1 TO 25
           READ NUMBER(I)
        NEXT I
1020    DATA 765,34,92,146,87,6,9412,3874,45,69, &
             56,23,44,182,67,906,645,237,684,9, &
             55,385,47,64,519
1030 RETURN

1200 Print_2_smallest:           ! Print the two smallest numbers
1210    PRINT 'Array of 25 numbers read from DATA statements'
        PRINT 'The two smallest numbers in the array were '; &
              SMALLEST; ' and '; NEXT_SMALLEST
        PRINT
1220 RETURN

1500 Find_2_smallest:            ! Find the two smallest numbers
1510 ! Use first element as starting value
        SMALLEST = NUMBER(1)
        NEXT_SMALLEST = NUMBER(1)
1520    FOR I = 2 TO 25
1530       IF NUMBER(I) <= SMALLEST
           THEN NEXT_SMALLEST = SMALLEST
                SMALLEST = NUMBER(I)
           END IF
1540       IF NUMBER(I) > SMALLEST AND NUMBER(I) < NEXT_SMALLEST
           THEN NEXT_SMALLEST = NUMBER(I)
           END IF
1550    NEXT I
1560 RETURN

32767 END

RUNNH

Array of 25 numbers read from DATA statements
The two smallest numbers in the array were  6 and  9
```

You will have to look carefully to see the difference: An equality symbol has been moved from statement 1530 to 1540. Now consider what happens if we reach statement 1530 with the following conditions:

```
NUMBER(I)      = 60
SMALLEST       = 70
NEXT_SMALLEST  = 80
```

The condition in statement 1530 is true, so the two statements in the ELSE clause will execute. The result is:

```
NUMBER(I)      = 60
SMALLEST       = 60
NEXT_SMALLEST  = 70
```

So far, this is correct. Unfortunately, the condition at statement 1540, which was false before, now becomes true, because SMALLEST was set equal to NUMBER(I). Therefore, the statement in the THEN clause of line 1540 executes. The results are as follows:

```
NUMBER(I)      = 60
SMALLEST       = 60
NEXT_SMALLEST  = 60
```

This is clearly wrong! With the equality symbol placed as in Figure 7-5, however, this error does not occur.

A better solution would be to use an ELSE before the second IF because the second conditional statement will not execute if the first one has already done so. An additional benefit is that the second condition can be simplified since the first would be known to be false. Lines 1530 and 1540 would be combined into one logical statement, as follows:

```
1530      IF NUMBER(I) < SMALLEST
          THEN
              NEXT_SMALLEST = SMALLEST
              SMALLEST = NUMBER(I)
          ELSE
              IF NUMBER(I) < NEXT_SMALLEST
              THEN NEXT_SMALLEST = NUMBER(I)
              END IF
          END IF
```

Be sure you understand these fine points as you will run into similar situations quite often. An awareness of these types of errors will allow you to find and remove them.

7.8 SORTING ONE-DIMENSIONAL ARRAYS

Sorting is the process of putting the elements of an array in numerical or alphabetical order. If the data are to be arranged from the lowest to the highest, then the sort is called an **ascending sort.** If from highest to lowest, it

Figure 7-6.
Bubble Sort of 10-Element Array: First Pass

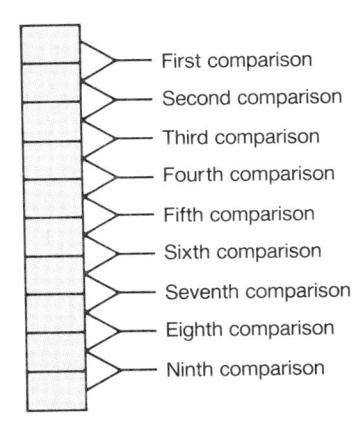

- First comparison
- Second comparison
- Third comparison
- Fourth comparison
- Fifth comparison
- Sixth comparison
- Seventh comparison
- Eighth comparison
- Ninth comparison

is called a **descending sort.** Many techniques are used to sort arrays. One of the most popular is called the **bubble sort,** in which adjacent elements are compared and interchanged if they are out of sequence.

Assume we are given an array with 10 real numbers, as diagrammed in Figure 7-6. We wish to sort the elements in ascending order; that is, with the smallest number in A(1) and the largest in A(10). A method we can use begins by comparing the first two numbers. If they are in the wrong sequence, we interchange them. Then we compare the second and third numbers and, if they are out of order, we interchange them. After these steps, the largest of the first three numbers in the array is the third element. This procedure is repeated seven more times. The last time it is done, the ninth element is compared with the tenth and, if necessary, those two elements are interchanged.

The end result of all of these comparisons and interchanges is that the largest number is now at the bottom of the list in the tenth position (Fig. 7-7). Note that none of the other elements of the array has been sorted yet. One of the characteristics of a bubble sort, or any of its variations, is that we know exactly *one* number is correctly positioned during each complete pass through the array.

Figure 7-7.
Bubble Sort of 10-Element Array: Second Pass

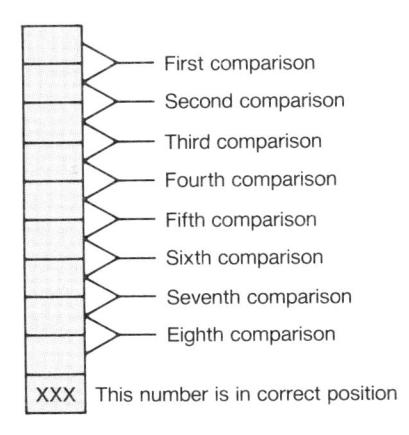

- First comparison
- Second comparison
- Third comparison
- Fourth comparison
- Fifth comparison
- Sixth comparison
- Seventh comparison
- Eighth comparison
- XXX This number is in correct position

The pseudocode for this first pass through the array is:

```
Compare 10 numbers:
   Loop I = 1 to 9 (9 comparisons with 10 numbers)
      If A(I) > A(I+1) then interchange them
   End of loop
End of comparing 10 numbers
```

Now that the tenth number is correctly placed, we have to do something about the first nine numbers, which are as yet unsorted. Because the tenth number is in its correct position, we will not concern ourselves with it. Only the first nine numbers need be sorted, as shown in Figure 7-7.

To get the largest of these nine numbers in Figure 7-7 to the ninth element of the array, we proceed as before, except that we need only eight comparisons for the nine numbers. The pseudocode is:

```
Compare 9 numbers:
   Loop I = 1 to 8 (8 comparisons for 9 numbers)
      If A(I) > A(I+1) then interchange them
   End of loop
End of comparing 9 numbers
```

We already had the largest number in the tenth position of the array. Now we have the next-to-largest in the ninth position. The first eight elements are still not sorted. You can see what comes next: We will need a loop that goes from 1 to 7 to place the eighth element, then a loop from 1 to 6 to place the seventh, a loop from 1 to 5, 1 to 4, 1 to 3, 1 to 2, and finally, a loop from 1 to 1. This final pass compares the first number to the second when there are only those two numbers left unsorted (see Fig. 7-8).

But we certainly do not want to write a program with a sequence of nine loops. Fortunately, when we have to perform nine loops, we can do so by putting those loops inside another loop.

Let's clarify this idea. If something has to be done nine times, we put it into a loop that goes from 1 to 9. Therefore, if a *loop* must be performed nine times, we can put that loop inside *another loop* that executes 9 times as its counter goes from 1 to 9:

```
Loop N = 1 TO 9
   Perform loop to do comparisons
End of loop
```

In this case, the inner loop performs the comparisons and interchanges. When N = 1, on the first pass through the array, we want to perform the loop that goes from 1 to 9. When N = 2, we want to perform the loop from 1 to 8, and so forth. When N = 9, we want to perform the final loop, which goes from 1 to 1.

We could write this in pseudocode as follows:

```
Loop N = 1 to 9
   Perform comparisons with loop from 1 to 10 - N
End N loop
```

Figure 7-8.
Bubble Sort of 10-Element Array: Remaining Passes to Complete the Sort

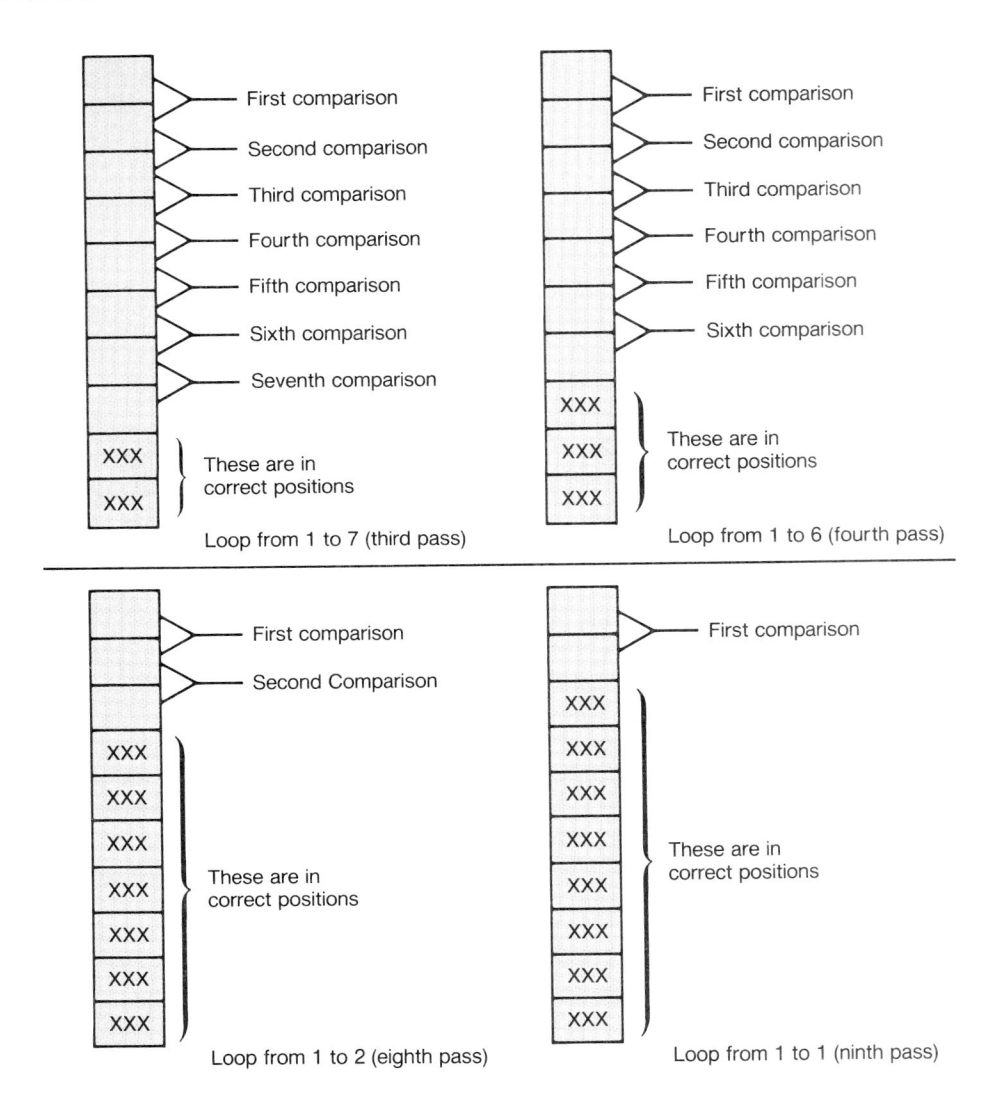

Loop from 1 to 7 (third pass)
- First comparison
- Second comparison
- Third comparison
- Fourth comparison
- Fifth comparison
- Sixth comparison
- Seventh comparison
- These are in correct positions

Loop from 1 to 6 (fourth pass)
- First comparison
- Second comparison
- Third comparison
- Fourth comparison
- Fifth comparison
- Sixth comparison
- These are in correct positions

Loop from 1 to 2 (eighth pass)
- First comparison
- Second Comparison
- These are in correct positions

Loop from 1 to 1 (ninth pass)
- First comparison
- These are in correct positions

This is all right, but we can do better. With the outer loop going from 1 to 9, the inner loop must go from 1 to 10 − N. (Why?) We can have the outer loop go from 9 to 1 instead by using a negative step of −1, which makes N equal to the number of comparisons in the inner loop. Let us name this variable `No.Comparisons`. The pseudocode will then look like this:

    Loop No.Comparisons = 9 to 1
        Perform comparisons with loop I = 1 to No.Comparisons
    End of No.Comparisons loop

This is more satisfying, having a certain elegance of style that the other method lacked. Now we put all of this pseudocode together:

Bubble sort:
   Loop No.Comparisons = 9 to 1 step −1
     Loop I = 1 to No.Comparisons
       If A(I) > A(I+1) then interchange them
     End of I loop
   End of No.Comparisons loop
End of bubble sort

The first time the outer loop is executed, the inner loop executes 9 times. For the second execution of the outer loop, the inner loop executes 8 times. This goes on until the ninth and last execution of the outer loop, when the inner loop executes once.

The only matter we have not yet discussed is how to interchange two numbers. This is a standard technique and requires a third variable, referred to as a **temporary variable.** Here is the logic:

Interchange two numbers:
   Store first number into temporary location
   Store second number into first number's location
   Store temporary into the second number's location
End of interchange

Our final program is shown in Figure 7-9.

Figure 7-9.
Program to Sort an Array

```
10  ! Sort an array
20      DECLARE INTEGER A(10), No.Comparisons, I, TEMP
30      GOSUB Array_input      ! Enter the array
40      GOSUB Bubble_sort      ! Sort the array
50      GOSUB Array_output     ! Print the array
60   EXIT PROGRAM
1000 Array_input:              ! Enter the array
1010     PRINT 'Enter 10 numbers for array'
         FOR I = 1 TO 10
            INPUT "Enter number"; A(I)
         NEXT I
1020 RETURN

1100 Array_output:             ! Print the array
1110     PRINT
         PRINT 'The sorted array is: '
         FOR I = 1 TO 10
            PRINT TAB(8); A(I)
         NEXT I
         PRINT
1120 RETURN

1500 Bubble_sort:              ! Bubble Sort
1510     FOR No.Comparisons = 9 TO 1 STEP −1
            FOR I = 1 TO No.Comparisons
```

Figure 7-9. (*Cont.*)

```
                        IF A(I) > A(I+1)
                        THEN
                            TEMP = A(I)
                            A(I) = A(I+1)
                            A(I+1) = TEMP
                        END IF
                    NEXT I
                NEXT No.Comparisons
1520 RETURN

32767 END

RUNNH
Enter 10 numbers for array
? 45
? 87
? 942
? 36
? 17
? 8
? 671
? 4
? 89
? 123
The sorted array is:
            4
            8
            17
            36
            45
            87
            89
            123
            671
            942
```

In subroutine `Bubble_sort` (line 1500), we have a loop within a loop. This is called a **nest of loops** or a **nested loop.** Study this nest carefully to be sure you understand it. The outer loop determines the number of comparisons that must be made to get the largest of the remaining numbers to the bottom of the unsorted list. The inner loop actually performs these comparisons and makes the necessary interchanges.

Sorting String Arrays

The previous program (Fig. 7-9) showed how a numerical array can be sorted. A string array, containing names for example, can be sorted using the same logic. The only difference is that the array name must be DECLAREd with the STRING data-type. If NAMES has been DECLAREd a STRING array, then line 1510 of the sort routine would then appear as follows:

```
1510    FOR No.Comparisons = 9 TO 1 STEP -1
           FOR I = 1 TO No.Comparisons
              IF NAMES(I) > NAMES(I+1)
              THEN
                   TEMP = NAMES(I)
                   NAMES(I) = NAMES(I+1)
                   NAMES(I+1) = TEMP
              END IF
           NEXT I
        NEXT No.Comparisons
```

It is important that TEMP also be DECLAREd as a STRING type.

When the computer compares strings, it compares them according to the ASCII (American Standard Code for Information Interchange) codes for their characters. Where strings contain more than two characters, their ASCII codes are compared starting at the leftmost character of each string. The comparisons proceed to the right, character by character, until two different ASCII codes are detected. The smaller code then determines which is the smaller string. Refer to appendix 3 on ASCII codes to see which characters are considered "smaller" than others. Note that upper case precede lower case letters. When comparing two strings that are identical except for case, the string in upper case would be "less than" or "smaller" than the one in lower case.

7.9 ASSOCIATED ARRAYS

Often we have two or more arrays in which corresponding elements of the two arrays are related in some manner. Such arrays are said to be **associated.** For example, one array might consist of social security numbers and another of names. If each name and its corresponding social security number are in the same position in their respective arrays, then the arrays are associated.

**Example 7.8
Sequential Search**

This program will enable the user to enter names, social security numbers, addresses, and telephone numbers. These will be read into four string arrays. Next, the program will prompt for a social security number. After this has been entered, the program will print the corresponding name, address, and telephone number. The user may enter additional social security numbers to repeat the process. The program ends when the user presses <Return> without entering a number (we call this a **null input**).

```
Associated arrays:
   Dimension the arrays
   Read the arrays
   Process requests
Stop

Process requests:
   Ask for social security number
   UNTIL social security number = ' ' (null)
      Search for social security number in array
```

7 ONE-DIMENSIONAL ARRAYS

      Print all associated data
      Ask for next social security number
     End of loop
    Return

To search for the social security number, we will use a technique called a **sequential search.** In this type of search, we start at the top of the array and look at every element in sequence. We stop looking after we find what we are searching for, or after we have looked at every element and still have not found a match. If we find a match, we return the position of the element where the match occurred. If not, we return a position of 0 and because no social security number is stored in the zero'th element, we know the search failed.

  The pseudocode for the sequential search is as follows:

    Sequential search:
     Start at first position of social security array
     UNTIL datum is found or we reach the last position
      of the array
      Go to next position
     End of loop
     If no match was found, set position to 0
    Return

**Figure 7-10.
Sequential Search
Technique for Associated
Arrays**

  The idea is to start looking for the desired datum beginning at the first element of the array. If the first element is not a match, we look at the next element's value, and so on. Eventually, we find what we have been looking for or we run out of elements. If we find the value, we will return its position by returning the subscript. If we run out of elements and, hence, the search fails, we have to let the rest of the program know that; so we return a 0, a nonexistent position in a one-based array. The code appears in Figure 7-10.

```
10  ! Associated arrays
20       DECLARE STRING    NAME.(500), SSN(500), ADDR(500), &
                           TEL(500), NAME.IN, SSN.FIND, &
                 INTEGER   I, POSN, NO.RECORDS
30       GOSUB Read_arrays      ! Read the arrays
40       GOSUB Process_reqs.    ! Process requests
50   EXIT PROGRAM

1000 Read_arrays:                ! Read the arrays
1010     I = 0                   ! Initialize subscripts
         GOSUB Read_rec          ! Read first record
1020     UNTIL NAME.IN = ''
             GOSUB Read_rec      ! Read next record
         NEXT
1030 RETURN

1200 Read_rec:                   ! Read a record
1210     READ NAME.IN
```

Figure 7-10. (*Cont.*)

```
1220    ! Read rest of data only if not sentinel
        IF NAME.IN <> ''
        THEN I = I + 1           ! Increase subscript
             NAME.(I) = NAME.IN
             READ SSN(I), ADDR(I), TEL(I)
        END IF
1230    NO.RECORDS = I           ! Records read so far
1240 RETURN

2000 Process_reqs.:              ! Process requests
2010    GOSUB Enter_ssn          ! Enter soc.sec.no.
2020    WHILE SSN.FIND <> ''
2030      GOSUB Find_ssn_posn ! Search for soc.sec.no.
2040      IF POSN = 0
          THEN PRINT SSN.FIND; ' not found in array'
          ELSE PRINT
               PRINT SSN(POSN); TAB(15); NAME.(POSN); &
                     TAB(40); ADDR(POSN); TAB(65); &
                     TEL(POSN)
              PRINT
          END IF
2050      GOSUB Enter_ssn     ! Enter next soc.sec.no.
2060    NEXT
2070 RETURN

2100 Enter_ssn:                  ! Enter soc.sec.no. to find
2110  ! Print all available social security numbers for reference
        PRINT \ PRINT
        PRINT "Social Security numbers available are :"
        FOR I = 1 TO NO.RECORDS
            PRINT SSN(I),
        NEXT I
        PRINT \ PRINT
2120  ! Enter social security number to find
        INPUT 'Enter soc.sec.no. <RETURN> to end'; SSN.FIND
        PRINT
2130 RETURN

2200 Find_ssn_posn:               ! Sequential search routine
                                  ! for social security number
2210    POSN = 1
        UNTIL SSN(POSN) = SSN.FIND OR POSN = NO.RECORDS
            POSN = POSN + 1
        NEXT
2220    IF SSN(POSN) <> SSN.FIND THEN POSN = 0   END IF
2230 RETURN

5000 ! DATA statements
5010    DATA Anne Boleyn,535-25-3999,123 Main St.,(205)555-6249
5020    DATA Edgar A. Poe,878-29-3378,45 Dungeon Lane,(122)244-3826
5030    DATA Simon LeGree,222-37-9999,27 Elm St.,(212)555-2212
5040    DATA Matty Hayes,115-99-0274,1 Moonlight Rd.,(515)345-3456
5050    DATA Daffy Duck,000-00-0000,20 Disney Blvd.,(902)617-5555
5060    DATA ''

32767 END
```

Line 2040 presents a special problem. Because the PRINT statement does not fit on one line, it must be continued on additional physical lines. These physical lines do not contain a complete statement, so the previous line must end with an ampersand.

The sequential search of Figure 7-10 is in subroutine `Find_ssn_posn` (line 2200). When we leave the loop of line 2210, it is for one of two reasons: we found the social security number or we reached the end of the list. If the match is found at the last element, both reasons could be true. Line 2220 resets `POSN` to 0 if a match is not found. Line 2040 in the print routine tests for this value.

We have blithely ignored a number of items. Chief among these concerns is the representation of social security numbers: do we use hyphens or not? The program will not work if we sometimes use hyphens and sometimes not. At present, we must be careful to be consistent. In chapter 9, we learn of other techniques that can be used to compensate for variations in input formats.

Example 7.9
Insertion Sort

Another sort routine is the **insertion sort.** We will use it to sort associated arrays. Assume we have a 10-element array that is already sorted. We want to add one additional value so that there are 11 elements, but want to keep the array sorted. We can compare the new value with the last element in the list, the tenth. If this element is greater than the new value, then we move it down to the eleventh position. Now we compare with the ninth element, and move that into the tenth position, if necessary. We continue in this manner until all elements larger than the new value have been moved down one position. The new value is then inserted in the array in its proper location, and the array remains sorted (see Fig. 7-11).

Figure 7-11.
Inserting a Number Into a Sorted Array

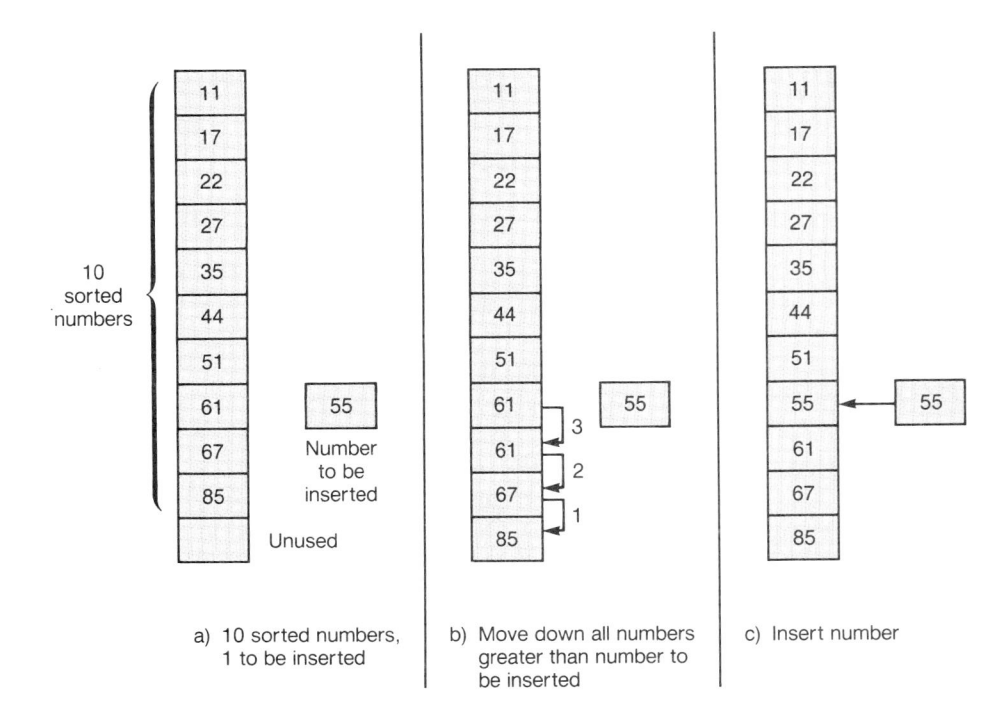

a) 10 sorted numbers, 1 to be inserted

b) Move down all numbers greater than number to be inserted

c) Insert number

Figure 7-12.
Inserting Next Value Into Partially Sorted Array

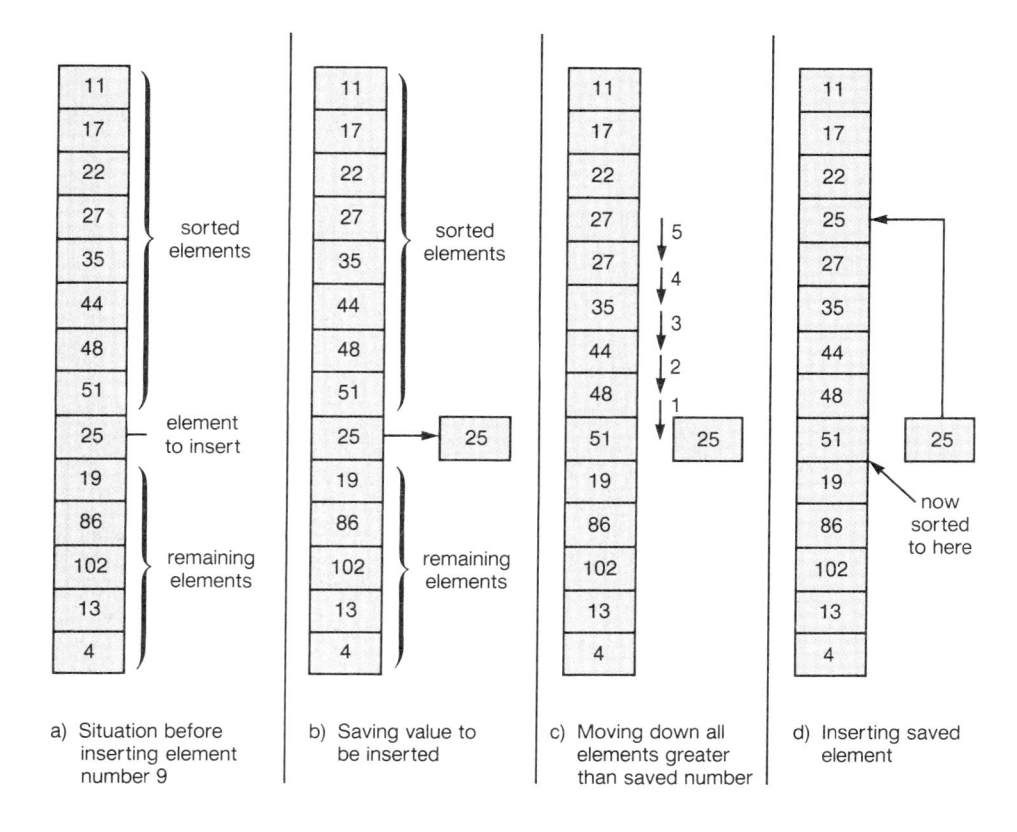

a) Situation before inserting element number 9

b) Saving value to be inserted

c) Moving down all elements greater than saved number

d) Inserting saved element

Suppose we are given an unsorted array and wish to sort it using an insertion sort. If we consider only the first element of the array, we have a list consisting of one element that is already sorted. Now consider the first two elements. The second element is a "new" value that must be inserted into the one-element "sorted" list above it. To do this, we use the procedure mentioned above. The result is a sorted list of two elements.

The third element is then considered a "new" value to be added to a sorted array of two elements. Again, the above procedure can be used.

We continue in this manner, treating each successive element as a new value to be added to the sorted list. After each element has been inserted, the sorted part of the list consists of one additional element. Eventually, the entire array will be sorted. (See Fig. 7-12.)

One matter we have not yet considered: If the element we are inserting is the smallest value thus far encountered, then all elements above it must be moved down one position. The new value will be inserted in the first position in the array. In our comparisons, we must make certain we do not go off the top of the array; that is, our comparisons must not involve negative subscripts. Comparisons must stop after the new value has been compared to the first element.

The pseudocode for the insertion sort is shown below.

Insertion sort:
   For second element to last element
      Insert element

```
            Next element
        Return
        Insert element:
            Save element in temporary variable
            Set pointer to previous element
            While element at pointer > temporary variable
                    and pointer > 0
                Move element at pointer to next location
                Subtract 1 from pointer
            End loop
            Move temporary variable into element after pointer
        Return
```

In Figure 7-13, we write only the code for the subroutine here (actually two subroutines). It could replace the code for the bubble sort in Figure 7-9.

The subroutine depends on the existence of A(0) and on its not being used to hold data. This is because the WHILE condition refers to `A(Pointer)`, and `Pointer` could have a value of 0. If A(0) had useful data, and the array were zero-based, then the logic would be more complicated. Let us leave well enough alone.

The subroutine of Figure 7-13 can be modified to permit its use with associated arrays. Suppose one array contains names and the other contains associated addresses. Whenever we move an element of one array, we must also move the corresponding element of the other.

The subroutines in Figure 7-14 are a modification of Figure 7-13. There are two associated arrays—`Names` and `Addresses`. The sort is by name. Two temporary variables are required—one to hold the name to be inserted, the other to hold its associated address.

Example 7.10
Binary Search

We conclude this chapter with one more useful example, the binary search. We have previously discussed and programmed the linear search, in which

Figure 7-13.
Subroutine for Insertion Sort

```
2000 Insertion_sort:
2010     FOR I = 2 TO No.of_elements
             GOSUB Insert_element
         NEXT I
2020 RETURN

2100 Insert_element:
2110     Hold = A(I)        ! Save element to be inserted
         Pointer = I - 1    ! Set pointer to previous element
2120 ! Move larger elements down
         WHILE A(Pointer) > Hold AND Pointer > 0
             A(Pointer + 1) = A(Pointer)
             Pointer = Pointer - 1
         NEXT
2130     A(Pointer + 1) = Hold   ! Insert element
2140 RETURN
```

Figure 7-14.
Subroutine for the Insertion Sort Technique for Associated arrays

```
2000 Insertion_sort:         ! Insertion sort, associated arrays
2010    FOR I = 2 TO No.of_elements
            GOSUB Insert_element
        NEXT I
2020 RETURN

2100 Insert_element:
2110    Name_Hold = Names(I)        ! Save name to be inserted
        Address_Hold = Address(I)   ! Save address to be inserted
        Pointer = I - 1             ! Pointer to previous element
2120 ! Move larger names, and associated addresses, down
        WHILE Names(Pointer) > Name_Hold AND Pointer > 0
            Names(Pointer + 1) = Names(Pointer)
            Address(Pointer + 1) = Address(Pointer)
            Pointer = Pointer - 1
        NEXT
2130 ! Insert Name and Address
        Names(Pointer + 1) = Name_Hold
        Address(Pointer + 1) = Pointer_Hold
2140 RETURN
```

every element is examined in sequence, starting with the first element in the array. If the array is large, this can take a considerable amount of time.

If the array we are searching is sorted, we have a much more efficient method available than the sequential search, namely, the **binary search.**

When you look for a name in the telephone book, you do not search sequentially. Instead, you make use of the fact that the names are sorted alphabetically to find the entry you want quickly. Similarly, the binary search makes use of the ordered array to locate a specific value.

Suppose we are trying to find a specific value. We can start by looking at the middle element of the array. There are three possibilities:

1. The middle element is the one for which we are looking. In that case, we are finished—the search is over.

2. The middle element is *larger* than the one for which we are looking. In this case, we can now search the elements in the *top* half of the array, and ignore the bottom half.

3. The middle element is *smaller* than the one for which we are looking. In this case, we can now search the elements in the *bottom* half of the array, and ignore the top half.

For the second and third cases, we can repeat the procedure with the appropriate half, leaving us with the same three possibilities again, except that we have now restricted the search to one-quarter of the array. And so on, until we find the element, or know for sure that it is not in the list (which happens after we have restricted ourselves to only one element and it is not the one we want).

A *flag* will be set if we find the value in the array. A flag is like a switch (it is even called a switch). Before something occurs, it has one value. After its occurrence, it has another value—that is our clue that we have found the element for which we were searcheng. We will call our flag Found. It will be initialized to 0; if we find our value, it will be changed to 1.

To keep track of the different areas of the array we are searching, we use the two variables Top and Bottom. Top is initially set to 1, the subscript of the first element. Bottom will be set to the subscript of the last element. Another variable, Middle, will be set to the subscript midway between these two. Whenever we want to restrict ourselves to the top part of the array, we will set Bottom to Middle - 1. Whenever we want the bottom part of the array, we set Top to Middle + 1. You can see that the variable Bottom moves up when we keep the top half, and the variable Top moves down when we keep the bottom half. If Top and Bottom ever pass each other, we will know that the value we want is not in the array.

The binary search will return the subscript of the element that contains the value we were seeking, or it will return a value of 0 if the value was not in the array. Assume a one-based array, whose number of elements is in the variable No.of_elements. We pseudocode the binary search as follows:

```
Binary search:
   Initialize Top to 1
   Initialize Bottom to No.of_elements
   Initialize Found to 0
   While Top and Bottom have not passed each other
      Find Middle (midway between Top and Bottom)
      If middle element = value then
         set Found to 1
      Else if middle element > value then
         set Bottom to Middle - 1 (keep top half)
      Else if middle element < value then
         set Top to Middle + 1 (keep bottom half)
      End If
   End loop
   If not found, set subscript to 0
   Else set subscript to Middle
Return
```

The code for this routine is in Figure 7-15. The array is called SSN (social security numbers). Any array, of any type, may be used instead.

Be careful in lines 1030 and 1040. If the NEXT of line 1040 is to be included in line 1030, then a second END IF is required after the one already in line 1030 for the following reason: An IF statement ends at an END IF or at a new line number. Since there is a nest of two IF statements in line 1030, if you don't use a new line number, you need two END IFs. With only one END IF, one IF statement is not terminated; therefore, the NEXT would be *in* the IF statement instead of *after* it.

Figure 7-15.
Binary Search Subroutine

```
1000 Binary_search:                  ! Binary search routine
1010 ! Initializations
     Top = 1                         ! Top, Bottom, and Found
     Bottom = No.of_elements         ! are all DECLAREd as
     Found = 0                       ! INTEGER
1020 WHILE Top <= Bottom AND Found = 0
        Middle = (Top + Bottom) / 2
1030    IF SSN(Middle) = Value THEN Found = 1
        ELSE IF SSN(Middle) > Value THEN Bottom = Middle - 1
        ELSE Top = Middle + 1
        END IF
1040 NEXT
1050 IF Found = 0 THEN Subscript = 0
     ELSE Subscript = Middle
1060 RETURN
```

SUMMARY

In this chapter, you learned how to use one-dimensional arrays. You also learned the concept of associated arrays, the bubble and insertion sorts, and the sequential and binary searches. To utilize arrays, we used a number of features of BASIC that we had not used previously.

1. The DECLARE statement reserves storage for array elements.
2. Arrays can be read with enumerative or controlled loops. Enumerative loops are used when it is known how many elements are to be read. Controlled loops are used when the last element is a sentinel and the array is to be only partially filled. Both INPUT and READ instructions can be used to enter elements into an array.
3. Arrays can be printed using loops. Enumerative loops are usually used because the number of elements is known.
4. The bubble and insertion sorts are techniques used to arrange elements of an array in a particular sequence. If the sequence is lowest to highest, then the sort is referred to as ascending. If the sequence is highest to lowest, then the sort is a descending sort. Character string arrays as well as numerical arrays can be sorted. The sort for string arrays is done according to the collating sequence of the computer, usually the ASCII sequence.
5. Sequential and binary searches are techniques that let you find a given value in an array. The elements of the array are compared to the desired value. If the value is found, the subscript indicating the position of the element within the array is returned. If it is not found, a zero is returned.
6. Associated arrays are two or more arrays in which elements in corresponding positions are related. The elements in a particular position are often the different fields of one record.

REVIEW QUESTIONS

1. What is an array?
2. How are the different elements of an array distinguished from one another?

3. Which statement is used to dimension an array?

4. If the statement DECLARE REAL A(50) is used in a program, what is the range of subscripts permitted for this array?

5. What is meant by a **one-based array?** What is meant by a **zero-based array?**

6. Discuss the difference between the subscript and value of an element. In the term A(5), is 5 the subscript or the value of the element? In the expression A(5) = 10, is the value of the element 5 or 10?

7. What is meant by the term **associated arrays?** When are they used?

8. What is a sort? Explain the difference between an ascending sort and a descending sort.

9. Explain the logic of the bubble sort as presented in this chapter.

10. Explain the logic of the insertion sort as presented in this chapter.

11. What is a search? Explain the logic of the sequential search technique as discussed in this chapter.

12. Explain the logic of the binary search technique as discussed in this chapter.

SYNTAX EXERCISES

The following problems all contain one or more syntax or logic errors. Find and correct them.

1.
```
1000 Read_array:
1010 FOR I = 1 TO No.elements
        INPUT A(1)
     NEXT I
```
2.
```
1000 Print array:
1010 FOR I = 1 TO No.Elements
        PRINT A(J)
     NEXT I
```
3. `100 SUM = A[1] + A[2] + A[3]`
4. `100 AVG = A[1] + A[2] + A[3] / 3`
5.
```
1000 ! Find sum of numbers
     FOR I = 1 TO 100
        SUM = 0
        SUM = SUM + A(I)
     NEXT I
```
6.
```
1000 ! Find product of numbers
     FOR I = 1 TO 100
        PRODUCT = 0
        PRODUCT = PRODUCT * A(I)
     NEXT I
```
7. `1000 FOR I = 1 TO 100 BY 2`
8. `1000 FOR I = 1 TO 100 BY -1`
9. `100 NAME(I) = NAME(J)`
10. `100 NAME(1) = "John Smith"`

PROGRAMMING EXERCISES

Write subroutines or programs to solve the following problems, as directed. All program output must be identified.

■   **1a.** Write a subroutine that finds the average of every second element of a 100-element array, starting with the first element.

1b. Write a program that lets you enter a 10-element array from the terminal, then finds the average of every other element beginning with the first, and the average of every other element beginning with the second. Print the array and both averages, providing suitable identification for all output.

2a. Write a subroutine that reads elements into a 100-element array from DATA statements. The DATA statements may contain fewer than 100 elements. A sentinel, −999, signals the end of the data.

2b. Enter elements into a 100-element array using DATA statements. The number of elements entered may be less than 100; use a sentinel. Find the average of every other element, starting with the first element, and the average of every other element starting with the second. Print all the elements of the array that were entered, and both averages, with suitable identification.

■   **3a.** Write a subroutine that finds the smallest element of an array of 31 elements.

3b. Write a program that allows you to enter into an array the average daily temperature for each day in January of this year. The data may be entered at the terminal, or come from DATA statements. The program is then to find and print the date that had the lowest average temperature and the date that had the highest.

4a. Enter a list of names into an array. Sort the list of names in ascending order. Print the original list of names and the list of names after sorting. At least 10 names should be used, with provision for up to 100. HINT: Make a copy of the NAMES array and sort the second copy.

4b. Same as problem 4a, but use an insertion sort.

5a. Three associated arrays contain names, addresses, and social security numbers, respectively. Write a subroutine that sorts the arrays by social security number, using a bubble sort.

5b. Same as problem 5a, but use an insertion sort.

5c. Enter 10 records from the terminal or from DATA statements. Each record is to contain a name, social security number, and address. The data are to be stored in three associated arrays.

Sort the records by name, keeping all associated data together. Sort them again, this time by social security number.

The printout should consist of the original data, the data after sorting by name, and the data after sorting by social security number. All output should be properly identified using headings.

6a. Enter a list of at least 10 names, addresses, and social security numbers into three associated arrays. The data may come from the terminal or from DATA statements. Now enter a social security number from the terminal. Using a sequential search, print the name and address of the person who has this social security number. Be sure to take into account the possibility that the social security number may not be found.

6b. Same as problem 6a, but use a binary search instead of a sequential search.

7. One variation of the bubble sort was presented in this chapter, but there is another variation that can sometimes save time.

What would it mean if we went through the array from top to bottom, comparing adjacent elements, but did not have to interchange any of them? A moment's reflection should convince you that the list would, of necessity, already be sorted at that point. We would not have to do any more comparisons.

To keep track of whether or not we did an interchange, we can use a flag. This is merely a variable that will be given one of two possible values. For instance, if we did an interchange, we could set the flag to YES, and if there is no interchange, the value could be NO. The logic for this version of the bubble sort would be:

```
Bubble sort:
    Set No.Comparisons to No.Elements - 1
    Set Interchange_Flag to "YES"(To get into loop)
    WHILE No.Comparisons >= 1 and Interchange_Flag = "YES"
        Set Interchange_Flag to "NO"  (No interchanges yet)
        FOR I = 1 TO No.Comparisons
            If A(I) > A(I+1) then
                Interchange elements and
                Set Interchange_Flag to "YES"
            End If
        End of I loop
        Subtract 1 from No.Comparisons
    End of WHILE loop
Return
```

If you compare this logic with that of Figure 7-9, you will see that the outer loop has been made a WHILE instead of a FOR loop. That way, the loop can be terminated if no interchanges were performed on the previous cycle, in addition to the criterion used previously.

a. Write a subroutine that will sort a 50-element array using the logic of this bubble sort.

b. Write the program using this logic. The array may be entered at the terminal, or be read from DATA statements. The second method will be easier, at least until the program is debugged.

8a. Given an array of 100 names, write a subroutine that counts the number of names beginning with the letter A. HINT: Compare each name to the letters A and B.

8b. Enter a list of names into an array from DATA statements or from the terminal. Print all names that begin with the letter A. The names are stored last name first. Write the program.

9. Enter a list of names into an array from the terminal or from DATA statements. Print all names that begin with the letter A, then all names that begin with B, and so on through the letter Z. (It is not necessary to sort the array to do this problem.)

HINT: Read the letters A through Z into an array, ALPHABET. Use a loop that executes 26 times, using a different element of this array each time in your comparisons.

10. The formula for standard deviation is:

$$\text{s.d.} = \sqrt{\frac{\Sigma(X(i) - \bar{x})^2}{n}}$$

where the summation symbol means to add up the values of the expression to the right, evaluated at elements X(1) through X(n) and

X(i) = element i in array X
$\bar{X}$ = the mean (average) of array X
n = the number of elements in array X.

a. Write a subroutine that will calculate the standard deviation, given an array X whose number of elements is stored in the variable `No.of_elements`.

b. Write a program that will read an unknown number of numeric values into array X (maximum of 100 elements). Use −999 as the end-of-data sentinel. Compute the standard deviation and print it.

11. Read 50 numbers into an array from the terminal or from DATA statements. The elements may be read in already sorted, or you may sort them after reading them in. Find the mean and median of the numbers. These parameters are defined as follows:

MEAN = (Sum of all elements)/(Number of elements)
MEDIAN = The element in the middle position of the array when the array is sorted. (If the array has an even number of elements, the median is the sum of the 2 middle elements divided by 2.)

■ **12a.** Given a sorted array, write a subroutine that will find the *mode*. The mode is defined as the value that appears most frequently.

12b. Refer to problem 11. Instead of the mean and median, write a program that will find and print the mode.

13. A program uses two associated arrays. The first, `TRANSACTION.CODE`, will contain numbers from 0 to 4. The second, `TRANSACTION.AMOUNT`, will contain the amounts of various bank transactions. If the code is 1, then the amount is the initial balance. If the code is 2, then the amount is a bank deposit, and it is added to the account balance. If the code is 3, then the amount is a withdrawal, and is subtracted from the balance. If the code is 4, then the transaction involves calculating and crediting interest. Finally, if the code is 0, this is the signal that there are no more transactions and output should begin.

Write the program. The interest rate to use in calculating interest will be read from a DATA statement. The transactions are to be entered and stored in the two arrays mentioned. A menu-driven routine is suggested. Each transaction will require entering the code and the amount. For a code of 4, the amount entered could be 0 or null. The last transaction will have a code of 0. Allow for 50 transactions, but you may enter fewer than 50.

Output will consist of the transaction type, not the code; the amount of the transaction; and the new balance after each transaction. Column headings should be used to make the output presentable.

14. A number of DATA statements have the following records. The first record is number of customers. For each customer record, there are four fields: social security number in the form XXX-XX-XXXX; name; address; and account balance. Read the customer data into associated arrays.

Additional input will come from the terminal and will consist of three items: a social security number; an integer, which will be 1 or 2; and an amount, which represents either a charge or a payment. If the integer is 1, then the amount is a charge to the individual's account and is added to the balance. If the integer is a 2, then the amount is a payment and is subtracted from the balance. The social security number will be used to determine whose balance is to be affected. The process is to be repeated until the social security number 000-00-0000 is entered. After that, all data are to be printed in a report showing name, social security number, and final balance for each customer.

    a. Write the program using a sequential search.

    b. Write the program using a binary search.

15. Set up a number of DATA statements, each with four items of information: part number, part description, quantity available, and unit cost. Read these into four associated arrays. Print a report in which each line has the following information: part number, part description, quantity on hand, unit cost, and total cost for all of that item. The output should include suitable column headings. At the end of the report, print a summary giving the total number of items (how many part numbers?), total quantity of all items, and total cost.

16. Write a simplified inventory control program. Inventory control is a method used by people in charge of warehouses to keep track of the amount of goods in storage. The program must keep track of the quantity and price of various items.

    Each item will have a part number. The part number will be the subscript of an array in which the quantity is kept. For example, the value of QUANTITY(26) will be the quantity of part number 26 on hand in the warehouse. The price and description of each part will be kept in an associated arrays called PRICE and PART.DESC; PRICE(26) will contain the price of part number 26 while PART.DESC(26) will contain the description of part number 26. There will be a maximum of 250 parts.

    When a shipment arrives, the quantity of each item received must be added to the quantity on hand. When a shipment goes out, the quantity of each part shipped must be subtracted from the quantity on hand. At various intervals, management will require a report that provides the quantity on hand, the cost of each item, and the totals for all items.

    The main program will display a menu that gives the user a choice of:

    1. Adding a new part number to the list

    2. Increasing the quantity on hand of an item

    3. Decreasing the quantity on hand of an item

    4. Changing the price of an item

    5. Preparing a report

    6. Ending the program

    Each of these choices will invoke a subroutine that will perform the indicated process. The report should print each part number, the quantity on hand, the price of each, and total value. After this information is printed for each part number, the total number of part numbers available, the total number of all parts, and the total value of all parts should be printed.

    a. Write the subroutine that prints the menu.

    b. Write each of the six subroutines that perform the above operations.

    c. Write the complete program. The output should be printed in a neat, clear manner, as if your job depended on it. (Someday, it might.)

17. A jail has 100 cells. The warden is celebrating his birthday and decides to release some of the prisoners. First, he opens all the cell doors. Then he closes every second one. Then he changes the current condition of every third one, closing the open doors and opening the closed ones. He repeats this for every fourth door, changing the state of each one. He continues doing this for every fifth door, every sixth door, and so on, until he gets to every hundredth door. Prisoners whose doors are open when he is done are permitted to leave.

a. Let the cell doors be represented by an array. Let a door that is open be represented by a value of 1, and one that is closed by -1. Given an array depicting 100 doors, some of which are open, and some of which are closed, write a subroutine that reverses the state of every fifth door, opening the closed ones, and closing the open ones.

b. Write a program that determines who can leave. Simulate the cells with a 100-element array. Print the cell numbers of the prisoners who are freed. After you have run the program, examine the cell number of every released prisoner. Can you detect a pattern in the numbers? (See part a.)

18. The Sieve of Eratosthenes is a very fast method for finding prime numbers (i.e., numbers that are divisible only by themselves and 1). The Sieve finds all prime numbers up to a specified maximum.

Assume that you want all prime numbers up to 1000. Begin by storing these numbers into an array. Now start eliminating all numbers that are not prime, using the following procedure:

1. Because 2 is a prime number, cross off every second number after 2 by replacing it with 0. Because 2 is the only even prime number, we need no longer concern ourselves with any even numbers.

2. The next number that has not been crossed out is 3. Three is a prime number, but its multiples are not. Therefore, we must cross out every multiple of 3 except 3 itself. The even multiples, 6, 12, 18, . . . , are already crossed out, so we only have to cross out the odd multiples which would be every sixth number starting at nine, 9, 15, 21, ... (Notice that 9 = 3 * 3 and 6 = 2 * 3.)

3. The number 4 has been crossed off the list by this time, so we know it is not prime. The next number not crossed out is 5, which is the next prime number. All its multiples must be crossed out. All even multiples, and all odd multiples up to 25 (5 * 5) are already crossed out. So we cross out every tenth number starting at 25: 25, 35, 45, 55, etc. (Notice that 25 = 5 * 5 and 10 = 2 * 5.)

4. We continue in this way, skipping over numbers that are already crossed out, and crossing out multiples of numbers that have not been crossed out, starting with the square of such numbers, and proceeding in steps equal to the number times 2.

5. The process continues until we reach the largest number whose square is less than or equal to 1000. In this case, that would be the number 31. We need go no further, because crossing out always begins with the square of the number we are at in the list. The numbers now remaining in the list are the prime numbers.

a. Write a subroutine that will find the prime numbers up to N, using the method of the Sieve of Eratosthenes.

b. Write a program that finds and prints all the prime numbers up to 1000, using the method of the Sieve of Eratosthenes.

ENRICHMENT TOPICS 7 — Variable Dimension and MAT Statements

VARIABLE DIMENSIONING

When an array is declared with a DECLARE statement, its size is basically fixed for the duration of the program. There are times when it is convenient to let the size of the array be determined at the time the program is run. We can use an executable DIMENSION statement for this purpose, or its abbreviation, DIM. Its syntax is:

sn DIM data-type array-name(dimension) [, . . .]

For example:

```
100 Array_size = 100
    DIM STRING  NAMES(Array_size), &
                REAL GRADES(Array_size), AVGS(Array_size)
    DIM INTEGER Codes(40)
```

As you can see, the DIM statement can use fixed dimensioning, the same as the DECLARE statement. However, one of the big advantages is that the dimensions in a DIM statement may be variables. This lets you enter the size of the array you need at the terminal, and then create arrays of that size. Consider the following program segment:

Example 7.11

```
10 ! Example illustrating variable dimensioning
20    DECLARE INTEGER ARRAY_SIZE
30    INPUT "Enter size of desired arrays"; ARRAY_SIZE
40    DIM STRING    NAMES(ARRAY_SIZE), &
          INTEGER   AVGS(ARRAY_SIZE), &
          REAL      GPA(ARRAY_SIZE)
```

There may be many DIM statements in a program. Each one can redimension any given array or arrays to change its size. This redimensioning takes place at the time that the DIM statement executes. *Be aware, however, that redimensioning an array will cause its previous values to be lost.*

MAT STATEMENTS

VAX-BASIC contains a number of statements that allow you to work with an entire array as a unit. These are called **MAT instructions,** some of which are described below.

Input Using MAT INPUT

VAX-BASIC has a method of input that allows an entire array, or part of an array, to be read with only one statement. The applicable instructions are MAT INPUT and MAT READ. Their syntax is:

> sn **MAT INPUT** array-name
> sn **MAT READ** array-name

where **array-name** is the symbolic name of an array. Note that you may not include an informational prompt in the MAT INPUT instruction; any prompt will have to be printed by a preceding PRINT instruction.

For example, `20 MAT INPUT A` will read all or part of array A.

The data you type to satisfy a MAT INPUT instruction must all be entered on one line *before* you press <Return>. If there is more data than you can type on one physical line on the terminal, you can terminate the physical line with an ampersand and enter additional numbers on succeeding lines. When the <Return> key is pressed without a preceding ampersand, all numbers that have been typed at the terminal up to that point are stored in the array.

This method of entering data is very different from the method described earlier when a loop is used. In that case, data had to be entered one value at a time. Each value had to be followed by a <Return>. When using MAT INPUT, all values are typed on one logical line, and one <Return> terminates all input.

Example 7.12

```
10 MAT INPUT A
```

If A is a 100-element array, we can now type up to 100 numbers at the terminal. The numbers will be read into successive elements of the array. The only prompt when this statement executes will be a question mark. If any other prompt is required, it must be printed with a separate PRINT statement.

If we type the following in response to the question mark:

```
6, 5, 8, 9, 7 <RETURN>
```

then A(1) will be 6, A(2) will be 5, A(3) will be 8, A(4) will be 9, and A(5) will be 7. The remaining 95 elements will be *unchanged* from their previous values, and the values will be zeros unless they have previously been assigned other values.

If we use a MAT INPUT instruction, but only partially fill the array, it may be very important to know how many elements have actually been transferred. Fortunately, VAX-BASIC gives us a suitable means of determining this important piece of information—the NUM variable.

The NUM Variable

We stated earlier that a MAT INPUT instruction can read either an entire array or only a part of it, leaving the remaining elements unchanged. If the

218 | VARIABLE DIMENSION AND MAT STATEMENTS

Figure 7-16
Program to Illustrate Use of the NUM Variable

```
10 ! Example illustrating MAT INPUT and NUM
20    DECLARE REAL A(100)
30    PRINT 'Enter up to 100 numbers' ! Prints a prompt for user
      MAT INPUT A
          ! The MAT INPUT statement causes NUM to be set
          ! to the number of elements actually entered
40    PRINT "Number of elements entered ="; NUM
50 END
```

array is dimensioned so that it can hold 100 elements, but we type only 25 elements in response to a MAT INPUT, then only those 25 elements are stored.

This leaves us with a problem. In many cases, it is important to know exactly how many numbers were read into the array. An example would be finding the average of these numbers. Fortunately, we have a way of obtaining this information from within the program. It is by means of a built-in variable called the **NUM variable.**

When a MAT INPUT instruction is executed, the built-in variable NUM is set equal to the number of elements actually read into the array. This variable can be used in loops, for example, and where it is necessary to know the actual number of elements read.

Figure 7-16 is a simple example illustrating the use of the NUM variable. When this program is run, it will prompt the user to type up to 100 numbers. Suppose only 30 numbers are typed before the <Return> key is pressed. We will then see the output line

```
Number of elements entered = 30
```

printed at the terminal CRT. The built-in variable NUM automatically counted the numbers that were entered while the MAT INPUT instruction was executing.

Example 7.13

We will write a program to read numbers into a 100-element array. There may be fewer than 100 numbers. The program will find the average of the numbers actually read in. The pseudocode is:

> Average of partially filled array:
>   Dimension the array
>   Read the array, setting NUM
>   Find the average
>   Print average
> Stop
>
> Find the average:
>   Initialize a sum

> Loop from 1 to NUM
> > Add element to sum
>
> End of loop
> Divide sum by NUM
>
> Return

You can see that the variable NUM is used as the final value for the loop counter to control the number of elements that will be added. Also, when we calculate the average, we will divide the sum by NUM. The code for this program follows:

```
10   ! Average of partially filled array
20       DECLARE REAL      A(100), AVG, SUM
30       GOSUB Input_rtn   ! Read the array
40       GOSUB Find_avg    ! Find the average
50       GOSUB Print_rtn   ! Print the average
60   EXIT PROGRAM

1000 Input_rtn:            ! Read the array
1010     PRINT 'Enter the array, up to 100 numbers'
         MAT INPUT A       ! Sets variable NUM
1020 RETURN

1100 Print_rtn:            ! Print the average
1110     PRINT
         PRINT TAB(25); 'There were '; NUM; ' numbers in the array'
         PRINT TAB(25); 'Their average was '; AVG
         PRINT
1120 RETURN

1500 Find_avg:             ! Find the average
1510     SUM = 0
         FOR I = 1 TO NUM
            SUM = SUM + A(I)
         NEXT I
1520     AVG = SUM / NUM
1530 RETURN

32767 END
```

A sample interaction when the program is run appears below.

```
runnh
Enter the array, up to 100 numbers
75, 80, 85, 90, 95

There were 5 numbers in the array
Their average was 85
```

INPUT USING MAT READ

The MAT READ instruction is similar to MAT INPUT, except that the data are read from DATA statements contained within the program. For example, the two statements:

```
100 MAT READ A
500 DATA 17,58,256,95,14
```

will cause the five numbers in statement 500 to be stored in the array A when statement 100 is executed. If array A is larger than the number of values in the DATA statements, then the excess elements in the array are left unchanged. If the DATA statements have more values than required to fill the array, then the extra values are available for assignment with later READ statements.

OUTPUT USING MAT PRINT

The MAT PRINT statement can be used to print an array. However, it can be used only when the entire array is to be printed. When only part of the array is desired, the MAT PRINT statement cannot be used; a loop is used instead.

Three variations of MAT PRINT can be used:

```
150 MAT PRINT D
150 MAT PRINT D,
150 MAT PRINT D;
```

The first statement will print all of array D, printing one number on each line of the output.

The second statement will also print all of array D, but notice the comma after the array name. Because of that comma, there will be five numbers printed on each line instead of only one (assuming that the margin has been set at 80). This generally makes the output easier to read.

Because of the semicolon, the third statement will print the entire array, but in *packed format*—putting as many numbers as possible on each line of output. All numbers will be separated by at least one blank so that they can be read. In some cases, however, a number at the end of one line could be continued on the next. This usually happens when the numbers are not integers, but it could also happen with integers, depending on the number of digits they contain. Elements of a string array printed in packed format will not have any spaces between values unless spaces are actually part of the data items.

Example 7.14

Read two 100-element arrays, A and B. Enter all the A's first, then all the B's. Now form a third array, C, by adding the corresponding elements of arrays A and B. That is, C(1) = A(1) + B(1), C(2) = A(2) + B(2), etc. Finally, print all elements of array C. As usual, we begin with the pseudocode:

    Adding arrays:
      Enter the arrays
      Add the arrays
      Print array C
    Stop

This translates into the following code:

```
10  ! Adding corresponding array elements
20      DECLARE REAL    A(10), B(10), C(10)
30      GOSUB Array_input    ! Enter the arrays
40      GOSUB Array_add      ! Add the arrays
50      GOSUB Print_routine  ! Print third array
60   EXIT PROGRAM

1000 Array_input:            ! Enter the arrays
1010     PRINT 'Enter 10 elements for A'
         MAT INPUT A
1020     PRINT 'Enter 10 elements for B'
         MAT INPUT B
1030 RETURN

1500 Array_add:              ! Add the arrays
1510     FOR I = 1 TO 10
             C(I) = A(I) + B(I)
         NEXT I
1520 RETURN

2000 Print_routine:          ! Print third array
2010     PRINT
         PRINT "Sums of corresponding elements are:"
         MAT PRINT C,        ! Print array C
         PRINT
2020 RETURN

32767 END
```

All three arrays must be dimensioned, not only the two being read. Array C must be dimensioned so that sufficient space in memory is allocated to store the results when they are calculated.

Each MAT INPUT is preceded by a PRINT instruction, which prints a prompt for the user. You cannot put a prompt into the MAT INPUT instruction as you can with the INPUT statement. The prompt must be printed separately with a PRINT instruction as shown.

Note the form of the MAT INPUT instructions that was used for entering the data, and the MAT PRINT instruction that was used to print the results with five numbers printed on each line.

MAT ASSIGNMENT STATEMENTS

In addition to the MAT input/output instructions of MAT INPUT, MAT READ, and MAT PRINT, VAX-BASIC has a number of other MAT instructions that can be used in assignment statements.

First, there are some statements that can be used to initialize arrays. They use special keywords to set all elements of an array to a specific value. The statements are as follows:

Statement	Purpose
MAT A = ZER	Set all elements of A to 0
MAT A = CON	Set all elements of A to 1
MAT B = NUL$	Set all elements of B to null strings

Array A in the above statements may be REAL or INTEGER; it may not be DECIMAL. Array B must be STRING type.

Second, we have some statements that assign one array to another, with some optional calculations performed along the way. One merely copies all elements of one array into another array. Two others add or subtract corresponding elements of two arrays, and put the result into a third. There is also a MAT statement that multiplies all elements of an array by a scalar quantity. The formats of these statements are:

Statement	Purpose
MAT A = B	Move all elements of B into A
MAT C = A + B	Add corresponding elements of A and B, store them in C
MAT C = A - B	Subtract corresponding elements of B from A, store differences in C
MAT B = (num-expr) * A	Multiply each element of A by the value of the numerical expression

The use of these statements is illustrated in Figure 7-17.

Figure 7-17
Program to Illustrate Use of MAT Assignment Statements

```
10 ! Program to illustrate use of MAT assignment statements
20    DECLARE INTEGER A(5) , B(5), C(5), D(5), E(5), F(5)
30    MAT A = CON          ! All elements of A set to 1
40    MAT B = (5) * A      ! All elements of B become 5
50    MAT READ C           ! C read from DATA statement below
60    MAT D = C + A        ! D becomes 501, 401, 301, 201, 101
70    MAT E = C - B        ! E becomes 495, 395, 295, 195, 95
80    MAT F = (3 / 50) * C ! F becomes 30, 24, 18, 12, 6
90    MAT PRINT A; B; C; D; E; F; ! Print the arrays
1000 DATA 500, 400, 300, 200, 100
32767 END
```

ARRAYS AS ARGUMENTS

An array can be passed to an external subprogram in the argument list. In the CALL statement, the array name is followed by parentheses, as shown in Example 7.15.

Example 7.15

```
30 DECLARE STRING  A(100), REAL B(50)
40 CALL SUBR (A(), B())
```

The subprogram itself would use the same scheme.

```
1000 ! Subprogram with arrays
1010    SUB SUBR (STRING A(), REAL X())
           ...
           ...
        END SUB
```

In the subprogram in Example 7.15, even though array A is matched with the argument A, their names are different entities. This is illustrated with the second array parameter, X, which is matched with the array argument B. Their names, however, are local. The array is called B in the main program and X in the subprogram.

Example 7.16 We will write a program using an external subprogram. The main program will read two arrays, form a third array that is the average of the correspond-

Figure 7-18.
Program That Passes Arrays to External Subroutines

```
10 ! Find average of corresponding elements of 2 arrays
20    DECLARE REAL A(20), B(20), C(20)
30    CALL Read_arrays (A(), B())              ! Read arrays A and B
40    CALL Calculate_C (A(), B(), C())         ! Calculate C
50    CALL Print_C (C())                       ! Print array C
60 END                                         ! End main program

1000 SUB Read_arrays (REAL A(), REAL B())      ! Read arrays A and B
1010    DECLARE INTEGER I
1020    FOR I = 1 TO 20
            INPUT "Enter value for array A"; A(I)
        NEXT I
1030    FOR I = 1 TO 20
            INPUT "Enter value for array B"; B(I)
        NEXT I
1040 END SUB

2000 SUB Calculate_C (REAL A(), REAL B(), REAL C())
2010    DECLARE INTEGER I
2020    FOR I = 1 TO 20
            C(I) = (A(I) + B(I))
        NEXT I
2030 END SUB

3000 SUB Print_C (REAL C())                    ! Print array C
3010    MARGIN 80
3020    DECLARE INTEGER I
3030    PRINT \ PRINT
        FOR I = 1 TO 20
            PRINT C(I),
        NEXT I
3040 END SUB
```

ing elements of the first two, then print the third array. All these processes will be accomplished using external subprograms. The program is shown in Figure 7-18.

Note that each subroutine in Figure 7-18 could have used a MAT statement instead of a loop. Notice how the parameters are declared in the parameter lists of the subprograms, while local variables are declared in DECLARE statements.

8 Terminal-Format Files

Outline

8.1 File Terminology
8.2 The OPEN Statement
8.3 Input/Output With Files
8.4 The CLOSE Statement
8.5 Setting the Margins
Summary
Review Questions
Syntax Exercises
Programming Exercises
Enrichment Topics
MAT Statements

Introduction Prior to this chapter, we have had no way to save the output of one program in a form where it could be used as input to another. Without this capability, computers would not be as important in science, business, and industry as they are today.

In modern computers, data are usually stored on disks in entities called **files.** Files are the topic of this chapter.

8 TERMINAL-FORMAT FILES

8.1 FILE TERMINOLOGY

A very important concept of any computer system is that of a **file.** A file may be compared to a book. Just as a book has paragraphs, a file has records. The fields of a record are analogous to words of a paragraph.

> Field: smallest subdivision; contains one value
> Record: a group of related fields
> File: a group of records

As an example, suppose a file contains the following information:

> Sam, 54, 89
> Joe, 87, 42
> Lil, 75, 82
> Nan, 92, 73

The file consists of four records, each with three fields. The first field of each record is a string field, and the remaining two fields are numeric. The programs that you have been writing and saving on your computer are stored as files, called **BASIC files.**

In this chapter you will learn how to create and read **data files:** files that contain the data required by your program, or that can permanently store the data generated by your program.

The way files are handled varies from one BASIC system to another. The techniques used in this chapter will work for BASIC on most machines by Digital Equipment Corporation, including VAX-BASIC.

VAX-BASIC supports many different types of files. We will mention, and briefly describe, only some of them. Most of these file types are said to be **record-oriented;** i.e., an entire record, consisting of one or more fields, is read from, or printed to the file as a unit. When reading a record from a file, the data pass through an intermediate area, called a **buffer;** the program then separates the record in the buffer into its component fields, and stores these fields in the program variables. When writing to such a file, the process is reversed. See Figure 8-1.

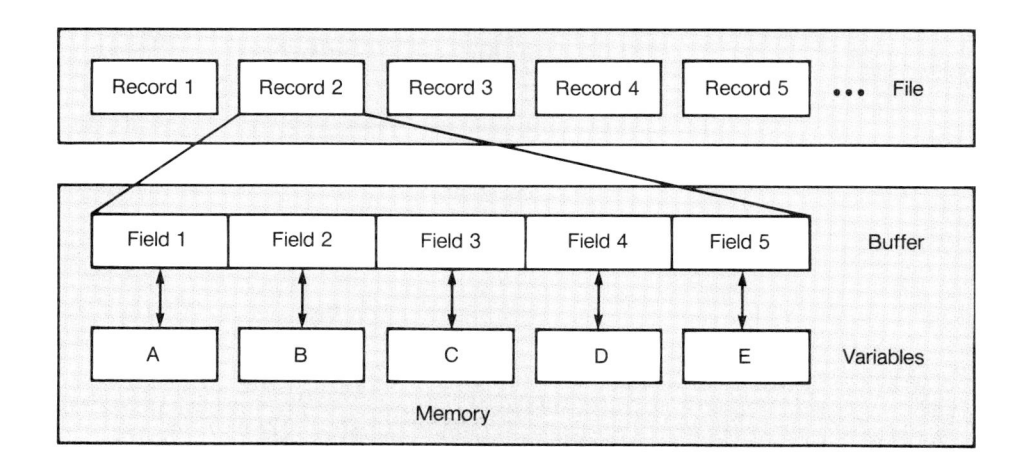

Figure 8-1.
File Buffering

Here are some record-oriented types of files:

1. **Sequential:** A sequential file consists of records that are written or read in sequence from first to last. To access the tenth record, it is necessary to first access the previous nine.
2. **Relative:** The records in the file are numbered sequentially, starting with 1. Therefore, it is possible to access any record by specifying by number which record is desired; it is not necessary to read or write any previous records. A file whose organization is relative is one type of **random access** file. Random access means that records may be accessed in any order. A file that has the relative file organization may also be accessed sequentially, if desired. Relative files will be discussed in chapter 12.
3. **Indexed:** The records in an indexed file contain a **key.** A key is a field that is used to identify the record. For example, the key for a particular file might be the social security number of the person associated with the record, or it might be the part number of the record in an inventory file. A record is accessed by specifying the key. The computer then makes the corresponding record available to the program. An indexed file is also random access because records may be accessed in any order.
4. **Block I/O:** This is a file organization that is more efficient than others. The file consists of a sequence of blocks, where each block consists of 512 bytes or characters. A block is read from the file into a buffer, or vice versa, as a unit. Instead of moving data from the buffer into program variables, the program manipulates data in the buffer directly. The mechanism for using block I/O files is a little more complicated than some of the other types. Block I/O files are also random access files. A block is read or written by specifying the block number.
5. **Virtual arrays:** VAX-BASIC treats virtual array files as if they were arrays. That is, the data are read or written with assignment statements using subscripted variables. No input or output instructions are used in referencing the data. Virtual arrays are a form of random access file.
6. **Terminal-Format:** The data in a terminal-format file are in the same format as data on a terminal; hence the nomenclature. A terminal-format file can be used instead of the terminal keyboard to provide input for a program, and it can be used instead of the screen or printer to receive output. Unlike the terminal, however, once something has been written to a terminal-format file, it can later be read as input to another program. Therefore, it is not necessary to type in the results of one program to be able to use them in another. A terminal-format file must be accessed sequentially.

We will study only the last of these file types, terminal-format files, in this chapter. As it happens, such files are relatively unimportant in production programs. However, they are the easiest to learn, and will give you a good background in file concepts. In chapter 12, we will learn of other, more important, file organizations.

8.2 THE OPEN STATEMENT

Before a file can be used, it must be opened. Opening a file associates a filename with a **channel** number and makes the data accessible. Picture the computer memory as being connected to an old-style telephone switchboard. Each of the sockets on the switchboard would be called a channel. The channels are numbered: channel 1, channel 2, and so on, as shown in Figure 8-2. The memory can read from or write to any file once the file has been connected to one of the channels. The OPEN statement connects a file to one of these channels (electronically, not physically).

The computer does not care which file is connected to which channel. When BASIC does file input, it reads from a channel. Whichever file is connected to that channel will supply the data. The purpose of the OPEN statement is to bridge the gap between the files and the channels. Consider several people who have been at the beach all day. They are so sunburned and so fatigued that they cannot lift their arms. There they sit at a soda counter, staring at the milkshakes that are set before them. Their mouths are the "channels" to their stomachs; the shakes are the "files" whose data they would like to ingest. But there is a gap between the channels and the files. The soda jerk, feeling pity at their plight, sticks one end of a straw in each mouth and the other into a glass. He has connected each "file" to a "channel." The "files" have been "opened." Any mouth could have been connected to any soda by appropriate placement of the straw.

So too, the OPEN statement connects a physical file to a channel. Once connected, the computer can send data between memory and the file via the channel.The OPEN statement has the following syntax:

>   [FOR INPUT]
> sn OPEN filename [   ]AS FILE #channel
>   [FOR OUTPUT]

The items in brackets are optional. If used, only one is permitted per OPEN statement.

On VAX machines, channel numbers may be in the range of 1 through 99. Some examples:

```
10 OPEN "DATA.FIL" FOR INPUT AS FILE #1
10 OPEN Out_file FOR OUTPUT AS FILE #2
10 OPEN "MASTER.FIL" AS FILE #3
10 OPEN In_file FOR INPUT AS FILE #In_channel
```

Figure 8-2.
Diagram of Files,
Channels, and Memory:
No Files Open.

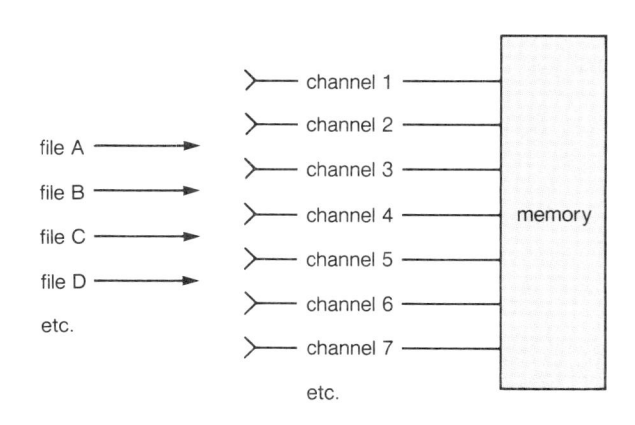

These and other examples are explained later, after some preliminary remarks concerning the OPEN statement.

The OPEN statement associates the filename with a channel number. You may select any channel number you like (within the allowable limits). On Monday you could use channel 1 for your file, while on Tuesday (or later on Monday) you could use channel 2. In the program, the channel number is used instead of the filename.

In the first example above, the filename is DATA.FIL. This is how it appears when you request a DIRectory listing of the files in your account. Because of the OPEN statement, the program will read from the file by reading from channel 1.

Opening a file FOR INPUT means that the file already exists and that we are going to read records from the file into memory. The file will be used instead of the keyboard to supply data to the program. The computer first checks the user's account directory to ascertain that the file exists. If it does not, then an error message is printed at the user's terminal.

Opening a file FOR OUTPUT means that the program will transfer data from memory to the file. The file will be used instead of the CRT screen or printer to receive output. The file will then store these data which can be used at some future time by another program. If a file is opened FOR OUTPUT and a file with the same name already exists in the user's account, then a new version of that file is created. The new file has no data in it initially.

If you accidentally open a file FOR OUTPUT when you meant FOR INPUT, and a file with that name already exists, be sure to DELete the new version, specifying the latest version number. Failure to do so will result in errors the next time you attempt to OPEN the file FOR INPUT. It could also be disastrous if you PURGE your account; only the latest, and useless, version will remain.

Normally, a file that has been opened FOR INPUT will be used with INPUT instructions. The INPUT instruction puts data into memory. A file that has been opened FOR OUTPUT will normally be used with PRINT instructions. The PRINT instruction takes data already in memory and "prints" it to an output device, in this case the file instead of the terminal.

A file that has been opened neither FOR INPUT nor FOR OUTPUT is handled as follows. The computer first searches the user's directory to see if the file already exists. If it does, the file is opened as if it had been opened FOR INPUT. If it does not exist, then a new file is created (containing no data) as if it had been opened FOR OUTPUT.

Example 8.1 | `10 OPEN "DATA.FIL" FOR INPUT AS FILE #1`

This example causes the user's directory to be searched for a file called DATA.FIL (Fig. 8-3). If the file is found, it is opened and associated with channel 1. It can then be used for input operations. (It can also be used for output operations, but this will overwrite some of the data already in the file.) If the file is not found, an error message is printed at the terminal.

Example 8.2 | `10 OPEN Out_file FOR OUTPUT AS FILE #2`

In this example, the user's directory is searched for the file whose name is stored in variable Out_file, a STRING variable. Note that Out_file

Figure 8-3.
Diagram of Files,
Channels, and Memory:
DATA.FIL Opened on
Channel 1.

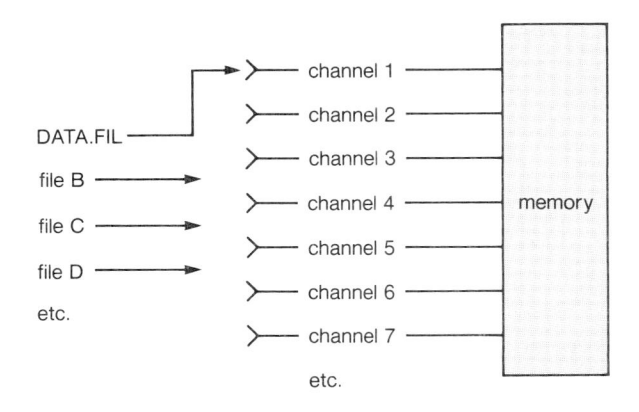

Figure 8-4.
Diagram of Files,
Channels, and Memory:
DATA.FIL Opened on
Channel 1 and OUT.FIL
Opened on Channel 2

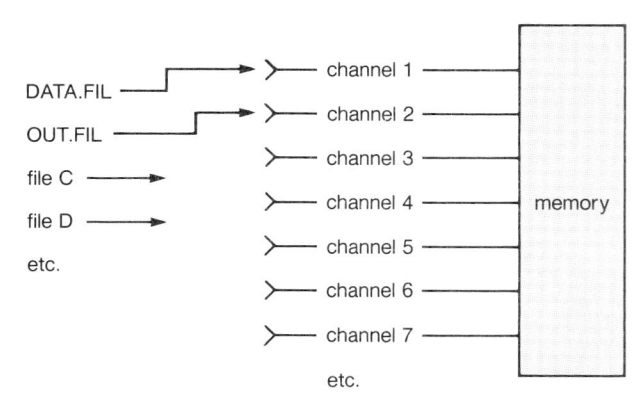

Figure 8-5.
Diagram of Files,
Channels, and Memory:
DATA.FIL Opened on
Channel 1; OUT.FIL
Opened on Channel 2; and
MASTER.FIL Opened on
Channel 3

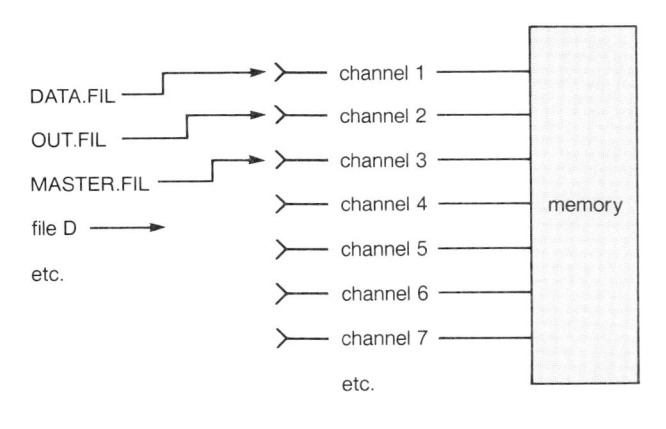

Figure 8-6.
Diagram of Files,
Channels, and Memory:
DATA.FIL Opened on
Channel 1; OUT.FIL
Opened on Channel 2;
MASTER.FIL Opened on
Channel 3; and DATA.IN
Opened on Channel 4

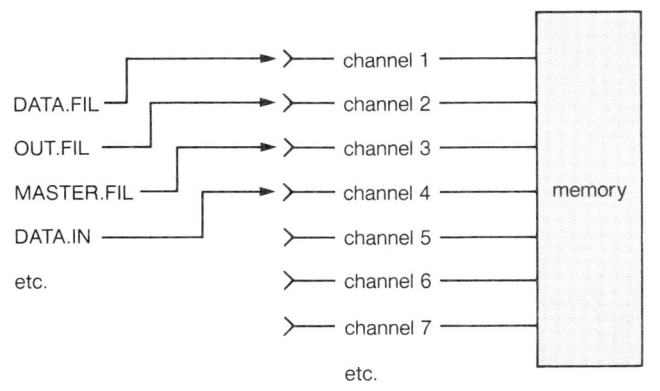

is a variable—it is not in quotes. `Out_file` could be entered using an INPUT instruction, for instance:

```
10    DECLARE STRING Out_file
20    INPUT "Enter file name "; Out_file
      OPEN Out_file FOR OUTPUT AS FILE #2
```

If the user typed OUT.FIL in response to the prompt Enter file name, then the file called OUT.FIL in the user's account would be connected to channel 2 (Fig. 8-4). The INPUT instruction would have to precede the OPEN statement. Once the OPEN statement executes, if the file with the entered filename exists, then a *new* version of the file is created and made ready for output instructions on channel 2. If the file is not found then version 1 of that file is created and is opened on channel 2.

Example 8.3

```
10    OPEN "MASTER.FIL" AS FILE #3
```

In this example, the file named "MASTER.FIL" is connected to channel 3 (Fig. 8-5). If such a file already exists, it is opened as if FOR INPUT had been used. If not, version 1 of the file is created, and opened as if FOR OUTPUT had been specified. Notice that if the program is run a second time, the file that was created the first time will now cause the statement to be treated as if FOR INPUT had been used.

Example 8.4

The channel number can be a variable in the OPEN statement. Consider the following OPEN statement:

```
10    DECLARE STRING In_file, INTEGER In_channel
20    INPUT "Enter the input file name "; In_file
      INPUT "Enter the channel number "; In_channel
      OPEN IN_FILE FOR INPUT AS FILE #In_channel
```

Both the filename and the channel number are first entered into variables. The OPEN statement then uses these variables to connect the typed-in filename to the typed-in channel number. If DATA.IN is typed in response to the first prompt, and the number 4 is typed in response to the second prompt, then file DATA.IN will be connected to channel 4 (Fig. 8-6).

8.3 INPUT/OUTPUT WITH FILES

Input and output using files is as easy as input and output using the terminal. All that is required is an OPEN statement that associates a filename with a channel number, and the use of that channel number in the INPUT and PRINT statements.

The syntax of these I/O statements is:

> **INPUT** #channel, list
> **PRINT** #channel, list

The # symbol is required in these statements.

Examples:

```
10 INPUT #1, A,B,C    ! read 3 nos. from channel 1
20 PRINT #2, X        ! print X to channel 2
```

The channel can be a number or an expression, and it can be either real or integer type. If it is a real type, it will be converted to an integer value by truncation of the fractional part. This is true in any statement that uses a channel number.

```
30 N = 5 \ M = 6
40 PRINT #N, A,B,C    ! Print to channel #5
50 INPUT #M, X,Y,Z    ! Read from channel #6
```

Channel numbers can be in the range of 1 through 99 in VAX-BASIC. In addition, channel 0 refers to the user's own terminal. That is:

```
10 PRINT A,B,C
```

is equivalent to:

```
10 PRINT #0, A,B,C
```

An OPEN statement is not useful for channel #0.

8.4 THE CLOSE STATEMENT

At the end of your program, you must disconnect the file from the channel. We call this **closing the file.** This is particularly important with an output file:

CAUTION! **If an output file is not closed, the last output data may not be printed to the file and may be lost.**

The syntax of the CLOSE statement is:

CLOSE #channel, #channel, . . .

Examples:

```
CLOSE #1              ! close channel 1
CLOSE 2               ! close channel 2
CLOSE #N,#M           ! close channels N and M
CLOSE 1,2,3,N,M       ! close all 5 channels
```

Note that the channel number is required in the CLOSE statement. The filename cannot be used. Unlike the INPUT and PRINT statements, the # symbol is optional in the OPEN and CLOSE statements.

8.5 SETTING THE MARGINS

A terminal file is very much like your CRT screen. Just as your screen has margins, so does your terminal file. There is a slight difference in these margin settings, however. The margins on your screen are usually set to 80 columns or they are not set at all (unlimited). A terminal file is usually set with a margin of 72. Thus if you print a record that is more than 72 characters long, it will appear in the file as more than one record. You will see this if you print the file to the screen or a printer.

Just as the margins on a terminal can be set, so can the margins on a terminal file. Use the MARGIN statement and a channel number:

   sn MARGIN #channel, margin

For example, the statement

```
40 MARGIN #2, 132
```

sets the margin of the file connected to channel #2 to 132. This lets you output records up to that length to the file. Incidentally, 132 is the maximum length permitted for a margin, unless we add another clause to the OPEN statement, which we will not do here.

Margins can be removed from the terminal file altogether. The computer then treats the file as one record of infinite length. This is accomplished with the NOMARGIN statement:

```
40 NOMARGIN #2
```

This statement will remove the margin limit for the file connected to channel 2.

8.6 EXAMPLES

Example 8.5   A file consists of records, each of which contains a name, social security number, hours worked, and hourly pay rate. The last record is a sentinel, with END in the first field and zeros in all the others. The sentinel is not to be processed. We wish to output social security number, name, hours worked, base pay, and salary to a file. The first record of this file will consist of headings, the same as we would use when outputing to the screen. The input file is called `EMPLYE.DAT`; the output file will be `EMPLYE.OUT`.

Let us pseudocode the solution:

```
Payroll:
    Open the input and output files
    Print headings to the output file
    Process the files
    Close the files
Stop
```

The main program will be:

```
10  ! Payroll from file
20       (reserved for DECLARE statement)
30       GOSUB Open_files     ! Open the files
40       GOSUB Headings       ! Print headings
50       GOSUB Process_files  ! Process the files
60       GOSUB Close_files    ! Close the files
70  EXIT PROGRAM
```

The subroutines `Open_files`, `Headings`, and `Close_files` are very short. We will present them when the final solution is written. But the subroutine `Process_files` requires some elaboration:

Process the files:
   Read first record
   Loop while name <> sentinel
     Find the salary
     Output the results
     Read next record
   End of loop
Return

The code for this subroutine will be:

```
2000  ! Process the files
2010       GOSUB Read_rec        ! Read a record
           WHILE NAME. <> 'END'
               SALARY = HRS.WORKED * PAY.RATE
               GOSUB Print_rtn   ! Print results
               GOSUB Read_rec    ! Read next record
           NEXT
2020  RETURN
```

Subroutines `Read_rec` and `Print_rtn` will perform the actual file input and output operations. They present no difficulty and are included in the final program (Fig. 8-7). The program requires file `EMPLYE.DAT` to have been created previously.

The output file can be viewed by leaving BASIC, and using the command TY EMPLYE.OUT from the VMS environment.

The program in Figure 8-7 has been written with I/O data abstraction. If we wish to change the program so that a different input file is used, all we need do is change the first OPEN statement in subroutine `Open_files`. Alternatively, if we want to save the output to a different file, we would change the second OPEN statement. No other changes would have to be made to any other part of the program.

Note also that the margin for the output file was increased to 80 columns. We did this immediately after we opened the file, in line 1020.

Example 8.6 | For this program, we want the same program logic as in Example 8.5, but we would like to be able to enter the names of the data files. We need only

Figure 8-7.
Payroll Program

```
10   ! Payroll from file
20       DECLARE STRING    NAME., SSN, &
             DECIMAL(7,2) HRS.WORKED, PAY.RATE, SALARY
30       GOSUB Open_files        ! Open the files
40       GOSUB Headings          ! Print headings
50       GOSUB Process_files     ! Process the files
60       GOSUB Close_files       ! Close the files
70   EXIT PROGRAM

1000 Open_files:                 ! Open the files.
1010   ! Open input file
       OPEN 'EMPLYE.DAT' FOR INPUT AS FILE #1
1020   ! Open output file
       OPEN 'EMPLYE.OUT' FOR OUTPUT AS FILE #2
       MARGIN #2, 80
1030 RETURN

1500 Headings:                   ! Print headings
1510    PRINT #2, TAB(5); 'SS#'; TAB(15); 'Name'; TAB(40); &
              'Hrs'; TAB(50); 'Rate'; TAB(60); 'Salary'
1520 ! Underline the column headings
        PRINT #2, TAB(5); '---'; TAB(15); '----'; &
              TAB(40); '---'; TAB(50); '----'; &
              TAB(60); '------'
1530    PRINT #2                 ! Skip a line (in the file)
1540 RETURN

2000 Process_files:              ! Process the files
2010    GOSUB Read_rec           ! Read a record
        WHILE NAME. <> 'END'
           SALARY = HRS.WORKED * PAY.RATE
           GOSUB Print_rtn       ! Print results
           GOSUB Read_rec        ! Read next record
        NEXT
2020 RETURN

2100 Read_rec:                   ! Read a record
2110  ! Input is from channel #1
        INPUT #1, NAME., SSN, HRS.WORKED, PAY.RATE
2120 RETURN

2200 Print_rtn:                  ! Print results
2210  ! Output is to channel #2
        PRINT #2, SSN; TAB(15); NAME.; TAB(40); HRS.WORKED; &
              TAB(50); PAY.RATE; TAB(60); SALARY
2220 RETURN

2500 Close_files:                ! Close the files
2510    CLOSE #1, #2
2520 RETURN

32767 END
```

change subroutine `Open_files` as follows:

```
1000 Open_files                    ! Open the files
1010   ! Get names of input and output files
       INPUT 'Enter input filename'; IN_FILE
       INPUT 'Enter output filename'; OUT_FILE
1020   ! Open input file
       OPEN IN_FILE FOR INPUT AS FILE #1
1030   ! Open output file
       OPEN OUT_FILE FOR OUTPUT AS FILE #2
       MARGIN #2, 80
1040 RETURN
```

IN_FILE and OUT_FILE would be variables of the STRING data-type in the DECLARE statement.

Assume that we run the program substituting the above subroutine. If we enter SALARY.IN at the first prompt and SALARY.OUT at the second, then the input data will be taken from the file SALARY.IN and the output (the results) will be written to file SALARY.OUT. The SALARY.IN file will have been previously created, and the SALARY.OUT file will be left in the user's account to be used for later processing or printed from the VMS environment, if desired.

One means of creating a terminal-format file is by writing a program that lets you enter data at the terminal and writes it to a file. When you close the file, the data will be ready to be read by another program.

Another way, which is sometimes better, is to use an editor. From the VMS environment, you can enter the same editor you have been using from BASIC, with one difference: you must specify a filename when you enter the editor from VMS. For example:

EDIT DATA.IN

Once you are in the editor, the commands you will use are the same ones you have been using. When you exit the editor, you will be back in the VMS environment, and the file you created will be in your account.

Example 8.7 This example illustrates some of the problems associated with files and some possible solutions.

We will create a file in which each record contains a name and an amount. A sentinel will be sent to the file as the last record. After the file has been created, we will reopen it for input, read each record, and print the name and the *integer* part of the number. When we try to run the program, however, it does not work. We will discuss the reasons after we write the program. Here is the logic:

    Create and read file:
      Create file
      Read file
    Stop

For "Create file" we have:

    Create file:
      Open the output file for output

      Loop until sentinel is entered
         Enter name and number from terminal
         Print name and number to file
      End of loop
      Close output file
   Return

For "Read file" we have:

Read file:
   Reopen the file, this time for input
   Read first record (priming read)
   Loop until sentinel is read
      Print name and integer part of number
      Read next record
   End of loop
   Close file
Stop

You may have noted that "Create file" does not have a priming read before its loop, while "Read file" does. This is because the first subroutine creates the output file, and we want the sentinel record to be included in that file. The second subroutine processes the data we put into the file, but we do not wish to process the sentinel record itself. Therefore, we must read the record and test for the sentinel before we process it. That is why we need the priming read before the loop and another read at the end of it.

The initial program is shown in Figure 8-8a. Bear in mind that it contains an error.

In line 2020, we have used the built-in function, INT, which, you may recall, returns the integer part of the number sent to it in the parentheses. Therefore, INT(56.784) is 56, while INT(NUMBER) is the integer part of the number stored in location NUMBER.

As we said earlier, there is a bug in this program. When we run the program, we might interact with the computer as follows:

```
Enter name, number (END,0 to end)? ABE LINCOLN,42.87
Enter name, number (END,0 to end)? BETTY BOOP,56.28
Enter name, number (END,0 to end)? CHARLIE TUNA,-14.3
Enter name, number (END,0 to end)? END,0
File created
```

The file DATA.DAT will contain the following records:

```
ABE LINCOLN      42.87
BETTY BOOP       56.28
CHARLIE TUNA    -14.3
END              0
```

Note carefully the following point: The output file contains no commas between items in the record. We have the first name, a blank, the second name, several blanks, and the number.

The lack of commas between fields in the file records causes the second part of the program to fail. When the INPUT instructions at line 2020 are

Figure 8-8a.
Program Containing an Error that Creates and Accesses a File

```
10  ! Create and read a file
20       DECLARE STRING   NAME_, REAL NUMBER
30       GOSUB Create_file     ! Create the file
40       GOSUB Read_file       ! Read the file
50    EXIT PROGRAM

1000 Create_file:              ! Create the file
1010    OPEN "DATA.DAT" FOR OUTPUT AS FILE #1
1020    WHILE NAME_ <> "END"
           INPUT 'Enter name, number (END,0 to end)'; NAME_, NUMBER
           PRINT #1, NAME_, NUMBER
        NEXT
1030    CLOSE 1                ! File complete
        PRINT 'File created'   ! Keep user informed
1040 RETURN

2000 Read_file:                ! Read the file
2010    OPEN "DATA.DAT" FOR INPUT AS FILE #1
2020    INPUT #1, NAME_, NUMBER ! Priming read
        WHILE NAME_ <> "END"
           PRINT NAME_, INT(NUMBER)
           INPUT #1, NAME_, NUMBER
        NEXT
2030    CLOSE #1
2040 RETURN

32767 END
```

executed, they read a string into the variable NAME_. Strings are ended with commas or carriage returns (end of line), not spaces. Therefore, the entire first record, including the number, is read into NAME_ with the priming read at line 2020. To get NUMBER, the computer will have to read the second record. But NUMBER is a numeric variable and the second record begins with a string, BETTY, so an error occurs and the program crashes.

There are three ways to fix this problem. The first is to include a comma in the output record by using the statement:

PRINT #1, NAME_; ',', NUMBER

at line 1020. Note the comma in quotation marks. This will put a comma into the record in the output file. The file will now look like this:

```
ABE LINCOLN,    42.87
BETTY BOOP,     56.28
CHARLIE TUNA,  -14.3
END,            0
```

The commas will serve as delimiters for the strings in the INPUT statements at line 2020.

A second solution is to use two PRINT statements in line 1020, so that the string is in one record, delimited with a carriage return, and the number is in another record. We replace the PRINT statement in line 1020 with:

```
PRINT #1, NAME_
PRINT #1, NUMBER
```

Each PRINT statement will create a new record, or line, in the output file. The file will contain the following records:

```
ABE LINCOLN
 42.87
BETTY BOOP
 56.28
CHARLIE TUNA
-14.3
END
 0
```

Each of the INPUT instructions at line 2020 will read two records to satisfy its list requirements. The first record will be read into `NAME_`, and the second into `NUMBER`.

The third, and best, method is to read the entire record, including name and number, into one string variable. String functions, discussed in chapter 9, can then separate the string into two strings: the part with the name and the part with the number. Then the string function VAL can convert the numeric string into an arithmetic value. We are not ready at this time to illustrate this solution. We will do so in chapter 9.

Study Example 8.7 carefully. It explains a great deal concerning the use of files. One version of the corrected program appears in Figure 8-8b.

There are two changes between this program and the previous version of Fig. 8-8a. One change is in the PRINT statement of line 1020. The other is in the WHILE conditions of lines 1020 and 2020. We have allowed the user to enter the sentinel END in either upper or lower case. This will eliminate the most anticipated error when the program is run. A TAB function has also been added to improve the appearance of the output.

Example 8.8   We are going to create a system of two programs. The first will allow a teacher to enter a name and five test marks for each of his students. The second program will calculate each student's average and letter grade, and then print the student's name, average, and letter grade.

The first program requires entering the data at the terminal and printing it to the file. As explained in Example 8.7, we will print a comma between each item in the record. The pseudocode is:

```
Create student file of test grades:
    Open the output file
    Loop until sentinel
        Enter data from terminal
        Print data to file, separated with commas
    End of loop
    Close file
Stop
```

Figure 8-8b.
Corrected Program to
Create and Access a File

```
10  ! Create and read a file
20      DECLARE STRING    NAME_, REAL NUMBER
30      GOSUB Create_file      ! Create the file
40      GOSUB Read_file        ! Read the file
50   EXIT PROGRAM

1000 Create_file:              ! Create the file
1010    OPEN "DATA.DAT" FOR OUTPUT AS FILE #1
1020    WHILE NAME_ <> "END" AND NAME_ <> "end"
          INPUT 'Enter name, number (END,0 to end)'; NAME_, NUMBER
          PRINT #1, NAME_; ',', NUMBER
        NEXT
1030    CLOSE 1                ! File complete
        PRINT
        PRINT 'File created'   ! Keep user informed
        PRINT
1040 RETURN

2000 Read_file:                ! Read the file
2010    OPEN "DATA.DAT" FOR INPUT AS FILE #1
2020    INPUT #1, NAME_, NUMBER ! Priming read
        WHILE NAME_ <> "END" AND NAME_ <> "end"
          PRINT TAB(25); NAME_, INT(NUMBER)
          INPUT #1, NAME_, NUMBER
        NEXT
2030    CLOSE #1
2040 RETURN

32767 END
```

This is a very simple program that involves only input and output. We will not decompose it into subroutines. The code follows. Note that a variable, COMMA, is defined to contain a comma. When a comma is to be printed, we merely print COMMA.

```
10 ! Create file of student test grades
20      DECLARE STRING    NAME_, COMMA, &
                INTEGER   GRADE1, GRADE2, GRADE3, GRADE4, GRADE5
30   ! Open the output file
        OPEN "CLASS.TST" FOR OUTPUT AS FILE 1
40      COMMA = ","            ! Define COMMA as a comma
50   ! Create the output file
        UNTIL NAME_ = "END" OR NAME_ = "end"    ! Start of loop
          INPUT "Enter name, 5 grades (END,0,0,0,0,0 to end) "; &
                NAME_, GRADE1, GRADE2, GRADE3, GRADE4, GRADE5
          PRINT #1, NAME_; COMMA; GRADE1; COMMA; GRADE2; &
                COMMA; GRADE3; COMMA; GRADE4; COMMA; GRADE5
        NEXT
60      CLOSE 1                ! Close file
70   END
```

When this program is run, the last record entered at the terminal must be the sentinel record, END, and the grades can all be zeros.

Now for the second program. The file we have just created, CLASS.TST, must be read. For each record, we must calculate the average and letter grade, and then print those together with the name. For more flexibility, we will allow the selection of the output filename at run time. Here is the pseudocode:

> Student grades from file:
>   Open the input and output files
>   Process student records
>   Close the files
> Stop

In creating the output file, we want the last record to be a sentinel. We will accomplish this by not using a priming read when we read the input file, so that the input sentinel record will be processed like any other record and transferred to the output file. For "Process student records" we have:

> Process student records:
>   Loop while not the sentinel
>   Read record from input file
>   Find student average
>   Assign letter grade based on average
>   Print result to output file
>   End of loop
> Return

The code will enable us to enter the output filename, but will use the previously created file CLASS.TST as the input file. In that way, the instructor will be able to direct the output to a different file each time the program is run.

In addition, we will perform an error check to protect the instructor from his own folly. If the teacher were to inadvertently enter the input filename when requested to enter the output filename, then the input file would be destroyed when the account is PURGEd. Therefore, we will check the name he enters. If it is the same as the input filename, we will inform him of that fact and ask that he enter a different output filename. This error check will be performed in a loop, and he will be unable to proceed until an acceptable name is entered. The pseudocode for this section is:

> Prompt for output filename
> While output filename = input filename
>   Print error message
>   Prompt for new output filename
> End of loop

This logic will be incorporated into the subroutine that opens the files. The remainder of the program is nearly the same as that of a problem done in an earlier chapter, so we will not show the pseudocode here.

Figure 8-9 is the code for this program. Keep in mind that the input file is called CLASS.TST.

8 TERMINAL-FORMAT FILES

Figure 8-9.
Class Grading Program

```
10  ! Program to calculate grades from a file
20      DECLARE STRING   NAME., OUT_FILE, GRADE, &
                INTEGER  TEST1, TEST2, TEST3, TEST4, TEST5, &
                REAL     AVG
30      GOSUB Open_files      ! Open the files
40      GOSUB Process_recs    ! Process student records
50      GOSUB Close_files     ! Close the files
60      PRINT \ PRINT "Done" \ PRINT
70   EXIT PROGRAM

1000 Open_files:              ! Open the files
1010 ! Get the output filename
        INPUT "Enter output filename "; OUT_FILE
        WHILE OUT_FILE = "CLASS.TST" OR OUT_FILE = "class.tst"
            PRINT
            PRINT "Cannot use CLASS.TST"
            INPUT "Enter output filename "; OUT_FILE
        NEXT
1020 ! Open the files
        OPEN "CLASS.TST" FOR INPUT AS FILE #1
        OPEN OUT_FILE FOR OUTPUT AS FILE #2
1030 RETURN

1100 Close_files:             ! Close the files
1110    CLOSE #1, #2
1120 RETURN

2000 Process_recs:            ! Process student record
2010    WHILE NAME. <> "END" AND NAME. <> "end"
            GOSUB Read_rec        ! Read student record
            GOSUB Find_avg        ! Find average
            GOSUB Assign_grade    ! Assign letter grade
            GOSUB Output_rtn      ! Output
        NEXT
2020 RETURN

2100 Read_rec:                ! Read student record
2110    INPUT #1, NAME., TEST1, TEST2, TEST3, TEST4, TEST5
2120 RETURN

2200 Find_avg:                ! Find average
2210    AVG = (TEST1 + TEST2 + TEST3 + TEST4 + TEST5) / 5
2220 ! Round AVG to nearest integer
        AVG = INT( AVG + .5)
2230 RETURN

2300 Assign_grade:            ! Assign letter grade
2310    IF AVG < 60 THEN GRADE = 'F'
        ELSE IF AVG < 70 THEN GRADE = 'D'
        ELSE IF AVG < 80 THEN GRADE = 'C'
        ELSE IF AVG < 90 THEN GRADE = 'B'
```

Figure 8-9. (*Cont.*)

```
         ELSE GRADE = 'A'
         END IF   END IF   END IF   END IF
2320 RETURN

2400 Output_rtn:              ! Output routine
2410    PRINT #2, NAME.; ',';AVG; ','; GRADE
2420 RETURN

32767 END
```

At line 2220, we have again used the INT function to find the integer part of a number. In this case, we use it to round the average to the nearest integer using a well-known technique: We add 0.5 to the quantity that is to be rounded, then take the integer part of the result. Because the INT function drops the fractional part no matter how large it is, adding 0.5 causes any number whose fractional part is larger than 0.5 to become the next higher integer. When the fraction is dropped, the number will be rounded up. On the other hand, if the number has a fractional part less than 0.5, adding one-half will not cause the integer part of the number to increase; dropping the fractional part will now have the effect of rounding down.

Note the manner in which letter grades have been assigned in statement 2310. Each ELSE means that all previous conditions have failed. This simplifies the assignment of the correct letter grade. As soon as one of the conditions is true, GRADE is assigned the correct grade and control passes to the RETURN statement. The final ELSE is for all averages that are 90 or higher, after all the other conditions have failed. A SELECT-CASE statement could have been used instead, as shown below:

```
2310       SELECT AVG
              CASE 0 TO 59
                 GRADE = 'F'
              CASE 60 TO 69
                 GRADE = 'D'
              CASE 70 TO 79
                 GRADE = 'C'
              CASE 80 TO 89
                 GRADE = 'B'
              CASE 90 TO 100
                 GRADE = 'A'
           END SELECT
```

Example 8.9 We will write a subroutine that will be able to open either a file or the user's keyboard as an input device. Remember that input from channel #0 is the same as input from the terminal. (Likewise, printing to channel #0 is the same as printing to the terminal.) The subroutine will ask the user for an input file name. If the user responds with a <Return>, the terminal will be opened for keyboard entry; if a file name is supplied, that file will be opened. The subroutine is coded below.

```
1000 Open_input_file:                  ! Open the input file
1010    INPUT "Enter filename, <Return> for keyboard"; In_file
1020    IF In_file = "" THEN Channel = 0
        ELSE
            Channel = 1
            OPEN In_file FOR INPUT AS FILE #Channel
        END IF
1030 RETURN
```

Channel is an INTEGER variable. It is set to 0 if the keyboard is selected and no file is OPENed for that case. On the other hand, if a file is to be used, the variable Channel is set to 1, and the file opened on that channel.

The input routine has to test the value of Channel. If it is 0, then a prompt must be printed for the user; if it is not 0, then a prompt should not be printed. The input routine can be coded as follows:

```
1200 Input_routine:                    ! Input from terminal or file
1210    ! Print prompt for keyboard input
        IF Channel = 0 THEN PRINT "Enter 3 numbers "; END IF
1220    ! Enter data from selected channel, possibly keyboard
        INPUT #Channel, A, B, C
1230 RETURN
```

You can see that the channel number is a variable in both the OPEN and INPUT statements. It is this that lets us select either the keyboard or the file as the source of the input data.

Output can be handled in a similar manner. Again, channel 0 will output to the terminal screen or printer. Any other channel can be opened to print to a disk file.

SUMMARY

In this chapter, we introduced the concept of files and gave several examples. A file is used whenever input or output does not use the user's terminal or printer. With files, I/O instructions can use a permanent file in the user's account for input or output data. In fact, the file can reside in an account different from that of the user. For instance, your teacher may want to create a data file in his account and ask you to write a program that will process the data in his file.

The following statements are needed to use files; specifically, terminal-format files.

1. The OPEN statement is used to gain access to a file. A file may be opened FOR INPUT, which allows data from the file to be read, or it may be opened FOR OUTPUT, which allows data to be written to the file. The syntax is:

OPEN file [FOR INPUT | FOR OUTPUT] AS FILE #channel

2. INPUT #channel and PRINT #channel are the I/O instructions needed to input from or print to the file. #channel is the FILE # as specified in the OPEN statement. The syntax is:

INPUT #channel, list
PRINT #channel, list

3. The CLOSE statement closes the file. This is especially important for an output file. Failure to close such a file may result in loss of data. The syntax is:

CLOSE [#]channel [, . . .]

REVIEW QUESTIONS

1. What is a field? What is a record? What is a file?
2. What is a sequential file? What is a random access file? How do they differ?
3. What is a terminal-format file?
4. What is the purpose of the OPEN statement?
5. What is the difference between opening a file FOR INPUT and opening it FOR OUTPUT?
6. What is the purpose of the CLOSE statement?
7. What are channel numbers? How are they used in I/O instructions?
8. Write an OPEN statement that would allow you to read data from the file CLASS.DAT.
9. Write an OPEN statement that would allow you to print data to a file whose name is stored in the variable OUT.FILE.
10. What is the range of channel numbers that can be used in an OPEN statement in VAX-BASIC?

SYNTAX EXERCISES

The following statements contain one or more errors. Find and correct them.

1. `30 OPEN "Input.dat" FOR INPUT AS #1`
2. `30 OPEN "Data.Dat" FOR OUTPUT AS #2`
3. `30 OPEN "Salaries' FOR INPUT`
4. `30 OPEN "Grades FOR OUTPUT" AS FILE #3`
5. `30 OPEN "Inventory FOR INPUT" AS FILE #5`
6. `30 INPUT "Enter filename"; Data_in`
   `   OPEN "Data_in" FOR INPUT AS FILE #1`
7. `30 INPUT "Enter filename"; Data_out`
   `   OPEN "Data_out" FOR OUTPUT AS FILE #2`
8. `1030 INPUT #1; A; B; C`
9. `1030 INPUT #2; NO.1, NO.2`
10. `1030 INPUT 1, Name, Address`
11. `1030 INPUT 5, Description, Price`
12. `2030 PRINT #2; A; B; C`
13. `2030 PRINT #3; Name, Address`
14. `2030 PRINT 1, No.1, No.2`
15. `2030 PRINT 3, Grade_1, Grade_2, Grade_3`

PROGRAMMING EXERCISES

Write subroutines or programs, properly modularized, that will solve the following problems.

■   **1a.** Write OPEN statements that will open an input file called STORY.DOC and an output file called FILE.OUT.

1b. A file called `STORY.DOC` contains a story. Read the file and print the story. The last record of the file is 'The end.'

2. Each record in a file called `SALES.DAT` contains:
   a. A social security number
   b. A name
   c. Five sales

The last record is a sentinel:

```
000-00-0000, 'NONAME', 0, 0, 0, 0, 0
```

Process the file as follows:

For each salesman, sum his sales and calculate his salary, which is $200.00 plus 10% of his total sales. Print the salesman's name, total sales, and salary.

3. Same as Exercise 2, but perform additional calculations to find the salesman who had the highest sales. Print the name of that salesman and a message that he is the winner of a trip to the Caribbean.

4a. Write a subroutine that reads numbers from a file connected to channel #1 and finds the smallest of these numbers. The last number in the file is the sentinel −999.

4b. Each record in a file called `GRADES` contains a name, a social security number, and five test marks. A sentinel containing the social security number 000-00-0000 is the last record. The instructor wants a program that processes the file and produces term grades. Specifically, he wants each student's term average and letter grade after dropping the lowest test mark. Output should consist of the social security number, the name, the term average, and the letter grade. The printout should have proper headings.

5a. Write a subroutine that uses the random number generator to create a file of 100 random integers in the range of 5000 to 10,000.

5b. Write a subroutine that reads the file created in part a, and find the largest number in the file.

5c. Write a program that does the following: Use the random number generator to create a file of 100 random integers in the range 5000 through 10,000. Close the file, reopen it FOR INPUT, read all the numbers, find the largest number, and print that number with suitable identification.

6a. Write a subroutine that reads 50 numbers from a file called `NUMBERS.DAT` and stores them into an array.

6b. Write a subroutine that reads 50 records, each containing a name and social security number, and stores them into two associated arrays.

6c. Enter 50 records from a file called `NUMBERS.DAT`. Each record is to contain a name, social security number, and address. The data are to be stored in three associated arrays.

Sort the records by name, keeping all associated data together. Then put the records into a new version of the original file. Write the program.

7. Read a file in which each record contains a name and a social security number. Create a file in which the records are sorted by name, and another file in which they are sorted by social security number. Be sure to keep each name with its corresponding social security number. The last record of the input file is XXXX, 000-00-0000. This record is to be written as the last record of each output file but is *not* to be included in the sorts.

8a. A file connected to channel 1 consists of an arbitrary number of alphabetically sorted words. Another file connected to channel 2 contains another sorted list of words. The last word in each file is the sentinel ZZZZ. Write a subroutine that reads the two files and writes the words to another file connected to channel 3 so that the third file is also sorted. This procedure is called a **merge**.

8b. Each of two files, WORDS.1 and WORDS.2, contains an alphabetically sorted list of words. Write a program that will merge the two files to produce a combined list of words, still in alphabetical order. The new file is to be called WORDS.ALL. The last word in each file, including the output file, is the sentinel ZZZZ. HINT: Comparing strings is identical to comparing numbers. The comparisons are done according to ASCII codes.

9a. A file connected to channel 5 contains an arbitrary number of 1's, followed by an arbitrary number of 2's, then an arbitrary number of 3's, and so on, up to an arbitrary number of 10's. Write a subroutine that counts the number of 1's, the number of 2's, and so on, and stores these counts in a 10-element array.

9b. Each record in a file contains the following data: department number, item number, number of units sold, and cost per unit. The file is sorted by department number. Write a program that will print a report with the following format:

DEPT NUMBER	ITEM NUMBER	UNITS SOLD	COST PER UNIT	SALES IN DOLLARS
1	1	20	10.00	200.00
1	2	30	15.00	450.00
1	3	10	50.00	500.00
TOTAL DEPT. 1		60		1150.00
2	5	20	25.00	500.00
2	7	5	40.00	200.00
TOTAL DEPT. 2		25		700.00
GRAND TOTALS		XXX		XXXXX.XX

Keep in mind that the file is sorted and that it contains all the data in the order required. The last record in the file is a sentinel 999, 999, 999, 999.

10. A file has records as follows: The first record is the number of customers, and subsequent records contain information regarding customers. For each customer, there are four fields: social security number in the form XXX-XX-XXXX; name; address; and account balance. Read these records into associated arrays of 100 elements.

Additional input will come from the terminal and will consist of three items: social security number; an integer, which will be a 1 or a 2; and an amount, which represents either a charge or a payment.

If the integer is 1, then the amount is a charge to the individual's account and is added to the balance. If the integer is a 2, then the amount is a payment and is subtracted from the balance. The social security number is used to determine whose balance is affected.

The process is to be repeated until the social security number 000-00-0000 is entered. After that, all data are to be printed in a report and the file rewritten to reflect the new balances. Be sure to make the first record equal to the number of customers.

11a. A file connected to channel 1 contains inventory records. Each record contains the quantity on hand and the price of a part in the warehouse. The last record contains a price of 0, and is an end-of-file sentinel.

Write a subroutine that will read the file and store the data into two associated arrays. Assume that the file contains no more than 100 different parts.

11b. Write a simplified inventory control program. Inventory control is used by people in charge of warehouses to keep track of the amount of goods in storage. The program will have to keep track of the quantity and price of various items, be able to update the contents of the file by rewriting it, and make periodic reports.

The data are kept in a file called `INVENTORY`. Each record contains the quantity, price, and description of one part in the warehouse. The program will have to give the user the following choices:

  a. Add a new part number to the list
  b. Increase the quantity on hand of an item
  c. Decrease the quantity on hand of an item
  d. Change the price of an item
  e. Prepare a report
  f. Read data from the file
  g. Write data to the file
  h. End the program

"Read" the file will mean storing the quantity, price, and description of each record into three associated arrays. The first record is for part number 1, and should be stored in the first element of each array. The second is for part number 2, and should be stored in the second element of each array, and so forth. Therefore, the part number is the subscript of the array in which the three items of each record are kept. For example, `QUANTITY(26)` will be the quantity of part number 26 on hand in the warehouse. The price of each part will be in the associated array called `PRICE`. `PRICE(26)` will be the price of part number 26. Of course, `PART.DESC(26)` would be the part description of part number 26—"right-angled frammis", for example.

Write a menu-driven program in which each function above is executed with a separate subroutine. For choice **e**, a report showing the part number, description, quantity, and price should be printed, with proper column headings.

The program should include a safety feature. If the user selects choice **h** to quit the program, he should first be reminded to save the data to a file, then asked if he really wants to quit. If he answers no, then he should be returned to the menu to make another selection.

12. A biologist wants to investigate the effect of noise pollution on the growth of rats. He takes 100 newborn rats and subjects each to a different constant noise level for two months. At the end of the two months, he weighs each rat and stores the data in a file `RAT.WGT`. Each record contains the noise level in db (decibels), and the weight of the corresponding rat in grams.

The biologist wants to calculate a measure called the **correlation coefficient.** Values of this measure are between -1 and $+1$. A correlation coefficient of 0 means that there is no relationship between noise level and weight; 1 means a perfect positive correlation—as noise level goes up, weight goes up proportionally; and -1 means a perfect negative correlation—as noise level goes up, weight goes down proportionally.

The correlation coefficient is calculated with the formula:

$$r = \frac{N\Sigma XY - (\Sigma X)(\Sigma Y)}{\sqrt{N\Sigma X^2 - (\Sigma X)^2} \sqrt{N\Sigma Y^2 - (\Sigma Y)^2}}$$

where

N = number of data points (in this case, 100)
ΣX = $X(1) + X(2) + \ldots + X(100)$, where the X's are the noise level
ΣY = $Y(1) + Y(2) + \ldots + Y(100)$, where the Y's are the weights
ΣX^2 = $X(1)^2 + X(2)^2 + \ldots + X(100)^2$
ΣY^2 = $Y(1)^2 + Y(2)^2 + \ldots + Y(100)^2$
ΣXY = $X(1) * Y(1) + X(2) * Y(2) + \ldots + X(100) * Y(100)$

a. Write a subroutine that reads the 100 records from the file into two associated arrays—one to store the decibel level and one to store the weight of the corresponding rat.
b. Write a subroutine that forms the five sums shown in the equation above for the 100 rats, given the two associated arrays formed in part a.
c. Write a subroutine that finds the correlation coefficient, given the five sums formed by the subroutine of part b.
d. Write a program that reads the records from the file into two associated arrays for noise level and weight, and then calculates and prints the correlation coefficient.

13. Refer to Exercise 12. Instead of the correlation coefficient, the biologist wants the equation of the straight line that best fits the 100 points of data. This line is called the **regression line,** and can be used to make predictions concerning the weight of untested rats. The regression line formula is:

$$\tilde{Y} = \mu_Y + b(X - \mu_X)$$

where

μ_X = the mean of the X's (noise levels)
μ_Y = the mean of the Y's (weights)
$\tilde{Y}$ = the estimate for a weight when a noise level, X, is given
b = the slope given by:

$$b = \frac{N\Sigma XY - \Sigma X \Sigma Y}{N\Sigma X^2 - (\Sigma X)^2}$$

where the summations are as defined in Exercise 12.

Write a program that reads the file into two associated arrays, then calculates and prints the two means μ_Y and μ_Y, and the slope b.

ENRICHMENT TOPICS 8

MAT File Statements

VAX-BASIC allows you to use MAT statements to read from, or write to, a file. The syntax of these statements is:

> **MAT INPUT #channel, array-name**

and

> **MAT PRINT #channel, array-name[,|;]**

The effect of these MAT statements is identical to the effect they have on the terminal, except they work with terminal-format files instead. For instance, note that the MAT PRINT statement may be followed by a comma or semicolon; the effect of either on the file is the same as it would be for the terminal—five items per line or packed format, respectively.

Care must be taken when using these statements. Just as data must be separated by commas when input is from the terminal, the input file for a MAT INPUT must have commas between data values. Just as all data must be entered at the terminal before pressing <Return>, all data in the file that will be entered into one array must appear in the file in one record before a <Return>.

A MAT PRINT to the file will print the entire array exactly as it would be printed to the terminal. In particular, data values will *not* be separated by commas, and each row of the array will be terminated with a <Return>, regardless of the MARGIN set for the file. This means that A FILE CREATED WITH A MAT PRINT CANNOT BE READ WITH A MAT INPUT.

B Programming Tool: Error Trapping

Outline

B.1 Error Traps—ON ERROR GO TO
B.2 Some Useful Built-in Variables
  ERR Built-in Variable
  ERL Built-in Variable
  ERT$ Built-in Function
B.3 Severity of Errors
B.4 The RESUME Statement
  RESUME Without Line Number
  RESUME With Line Number
B.5 Returning Errors to the System
B.6 Examples
B.7 Error Handler Criteria
Review Questions
Programming Exercises
Enrichment Topics
  Error Trapping in Subprograms
    ON ERROR GO BACK
    The ERN$ Built-in Variable

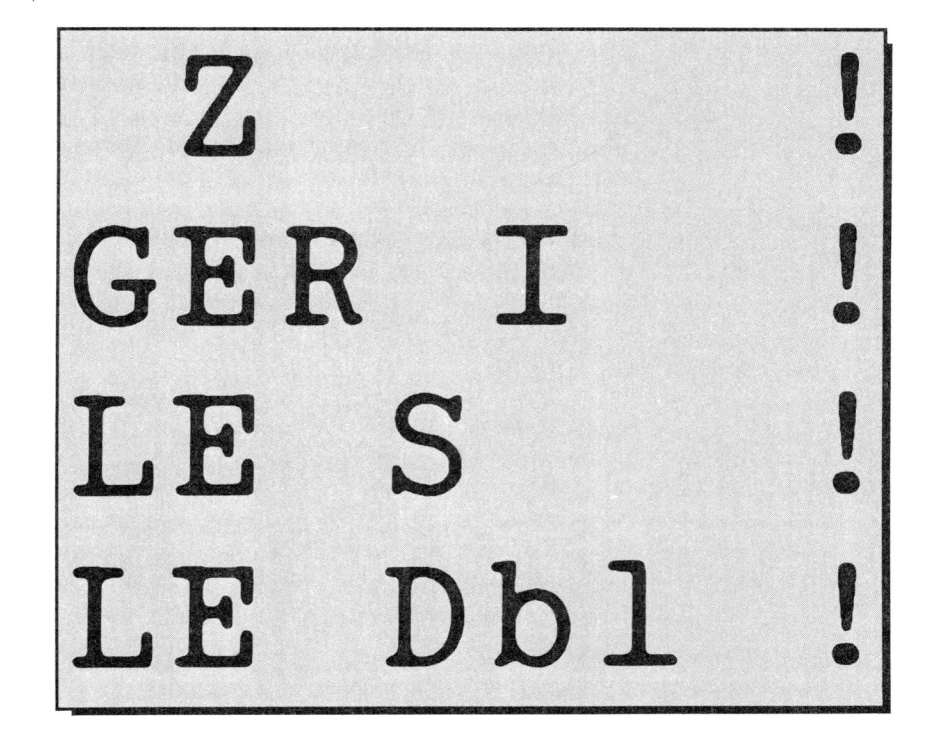

Introduction This chapter is optional. It contains material that is important, but can be omitted in a first course. Careless use of the material taught in this chapter may lead to unstructured programs. Be careful!

By now, you may have discovered that your programs frequently "crash" because of errors. Sometimes, you would like to ignore the error after it occurs and continue executing the program. To do so, you must find a means of preventing the program from being aborted by the system. This is called **error trapping** and is the subject of this chapter.

B.1 ERROR TRAPS—ON ERROR GO TO

When you were little, you may have been told: "Do not go into the street or you will be punished." Did you get punished immediately? Later? At all? That depends on what you did. A rule was set up: If a certain event occurs from this point on, then a certain action will take place. An error trap was set up.

An error trap is a rule you establish within your program. By means of the command, shown below, you tell the computer, "If an error should take place in my program from this point on, please invoke an error routine that I have written, and I will handle the error myself." The statement used to set up this rule is:

```
ON ERROR GOTO Error_handler
```

Note that GOTO may be written as two words, GO TO. `Error_handler` is a user-defined arbitrary name. It is the label of the error routine you will write in which you plan to process errors. An error routine is similar to a subroutine, but there are some significant differences, which will be discussed later.

You may have several error routines in your program, if desired. When your program first starts to execute, you can use the statement

```
ON ERROR GOTO Error_routine_1
```

If an error occurs, `Error_routine_1` will be used to handle the error. Later in the program, you can execute the statement

```
ON ERROR GOTO Error_routine_2
```

and from then on, `Error_routine_2` will be used to handle errors. Usually, you will have only one error handler in your program, if you have one at all.

You may override all of your error routines and return error handling back to BASIC by executing the statement

```
ON ERROR GOTO 0
```

Because the ON ERROR statement sets up the rule as to which error handler is to be used, the statement must execute *before* an error occurs. Therefore, it will usually be placed in the main program as the *first* executable statement. The error handler itself may be placed anywhere in the program; like a subroutine, it will not be executed until it is invoked. We will put our error routines at line 19000 in our programs, as recommended by DEC in its program protocol.

B.2 SOME USEFUL BUILT-IN VARIABLES

Before we begin to write our error routines, we will learn about three significant built-in variables that will be of use when an error occurs in our program. They are ERR, ERL, and ERT$.

ERR Built-in Variable

Each error that can occur in a BASIC program has been assigned an error number (refer to appendix 2). When an error occurs, the built-in variable ERR is set to the error number. So, if you attempted division by zero, the ERR variable would be set to 61, the division-by-zero error number. If you attempted to read a file that had no more data, then ERR would be set to 11. The STOP instruction you have been using to debug your programs (which causes that strange two-line message) is also considered an "error" by BASIC. It causes ERR to take on the value 123. As you will see, this particular STOP "error" is only a warning, and it is possible to recover from a warning. In this case, you can continue by typing CONT.

We will be using ERR in our error routine to determine the type of error that was trapped.

ERL Built-in Variable

When an error occurs, the ERL variable is set equal to the line number of the statement that caused the error. So, if line number 1050 contained a statement that attempted division by zero, then ERL would be set to 1050. (ERR would be 61, as described above.)

ERT$ Built-in Function

The ERT$ function returns the error message that corresponds to a particular error, as listed in appendix 2. The statement

```
Message = ERT$(61)
```

would store the string ?Division by 0 in the STRING variable Message. ERT$(ERR) returns the error text corresponding to the error number in variable ERR. In fact, appendix 2 was created by running the following program.

```
10  ! Create error text file
20    DECLARE INTEGER I
30    OPEN "ERROR.TXT" FOR OUTPUT AS FILE #1
40    FOR I = 0 TO 255
          PRINT #1, I, ERT$(I)
      NEXT I
50    CLOSE #1
60  END
```

Different versions of VAX-BASIC may have different errors defined. The errors that apply to your system may always be determined by running the above program on your machine, and examining the file ERROR.TXT when it has finished executing.

B.3 SEVERITY OF ERRORS

As you examine the error messages in appendix 2, you will see that some error messages are preceded by a question mark, ?, others by a percent symbol, %, and others by neither. These symbols indicate the severity of the error.

If an error message is preceded by a question mark, the error can be trapped. You can supply an error handler to fix the error, or you can bypass it and continue processing.

If an error message is preceded by a percent symbol, the error is fatal and cannot be fixed with an error handler. The program is destined to abort.

If the error message is preceded by neither of these, the error is merely a warning. Execution may continue even if you do not trap the error and supply an error handler. As mentioned above, one example is STOP, error number 123. As you already know, you can continue executing your program after a STOP by typing CONT. **You cannot trap a warning in a user-defined error handler.** The BASIC system will always handle such an "error."

B.4 THE RESUME STATEMENT

Before we learn how to write an error handler, let us learn how to exit one. There are two ways to exit: One way clears the error, so that as far as the system is concerned, there is no error. The other way leaves the error set; on exiting the error handler, the system detects that there is still an error, and BASIC handles the error in its usual way.

The RESUME statement is used to exit from an error handler. **It clears the error,** and lets you resume execution at any statement you want. There are two forms of this statement. They are:

RESUME

and

RESUME line-number

RESUME Without Line Number

A RESUME statement without a line number is used if your error handler was able to fix the error that was trapped: It clears the error and *returns control to the first statement of the logical line* in which the error occurred. Consider the following code:

```
1040 C = 0
1050 A = 10
     B = 20
     SUM = A + B
     QUOTIENT = SUM / C
     PRINT QUOTIENT
```

When line 1050 executes, the statement QUOTIENT = SUM / C causes a division-by-zero error. If we trap this error and leave the error handler with the RESUME statement, line 1050 will execute all over again, from the statement A = 10. If we change the value of C in our error handler to some non-zero value, the program will be able to continue executing. Of course, this change may give us incorrect results. For this reason, we will not usually use RESUME without a line number.

RESUME With Line Number

The RESUME statement with a line number clears the error and allows us to resume execution at a line different from the one that caused the error. Suppose we again have line 1050, as shown above. This time, let us exit the error routine with the statement

```
RESUME 1060
```

Instead of resuming at line 1050 as before, we will now resume at line 1060. This gets us past the point of the error and lets our program continue executing.

An error handler, by means of the built-in variables explained earlier, will include code to determine both the type of error and its source. Therefore, any anticipated errors can be handled and the program RESUMEd at the correct spot.

B.5 RETURNING ERRORS TO THE SYSTEM

Suppose that we have trapped an error and are in our error handler, but the error is not one that we have anticipated or for which we have provided. We would like to exit our error handler and have BASIC handle the error the way it normally would. We can do this by exiting the error routine with the statement

```
ON ERROR GOTO 0
```

Because we did not execute a RESUME, **the error is still set.** The above statement cancels our error trap, and tells BASIC to handle all errors. Since the error is still pending, BASIC immediately handles it, giving its usual error message and traceback information.

IMPORTANT! | An error handler must always be exited with a RESUME or ON ERROR GOTO statement. Anything else is an error!

B.6 EXAMPLES

We are finally in a position to write a few error handlers.

Trapping the End-Of-File Condition

In chapter 8, we learned about terminal-format files. To signify the end of the file, we used a sentinel record. Unfortunately, not all files in real situations have such a record. The more usual case is to process records until an

256 | PROGRAMMING TOOL: ERROR TRAPPING

"end-of-file" condition occurs. If we do not trap this condition, the program will abort with an error message. We will trap this error, and write an error handler that will allow processing to continue.

Example B.1

We will write a program that reads a file into an array. The array will have 100 elements, but the file may have fewer than 100 numbers. We will read as much into the array as possible and then end the program without further processing; there will be no output.

Our error handler will test for the end-of-file error (number 11 in appendix 2), and for the statement number that caused the error. If they correspond to the expected values, we will resume processing with the statement *after* the statement that caused the error. If any other error or any other statement is involved, we will return the error to BASIC for the system to handle. Here is the code for the program.

```
10  ! Program to illustrate end-of-file error trap
20        DECLARE INTEGER EOF, I, No.of_elements, &
                  REAL A(100)
30     ! Set error trap
          ON ERROR GOTO Error_handler
40        GOSUB Open_file                ! Open input file
50        GOSUB Read_array               ! Read the array
60     ! Remainder of program would follow
70  EXIT PROGRAM

1000 Open_file:                          ! Open input file
1010      OPEN "GRADES." FOR INPUT AS FILE #1
1020 RETURN

1100 Read_array:                         ! Read the array
1110      EOF = 0                        ! End-of-file flag,
                                         ! becomes 1 in error handler
1120      I = 0
          WHILE EOF = 0 AND I < 100
              I = I + 1
              INPUT #1, A(I)
          NEXT
1130      IF EOF = 0 THEN No.of_elements = I
          ELSE No.of_elements = I - 1
          END IF
1140 RETURN

19000 Error_handler:
19010     IF ERR = 11 AND ERL = 1120     ! End-of-file
          THEN
              EOF = 1
              RESUME 1130
          ELSE                           ! All other errors
              ON ERROR GO TO 0           ! Let BASIC handle it
          END IF
19020 ! End of error handler

32767 END                                ! End of program
```

The error handler RESUMEs at statement 1130, the first statement after the loop, which ends reading the file.

Line 1130 is interesting. If we do not run out of data in the file, then we leave the loop with EOF = 0 and I = 100. Therefore, the number of elements is equal to I. Now suppose that we do not have 100 numbers in the file. Perhaps there are only 50. After we have read all 50 numbers, we enter the loop again and I becomes 51. The error trap springs, setting EOF = 1, and we leave the loop. Since no datum was read this last time around the loop, the number of elements is equal to I - 1. We test the value of EOF and take appropriate action.

The ELSE ON ERROR GOTO 0 is very important. If an error were raised somewhere else in the program, the error would be trapped, but we have not programmed our error handler to handle it. What will happen is most unpredictable. Therefore, we use the above ELSE clause to refer the error back to BASIC for handling.

Example B.2 We now write an error routine that traps all errors; prints the error number, an error message, and the line number in which the error occurred; and aborts the program after printing a suitable message:

```
19000 Error_handler:
19010     PRINT "Error"; ERR, ERT$(ERR); &
                    " has occurred in line"; ERL
19020     RESUME 32767           ! End program
19030 ! End of error handler
```

For all trappable errors, an informatory message, such as

```
Error 5 ?Can't find file or account has occurred in line 1010
```

is printed at the terminal. (The above would be printed if you attempted to open a non-existent file, for instance.)

Example B.3 We will write an error handler using a SELECT-CASE statement. The handler will check for the end-of-file condition, an incorrect filename, and a number of calculation errors. All errors not provided for will be returned to BASIC for handling. This error handler is written as follows:

```
19000 Error_handler:
19010 SELECT ERR
         CASE 11               ! End-of-file
            EOF = 1
            RESUME 1130
         CASE 5                ! Can't find file or account
            PRINT
            PRINT ERT$(ERR)
            INPUT "Reenter filename "; IN_FILE
            RESUME             ! Resume at OPEN statement
         CASE 52 to 54         ! Various illegal numbers
            PRINT "Illegal number in line "; ERL
            PRINT "Error "; ERR, ERT$(ERR)
            RESUME 32767       ! Abort program
```

```
           CASE 72 TO 89         ! Various program errors
              PRINT "Error in program in line "; ERL
              PRINT "Error "; ERR, ERT$(ERR)
              RESUME 32767       ! Abort program
           CASE ELSE
              ON ERROR GOTO 0
        END SELECT
19020 ! End error handler
```

B.7 ERROR HANDLER CRITERIA

1. An error handler must be exited with a RESUME or ON ERROR GOTO statement.

2. A RESUME leaves the error handler with the error cleared. An ON ERROR GOTO leaves it with the error set and pending.

3. An error handler *must handle all errors or pass the handling of some errors to another handler with the ON ERROR GOTO*. The ON ERROR GOTO 0 statement passes the error to BASIC, while ON ERROR GOTO label passes the error to another user-defined error handler.

4. It is illegal to "drop through" an error handler to a statement after the error handler. To reach such a statement, you must RESUME to that statement (see criterion 1).

IMPORTANT! Error handlers allow you to jump to a new point in a program. *This violates the concept of a structured program.* Where error handlers are used, great care should be taken to restrict severely the range of this jump. You should generally *RESUME to a statement immediately following the one that caused the error, or to one very near it.* You should certainly RESUME to a statement in the same subroutine as the statement that caused the error. While error trapping may be unavoidable, remember that it is always important to know how you got to a particular statement. If you get sloppy with an error handler, this may no longer be possible.

REVIEW QUESTIONS

1. What is an error trap? How do error traps differ from other parts of a program?
2. How is an error trap set in a VAX-BASIC program?
3. What are ERR, ERL, and ERT$ used for? Where are they normally used?
4. What are the two ways used to leave an error handler? How do they differ?
5. What is the meaning of the ? and % symbols preceding the error messages printed by the ERT$ function? What does no symbol preceding the error messages mean?

PROGRAMMING EXERCISES

Program any of the programming exercises of chapter 8 that read from a file using a sentinel; use an end-of-file trap instead.

ENRICHMENT TOPICS B

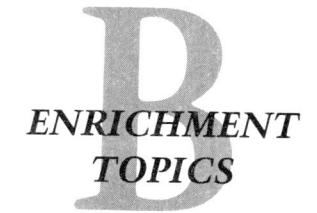

Error Trapping in Subprograms

Error traps may be used in subprograms. When a subprogram contains an error trap and error handler, all errors in the subprogram may be handled by its own error handler. When the subprogram returns control back to the invoking procedure, the invoking procedure's error handler will resume handling errors. Every time a subprogram is invoked, think of its error handler being placed on top of the previous one. When you leave the subprogram, its error handler is peeled off the top, uncovering the previous one.

A RESUME in a subprogram may only RESUME to a statement within the subprogram.

An ON ERROR GOTO 0 statement in the subprogram's error handler returns error handling to BASIC, usually resulting in an error message and program abort.

ON ERROR GO BACK

The statement ON ERROR GO BACK in the error handler of a subprogram leaves the error set and returns it to the invoking procedure for its error handler to process. If the invoking procedure has no error handler, then BASIC will handle the error.

So, just as the ON ERROR GOTO 0 statement in the main program returns the error to BASIC to handle, ON ERROR GO BACK refers the error to the previous subprogram or main program. In fact, if you execute ON ERROR GO BACK from the main program, it will do the same as ON ERROR GOTO 0, because the previous level from the main program is the BASIC system.

The ERN$ Built-in Variable

When an error occurs in a subprogram, the built-in variable ERN$ will contain the name of the subprogram. If, for instance, you had called the subprogram `Bubble_sort`, which contains an error trap and error handler, with the statement

```
CALL Bubble_sort
```

260 | ERROR TRAPPING IN SUBPROGRAMS

and an error occurs during execution of this routine, then the statements

```
PRINT "Error "; ERR, ERT$(ERR);
PRINT " has occurred in "; ERN$
```

will print the error number, the error text, and the name of the subprogram, Bubble_sort.

Example IM.4 | This example illustrates the use of error traps in both the main program and a subprogram. The main program handles the end-of-file and incorrect file name errors, passing all others to BASIC. The subroutine handles the division-by-zero error, passing all others back to the main program. The code is shown below:

```
10 ! Program to find average of array elements
   ! Array read from file
   ! Error handlers in main program and subprogram
20    DECLARE REAL A(100), AVG, &
              INTEGER I, No.of_elements, EOF, &
              STRING Filename
30    ON ERROR GOTO Error_handler
40    GOSUB Open_input_file
50    GOSUB Read_array
60    CALL Find_avg (A(), No.of_elements, AVG)
70    GOSUB Print_avg
80 EXIT PROGRAM

1000 Open_input_file:
1010    INPUT "Enter file name "; Filename
1020    OPEN Filename FOR INPUT AS FILE #1
1030 RETURN

1100 Read_array:
1120    I = 0 \ EOF = 0
        WHILE EOF = 0 AND I < 100
           I = I + 1
           INPUT #1, A(I)
        NEXT
1130    IF EOF = 0 THEN No.of_elements = I
        ELSE No.of_elements = I - 1
1140 RETURN

1200 Print_avg:
1210    PRINT \ PRINT
        PRINT "The average is"; AVG
        PRINT
1220 RETURN

9000 Error_handler:
9010    SELECT ERR
           CASE 5                    ! Can't find file
              PRINT
              PRINT ERT$(ERR)
```

```
              INPUT "Reenter filename "; Filename
              RESUME                ! Resume at OPEN statement
          CASE 11                   ! End of file
              EOF = 1
              RESUME 1130
          CASE ELSE                 ! All other errors
              ON ERROR GOTO 0
       END SELECT
9020 ! End error handler

9999 END                            ! End of main program

10000 SUB Find_avg (REAL A(), INTEGER No.elems, REAL AVG)
10010    DECLARE INTEGER I
10020    ON ERROR GOTO Error_routine
10030    SUM = 0
         FOR I = 1 TO No.elems
            SUM = SUM + A(I)
         NEXT I
10040    AVG = SUM / No.elems
10050 EXIT SUB                      ! Leave SUBprogram

19000 Error_routine:
19010    IF ERR = 61                ! Division by 0
         THEN
            PRINT
            PRINT "No numbers read. Average set to 0"
            AVG = 0
            RESUME 10050
         ELSE                       ! All other errors
            ON ERROR GO BACK        ! Let main program handle it
         END IF
19999 END SUB
```

A new statement EXIT SUB has been introduced at line 10050. This statement acts like an END SUB statement and returns control back to the invoking procedure. EXIT SUB must be used because END SUB must be the last line of the subprogram, and the error handler must appear before the END SUB (see lines 19000 to 19999).

In this program, the error routine in the subprogram has a different label from the one in the main program. There was no need for this; they could both have the same label because all identifiers in the subprogram are local to the subprogram. For example, the variable I in the subprogram is different from the one in the main program.

9 String Processing

Outline

9.1 The LINPUT Instruction
9.2 Combining Strings—Concatenation
9.3 The Length Function—LEN
9.4 The SEG$ Function
9.5 Searching for a Substring—The POS Function
9.6 Editing Strings—The EDIT$ Function
9.7 The VAL Function
9.8 Comparing Strings
Summary
Review Questions
Syntax Exercises
Programming Exercises

```
type, -1
ype, -32
type, -2
ype, sys
```

Introduction A lot of computer work involves character data rather than numeric data. Word processors are used to create documents, such as this book; "fail-safe" input routines accept characters instead of numbers, then convert them to numeric format for processing; output routines put data into specific formats to improve appearance; and there are many other applications.

The manipulation of character data is called **string processing.** There are many operations that can be performed on strings: They can be combined, taken apart, compared, and/or converted from one form to another. This chapter will discuss a number of these operations.

9.1 THE LINPUT INSTRUCTION

A **string** is defined as any sequence of characters. In string processing, often an entire line, up to a <Return>, must be read into one string variable. This presents a problem if the line contains commas because the INPUT instruction we have used so far reads only to the first comma. To overcome this limitation, we can use the LINPUT instruction. The syntax of the LINPUT instruction is:

> sn LINPUT [prompt;] list of string variables
> sn LINPUT #channel, list of string variables

The prompt is optional as indicated by placing it in brackets. If present, it may be followed by a comma instead of a semicolon. Examples are:

```
10 LINPUT "Enter two strings "; STRING_1, STRING_2
20 LINPUT #1, SENTENCE
```

The first example prints a prompt and then gets the data from the user's terminal. All characters typed at the terminal up to the first <Return>, including commas, are put into the variable called STRING_1. All characters typed up to the second <Return> are put into the variable called STRING_2. Both STRING_1 and STRING_2 must be of the STRING data-type.

In the second example, the computer looks into the terminal-format file connected to channel 1. Everything up to the first <Return> in that file, including commas, is put into the variable called SENTENCE, which must be of the STRING data-type.

There is also an INPUT LINE instruction that may be used instead of LINPUT. The only difference between the two is that, when using INPUT LINE, the <Return> at the end of the line is considered part of the string and is stored in the string variable. Therefore, if LINPUT and INPUT LINE are both used to read the same string, the length of the string stored by INPUT LINE will be one character longer (the <Return>) than that stored by LINPUT.

Examples of the INPUT LINE statement are:

```
10 INPUT LINE "Enter two strings "; STRING_1, STRING_2
20 INPUT LINE #1, SENTENCE
```

9.2 COMBINING STRINGS—CONCATENATION

Two strings can be combined into one by an operation called **concatenation.** The symbol for this operation is the plus, +, sign. The effect of concatenation is to join the second string to the end of the first.

Example 9.1
```
10   DECLARE STRING A,B,C
20   A = "STEVEN"
     B = "SON"
     C = A + B
     PRINT C      ! Prints STEVENSON
30   END
```

The computer will print STEVENSON at the terminal, because A and B were concatenated to form C.

9.3 THE LENGTH FUNCTION—LEN

It is sometimes necessary to know how many characters a string contains. The LEN function returns the number of characters in the string. Its syntax is:

LEN (string)

Example 9.2

```
10 DECLARE STRING A
20 A = "STEVENSON"
30 PRINT "Length of string "; A; " = "; LEN (A)
40 END
```

Length of string STEVENSON = 9 is printed at the terminal, because there are nine characters in the name STEVENSON (all of them letters).

9.4 THE SEG$ FUNCTION

The SEG$ function[1] can be used to obtain a substring from a given string. It requires three arguments: the first is the string from which the substring is obtained; the second is the position within this string of the first character of the substring; and the third is the position of the final character of the substring. The syntax of this function is:

SEG$ (string, first-position, last-position)

For example, to obtain a copy of the substring that starts in position 5 and ends in position 10 (6 characters) of the string stored in the STRING variable Sentence, you would use the statement

```
Substring = SEG$ (Sentence, 5, 10)
```

The SEG$ function copies the substring it returns; it does not remove it from the original string.

To obtain a substring that starts at the beginning of the string, set the second argument to 1. For example,

```
Substring = SEG$ (String_, 1, 10)
```

will store the first 10 characters of String_ in Substring.

---

[1] The SEG$ function takes the place of the LEFT$, RIGHT$, and MID$ functions of BASIC-PLUS and BASIC-PLUS-2. While VAX-BASIC supports LEFT$, RIGHT$, and MID$ to maintain compatibility with those dialects, DEC recommends that SEG$ be used in all new programming efforts.

To obtain a substring that consists of the last characters of a string, starting at a given point, make the third argument equal to the length of the string. For example,

```
Substring = SEG$ (String_, 15, LEN (String_))
```

will copy all characters of String_, starting at the fifteenth character and extending to the end of String_, into Substring.

Example 9.3
```
10   DECLARE STRING A, B, C, D
20   D = "STEVENSON"
     A = SEG$ (D,1,5)
     B = SEG$ (D,7,9)
     C = SEG$ (D,3,6)
30   PRINT "FIRST  = "; A    ! Prints FIRST  = STEVE
     PRINT "SECOND = "; B    ! Prints SECOND = SON
     PRINT "THIRD  = "; C    ! Prints THIRD  = EVEN
40   END
```

The program segment above prints

```
FIRST  = STEVE
SECOND = SON
THIRD  = EVEN
```

at the terminal. SEG$(D,1,5) returns the first five characters of D, which contains the name STEVENSON. The result, STEVE, is assigned to A.

SEG$(D,7,9) takes the seventh through the ninth (last) character of D. We could have used SEG$(D,7,LEN(D)) instead. The substring returned is assigned to B.

SEG$(D,3,6) copies the third through sixth characters of D; this substring, EVEN, is then assigned to C. Note that D is unchanged and still contains STEVENSON.

9.5 SEARCHING FOR A SUBSTRING—THE POS FUNCTION

In string processing, we often need to know whether a string contains a given substring and, if so, where the substring begins. For example, does a sentence contain the word "kumquat" and, if so, where is it?

A function that can be used for this purpose is the POS function.[2] The syntax of this function is:

POS (string, substring, posn)

where

    string   = the string in which the search takes place
    substring = the string being searched for
    posn   = the position in the string where the search begins

---

[2] VAX-BASIC also supports the INSTR function for compatibility with BASIC-PLUS and BASIC-PLUS-2, but DEC recommends using POS for new development.

The computer starts at position posn of the string and begins its search for the substring. If it finds the substring, the position of the first character of the substring is returned. If it does not find the substring, the number 0 is returned. Note that the POS function returns a number, not a string.

Example 9.4

```
10 DECLARE STRING A, INTEGER N1, N2, N3, N4
20 A = "STEVENSON"
30 N1 = POS (A, "E", 1)        ! N1 becomes 3
40 N2 = POS (A, "E", N1+1)     ! N2 becomes 5
50 N3 = POS (A, "EN", 1)       ! N3 becomes 5
60 N4 = POS (A, "EVER", 1)     ! N4 becomes 0
70 PRINT N1, N2, N3, N4
80 END
```

Statement 30 of this program starts searching from position 1 of A, which contains STEVENSON, and looks for the letter E. It finds the first one at position 3; therefore, N1 becomes 3.

Statement 40 starts its search at position N1+1, which is position 4, and again looks for an E. It finds one at position 5, so N2 becomes 5.

Statement 50 starts again at position 1 of A (which is still STEVENSON) and looks for the string EN. The first, and only, instance of the combination EN begins at position 5. Therefore, N3 becomes 5.

Statement 60 again starts at the beginning of A and looks for the word EVER. Because EVER does not occur in STEVENSON, the search fails, and N4 becomes 0.

Statement 70 causes the following output at the terminal:

```
3              5              5              0
```

Notice that the POS function always searches for the first occurrence of the substring in the string at or after the position given in the third argument.

Example 9.5

This program will enable us to enter from the terminal a name consisting of a first name and a last name separated by a blank. The program will reverse the order of the names, printing the last name, a comma, a blank, and finally the first name.

This program would be trivial if we were to read each part of the name into a separate variable—but that wouldn't be any fun at all. What we will do instead is read the entire name into one variable, then separate the name into its component parts, and finally reassemble the name the way we would like it to appear. Here is the plan:

    Interchange first and last names:
      Enter the name
      Find the position of the blank
      Extract all characters up to the blank as the first name
      Extract all characters after the blank as the last name
      Concatenate last name, a comma, a blank, first name
      Print result
    Stop

9 STRING PROCESSING

The resulting program is as follows:

```
10 ! Interchanging first and last names
20     DECLARE STRING    Name_, First, Last, New_name, &
               INTEGER   Posn_blank, Name_length
30     INPUT 'Enter first, last name'; Name_
40     Name_length = LEN (Name_)
50     Posn_blank = POS (Name_, " ", 1)            ! Find the blank
60     First = SEG$ (Name_, 1, Posn_blank-1)       ! Get first name
70     Last = SEG$ (Name_, Posn_blank+1, Name_length) ! Get last name
80     New_name = Last + ", " + First              ! Form new name
90     PRINT TAB(24); New_name
100 END

RUNNH
Enter first, last name? Joe Cool
                        Cool, Joe
```

Notice how the first name consists of all characters from the beginning of Name_ through position Posn_blank-1. The blank between the names is at position Posn_blank, so Posn_blank-1 is the position of the last letter of the first name. Similarly, Posn_blank+1 is the position immediately after the blank. This is the location of the first letter of the last name.

Statement 80 takes the last name, concatenates a comma-and-blank combination, and then concatenates the first name to the rest. If the input were JOHN HANCOCK, then the output would be HANCOCK, JOHN.

Example 9.6 We'll complicate matters slightly by including a middle name in the program of Example 9.5. We want output to consist of the last name, a comma, a blank, the first name, a blank, and finally the middle initial followed by a period. Input will consist of the complete name, including the full middle name, not just the initial. For example, if the input is

THOMAS ALVA EDISON

then the output should be

EDISON, THOMAS A.

Here is the pseudocode:

    Rearranging name:
      Enter entire name
      Find position of first blank
      Get everything up to first blank as first name
      Get first character after first blank as middle initial
      Find position of second blank
      Get everything after second blank as last name
      Reassemble name
      Print result
    Stop

9.5 SEARCHING FOR A SUBSTRING—THE POS FUNCTION

Our plan is executed as follows:

```
10  ! Name reversal with middle initial
20      DECLARE STRING   Name_, First, Middle, Last, New_name, &
                INTEGER   Blank1, Blank2
30      INPUT "Enter first, middle, last name "; Name_
40      Blank1 = POS (Name_, " ", 1)              ! Find first blank
50      First = SEG$ (Name_, 1, Blank1-1)          ! Get first name
60      Middle = SEG$ (Name_, Blank1+1, Blank1+1)  ! Get middle initial
70      Blank2 = POS (Name_, " ", Blank1+1)        ! Find second blank
80      Last = SEG$ (Name_, Blank2+1, LEN (Name_)) ! Get last name
90      New_name = Last + ", " + First + " " + Middle + "."
                                                   ! Reassemble name
100     PRINT TAB(33); New_name
110     END

RUNNH
Enter first, middle, last name? Thomas Alva Edison
                                Edison, Thomas A.
```

In line 50, the first name includes everything up to the position before the first blank. Line 60 takes the position after the first blank as the middle initial. You will notice that the first and last positions specified for the substring are the same.

Line 70 finds the position of the second blank. Line 80 takes everything to the right of the second blank as the last name.

You can see that we are concatenating six strings in statement 90. First we have the last name, then a comma-and-blank combination, the first name, a space, the middle initial, and finally a period after the middle initial. Line 100 prints the reassembled name.

Example 9.7 We will read sentences from a file called STRING.DAT and count the number of words in each sentence. Each record of the file contains one sentence. After we have counted the number of words in a sentence, we will print the number of words it contains. After all sentences have had their words counted, we will print the total number of sentences and the total number of words in all sentences combined. We will use an end-of-file trap, as discussed in the Intermezzo.

NOTE! **A STRING variable in VAX-BASIC may store up to 65535 characters. That is large enough for even the world's longest run-on sentence.**

In pseudocode we have:

Sentence and word counts:
  Open the file
  Process the file
  Close the file
Stop

The code for the main program is simple enough. We will wait until the final program is shown (Fig. 9-1) before presenting it.

For "Process the file" we have:

>Process the file:
>   Initialize for cumulative counts
>   Read sentence
>   WHILE not end-of-file
>   Count words in sentence
>   Print number of words in sentence
>   Adjust cumulative counts
>   Read next sentence
>   End of loop
>   Print cumulative counts
>Return

The code for this subroutine is:

```
2000 Process_file:                  ! Process the file
2010    GOSUB Initialize            ! Initialize for cumulative counts
2020    EOF = 0
        GOSUB Read_sentence         ! Priming read
        WHILE EOF = 0               ! Set to 1 in error handler
          GOSUB Count_words         ! Count words in sentence
          GOSUB Print_words         ! Print number of words
          GOSUB Cum_counts          ! Adjust cumulative counts
          GOSUB Read_sentence       ! Read sentence (could cause eof)
        NEXT
2030    GOSUB Print_cum_counts      ! Print cumulative totals
2040 RETURN
```

To count the number of words, we can find the blank between the first two words and add 1 to the word count. Then we can find the next blank, increment the word count, and repeat the process until there are no more blanks in the sentence. Because a sentence has one more word than blanks between words, we increase the word count by 1 after we run out of blanks. The pseudocode for this is:

>Count words in sentence:
>   Initialize word count to 0
>   UNTIL no more blanks
>   Find position of next blank
>   Add 1 to word count
>   End of loop
>Return

As mentioned, we increase the word count *after* we look for a blank. That means that if we do not find a blank, we still increase the word count by 1. This takes care of the last word, which is not followed by a blank. Make sure you understand how the last word is counted; it is easy to make an **"off-by-one"** error here.

The code for this subroutine is shown below:

```
2300 Count_words:                    ! Count words in sentence
2310 ! Initializations
        Word_count = 0
        Blank_pos = 1
2320    UNTIL Blank_pos = 0
           Blank_pos = POS (Sentence, ' ', Blank_pos + 1)
           Word_count = Word_count + 1
        NEXT
2330 RETURN
```

Note that `Blank_pos` was initialized to 1 so that we would get into the loop. Without that initialization, the subroutine would return a count of 0 for every sentence.

Figure 9-1.
Program to Count Words

We are ready for the complete program as shown in Figure 9-1.

```
10 ! Sentence and word counts
20    DECLARE STRING  In_file, Out_file, Sentence,    &
              INTEGER Word_count, Total_word_count,   &
                      Total_sentence_count, Blank_pos
30    ON ERROR GOTO Error_routine ! Set error trap
40    GOSUB Open_files             ! Open the files
50    GOSUB Process_file           ! Process the file
60    GOSUB Close_files            ! Close the files
70    EXIT PROGRAM

1000 Open_files:                    ! Open the files
1010 ! Open the input file
        INPUT 'Enter input filename'; In_file
        OPEN In_file FOR INPUT AS FILE #1
1020 ! Open the output file
        INPUT 'Enter output filename'; Out_file
        OPEN Out_file FOR OUTPUT AS FILE #2
1030 RETURN

1200 Close_files:                   ! Close the files
1210    CLOSE #1, #2
1220 RETURN

2000 Process_file:                  ! Process the file
2010    GOSUB Initialize            ! Initialize for cumulative counts
2020    EOF = 0
        GOSUB Read_sentence         ! Priming read
        WHILE EOF = 0               ! Set to 1 in error handler
           GOSUB Count_words        ! Count words in sentence
           GOSUB Print_words        ! Print number of words
           GOSUB Cum_counts         ! Adjust cumulative counts
           GOSUB Read_sentence      ! Read sentence (could cause eof)
        NEXT
2030    GOSUB Print_cum_counts ! Print cumulative totals
2040 RETURN
```

Figure 9-1. (*Cont.*)

```
2100 Initialize:                   ! Initialize cumulative counts
2110    Total_word_count = 0
        Total_sentence_count = 0
2120 RETURN

2200 Read_sentence:                ! Read a sentence
2210    LINPUT #1, Sentence        ! Note use of LINPUT
2220 RETURN

2300 Count_words:                  ! Count words in sentence
2310 ! Initializations
        Word_count = 0
        Blank_pos = 1
2320    UNTIL Blank_pos = 0
           Blank_pos = POS (Sentence, ' ', Blank_pos + 1)
           Word_count = Word_count + 1
        NEXT
2330 RETURN

2400 Print_words:                  ! Print number of words
2410    PRINT #2, 'Number of words this sentence = '; Word_count
2420 RETURN

2500 Cum_counts:                   ! Adjust cumulative counts
2510    Total_word_count = Total_word_count + Word_count
        Total_sentence_count = Total_sentence_count + 1
2520 RETURN

2600 Print_cum_counts:             ! Print cumulative totals
2610    PRINT #2 \ PRINT #2        ! Skip 2 lines
2620    PRINT #2, 'Total word count = '; Total_word_count
        PRINT #2, 'Number of sentences = '; Total_sentence_count
2630 RETURN

19000 Error_routine:
19010    IF ERR = 11 and ERL = 2210 THEN
            EOF = 1
            RESUME 2220
         ELSE
            ON ERROR GOTO 0
         END IF
19020 ! End error handler

32767 END
```

If the data come from the terminal instead of a file, this could be handled by using variables as channel numbers. The subroutine used to open the file would be as shown below.

```
1000 Open_files:                        ! Open the files
1010 ! Open the input file
        INPUT 'Enter input filename <Keyboard>'; In_file
```

```
             IF In_file = "" THEN In_channel = 0
             ELSE
                 In_channel = 1
                 OPEN In_file FOR INPUT AS FILE #1
             END IF
1020    ! Open the output file
         INPUT 'Enter output filename <Screen>'; Out_file
         IF Out_file = "" THEN Out_channel = 0
         ELSE
             Out_channel = 2
             OPEN Out_file FOR OUTPUT AS FILE #2
         END IF
1030 RETURN
```

If the user wants the default devices, Keyboard or Screen, he simply presses the <Return> key, and channel 0 will be opened for that device. For any other response, the selected file will be opened.

The input and output routines will require alteration, as follows:

```
2200 Read_sentence:                     ! Read a sentence
2210    IF In_channel = 0 THEN
            PRINT
            PRINT "Enter sentence"       ! Print prompt for user
        END IF
        LINPUT #In_channel, Sentence     ! Note use of LINPUT and
2220 RETURN                              ! variable channel number
2400 Print_words:                        ! Print number of words
2410    PRINT #Out_channel, &
            'Number of words this sentence = '; word_count
            ! Note use of variable channel number
2420 RETURN
```

The two variables `In_channel` and `Out_channel` must be declared INTEGER type.

9.6 EDITING STRINGS—THE EDIT$ FUNCTION

The built-in function EDIT$ will accept a string and return an edited version of the same string. The type of editing performed is determined by one of the arguments, the code argument, that is sent to the function. The syntax of the EDIT$ function reference is:

EDIT$ (string, code)

For example, the statement

`String_ = EDIT$ (String_, 32)`

converts all lower case letters in the variable `String_` to upper case, as determined by the second argument, 32. All of the codes and their purposes are shown in Figure 9-2.

Figure 9-2.
Table of EDIT$ Codes and Their Purposes

CODE	PURPOSE
1	Clears bit 0 for each character
2	Discards spaces and tabs
4	Discards carriage returns, line feeds, form feeds, and nulls
8	Discards leading spaces and tabs
16	Converts multiple spaces and tabs to a single space
32	Converts lower case letters to upper case
64	Converts brackets to parentheses
128	Discards trailing spaces and tabs
256	Suppresses editing for characters within quotation marks

For example, to discard all trailing spaces and tabs from the string stored in the variable Sentence, and to store the resulting string in the variable New_sentence, use the instruction

```
New_sentence = EDIT$(Sentence, 128)
```

To perform more than one editing function on a string, add the corresponding codes. For example, to discard all leading and trailing spaces and tabs, to convert all lower case letters to upper case, and to convert all multiple spaces and tabs to a single space in the string stored in variable Paragraph, use the code 184, calculated as follows:

8	Discard leading spaces and tabs
16	Convert multiple spaces and tabs to a single space
32	Convert lower-case to upper-case
128	Discard trailing spaces and tabs
184	Code to be used

A statement that does the editing is then:

```
Paragraph = EDIT$ (Paragraph, 184)
```

Example 9.8

We want to read a string and count the number of characters it contains. We do not wish to include any characters other than those we can see—that is, we want to ignore blanks, tabs, returns, and so on.

The easiest way to solve this problem is to edit the unwanted characters out of the string and find the length of the string that is left. The code for the program is shown in Figure 9-3.

Output from this program might be as follows:

```
Enter string ? The quick brown fox
Number of characters in old string = 19
Number of characters in new string = 16
```

We will use the EDIT$ function in a more practical way later on in this chapter.

Figure 9-3.
Program to Count
Characters in a String

```
10  ! Program to count characters in string
20      DECLARE STRING String_, New_string, &
                INTEGER Length_old, Length_new
30      INPUT "Enter string "; String_
40      New_string = EDIT$ (String_, 6)  ! 2 = Remove spaces and tabs
                                         ! 4 = Remove returns, etc.
50      Length_old = LEN (String_)
        Length_new = LEN (New_string)
60      PRINT "Number of characters in old string ="; Length_old
        PRINT "Number of characters in new string ="; Length_new
70      END
```

9.7 THE VAL FUNCTION

The VAL function is used to convert a numerical string into an arithmetic value. A numerical string looks like a number, but because it is a string containing digits in character form, it cannot be used in any arithmetic calculations.[3] The VAL function solves this problem.

There are actually two VAL functions. One returns its result in REAL data format, the other in INTEGER format. Their syntax is:

VAL (string)
VAL% (string)

where **string** is a numerical string constant or a string variable that contains a numerical string. The VAL function returns a real arithmetic value, while VAL% returns an integer value.

The argument passed to the VAL function may contain the digits 0 through 9, the symbols +, −, or . (the period), or the letter E. That is, it must look like a real fixed point or floating point number.

The argument passed to the VAL% function may contain the digits 0 through 9, and the symbols + or −. In other words, it must be a string that looks like an integer.

Example 9.9

```
10  ! Program illustrating string to numeric conversion
20      DECLARE STRING STR_1, STR_2, REAL NUM_1, NUM_2, NUM_3
30      ! Assign numeric string values
        STR_1 = '234.98'            ! Cannot add STR_1
        STR_2 = '52.49'             ! and STR_2 to get sum
```

---

[3] There are built-in functions in VAX-BASIC that let you perform arithmetic with strings. These will be described in chapter 13 on built-in functions, but they are not otherwise used in this text.

```
40        ! Convert to arithmetic values
          NUM_1 = VAL (STR_1)           ! NUM_1 becomes 234.98
          NUM_2 = VAL (STR_2)           ! NUM_2 becomes 52.49
50        ! Add the numbers
          NUM_3 = NUM_1 + NUM_2         ! Forms sum of numbers
60 END
```

You should realize that only numerical strings—strings that look like numbers—can be converted to arithmetical numbers. If the string contains any characters that are illegal in BASIC if contained in a number, or if the characters are arranged so that they do not represent a number, then an error occurs when the VAL function attempts to convert the string. (The error can be trapped, however.) Even commas included in the numeric string, as in 15,000, will cause an error.

Example 9.10

In an example in chapter 8, we created a file in which each record consisted of a name and a number. When the file was created, we had to insert a comma between the name and the number so that we could put the name and number into separate variables when we read the file. The PRINT statement

```
PRINT #1, NAME_; ','; NUMBER
```

was used, with a comma printed between the output values.

Let us assume that the comma has not been placed in the record. That is, the record has been written with the statement:

```
PRINT #1, NAME_, NUMBER
```

Let us further assume that each name consists of a first name and a last name, with exactly one blank between them, and that the number is preceded by an arbitrary number of blanks. As an example, a record might be:

```
John Smith      72
```

We want to read this record into a string variable, then divide the variable into its two parts: the name and the number. Remember that, when we try to read the name, the number comes along as well, because a string is delimited only by a comma or a carriage return. As there is no comma in the above record, the entire record is read when we try to read the name.

The logic for this part of the program would be:

> Read the record
> Break record into name and number

This is further decomposed into:

> Break record into name and number:
>   Find position of second blank
>   Take everything to second blank as name
>   Convert remainder of string to arithmetic
> Return

Assuming that the input statement has the form:

INPUT #1, Recrd

and the subroutine begins at line 1500, the code for the subroutine required would be:

```
1500 Decompose_record:    ! Break record into name and number
1510    Blank_1 = POS (Recrd, ' ', 1)
        Blank_2 = POS (Recrd, ' ', Blank_1+1)
1520    Name_ = SEG$ (Recrd, 1, Blank_2-1)
        Number_string = SEG$ (Recrd, Blank_2, LEN (Recrd))
        Number_value = VAL (Number_string)
1530 RETURN
```

You can see that, after the second blank is found, everything to its right is a numerical string that is put into the string variable Number_string. This string is then converted to an arithmetic value, using the VAL function, and stored into the real variable Number_value. Number_string will be DECLAREd as type STRING, and Number_value as type REAL. The number can now be used in arithmetic operations.

If we had wanted the value converted into integer form instead of real, we could have used VAL% in line 1520 above. In that case, it would make sense to declare Number_value to be of the INTEGER data-type.

Example 9.11 Figure 9-4 is a program that can read a file whose records consist of three fields: a first name, a last name, and a number. The first two fields are separated by one blank. There is at least one blank following the second field before the number. The last record is a sentinel, which contains the word END, followed by a blank and perhaps additional characters:

END (possible other characters)

(An end-of-file trap could be used, but we will not.) The condition that tests for the sentinel looks at the first four characters of each record to see if they are END<blank>. If they are, the sentinel record has been read. We look for END<blank> rather than simply END because a person's name could conceivably begin with the three letters END. Our program will use the EDIT$ function to look for this sentinel in upper case, lower case, or any combination. The program is written in Figure 9-4.

9.8 COMPARING STRINGS

We know that we can compare numbers using IF-THEN or IF-THEN-ELSE structures. If we have two variables, A and B, and want to know which contains the smaller number, we can use a statement such as:

```
IF A < B THEN PRINT 'A is smaller'
ELSE IF A > B THEN PRINT 'B is smaller'
ELSE PRINT 'A and B are equal'
```

Figure 9-4.
Program to Read Records Containing Fields Not Separated by Commas

```
10  ! Read a file with no commas between fields
20      DECLARE STRING   Recrd, Name_, Number_string, In_file, &
                REAL     Number_value, &
                INTEGER  Blank_1, Blank_2
30      GOSUB Open_files    ! Open the file
40      GOSUB Get_record    ! Get first record
50      WHILE SEG$ (Recrd,1,4) <> 'END '
            GOSUB Decompose_record    ! Break record into name
                                      ! and number
            GOSUB Print_record        ! Print record
            GOSUB Get_record          ! Read next record
        NEXT
60   EXIT PROGRAM

1000 Open_files:                       ! Open the file
1010    INPUT 'Enter input filename'; In_file
        OPEN In_file FOR INPUT AS FILE #1
1020 RETURN

1100 Get_record:                       ! Read a record
1110    INPUT #1, Recrd
1120    Recrd = EDIT$(Recrd,56)        ! Convert to upper-case
                                       ! Remove excess blanks
1130 RETURN

1200 Print_record:                     ! Print a record
1210    PRINT TAB(20); 'Name    = '; Name_
        PRINT TAB(20); 'Number ='; Number_value
        PRINT
1220 RETURN

1500 Decompose_record:   ! Break record into name and number
     ! Recrd has no leading or trailing blanks
     ! Multiple blanks replaced with single blank
1510    Blank_1 = POS (Recrd, ' ', 1)
        Blank_2 = POS (Recrd, ' ', Blank_1+1)
1520    Name_ = SEG$ (Recrd, 1, Blank_2-1)
        Number_string = SEG$ (Recrd, Blank_2, LEN (Recrd))
        Number_value = VAL (Number_string)
1530 RETURN

32767 END
```

Strings can be compared in the same way numbers are compared. Each character is stored in the computer using a numerical code (usually ASCII code as listed in appendix 3). The computer compares two characters according to their ASCII codes: The character assigned the smaller code is considered the smaller character.

Consider the following program statements:

```
10    FIRST = 'A'
      SECOND = 'B'

20    IF FIRST < SECOND THEN PRINT 'FIRST precedes SECOND'
      ELSE IF FIRST > SECOND THEN PRINT 'SECOND precedes FIRST'
      ELSE PRINT 'FIRST equals SECOND'
      END IF  END IF
```

Because A comes before B in the ASCII table, the above program segment will print "FIRST precedes SECOND" at the terminal.

Any characters can be compared, not just alphabetic ones. If line 10 above had been:

```
10    FIRST = '+'
      SECOND = '.'
```

then FIRST would precede SECOND because the ASCII code of the + sign is 43, while that of the period is 46.

Strings containing more than one character can be similarly compared. Consider the following statements:

```
10    NAME.1 = 'SMITH, JOHN'
      NAME.2 = 'JONES, TOM'

20    IF NAME.1 < NAME.2 THEN PRINT 'NAME.1 is first'
      ELSE IF NAME.1 > NAME.2 THEN PRINT 'NAME.2 is first'
      ELSE PRINT 'Names are equal'
      END IF  END IF
```

The computer compares the two strings, one character at a time, starting at the left-most characters of both. As soon as the two characters being compared are different, their ASCII codes determine which is the "smaller" string.

Because "JONES, TOM" comes before "SMITH, JOHN" alphabetically and in ASCII, the message "NAME.2 is first" will be printed.

This technique for comparing strings can be used to sort a list of names stored in a string array. Such an exercise will be left as an end-of-chapter assignment.

Example 9.12 | In this example, we will enter a string from the terminal, check each character to be sure that it is a digit, and finally convert the string to numeric if all characters are digits. This type of test can be used to ensure that the correct type of data is entered before processing continues. The pseudocode is:

> Check input for validity:
>   Input string
>   Test string for digits
>   If all digits, convert to arithmetic
> Stop

There are several ways of checking for digits. We will choose a simple method, albeit not the most efficient one. The pseudocode will be:

> Test string for digits:
> Initialize ALL.DIGITS to "TRUE"
> If any character is not a digit, set ALL.DIGITS to "FALSE"
> Return

ALL.DIGITS is an example of a flag. Its value determines whether or not a particular event has occurred. Specifically, if a non-digit is found, the flag is set to "FALSE", thus becoming a signal that the string is not numeric.

If the entire procedure is written as a subroutine at line 1000, the code will be as follows. (Note that STRING is a reserved word, so we have used STRNG here.)

```
1000 Validity_test:                   ! Check input for validity
1010   INPUT 'Enter string'; STRNG
1020   GOSUB Digit_check              ! Test string for digits
1030   IF ALL.DIGITS = "TRUE" THEN NUMBER = VAL (STRNG)
       ELSE PRINT "String not numeric. Cannot convert"
       END IF
1040 RETURN

1100 Digit_check:                     ! Test string for digits
1110   ALL.DIGITS = "TRUE"
1120   FOR I = 1 TO LEN (STRNG)
1130      CHARACTER = SEG$ (STRNG, I, I)
1140      IF CHARACTER < '0' OR CHARACTER > '9'
          THEN ALL.DIGITS = "FALSE"
          END IF
1150   NEXT I
1160 RETURN
```

Note line 1140, where we compare CHARACTER to the characters '0' and '9'. These are not the *numbers* 0 and 9; they are in quotation marks and are numeric strings. The computer compares the ASCII equivalent of CHARACTER to the ASCII equivalent of the character 0 (which is 48). It then compares CHARACTER to the ASCII equivalent of the character 9 (which is 57). If either test is true, then CHARACTER is not a digit, and the ALL.DIGITS flag is set to "FALSE."

Note that the variable ALL.DIGITS has only two possible values, TRUE and FALSE. Its purpose is to record an event that occurred, in this case the appearance of a non-digit character.

We did not check for a minus sign, so all negative numbers will be rejected. You may modify the program to include negative numbers. We also did not check to see if there might be a decimal point. This, too, is left as an exercise.

Example 9.13 | This example involves some text editing. We will read a number of strings, and in each string where the word "man" appears we will replace it with the word "person". The strings will be read from a file, and a sentinel string consisting of the words END OF FILE will be the last string. The output will be sent to a new file, and we will end that file with the same sentinel.

Pseudocode for the various modules follows.

    Word replacement in files:
       Open input and output files
       Process files
       Close files
    Stop

    Process files:
       While sentence <> END OF FILE
          Read a sentence
          Replace every MAN with PERSON
          Print sentence
       End of loop
    Return

    Replace every MAN with PERSON:
       Find position of MAN
       While MAN is found
          Replace MAN with PERSON
          Find next position of MAN
       End of loop
    Return

We will assume that all strings are in capital letters, and all replacements will be made with capital letters. The logic required to preserve case is much more complex than we wish to discuss here. The code for this program is shown in Figure 9-5.

You should be aware of a number of fine points concerning subroutine 2100. First, we searched for the word " MAN " (including blanks), not "MAN". The blanks before and after the word are necessary so that we do not change MANAGEMENT to PERSONAGEMENT or PERMANENT to PERPERSONENT.

Second, `Posn` is the position of the first blank in the string " MAN " and `Posn+4` is the position of the second blank. When we concatenate to form the new sentence, we take everything up to the first blank, the word `PERSON`, and then everything from the second blank. This leaves out the word `MAN`, which has been replaced.

Third, each new search begins at `Posn+8`, which is the position of the first letter of the word following `PERSON` in the new sentence.

The above program assumes that all strings are shorter than the maximum length allowed. For our terminal-format files, this will be the margin we set, namely 132. (Remember that STRING variables in VAX-BASIC may be as long as 65535 characters.) We used LINPUT in case any of the strings contain commas. Otherwise, only the part of the string before the comma would be read into `Sentence`. The rest of the record would be ignored and never processed.

Figure 9-5.
Program to Replace Words in a File

```
10  ! Word replacement in files
20       DECLARE STRING    In_file, Out_file, Sentence, &
                 INTEGER   Posn
30       GOSUB Open_files       ! Open the files
40       GOSUB Process_files    ! Process the files
50       GOSUB Close_files      ! Close the files
60    EXIT PROGRAM

1000 Open_files:                ! Open the files
1010   INPUT 'Enter input filename '; In_file
       OPEN In_file FOR INPUT AS FILE #1
1020   INPUT 'Enter output filename'; Out_file
       WHILE In_file = Out_file
         PRINT
         PRINT 'Cannot use '; In_file
         INPUT 'Enter output filename'; Out_file
       NEXT
       OPEN Out_file FOR OUTPUT AS FILE #2
1030 ! Set margins for terminal format files
       MARGIN #1, 132
       MARGIN #2, 132
1040 RETURN

1100 Close_files:               ! Close the files
1110   CLOSE #1, #2
1120 RETURN

2000 Process_files:             ! Process the files
2010   Sentence = ' '           ! To guarantee entry into loop
       WHILE Sentence <> 'END OF FILE.'
         LINPUT #1, Sentence
         GOSUB Substitute       ! Replace MAN with PERSON
         PRINT #2, Sentence
       NEXT
2020 RETURN

2100 Substitute:                ! Replace MAN with PERSON
2110   Posn = POS (Sentence, ' MAN ', 1)
       WHILE Posn <> 0
         Sentence = SEG$(Sentence,1,Posn) + 'PERSON' &
                      + SEG$(Sentence,Posn+4,LEN (Sentence))
         Posn = POS (Sentence, ' MAN ', Posn+8)
       NEXT
2120 RETURN

32767 END
```

The program contains some deficiencies. It will not find the word " MAN." at the end of a sentence, because there is no blank after the word. Also, it will only find upper case instances of " MAN " because the ASCII codes for upper case are different from lower case. We would have to look for " man " to replace the lower case occurrences, or use the EDIT$ function to convert lower to upper case in the Sentence.

Example 9.14 | The final example in this chapter is sufficiently complex that it will very likely contain errors, even if it is programmed by a very meticulous individual. We will handle it the way we handled the examples in the chapter on debugging: write it first, then go through an entire debugging process.

The program determines whether an input string is a **palindrome.** A palindrome is a sentence or paragraph that reads the same forward and backward. For example, there is Adam's introduction to Eve: "Madam, I'm Adam." Another example is: "A man, a plan, a canal, Panama," which was said of Teddy Roosevelt on building the Panama Canal. (Your library may have a book on palindromes. Entire short stories have been written in this form.)

This is the way it should work: The program looks at the character at each end of the string and compares the two. If they are the same character, then the next characters at each end are examined. If they are not the same, then a flag is set to indicate that the string is not a palindrome. We continue until either the middle of the string is reached or we have determined that the string is not a palindrome. After we leave the loop, the flag is tested and an appropriate message is printed. The pseudocode is:

```
Find palindromes:
    Enter the string
    Test for palindrome
    Print result
Stop

Test for palindrome:
    Until middle is reached or not a palindrome
        Get letter from each end
        If letters not equal, then not a palindrome
    End of loop
Return

Get letter from each end:
    Get next character from left
    Get next character from right
Return
```

The program has been written, as shown in Figure 9-6, but it does not work so STOP's have been inserted into the program.

In subroutine 1000, we again use a flag—this time called Palindrome. Its purpose is to signal the occurrence of two unequal letters.

As indicated, the program does not work. When we enter the string "Madam, I'm Adam," which is a palindrome, the program prints the message that it is not. Notice that the string contains commas; hence the use of

9 STRING PROCESSING

Figure 9-6.
Palindrome Program with Errors

```
10 ! Find palindromes
20     DECLARE STRING    Strng, Palindrome, Left_letter, &
                         Right_letter, &
               INTEGER   Left_posn, Right_posn
30     PRINT 'Enter string to test'
       LINPUT Strng
34 STOP ! For debugging
40     GOSUB Test_string      ! Test Strng for palindrome
50     PRINT
       IF Palindrome = 'YES'
       THEN PRINT Strng; ' is a palindrome'
       ELSE PRINT Strng; ' is not a palindrome'
       END IF
       PRINT
60     EXIT PROGRAM

1000 Test_string:              ! Test for palindrome
1010   ! Start pointers at each end of Strng
         Left_posn = 1
         Right_posn = LEN (Strng)
1020   ! Initialize palindrome flag
         Palindrome = 'YES'
1030     UNTIL Right_posn <= Left_posn OR Palindrome = 'NO'
           GOSUB Get_letters ! Get letter from each end
1040       IF Left_letter <> Right_letter
             THEN Palindrome = 'NO'
           END IF
1050       Left_posn = Left_posn + 1
           Right_posn = Right_posn - 1
1060     NEXT
1070 RETURN

1100 Get_letters:              ! Get letter from each end
1110   ! Get letter from left end
         Left_letter = SEG$ (Strng, Left_posn, Left_posn)
1120   ! Get letter from right end
         Right_letter = SEG$ (Strng, Right_posn, Right_posn)
1124 STOP ! For debugging
1130 RETURN

32767 END
```

LINPUT instead of INPUT. Let us run the program. Remember, our entries are underlined; the computer's responses are not.

```
RUNNH
Enter string to test? Madam, I'm Adam

Stop at line 34   (The actual message printed is more involved)
Ready
```

```
PRINT STRNG
```
Madam, I'm Adam

Ready

```
CONT
```

Stop at line 1124

Ready

```
PRINT LEFT_LETTER, RIGHT_LETTER
M            m
```

Ready

At this point, we should already see what is wrong. The first letter is a capital M, while the last letter is a lower case m. Referring to appendix 3, we see that the ASCII codes for the two are different—the computer thinks they are different letters!

We will compensate for the computer's pedantry by editing the input string to convert it to capital letters. At the same time, we will remove leading and trailing blanks. This will add a statement to line 30, as follows:

```
30      PRINT 'Enter string to test'
        LINPUT Strng
        Strng = EDIT$ (Strng, 168)
```

Since this is already three statements long, we will replace line 30 with a GOSUB statement, and use a subroutine for input, as follows:

```
30      GOSUB Input_string
```

and

```
1200 Input_string:
1210    PRINT 'Enter string to test'
        LINPUT Strng
        Strng = EDIT$ (Strng, 168)
1220 RETURN
```

We take out the STOP's, and run the program again. The program still does not work. It still says the string is not a palindrome. We put our STOP's back in, and this time we have the following interaction:

```
RUN
```

Enter string to test? Madam, I'm Adam
Stop at line 34

Ready

<u>PRINT STRNG</u>
MADAM, I'M ADAM   (Notice the conversion to upper-case)

Ready

<u>CONT</u>
Stop at line 1124

Ready

<u>PRINT LEFT_LETTER, RIGHT_LETTER</u>
M   M

Ready

<u>CONT</u>
Stop at line 1124

Ready

<u>PRINT LEFT_LETTER, RIGHT_LETTER</u>
A   A

Ready

<u>CONT</u>
Stop at line 1124

Ready

<u>PRINT LEFT_LETTER, RIGHT_LETTER</u>
D   D

Ready

<u>CONT</u>
Stop at line 1124

Ready

<u>PRINT LEFT_LETTER, RIGHT_LETTER</u>
A   A

Ready

<u>CONT</u>
Stop at line 1124

Ready

<u>PRINT LEFT_LETTER, RIGHT_LETTER</u>
M

Ready

What happened here? The left letter is M, as it should be, but where is the right letter?

Looking carefully at the string we entered, we should see the problem now. There is a blank before the word ADAM. As far as the computer is concerned, a blank is a character; it has its own ASCII code, 32. Again, the computer is not capable of knowing that we wanted to consider only letters, not spaces or punctuation. Notice that the comma and the apostrophe will also give us problems.

It is far too inconvenient for us to enter strings that do not contain blanks or other punctuation. We will, instead, tell the computer to ignore them. (If there is no punctuation, then we have a simple solution: use EDIT$ with a code of 2 to discard all spaces.) In subroutine 1100, we will add loops at lines 1110 and 1120 that will pass over any blanks or punctuation characters. When subroutine 1100 sends back two characters, they will be letters.

Subroutine 1100 will now be as follows:

```
1100 Get_letters:            ! Get letter from each end
1110    ! Get letter from left end
        Left_letter = SEG$ (Strng, Left_posn, Left_posn)
        UNTIL Left_letter >= 'A' AND Left_letter <= 'Z'
          Left_posn = Left_posn + 1
          Left_letter = SEG$ (Strng, Left_posn, Left_posn)
        NEXT
1120    ! Get letter from right end
        Right_letter = SEG$ (Strng, Right_posn, Right_posn)
        UNTIL Right_letter >= 'A' AND Right_letter <= 'Z'
          Right_posn = Right_posn - 1
          Right_letter = SEG$ (Strng, Right_posn, Right_posn)
        NEXT
1130 RETURN
```

As you can see, after we get a character, we check it against the letters A and Z. If the character is not in the range of those letters, we get the next character, and continue to do so until we have a letter.

Finally, we take out all the STOP statements, run the program, enter the string Madam, I'm Adam, and the program tells us that we have a palindrome. The complete, corrected program is presented in Figure 9-7.

Figure 9-7.
Corrected Palindrome Program

```
10 ! Find palindromes
20    DECLARE STRING   In_String, Strng, Palindrome, &
                       Left_letter, Right_letter, &
              INTEGER  Left_posn, Right_posn
30    GOSUB Input_string    ! Enter string to test
40    GOSUB Test_string     ! Test Strng for palindrome
50    PRINT
      IF Palindrome = 'YES'
      THEN PRINT In_String; ' is a palindrome'
      ELSE PRINT In_String; ' is not a palindrome'
      END IF
      PRINT
60    EXIT PROGRAM
```

Figure 9-7. (*Cont.*)

```
1000 Test_string:                  ! Test for palindrome
1010   ! Start pointers at each end of Strng
          Left_posn = 1
          Right_posn = LEN (Strng)
1020   ! Initialize palindrome flag
          Palindrome = 'YES'
1030      UNTIL Right_posn <= Left_posn OR Palindrome = 'NO'
             GOSUB Get_letters ! Get letter from each end
1040         IF Left_letter <> Right_letter
             THEN Palindrome = 'NO'
             END IF
1050         Left_posn = Left_posn + 1
             Right_posn = Right_posn - 1
1060      NEXT
1070 RETURN

1100 Get_letters:                  ! Get letter from each end
1110   ! Get letter from left end
          Left_letter = SEG$ (Strng, Left_posn, Left_posn)
          UNTIL Left_letter >= 'A' AND Left_letter <= 'Z'
            Left_posn = Left_posn + 1
            Left_letter = SEG$ (Strng, Left_posn, Left_posn)
          NEXT
1120   ! Get letter from right end
          Right_letter = SEG$ (Strng, Right_posn, Right_posn)
          UNTIL Right_letter >= 'A' AND Right_letter <= 'Z'
            Right_posn = Right_posn - 1
            Right_letter = SEG$ (Strng, Right_posn, Right_posn)
          NEXT
1130 RETURN

1200 Input_string:                 ! Enter string to test
1210     PRINT 'Enter string to test for palindrome'
         LINPUT In_String
         Strng = EDIT$ (In_String, 168)
1220 RETURN

32767 END
```

SUMMARY

In this chapter, you learned a number of functions and one operation that allow us to deal with character strings:

1. LINPUT: Instructions used to enter an entire record into a string variable. The record contains everything typed at the terminal or read from a file until a carriage return is encountered. Commas are not delimiters for this statement. Syntax:

> **LINPUT** [prompt;] string [, . . .]
> **LINPUT** #channel, string [, . . .]

2. Concatenation: A string operation whose symbol is the plus sign, +. It is used to combine two or more strings into one. Syntax:

    string + string

3. The LEN function: Used to determine the length of a string in terms of the number of characters it contains. Syntax:

    LEN (string)

4. The POS function: Used to find the location of a substring within a given string. The position where the search begins is specified by the third argument. Syntax:

    POS (string, substring, start-position)

5. The SEG$ function: Used to copy part of a string from a given starting position up to a designated ending position. Syntax:

    SEG$ (string, start-position, end-position)

6. The VAL and VAL% functions: Used to convert a numerical string into an arithmetical value. Syntax:

    VAL (numeric-string)
    VAL% (numeric string)

7. Comparisons: Strings are compared according to their ASCII codes (see appendix 3). Upper and lower case letters have different ASCII codes.

8. The EDIT$ function: Used to perform some simple, basic editing on strings. Syntax:

    EDIT$ (string, code)

The codes determine the type of editing that will be done. They are:

2	Discards spaces and tabs
4	Discards carriage returns, line feeds, form feeds, and nulls
8	Discards leading spaces and tabs
16	Converts multiple spaces and tabs to a single space
32	Converts lowercase letters to upper case
64	Converts brackets to parentheses
128	Discards trailing spaces and tabs
256	Suppresses editing for characters within quotation marks

REVIEW QUESTIONS

1. What is meant by string processing?
2. Which function is used to find the length of a string? What is its syntax?
3. Which function is used to copy all characters of a string from one specified position to another? What is its syntax? What do the arguments stand for? (The arguments are the items in parentheses.)

4. How do you copy all characters of a string up to a specified position? How do you copy all characters after a specified position?

5. What do we call the operation that joins two strings to form one? What symbol is used for this operation?

6. What is the purpose of the VAL function? What is its syntax? What characters are permitted to be in the string that is sent as the argument to the VAL function? What is the difference between VAL and VAL%?

7. When would you use the LINPUT instruction? How does it differ from INPUT?

8. What is the purpose of the EDIT$ function? What is its syntax?

9. What are the codes used in the EDIT$ function? What is the function of each code?

10. How can the EDIT$ function perform more than one editing function at a time?

11. What is the argument you would use in the EDIT$ function to remove leading and trailing tabs and spaces, and to change all multiple tabs and spaces to a single space?

12. What is meant by ASCII code? What are the ASCII codes for the alphabet? What is the ASCII code for a comma?

SYNTAX EXERCISES

The following statements all contain one or more errors. Find them and fix them.

1. 1010 LINPUT "Enter string "; String
2. 1010 LINPUT "Enter name "; Name
3. 1010 LINPUT 1, Record(I)
4. 1010 LINPUT 2, Address(I)
5. 20 DECLARE STRING Number
   2020 Number = 1234 + 5678
6. 20 DECLARE STRING ID, Name_
   2020 ID = 999-01-4321 + Name_
7. 1050 L = LENGTH (Name_)
8. 1060 Total_length = LENGTH(Name) + LENGTH(Address)
9. 3030 First_name = SEG$ (1, Blank_posn, Name_)
10. 3030 Last_name = SEG$ (Blank_posn, LEN (Name_), Name_)
11. 2030 String_ = "123.45" \ Number = VAL% (String_)
12. 2030 String_ = "672-100" \ Number = VAL (String_)
13. 2220 New = EDIT$ (4, Old)
14. 2220 New = EDIT (string_, 160

PROGRAMMING EXERCISES

Write programs or subroutines, as directed, to solve the following problems.

■   **1a.** Write a subroutine that accepts a name, first name first, and reverses it so that the order is last name, comma, space, first name.

1b. Enter a name at the terminal into a string variable: the first name, a space, then the last name. The name is to be decomposed into separate first and last names. These are to be reassembled into one name in the following order: last name, comma, space, first name. Store the result into another string variable. Print the name in its original order and in its reversed order.

2a. Write a subroutine that accepts a string containing first, middle, and last name. The subroutine will reverse the names so that they are last name, comma, space, first name, space, middle name.

2b. Enter a name from the terminal in the following order: first name, middle name, last name. Store this into a string variable. Now decompose the name into its three parts and store them separately. Reassemble the name in the order last name, comma, space, first name, space, middle name. This is to be stored into another string variable. Print the original name, the separate parts, and the reordered name, all suitably identified.

3a. Write a subroutine that accepts a string and checks each character to see if they are all letters of the alphabet. If they are, the subroutine is to return a flag containing the string "ALPHA"; if not, the flag is to return "NON-ALPHA".

3b. Enter a string with a LINPUT statement. Check each character of the string to make sure that it is an alphabetic character or a blank. If all characters meet this requirement, print the message "String OK." If not, print the message "String contains illegal characters." Write the program.

4a. Write a subroutine that examines a string to see if it is numeric. A flag containing "NUMERIC" is to be returned if it is; "NON-NUMERIC" if it is not. Legal characters are digits, decimal points, and prefix minus signs.

4b. Write a program that enables you to enter a string from a terminal into a string variable, then invokes a subroutine to determine if the string is a number. The number can be positive or negative and can contain a decimal point. If the string is numeric, print a message to that effect. If not, print a different message. The main program should be written to allow entering any number of strings until a sentinel XXX is entered.

5a. Write a subroutine that accepts a string and finds the number of times the letter e appears. Return this count.

5b. Enter a sentence into a string variable from the terminal or a DATA statement. Count the number of times the letter e appears in the string. Find what percentage of the letters are e by dividing the number of e's by the total number of letters. Calculate this percentage in two different ways: counting blanks between words in the total number of letters, and not counting blanks. Print the total number of e's, and the percentages obtained from the two methods of counting blanks.

6. Enter a sentence from the terminal into a string variable. Count the number of times each letter appears, and store this number into a 26-element integer array. Print each letter and the number of times it occurred. HINT: Read the 26 letters of the alphabet into an array, using READ and DATA statements.

7. Write a program that lets you enter names from a file, last name first, and prints the number of names with the first name JOHN. Use an end-of-file trap to signify the end of the data. If you have not learned how to trap errors, use the sentinel XXXX.

8. Read words one at a time from a file called WORDS.IN or from DATA statements. Print as many words on a line as possible, not to exceed 60 characters per line. Continue in a similar fashion, line after line until all words have been printed. Use an end-of-file trap, or the sentinel, ZZZZ.

9. Read strings from a file called `RECORD.DAT` or from DATA statements. Each string can have more than one word. Print as many words on a line as possible, not to exceed 60 characters per line. Continue until end-of-file (or the sentinel string ZZZZ if you have not learned error trapping).

10. A file `DATA.DAT` has a large number of records that include the word MAN in a number of places. Create a new file in which each occurrence of that word is replaced by PERSON. The new file can be called `DATA2.DAT`. (Avoid replacing the string MAN where it is part of a larger word.) Take into account the possibility that the word could be the last one in a sentence. Print the contents of the newly created file. Preferably, use an end-of-file trap. If not, use the sentinel XXXX.

11. You just got a job with the FBI as a message decoder. You must write a program that will take as input a coded message and translate it into English. There is a master translation string that looks like this:

`TRANSL_STRING = "GKPMBETWUNJHIRZYQCVSLFAOXD "`

You receive a message that consists of numbers between 1 and 27. Each number represents a letter. To decode the message, you must find the letter in the translation string that is in the position of the received number. (99 is the end-of-message code.)

For example, if the input is 12,6,21,21,24,99, then the message is HELLO. The twelfth letter of the translation string is H, the sixth is E, and so on. The twenty-seventh is a blank.

a. Write a subroutine that accepts the sequence of numbers and returns the decoded message.

b. Write a program that enables you to enter a sequence of numbers, decodes the message, and then prints the message at the terminal. Assume that all numbers entered are in the range 1 through 27 or 99.

12. Same as Exercise 11, but check each number entered to be certain that it is between 1 and 27 or 99. If a number is not in this range, an error message should be printed and the program terminated.

13. This problem uses a translation string as in Exercise 11. The input consists of numbers that correspond to letters in the translation string, as before, but the message is a mirror image of what it should be. For example, the numbers 24,21,21,6,12,99 translate to OLLEH, which is the reverse of what the message should be: HELLO. Read a numerically coded message, use the translation table of Exercise 11 to decode it, reverse all the letters to make the message readable, and print it.

14. Refer to the translation table of Exercise 11. Read an uncoded message and use the table to encode it. The output will be a sequence of numbers, separated by commas, representing the coded message and terminated by the number 99.

15a. Write a subroutine that accepts a name, social security number, and five numbers in string variables. The subroutine is to combine these strings into one string, as follows:

1. The name in the first 20 positions
2. The social security number in the next 11
3. The five numbers using the next 5 columns each

HINT: Padding is to be done with blanks to bring everything up to the required length.

15b. Write a program that can create a file called `CLASS.DAT`. Each record of the file must be one string containing a name in the first 20 characters (the name should be padded with blanks on the right, if necessary, to make it 20 characters long), a social security number in the next 11 characters, and 5 numbers of 5 columns each. The data are entered from the terminal as separate items: name, social security number, and 5 numerical strings. The program assembles the string for output, padding with blanks as needed, and writes the result to the file. This continues until the sentinel END is entered at the terminal. The sentinel need not be written to the file.

16. A file, `CLASS.DAT`, contains records with the following format: The first 20 characters contain a student's name; the next 11 contain the social security number; each of the next five fields is 5 characters long and contains a number representing the student's score on one of five high school achievement tests. There are no commas separating the seven fields. (Instead of a file, the records could be contained in DATA statements.) An end-of-file trap should be used or the sentinel END.

Read each record into a string. Separate the string into its seven component parts. For each record, print the social security number and name on one line, the five achievement scores on a second line, the highest and lowest scores on a third line, and the average of the five scores on a fourth line. Include a blank line after each student's printout. HINT: Because arithmetic will be performed with the scores, you will have to use the VAL function to convert the numeric strings into a form suitable for arithmetic.

17. A file `MAILNG.LST` contains a mailing list. (You may use a set of DATA statements instead of a file, if you prefer.) Each record has the following format:

  Cols 1–20 : Name
  Cols 21–50 : Address
  Cols 51–75 : City, state, and zip code
  Cols 76–77 : A two-character category code

The category codes are to permit selection of a certain group of names from the list. For example, the code FM might mean family; everyone whose code is FM would receive a New Year's card. Another code might be SS, service stations that you call when your car breaks down. These would probably not get New Year's cards. There can be many such codes.

  a. Write a subroutine that receives a string containing one record as described above. The subroutine is to decompose the string into its four component parts.

  b. Write a program that reads each record (or DATA statement). Use an end-of-file trap or a sentinel record containing XXXX in the name field.

Print the name and address of each person whose category code is FM.

18. Refer to exercise 17. Write a program thet can be used to create the file `MAILNG.LST`. Data are entered at the terminal. The program then creates records of the type specified in Exercise 17 and writes them to the file. The program ends when the name XXXX is entered at the terminal. The necessary sentinel must then be written to the file, the file closed, and the program ended.

10 Two-Dimensional Arrays

Outline

10.1 Rows, Columns, and Dimensioning
10.2 Reading a Two-Dimensional Array
　Entering Individual Elements
　Using a Nest of Loops
10.3 Printing Arrays
10.4 Calculating with Arrays
Summary
Review Questions
Syntax Exercises
Programming Exercises
Enrichment Topics
　Passing Arrays to Subprograms
　Arrays of Higher Dimensions
　MAT Instructions
　　Using MAT INPUT and MAT READ
　　NUM and NUM2 Built-in Variables
　　Using MAT PRINT

Introduction In this chapter, you will learn about another technique for storing large quantities of data. As with one-dimensional arrays, the data are stored under one name. However, the data are stored as a table with rows and columns—a **two-dimensional array**.

10.1 ROWS, COLUMNS, AND DIMENSIONING

A two-dimensional array is defined as a block of storage locations with one name. The block is conceptually arranged into rows and columns. Reference to one element of the array, sometimes called a **matrix,** requires two subscripts: one to specify the row number, the other the column number. For example, A(3,5) is the element in the third row, fifth column, of Figure 10-1, a 4×6 array consisting of four rows and six columns.

As with one-dimensional arrays, subscripts can be 0, resulting in a zero'th row and a zero'th column. Arrays that use the zero'th row and column for data are called **zero-based;** those that do not, and consider row 1 and column 1 as the first row and column, are called **one-based.** Henceforth, we will treat all arrays as one-based.

Which are the rows and which are the columns is a matter that often confuses beginners. Referring to Figure 10-1, you can see that each row is a horizontal "slice" or **cross-section** of the array. Rows are assigned numbers from top to bottom. Similarly, the columns are vertical cross-sections of the array. Each column is a vertical set of elements. The columns are numbered from left to right.

Study Figure 10-1 until you are sure you understand which numbers refer to the rows and which refer to the columns. The examples in this chapter should also help to clarify the matrix concept if you are not already familiar with it.

A two-dimensional array, like a one-dimensional array, is dimensioned with a DECLARE statement. (A DIM statement must be used if variable dimensioning is required—see chapter 7 Enrichment Topics.) However, two dimensions must be supplied for the array: the first specifies the number of rows and the second the number of columns.

Example 10.1

```
10 DECLARE REAL      A(10,50), &
           INTEGER   B(25,6), &
           STRING    N(50,2)
```

In this example, storage is reserved for three arrays: a real array, A, which has 10 rows and 50 columns; an integer array, B, which has 25 rows and 6

Figure 10-1.
Diagram of a
Two-Dimensional Array.

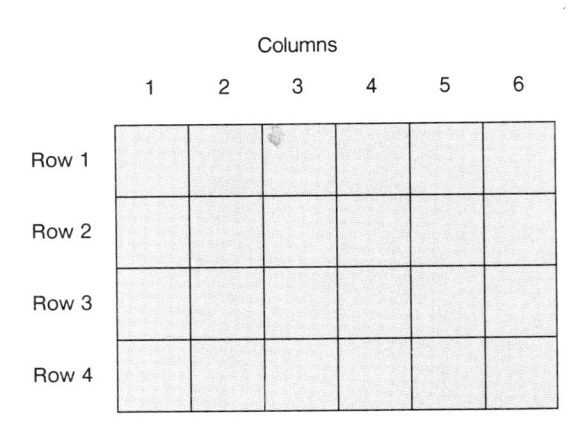

columns; and a string array, N, which has 50 rows and 2 columns. Such a string array might be used to store names in the first column, for instance, with corresponding addresses in the second. (Remember that we are dealing only with one-based array concepts. In actuality, memory is reserved for one additional row and one additional column in all of these arrays, the zero'th row and column.)

Two-dimensional arrays are used whenever it is natural to think of data in terms of groups and subgroups. For example, consider a class consisting of 25 students, with each student taking four tests. The test grades can be stored in an array of 25 rows and 4 columns: one row for each student, and one column for each test taken by that student.

Another example would be an array in which each row represented one salesman, while each column represented the sales he made in a particular month. If there were 50 salesmen, the array representing these data would be a 50×12 array, with one row for each salesman and one column for each month of the year.

10.2 READING A TWO-DIMENSIONAL ARRAY

Two-dimensional arrays can be read into memory in a number of ways. Two are described below.

Entering Individual Elements

Specific elements of an array can be read by specifying the row and column number of the element. For example:

```
INPUT A(1,1), A(2,1), A(1,2)
```

This instruction reads three numbers from the terminal into array A. The first is stored in row 1, column 1, the second in row 2, column 1; and the third in row 1, column 2.

Using a Nest of Loops

Because a two-dimensional array has both rows and columns, two subscripts are necessary to refer to a single element. The values for the subscripts can be supplied by the loop counters of two nested FOR statements. When one loop contains another loop, we say that the loops are **nested.** The nesting can be several levels deep. The following example is a set of two nested loops.

Example 10.2

```
10   DECLARE REAL A(5,10), INTEGER ROW, COL
20   FOR ROW = 1 TO 5      ! Row number
       FOR COL = 1 TO 10   ! Column number
         INPUT 'Enter No.', A(ROW,COL)
       NEXT COL
     NEXT ROW
```

In this example, we read values into a 5×10 array (5 rows, 10 columns). First, ROW, representing the row number, is set to a value of 1. Then COL, the column number, takes on each value from 1 to 10. In this way, the entire first row is read into the array horizontally since the row number doesn't change until columns 1 through 10 have been read.

After this first row has been entered, ROW becomes 2. The inner loop again takes on each value from 1 to 10, causing the second row to be read. This loop repeats for each row as ROW goes from 1 to 5. Therefore, the numbers are read into the array horizontally, or in **row-order**.

We can read the elements into the array vertically, or in **column-order**, by interchanging the two FOR statements:

```
20   FOR COL = 1 TO 10  ! Column number
       FOR ROW = 1 TO 5 ! Row number
         INPUT 'Enter No.', A(ROW,COL)
       NEXT ROW
     NEXT COL
```

Here the column number is selected first, after which the row number goes from 1 to 5. As the row number increases, we move down a column. The result is that the array is read in column-order. Notice that the subscripts have not reversed order in the array element; only the loops have. The first subscript is still ROW, the row number, and the second is still COL, the column number. *In any reference to an array element, the row number always precedes the column number.*

Example 10.2 used the variable names ROW and COL as the loop variables to make it clear what these variables represented. Any other numeric variables could be used instead and the loops would work just as well. The only loss would be to the user, as the program would not be as clear.

10.3 PRINTING ARRAYS

Arrays can be printed using statements similar to those used for reading arrays. Specific elements can be printed, or a nest of loops can be used to print an entire array or part of one.

Example 10.3

```
100   PRINT A(10,1), A(10,2), A(10,3)
200   FOR ROW = 1 TO 10
        FOR COLUMN = 1 TO 5
          PRINT A(ROW,COLUMN);
        NEXT COLUMN
        PRINT
      NEXT ROW
```

Line 100 will cause the first three elements in row 10 of array A to be printed in three fields of one line (note the commas used as separators). Line 200 will print 10 rows, with five numbers in each row in packed format (note the semicolon at the end of the first PRINT statement in line 200). Because more than five numbers would normally fit on one line, we have to make sure we end one line before we print another. That is the purpose of the `PRINT` statement between `NEXT COLUMN` and `NEXT ROW`. That `PRINT` statement does not print any values, but because it is not followed by a comma or semicolon, the next `PRINT` statement that executes will output on a new line.

If a comma had terminated the `PRINT A(ROW,COLUMN);` statement in line 200 instead of a semicolon, then one element of the array would be printed every 14 columns, in each field of the output line.

10.4 CALCULATING WITH ARRAYS

Calculating with two-dimensional arrays is similar to calculating with one-dimensional arrays except that a nest of at least two loops is usually required. As with reading or printing a two-dimensional array, the loop counter of one loop generally selects the row number to be used, while the other loop counter selects the column number.

IMPORTANT! When loops are nested, one loop *must* be entirely within the other. The loop that starts LAST must end FIRST, as shown in the following example.

```
FOR I = 1 to 50
       .
       .
       .
     FOR J = 1 to 10
            .
            .
            .
     NEXT J
       .
       .
       .
NEXT I
```

The following statements would be illegal, because the loops overlap each other:

```
FOR I = 1 to 50
       .
       .
       .
     FOR J = 1 to 10
            .
            .
            .
     NEXT I
       .
       .
       .
NEXT J
```

Example 10.4

A teacher gives five tests to each student in his class. He has a maximum of 40 students, but often has fewer. He needs a program that will allow him to enter all of the students' grades into an array, then calculate each student's average and store it in a one-dimensional array. Finally, the program should print each student's number (from 1 to the total number of students) followed by the student's average.

In pseudocode we have:

```
Class grading program:
    Input the student grades
    Calculate the student averages
    Print student numbers and averages
Stop
```

Expanding the central calculation gives:

```
Calculate the student averages:
    Loop student = 1 to number of students
        Find student (row) average
        Store into array of averages
    Next student
Return
```

The pseudocode statement "Find student (row) average" can be further expanded:

```
Find student (row) average:
    Initialize sum to 0
    Loop test = 1 to 5
        Sum = sum + grade
    Next test
    Avg = Sum/5
Return
```

We eventually arrive at the program shown in Figure 10-2.

In line 1010 of this program, we use NO.OF.STUDENTS as the row subscript number of the array. It is initialized to zero, and we then read one number into the simple variable, TEST. If that number is not the sentinel, we increase the row subscript; store that first number into column 1 of the array, then get the remaining four numbers of the row, which are stored in columns 2 through 5. That completes the data required for one student. At

Figure 10-2.
Class Grading Program

```
10  ! Class grading program
20      DECLARE INTEGER   GRADE(40,5), TEST, NO.OF.STUDENTS, &
                          SUM.TESTS, STUDENT, COL, &
                REAL      AVGS(40)
30      GOSUB Enter_grades     ! Enter student grades
40      GOSUB Find_avgs        ! Calculate student averages
50      GOSUB Print_avgs       ! Print student averages
60  EXIT PROGRAM
```

Figure 10-2. (*Cont.*)

```
1000 Enter_grades:              ! Enter student grades
1010    NO.OF.STUDENTS = 0
        PRINT \ PRINT 'Student no.'; NO.OF.STUDENTS + 1
        INPUT 'Enter test, -999 to end'; TEST
        WHILE TEST <> -999
           NO.OF.STUDENTS = NO.OF.STUDENTS + 1
           GRADE(NO.OF.STUDENTS, 1) = TEST
           FOR COL = 2 TO 5
              INPUT 'Enter test            '; &
                 GRADE(NO.OF.STUDENTS, COL)
           NEXT COL
           PRINT \ PRINT 'Student no.'; NO.OF.STUDENTS + 1
           INPUT 'Enter test, -999 to end'; TEST
        NEXT
        ! Note: NO.OF.STUDENTS now contains no. of rows read
1020 RETURN

1100 Print_avgs:                ! Print student averages
1110 ! Print headings
        PRINT
        PRINT TAB(20); 'St.no.'; TAB(30); 'Average'
        PRINT
1120 ! Print student numbers and averages
        FOR STUDENT = 1 TO NO.OF.STUDENTS
           PRINT TAB(21); STUDENT; TAB(32); AVGS(STUDENT)
        NEXT STUDENT
1130 RETURN

1500 Find_avgs:                 ! Find student average
1510    FOR STUDENT = 1 TO NO.OF.STUDENTS
1520       ! Find sum of students tests
           SUM.TESTS = 0
           FOR TEST = 1 TO 5
              SUM.TESTS = SUM.TESTS + GRADE(STUDENT,TEST)
           NEXT TEST
1530       ! Find average and store it
           AVGS(STUDENT) = SUM.TESTS / 5
1540    NEXT STUDENT
1550 RETURN

32767 END

runnh
Student no. 1
Enter test, -999 to end? 39
Enter test              ? 87
Enter test              ? 98
Enter test              ? 79
Enter test              ? 90
```

Figure 10-2. (*Cont.*)

```
Student no. 2
Enter test, -999 to end? 56
Enter test              ? 98
Enter test              ? 89
Enter test              ? 78
Enter test              ? 45

Student no. 3
Enter test, -999 to end? 52
Enter test              ? 76
Enter test              ? 84
Enter test              ? 89
Enter test              ? 90

Student no.4
Enter test, -999 to end? -999

              St.no.    Average
                1        78.6
                2        73.2
                3        78.2
```

the bottom of the loop, we again read one number into the simple variable, TEST. We then return to the top of the loop, where that number is compared to the sentinel again, and repeat. Eventually, we leave the loop when the sentinel is read.

Assume that the input consists of the following data:

```
70,80,90,60,100
75,75,75,75,75
85,90,80,95,100
```

Then the output of the program will be:

```
              St.No.    Average
                1          80
                2          75
                3          90
```

Example 10.5 We will modify the previous problem in three ways.

First, to relieve the teacher of the drudgery of having to enter the grades from the terminal each time the program is run, we will read the data from a file called GRADES.DAT. The five grades for each student will be in one record and will be separated with commas. We will read an entire record into a string variable with the LINPUT statement, then use string functions to separate the grades. We will use an end-of-file trap to determine when the last student's grades have been read.

Second, the average for each student will be calculated after dropping the lowest grade; only the four best grades of each student will be used to calculate his average.

Third, the class average will be found, using *all* grades; that is, the lowest will not be dropped.

The pseudocode for the main program is:

   Grades, dropping lowest, from file:
     Open the file
     Read the data
     Close the file
     Find averages
     Print results
   Stop

To find the averages, we have:

   Find averages:
     Initialize for class total
     For all students
       Find average, dropping lowest
       Accumulate for class average
     End of loop
     Find class average
   Stop

To find the average while dropping the lowest test, we first add all the tests together; then find the lowest test and subtract it from the sum; and finally divide the result by one less than the number of tests. In pseudocode, the solution requires the following steps:

   Find average, dropping lowest:
     Add all grades
     Find lowest grade
     Subtract lowest from sum
     Divide to find average
   Return

To find the lowest grade, we use the student's first test mark as a trial value. We then compare each of the other tests to that one. If a lower test is found, that becomes the new low value. The pseudocode is as follows:

   Find lowest test of student:
     Lowest = first test
     Loop from test 2 to 5
       If test < lowest then lowest = test
     End of loop
   Return

At the end of this loop, the variable Lowest will be equal to the lowest test of the five. The rest of the logic is straightforward, so we will proceed directly to the program, which appears in Figure 10-3.

Figure 10-3.
Modified Class Grading Program

```
10  ! Grades, dropping lowest, read from file
20      DECLARE INTEGER    Grades(40,5), Student, No.Students, &
                           Test, Sum, Lowest, Class_Sum, &
                           Comma_Before, Comma_After, Eof, &
                DECIMAL(4,1) Student_Avg(40), Class_Avg, &
                STRING     In_File, Five_Grades, Grade_String
30      ON ERROR GOTO Error_Routine
40      GOSUB Open_file              ! Open the file
50      GOSUB Read_file              ! Read the file
60      GOSUB Close_file             ! Close the file
70      GOSUB Find_avgs              ! Find the averages
80      GOSUB Print_avgs             ! Print the averages
90   EXIT PROGRAM

1000 Open_file:                      ! Open the file
1010    INPUT 'Enter filename '; In_File
1020    OPEN In_File FOR INPUT AS FILE #1
1030 RETURN

1100 Read_file:                      ! Read the file
1110    Student = 1
        Eof = 0                      ! Not End-of-file
        GOSUB Read_rec               ! Read first record
        WHILE NOT Eof = 1            ! Set to 1 in Error_Routine
          Student = Student + 1
          GOSUB Read_rec             ! Read next record
        NEXT
1120    No.Students = Student - 1    ! Don't count End-of-file
1130 RETURN

1200 Close_file:                     ! Close the file
1210    CLOSE #1
1220 RETURN

1300 Read_rec:                       ! Read a record
     ! Also break record into component parts
1310    LINPUT #1, Five_Grades
1320    Comma_Before = 0 \ Comma_After = 0
1330 ! Get first four grades from string
        FOR Test = 1 TO 4
          Comma_Before = Comma_After
          Comma_After = POS(Five_Grades, ",", Comma_Before + 1)
          Grade_String = SEG$(Five_Grades, Comma_Before + 1, &
                                           Comma_After - 1)
          Grades(Student, Test) = VAL(Grade_String)
        NEXT Test
1340 ! Get fifth grade, after last comma
        Grade_String = SEG$(Five_grades, Comma_After + 1, &
                                         LEN(Five_Grades))
        Grades(Student, 5) = VAL(Grade_String)
1350 RETURN
```

Figure 10-3. (*Cont.*)

```
1400 Print_avgs:                    ! Print all averages
1410   PRINT
       PRINT TAB(20); 'Student';TAB(30); 'Average'
       PRINT                         ! Heading
1420   FOR Student = 1 TO No.Students
          PRINT TAB(22); Student; TAB(30); Student_Avg(Student)
       NEXT Student
1430   PRINT
       PRINT TAB(20); 'Class average = '; Class_Avg
       PRINT
1440 RETURN

1500 Student_avg:              ! Find average, dropping lowest
1510   ! Sum the grades
       Sum = 0
       FOR Test = 1 TO 5
          Sum = Sum + Grades(Student, Test)
       NEXT Test
1520   ! Find lowest test
       Lowest = Grades(Student,1)
       FOR Test = 2 TO 5
          IF Grades(Student,Test) < Lowest
          THEN Lowest = Grades(Student,Test)
          END IF
       NEXT Test
1530   Student_Avg(Student) = (Sum - Lowest) / 4
1540 RETURN

2000 Find_avgs:                    ! Find averages
2010   Class_Sum = 0               ! Initialize for class average
2020   FOR Student = 1 TO No.Students
          GOSUB Student_avg   ! Find average, dropping lowest
                              ! and Sum of student grades
          Class_Sum = Class_Sum + Sum / 5
       NEXT Student
2030   Class_Avg = Class_Sum / No.Students
2040 RETURN

19000 Error_Routine:
19010    IF ERR = 5 AND ERL = 1020 THEN       ! Can't find file
            PRINT
            INPUT "Can't find file. Please reenter"; In_File
            RESUME
         ELSE IF ERR = 11 AND ERL = 1310 THEN ! End-of-file
            Eof = 1
            RESUME 1350
         ELSE                                 ! All others
            ON ERROR GOTO 0
         END IF
19020 ! End Error_Routine

32767 END
```

The class average was found by adding all of the individual student averages—without dropping the lowest grade—and dividing by the number of students. Here the student average was found by dividing the sum of the student's grades by 5 in line 2020. The program is easily modified so that input could be accepted from the terminal, as in the previous example.

SUMMARY

In this chapter, you learned how to use two-dimensional arrays:

1. The DECLARE statement is required to reserve storage for a two-dimensional array. Two numbers must follow the array name: the first specifies the number of rows, the second the number of columns.
2. Arrays can be read with INPUT or READ instructions. A nest of loops is usually required. The outer loop normally controls the row number, while the inner loop controls the column number.
3. Two-dimensional arrays can be printed by using nested loops to print element by element. The loop variable of the outer loop usually controls the row number, while the inner loop controls the column number.

REVIEW QUESTIONS

1. What is a two-dimensional array?
2. What is the purpose of the DECLARE statement regarding two-dimensional arrays? What does the first subscript in the DECLARE statement specify? What does the second subscript specify?
3. An array is dimensioned with the statement DECLARE A(5,8). How many rows does it have? How many columns? If the zero'th elements are taken into account, how many rows and columns does it have?
4. To enter data into an array by rows, using a nest of loops, does the outer loop control the rows or the columns?
5. To enter data into an array by columns, using a nest of loops, does the outer loop control the row or column number?
6. To print an array by rows, a nest of loops can be used. Does the outer loop control the row or column numbers?
7. Can a two-dimensional array store strings? What determines whether or not it can store strings?

SYNTAX EXERCISES

The following contain one or more errors. Find and correct them.

1. `20 DECLARE Sales(50,12)`
2. `20 DECLARE Grades(35,5)`
3. `20 DECLARE REAL Earnings(50,12)`
4. `20 DECLARE INTEGER Survey(10,10)`
5. `20 DECLARE STRING ID(25,2)`
   `1020 INPUT "Enter row 1 "; ID(1)`
6. `20 DECLARE INTEGER Numbers(20,10)`
   `2020 PRINT Numbers(5)          ! Print row 5`

7. ```
   2030 ! Output
        FOR ROW = 1 TO 10
            FOR COLUMN = 1 TO 20
                PRINT A(ROW,COLUMN)
            NEXT ROW
        NEXT COLUMN
   ```
8. ```
   1030 ! Input
        FOR COLUMN = 1 TO 5
            FOR ROW = 1 TO 10
                INPUT "Enter number "; Maze(ROW,COLUMN)
            NEXT COLUMN
        NEXT ROW
   ```
9. ```
   20 DECLARE REAL Quantity(100,12)
   3020 Sum = 0
        FOR I = 1 TO 12
            FOR J = 1 TO 100
                SUM = SUM + Quantity(I,J)
            NEXT J
        NEXT I
   ```
10. ```
    20 DECLARE INTEGER Salaries(100,12)
    3020 Sum = 0
         FOR Month = 1 TO 12
             FOR Person = 1 TO 100
                 Sum = Sum + Salaries(Month, Person)
             NEXT Person
         NEXT Month
    ```

PROGRAMMING EXERCISES

Write subroutines or programs, as directed, that will solve the following problems. All output should be identified.

1a. Write a subroutine that will find the average of each row of a 10×6 (10 rows, 6 columns) array, and store these averages in a 10-element, one-dimensional array.

1b. Write a subroutine that will find the average of each column of a 10×6 array, and store these in a 6-element, one-dimensional array.

1c. Read a 10 rows by 6 columns (10×6) two-dimensional array. Form a 10-element, one-dimensional array by averaging the elements in each row. Form a 6-element array by averaging the elements in each column. Print each row of the two-dimensional array, followed on the same line by the row-average from the row average array. (This means that you will print seven numbers on each row.) After printing these ten rows, skip a line and print the column averages under their respective columns.

2. Same as Exercise 1c, except that the lowest number of each row is to be dropped when computing the row averages.

3a. Write a subroutine that receives an 8×5 array and interchanges all the rows and columns to form a 5×8 array. That means, row 1 of the original should become column 1, row 2 should become column 2, and so on. This is called finding the **transpose** of the original array.

3b. Read an 8×5 two-dimensional array A. Form a 5×8 array B by interchanging the rows and columns of A. Print both arrays.

■ **4a.** Write a subroutine that accepts a 10×20 array and divides every element in a given row by the first element in that row.

4b. Read a 10×20 array from file `ARR10.20`. Divide every element in a given row by the first element in that row. Write the array to file `ARR10.20`, creating a new version of that file. HINT: Store the first element of each row before you start dividing that row. Once the first element is divided by itself, its value will be 1.

5. Read numbers that represent prices into the first column of a 50×3 array. The data may be entered from the terminal, DATA statements, or a file, but a file called `PRICES.DAT` is preferred. Calculate the tax for each price (6.25%) and put it into column 2. Add the tax to the price and store it in column 3. Print the array under suitable column headings.

6. Similar to Exercise 5, except for the following additional items:
  a. A one-dimensional string array associated with the above array contains a description of the item whose price is in column 1 of the two-dimensional, three-column array.
  b. The data for the arrays are to be read from a file called `INVENT.ORY`. Each record of the file will contain the description of the item followed by its price. The two will be separated in the file by a comma.

  As in Exercise 5, the program should calculate the tax (6.25%) and total price, storing them in columns 2 and 3, respectively. Output should consist of the part description, its base price, the tax, and the total price, all under suitable column headings.

7. Same as Exercise 6, except that the input file does not have a comma between items in a record; the part description is followed by a blank and then the base price. The entire record, including description and price, must be read into a string variable. String functions must then be used to separate the string into the two parts: item description and price. These will then be stored into the proper array. Output is to be as described in Exercise 6.

8. Store integers into a 10×10 array. You may use the random number generator, a file, or DATA statements, or you may enter the numbers at the keyboard. Add the elements on the perimeter (first row, first column, last row, last column). Then add up all the elements on the diagonals. Print the sums, suitably identified.

9. A two-dimensional string array has 50 rows and 3 columns. Each row contains data for one person. Column 1 contains the name, column 2 contains the address, and column 3 contains the telephone number.

■ **a.** Write a subroutine that accepts this array and sorts it by name. If the name in column 1 must be moved to a new row, be sure to move the address and telephone number along with it. Use a bubble sort (see chapter 7).
  b. Same as part a, but use an insertion sort (see chapter 7).
  c. Read data into the array from a file, `ID.DAT`, or from DATA statements. Use an end-of-file trap or the sentinel record X,X,X to denote the end of data.

  The program is to sort the array by name, keeping each name with its address and telephone number. After sorting, the array is to be printed under suitable column headings, one row per line. If files are used as input, a new version of the file is to be written from the sorted array. Use a bubble sort or insertion sort as directed by your instructor.

10. A file `ID.DAT` contains data for a two-dimensional array, as described in exercise 9. The data in the array are already sorted (possibly as a result of doing exercise 9).

a. Write a subroutine to which the array and a name are sent. The subroutine searches column 1 of the array for the given name. If it is found in the array, it will return the corresponding row number. If not, it will return 0. Use a binary search or sequential search, as directed by your instructor.

b. Write a program that reads the file into a two-dimensional, 50×3 array, using an end-of-file trap (or a sentinel). The program will then ask the user to enter a name. The array will be searched for that name. If it is found, the name, address, and telephone number should be printed. If not, a message informing the user that the name does not exist should be printed.

Extra recognition: Make the program insensitive to case.

11. A company manufactures five different products. It has fewer than 100 salesmen who sell these products. Read the following data for each salesman into a two-dimensional array, SALES, from a file, SALES.DAT, or DATA statements.

    salesman number
    units of product 1 sold
    units of product 2 sold
    units of product 3 sold
    units of product 4 sold
    units of product 5 sold

Dimension array SALES as 100×6. Each salesman's data will occupy one row of the array. The five products have the following unit prices:

PRODUCT	PRICE
1	$27.50
2	$43.43
3	$82.34
4	$10.00
5	$55.53

Read these prices from DATA statements into a one-dimensional array, UNIT.PRICE.

Now sort array SALES by salesman number. That is, put the salesmen's numbers in numerical order. When an interchange has to take place, be sure to interchange the entire row.

Next, find the gross sales for each salesman by multiplying the number of each item sold by the unit price and summing the results. Produce a report with the following appearance:

Salesman Number	Sales of products in units					Gross sales in dollars
	1	2	3	4	5	
###	###	###	###	###	###	$##,###.##
.	.	.	.	.	.	.
.	.	.	.	.	.	.
.	.	.	.	.	.	.
TOTALS	####	####	####	####	####	$###,###.##

The last row is calculated by summing the columns. HINTS: You might consider using column 0 of array SALES for the salesman's number. Add as many additional arrays for intermediate results as required.

12. A company has 10 workers. Each worker produces widgets at his own pace. The number of widgets produced by each worker every month is recorded. At the end of the year, the boss gives bonuses to some of the employees. The worker who produced the most widgets in a given month is given a bonus equal to 1% of his salary. Twelve such awards are given out, one for each month, and a person may get more than one such bonus. In addition, a bonus of 5% is given to the person who produced the most widgets that year.

The data to be read are contained in the 10 DATA statements that follow. (Alternatively, your instructor may wish to set up a data file for you to use.) Each DATA statement contains the employee's name followed by the number of widgets produced for each month of that year. The names are to be read into a 10-element string array and the monthly widget production figures into an associated two-dimensional 10×12 array.

For each month, identify the worker who made the most widgets. Print his name with a message indicating that he gets a 1% bonus. Then find the worker who had the highest yearly widget production. Print his name, indicating that he gets a 5% bonus. The DATA statements are:

```
DATA Sam,281,241,407,242,245,407,308,388,374,430,417,290
DATA Sally,382,274,434,430,261,201,435,378,239,450,370,476
DATA Joe,339,448,371,449,450,461,414,374,421,312,335,225
DATA Hillary,224,412,397,381,481,386,495,268,213,478,268,486
DATA Alfred,392,484,401,419,327,288,264,476,365,285,365,244
DATA Kim,352,445,348,251,398,445,327,452,347,225,313,459
DATA Xavier,242,416,477,496,266,373,242,219,254,341,412,441
DATA Bea,487,493,311,468,203,385,414,210,489,467,367,376
DATA Carol,405,466,278,335,462,370,245,394,269,212,371,370
DATA Chet,450,298,390,213,404,367,311,361,227,471,312,301
```

HINT: Use as many additional arrays as necessary to store intermediate results.

13. A chessboard has 64 squares arranged as eight rows and eight columns. We can represent such a board as a two-dimensional array. The subscripts of the array are the row and column numbers of the squares on the board. That is, if the array is called BOARD, then BOARD(5,7) would represent the square in the fifth row, seventh column, of the chessboard. Let a rook be placed on BOARD(4,4) with no other pieces on the board. Use a random number generator to place an opposing piece on the board. Have your program determine whether the rook is in a position to remove the opposing piece. If it can, print Piece attacked. If not, print Piece safe. A rook can move horizontally (left and right) or vertically (forward and back). A rook can remove any piece in its path. The program should repeat, placing pieces on the board ten times.

14. Same as Exercise 13, except use a queen instead of a rook. The queen can move horizontally, vertically, or diagonally. It can remove any piece in its path.

15a. Same as Exercise 13, except use the random number generator to place both the rook and its opponent.

15b. Same as part a, but use a queen instead of a rook, as in Exercise 14.

16. A mouse is in the middle of a table that is 30 inches wide by 60 inches long. The mouse has just finished drinking a martini which someone had left, and is now blind-drunk. Every 10 seconds, the mouse staggers a random number of steps in a random direction. The number of steps is between 3 and 10, and each step is 1 inch long. The direction is always parallel to one side of the table, never diagonal. Let the mouse stagger along for 5 minutes (300 seconds) or until it falls off the table, whichever comes first.

Write a program to simulate the mouse's predicament. The table can be a two-dimensional array. The mouse can start at the center, TABLE(15,30). A random number generator can simulate the number of steps and the direction of the mouse's meanderings. The program should print whether or not the mouse remains on the table after five minutes and its location, or at what time it falls off, if that is its unfortunate fate.

ENRICHMENT TOPICS 10

More On Arrays

VARIABLE DIMENSIONING

Two-dimensional arrays can be declared using variable dimensioning with the DIM statement. See the chapter 7 enrichment topics.

PASSING ARRAYS TO SUBPROGRAMS

A two-dimensional array can be passed to a subprogram. In the CALL statement, the array name is followed by parentheses. If the array is one-dimensional, only the parentheses are used. If two-dimensional, then a comma is included in the parentheses.

In the SUB statement argument list, the same protocol is used. In addition, the array parameters may (and should) be explicitly typed.

Example 10.6

```
30     DECLARE STRING A(100), REAL B(10,50)
40     CALL SUBR (A(), B(,))           ! Invoke the subprogram

1000 ! Subprogram with arrays
1010    SUB SUBR (STRING A(), REAL X(,))
           ...
           ...
           ...
        END SUB
```

In this subprogram, even though parameter array A is matched with the argument array A, their names are different entities. This is illustrated with the second array, X. This two-dimensional array is matched with the two-dimensional array B, but their names are local. The array is called B in the main program and X in the subprogram. See chapter 14 for a more complete discussion of arguments and parameters.

Example 10.7

We will write a program that reads a two-dimensional array and uses subprograms to read the array, find the average of each row, and print the row averages. The row averages will be stored in a one-dimensional array and returned to the main program by the subprogram.

The logic is simple; here is the code.

Figure 10-4.
Program Using Subprogram with Arrays

```
10   ! Program to find row averages using subprogram
20     DECLARE REAL A(50,10), Row_avgs(50)
30     CALL Read_array (A( , ))
40     CALL Find_row_avgs (A( , ), Row_avgs( ))
50     CALL Print_row_avgs (Row_avgs( ))
60   END

1000 SUB Read_array (REAL A( , ))
1010    DECLARE INTEGER Row, Column
1020    OPEN "ARRAY.DAT" FOR INPUT AS FILE #1
1030    FOR Row = 1 TO 50
            FOR Column = 1 TO 10
1035            INPUT #1, A(Row,Column)
            NEXT Column
        NEXT Row
1040    CLOSE #1
1050 END SUB

2000 SUB Find_row_avgs (REAL A( , ), REAL Row_avgs( ))
2010    DECLARE INTEGER Row, Column, REAL Sum
2020    FOR Row = 1 TO 50
            Sum = 0
            FOR Column = 1 TO 10
                Sum = Sum + A(Row, Column)
            NEXT Column
            Row_avgs(Row) = Sum / 10
        NEXT Row
2030 END SUB

3000 SUB Print_row_avgs (REAL Row_avgs( ))
3010    DECLARE INTEGER Row
3020    ! Print heading
        PRINT TAB(20); "Row"; TAB(30); "Average"
        PRINT TAB(20); "---"; TAB(30); "-------"
        PRINT
3030    FOR Row = 1 TO 50
            PRINT TAB(20); Row; TAB(30); Row_avgs(Row)
        NEXT Row
3040 END SUB
```

ARRAYS OF HIGHER DIMENSIONS

VAX-BASIC allows arrays to be dimensioned with up to 32 dimensions. Use of such high-dimensioned arrays is beyond the scope of this book.

MAT INSTRUCTIONS

Using MAT INPUT and MAT READ

VAX-BASIC has several MAT instructions that let you enter an entire array with only one instruction. These are the MAT INPUT, MAT LINPUT, and MAT READ instructions. The syntax for these statements is:

```
MAT INPUT array-name [, . . .]
MAT INPUT #channel, array-name [, . . .]
MAT LINPUT string-array-name [, . . .]
MAT LINPUT #channel, string-array-name [, . . .]
MAT READ array-name [, . . .]
```

Examples are:

```
MAT INPUT GRADES
MAT INPUT #1, A, B
MAT LINPUT NAMES, ADDRESSES
MAT LINPUT #2, SENTENCES
MAT READ X
```

Each variable in the examples above will have been DECLAREd (or DIMensioned) as an array. An explanation of each instruction follows.

MAT INPUT

The MAT INPUT instruction can read either an entire or partial array. When the MAT INPUT instruction executes, a question mark will appear at the terminal. The user may then type as much data as desired. The data will be entered into the array by rows, row 1 first, then row 2, and so on. If fewer elements are supplied than the array can hold, the remaining elements retain their previous value (which is 0 if they have never been assigned). If more data are supplied than the array can hold, the excess values are ignored. All data for the array must be entered before <Return> is pressed.

Assume that the following statements appear in a program:

```
10 DECLARE INTEGER GRADES(40,5)
20 PRINT "Enter 5 grades for each student"
   MAT INPUT GRADES
```

The first 5 numbers the user types will fill row 1, the next 5 will fill row 2, and so on. If 100 numbers are typed, then the first 20 rows of the array will receive those numbers. The remaining 20 rows will be as they were prior to the input instruction.

If 102 numbers had been entered, then the first 20 rows would be completely filled and the twenty-first row would have only 2 columns filled.

When entering data in response to a MAT INPUT instruction, the values must be separated by commas. If the data do not fit on one physical line, then an ampersand must be used at the end of the line so that the data may be continued on the next line. The following could be entered in response to the MAT INPUT instruction above:

```
78, 87, 92, 88, 75, &
65, 77, 82, 81, 76, &
95, 98, 89, 93, 100, &
65, 75, 72, 68, 73
```

The first 4 rows of the 40-row array would be filled, while the remaining 36 rows would remain unchanged.

If there are additional array names in the MAT INPUT instruction, then data for the second array can begin after the <Return> is pressed for the first array, data for the third commences after the <Return> for the second, and so on.

None of the MAT INPUT instructions may have an included prompt. Any desired prompt must be printed with a PRINT instruction prior to execution of the MAT INPUT statement.

> **NOTE!** **MAT instructions, including all those mentioned below, may be used only with one- or two-dimensional arrays. Arrays of higher order, which are not discussed in this text, must be handled with other types of instructions.**

MAT INPUT

The MAT INPUT # instruction is the same as the MAT INPUT instruction except for one major difference: the data will come from the file attached to the specified channel.

MAT LINPUT

This instruction is used with STRING arrays. An entire line, up to but not including the <Return>, is stored in each element of the array. After each <Return> is pressed, the MAT LINPUT instruction prints another question mark to prompt the user for more input. This continues until the array is completely filled. Consider the following instructions:

```
10 DECLARE STRING INFO(4,2)
20 PRINT "Enter name, then address"
   MAT LINPUT INFO
```

When line 20 executes, you may interact with the computer as shown below. (Your responses are underlined.)

```
Enter name, then address
?Bird, Tweety
?Gilded Cage, CA
?Runner, Road
?Mesa Flats, CO
?Bear, Yogi
?Jellystone Park, WY
?Duck, Donald
?Somewhere, VT
```

> **NOTE!** **The LINPUT instruction requires that the entire array be filled. It is filled by rows, one after the other. If more than one array is specified in the input instruction, then question mark prompts continue to appear at the terminal until all arrays have been supplied data.**

MAT LINPUT

This instruction is like the MAT LINPUT instruction except that data come from the file associated with the specified channel.

MAT READ

Data for the MAT READ instruction come from DATA statements within the program. If there are not enough data for the array in the DATA statements supplied, then the remaining elements in the array are unaltered. If there are more elements than necessary, the extra data are available for additional READ statements. As an example:

```
10 DECLARE REAL A(10,3)
20 MAT READ A
100 DATA 23,45,42,76,85,67,45,87,93,40,80
```

After these instructions, A(1,1) = 23, A(1,2) = 45, A(1,3) = 42, A(2,1) = 76, A(2,2) = 85, A(2,3) = 67, A(3,1) = 45, A(3,2) = 87, A(3,3) = 93, A(4,1) = 40, and A(4,2) = 80. Remaining elements in the array will be unchanged from their previous values (which will be 0 unless previously assigned other values).

NUM AND NUM2 BUILT-IN VARIABLES

After a MAT INPUT instruction, the built-in variable NUM is set to the total number of rows read, while NUM2 is set to the number of elements read into the last, incomplete row. If there are no incomplete rows, the value of NUM2 will be zero.

Example 10.8

```
10   DECLARE REAL A(50,5)
20   PRINT 'Enter numbers for a 50×5 array'
     MAT INPUT A
30   PRINT 'No. of Rows Read = '; NUM
40   PRINT 'No. of Elements in Last Row = '; NUM2
```

When these statements are executed, we will be allowed to enter up to 250 numbers, because that is how many numbers the array can store (50×5). If we were to enter only 123 numbers, however, the output of the program would be:

```
No. of Rows Read =  25
No. of Elements in Last Row =  3
```

We have entered 24 complete rows with 5 numbers in each row, equaling 120 numbers, plus the three numbers in the last row. Thus the number of rows read, including the final incomplete row, is 25.

The NUM and NUM2 variables can also be used in calculations within the program or as loop control limits. For example, after an array has been partially filled, a loop to perform calculations on the rows read in could be controlled with the following statements:

```
100 MAT INPUT A
    NO.ROWS = NUM
110 FOR ROW = 1 to NO.ROWS
        Loop statements
    NEXT ROW
```

USING MAT PRINT

An entire array, or part of an array containing complete rows, may be printed with a single MAT PRINT statement. Output may be in several forms. To print an entire array at the user's terminal, the following statements may be used:

MAT PRINT array-name
MAT PRINT array-name,
MAT PRINT array-name;

A MAT PRINT always starts printing an array on a new line. The first statement will print each element of the array on a new line.

The second statement, which is followed by a comma after the array name, causes five values to be printed on each line (assuming the MARGIN has been set at 80) at the predefined tab stops. However, each row of the array is started on a new line even if there is still room on the previous line.

The third version above has a semicolon after the array name. This produces output in packed format, with as much data printed on one line as possible. In any case, each new row of the array is printed starting on a new line at the terminal.

Examples are:

```
10  DECLARE REAL    NUMBERS(10,5), &
            STRING  NAMES_ADDRS(25,2), &
            INTEGER GRADES(40,5)
    ...
100 MAT PRINT NUMBERS
110 MAT PRINT NAMES_ADDRESSES,
120 MAT PRINT GRADES;
```

Part of an array may be printed by including subscripts after the array name. The column subscript should be the same as in the DECLARE statement. The row subscript should be the same as the number of rows you wish to print. Consider the following statements:

```
10 DECLARE INTEGER GRADES(40,5), No.students
20 PRINT 'Enter 5 grades for each student'
   MAT INPUT GRADES
   No.Students = NUM
       ...
       ...
90 PRINT 'Student grades are:'
   MAT PRINT GRADES(No.Students,5);
```

NUM was set when the MAT INPUT instruction executed. Its value was stored in the variable No.Students. The MAT PRINT instruction now prints only the number of rows that were entered.

The output can also be directed to a terminal-format file by including a channel number in any of the statements above. Examples are:

```
100 MAT PRINT #1, NUMBERS
110 MAT PRINT #2, NAMES_ADDRESSES,
120 MAT PRINT #3, GRADES;
130 MAT PRINT #4, GRADES(No.Students,5);
```

11 Print Using

Outline

11.1 The PRINT USING Instruction
11.2 Formatting Characters
  Quotation Mark—'
  Left Justify—'L
  Right Justify—'R
  Center Justify—'C
  Extended Field—'E
  Numeric Field—#
  Decimal Point—.
  Comma—,
  Floating Dollar Sign—$$
  Asterisk fill—**
  Other Editing Characters
11.3 Matching Headings with Data Lines
  Other Formats
11.4 PRINT USING for Terminal-Format Files
Summary
Review Questions
Syntax Exercises
Programming Exercises

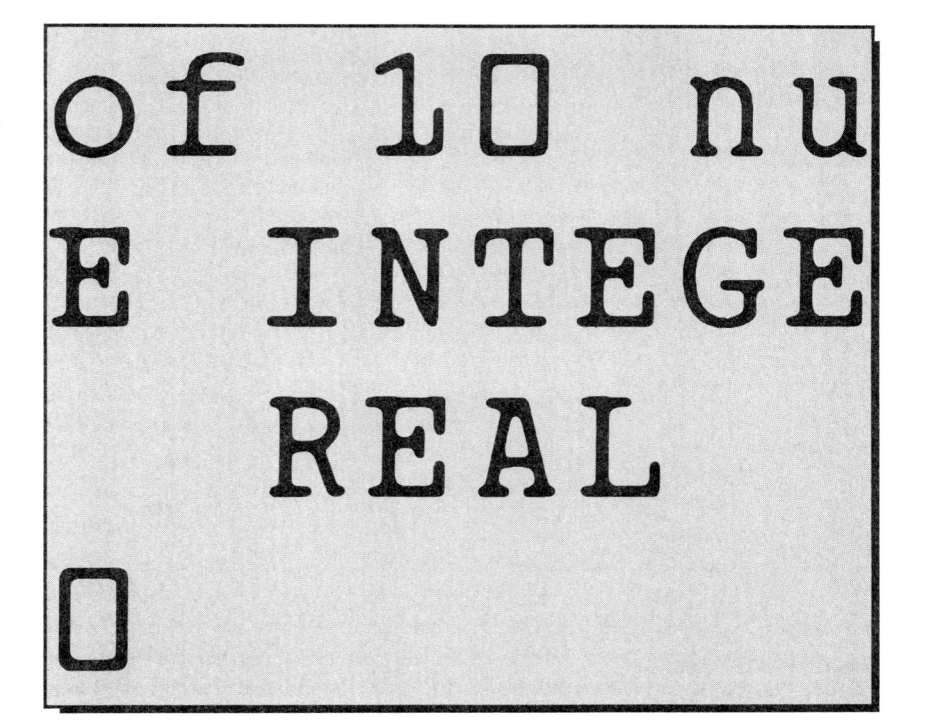

Introduction This chapter describes a statement that allows you to have greater control of print formatting than was available with previously described I/O. The chapter can be skipped entirely if you wish, or sections of it can be learned as the need arises.

The PRINT USING statement, with appropriate format specifications, allows exact control of the number of characters printed for character data and the number of decimal places printed for numeric data. In addition, various editing characters can be included in the output.

11.1 THE PRINT USING INSTRUCTION

The syntax of the PRINT USING statement is as follows:

sn PRINT USING format-string, list

where **format-string** is a string of format characters and **list** is an output list.

The format-string may be a **string literal** (constant containing a sequence of characters) or a **string variable.** If it is a string literal, the string must be enclosed in quotes. The characters it contains determine the appearance of the output.

IMPORTANT! If the format-string literal itself contains single quotes within it, then only double quotes may be used to enclose the string; single quotes would not be permitted as enclosures. It is always safe to use double quotes.

Here are four examples of the PRINT USING statement:

```
20    DECLARE STRING A, B, C, &
              REAL Salary, &
              INTEGER X, Code
100   PRINT USING "###", X
150   PRINT USING A, X, B, C
200   PRINT USING "'L ##.##", B, 25
250   PRINT USING '$$#,###,###.##   ###', Salary, Code
```

In these examples, the first string constant or variable that follows the word USING contains the format information. The rest of the statement, after the comma, is the list of constants or variables to be printed using that format. Line 100 prints variable X in three columns exactly (assuming it will fit). Line 150 prints the variables X, B, and C according to a format specified in the string variable A. (Notice that A is a STRING variable and will contain the format-string.)

Line 200 prints the first two characters of string variable B (because of the 'L as explained later in this chapter), and also prints the number 25 with two places after the decimal point (25.00). A single quote is part of the format-string, so the string had to be enclosed in double quotes as shown. Line 250 has a format-string that does not include a single quote, so we have enclosed the string in single quotes for illustrative purposes. But as a general rule, you are urged to use double quotes for format-strings to avoid possible errors.

11.2 FORMATTING CHARACTERS

Each of the formatting characters and their uses are now described. To help understand the output, a scale will be used, as shown below.

```
0++++5+++10+++15+++20+++25+++30+++35+++40+++45+++50
```

This scale corresponds to the columns of a zero-based line. Please be aware that this scale will **not** be printed when you actually run the examples; it is for reference purposes only.

Quotation Mark—'

The quotation mark identifies a one-character field and also starts a multi-character string field. Used alone, it causes the first character of the output string to be printed.

Example 11.1

```
10 DECLARE STRING A, B, C
20    A = 'ABC'
      B = 'DEF'
      C = 'GHI'
30    PRINT USING "'  '  '", A, B, C
32767 END
```

prints

```
0++++5+++10+++15+++20+++25+++30+++35+++40+++45+++50
A  D  G
```

The first character of each of the three strings contained in A, B, and C is printed. Each character replaces a single quote in the format string. Because there are two blanks between the quotes, there are two blanks between each of the letters in the output.

Notice that double quotes are used to enclose the format-string in line 30. Single quotes, as used in line 20, are not permitted in line 30 because they are used as formatting characters.

We also could have assigned the format string to a string variable and used the name of the variable instead of the string literal in the PRINT USING statement, as shown in Example 11.2.

Example 11.2

```
10 DECLARE STRING A, B, C, FORMAT_STRING
20    A = 'ABC'
      B = 'DEF'
      C = 'GHI'
30    FORMAT_STRING = "'  '  '"
      PRINT USING FORMAT_STRING, A, B, C
32767 END
```

This again prints

```
0++++5+++10+++15+++20+++25+++30+++35+++40+++45+++50
A  D  G
```

Left Justify—'L

A single quote followed by one or more L's, either upper or lower case, designates a field that will print left-justified characters. The quote represents one character and each L represents one character in the output field. If the datum being printed has fewer characters than the field width, then it will be printed left-justified, with blanks padding the rest of the field. However, if the datum is larger than the field, then it will be truncated to fit the field. Only the left-most characters will be printed.

Example 11.3

```
10 DECLARE STRING A, B, C, D, FORM
20    A = 'ABCDE'
      B = 'FGHIJ'
      C = 'KLMNO'
      D = 'PQRST'
30    FORM = "'L  'LLLLLLLLL  'LLL  'LL"
40 PRINT USING FORM, A, B, C, D
32767 END
```

prints the following:

```
0++++5+++10+++15+++20+++25+++30+++35+++40+++45+++50
AB  FGHIJ       KLMN  PQR
```

where FORM is the string variable that contains the format. Notice that there are two spaces between each field in the format string, so there are two blanks between the fields in the output.

The first field is a quote followed by an L, so the first two letters of the first variable, A, are printed.

The second format specification consists of a quote followed by nine L's. This is, therefore, a field of ten characters. Because B contains only five characters, they are printed at the far left of the ten-character field. The remaining five positions in the field are made blanks.

The third field specification consists of a quote followed by three L's—a four-character field. Variable C is printed using this specification. But because the field contains only four positions, only four characters of the string are printed.

The fourth field consists of three positions and is used to print the first three letters of the last variable, D.

Right Justify—'R

The right-justify field is handled just like the left-justify field, except that output will be right-justified. It is used for string output.

Example 11.4

```
10 DECLARE STRING A, B, C, D, FORM
20    A = 'ABCDE'
      B = 'FGHIJ'
      C = 'KLMNO'
      D = 'PQRST'
30    FORM = "'R  'RRRRRRRRR  'RRR  'RR"
40 PRINT USING FORM, A, B, C, D
32767 END
```

prints the following:

```
0++++5+++10+++15+++20+++25+++30+++35+++40+++45+++50
AB        FGHIJ KLMN PQR
```

This output is similar to that of Example 11.3, but the string contained in variable B, which is shorter than the ten-position field allotted to it, is printed in the right-most positions, instead of the left-most.

Center Justify—'C

Center justify, as its name implies, lets you create a field in which output data will be centered. The single quote and each C (upper or lower case) designate one position of the field. If the datum cannot be exactly centered because it has an even number of characters, it will be offset to the left. In other words, there will be one more space padded on the right than on the left.

Example 11.5

```
10 DECLARE STRING A, B, C, D, FORMAT_STRING
20    A = 'ABCDE'
      B = 'FGHIJ'
      C = 'KLMNO'
      D = 'PQRST'
30    FORMAT_STRING = "'C 'CCCCCCCC 'CCC 'CC"
40 PRINT USING FORMAT_STRING, A, B, C, D
32767 END
```

prints the following:

```
0++++5+++10+++15+++20+++25+++30+++35+++40+++45+++50
AB      FGHIJ      KLMN PQR
```

where FGHIJ has been printed in the center of its ten-column field, with two blanks padded at its left and three at its right.

Extended Field—'E

The left-, right-, and center-justify formats define fields of fixed length. If the string being printed in a field is longer than the field's defined length, it is truncated on the right, with only the left-most characters printed, equal to the width of the field.

In contrast, the extended field format defines a field of minimum length, but this field can expand to the size of the datum if the string is longer than the field width. Therefore, when the extended field format is used, no characters in the datum will be truncated—all will be printed. If the defined field is larger than the string, then the string will be left-justified within the field.

Example 11.6

```
10 DECLARE STRING A, B, C, D, EXTENDED_FORMAT
20    A = 'ABCDE'
      B = 'FGHIJ'
      C = 'KLMNO'
      D = 'PQRST'
30    EXTENDED_FORMAT = "'E   'EEEEEEEE   'EEE   'EE"
40 PRINT USING EXTENDED_FORMAT, A, B, C, D
32767 END
```

prints the following:

```
0++++5+++10+++15+++20+++25+++30+++35+++40+++45+++50
ABCDE   FGHIJ        KLMNO   PQRST
```

The first field, which was defined as two characters, has been extended to five to accommodate the string ABCDE.

The second field, which was defined as ten characters in width, had only five letters in the datum, so all five, FGHIJ, were printed and, according to the rules for extended fields, five additional blanks were padded in at the right.

The third and fourth fields were also extended to fit the data.

The blanks between format definitions in the variable EXTENDED_FORMAT cause the two blanks that appear between items in the output. Without those blanks, one field would run directly into another.

Numeric Field—#

The # character in a format string designates a numeric position. Several successive characters, with some additional optional characters to be described, define a numeric field. For example, the format string "###" defines a three-digit numeric field.

Example 11.7

```
10 DECLARE REAL A, B, C, STRING FORM
20 A = 26.84 \ B = 35.2 \ C = 18
30 FORM = "###   ###   ###"
40 PRINT USING FORM, A,B,C
```

prints this output:

```
0++++5+++10+++15+++20+++25+++30+++35+++40+++45+++50
 27    35    18
```

Although each number printed consists of only two digits, three columns have been used for each number because each format consists of three # symbols. The leading column is a blank because each number contains only two digits before the decimal point. In addition, because there are two blanks between each numeric field in the format, two additional blanks are inserted between the numbers in the output. The numbers are rounded to the nearest integer when printed because no provision has been made for a decimal point in the format specification.

Numeric fields can contain a number of editing characters, as discussed in the following sections.

Decimal Point—.

A decimal point in a numeric field determines the position of the decimal point in the printed number.

Example 11.8
```
10    A = 11/3
20    PRINT USING "###.##", A
32767 END
```

prints

```
0++++5+++10+++15+++20+++25+++30+++35+++40+++45+++50
  3.67
```

The number in A, which is stored by the computer as 3.666666, has been rounded to two decimal places for printing because the format string has only two # characters after the decimal point. Because there are three # symbols preceding the decimal point in the format, but the number has only one digit before the decimal point, there are two leading blanks before the number.

Comma—,

The comma is another editing symbol used in a numeric field. It consists of a single comma placed in a numeric field format after the first # symbol, but before the decimal point, if any. When the value is printed, a comma will be placed before every third digit to the left of the decimal point. (Hence, it follows that the comma will be printed only if the number has at least four digits to the left of the decimal point.) Note that even if the format-string field contains only one comma, a seven-digit number will be printed with two, one before each three digits to the left of the decimal point.

Example 11.9
```
10 DECLARE REAL A, B, C, STRING OUTPUT_FORMAT
20    A = 974
      B = 5287
      C = 4765
30    OUTPUT_FORMAT = '####,###   #,####.#   ####,.##'
40    PRINT USING OUTPUT_FORMAT, A, B, C
32767 END
```

prints the following numbers:

```
0++++5+++10+++15+++20+++25+++30+++35+++40+++45+++50
      974    5,287.0    4,765.00
```

All # symbols and commas that are not used become blanks in the output line. Notice that the commas in the first format specification do not appear on the output because the number has only three digits.

As you can see, it does not matter exactly where the comma is placed, as long as it is after the first # symbol and before the decimal point, if any. For convenience, and to make the format-string clear, most programmers normally put commas in their formats where they will appear in the output, as follows:

```
30    OUTPUT_FORMAT = '####,###    ##,###.#    #,###.##'
```

There is no reason not to do so and it will be less confusing.

Floating Dollar Sign—$$

A numeric format string that begins with two dollar signs causes a dollar sign to appear before the first printed digit. However, if the number is sufficiently large, then the positions occupied by the dollar signs may be used for digits instead.

Example 11.10

```
10    DECLARE REAL A, B, C, STRING FORM
20    A = 528639 \ B = 37 \ C = 5287.1
30    FORM = '$$#,###.##'
40    PRINT USING FORM, A
      PRINT USING FORM, B
      PRINT USING FORM, C
32767 END
```

prints this output:

```
0++++5+++10+++15+++20+++25+++30+++35+++40+++45+++50
528,639.00
    $37.00
 $5,287.10
```

As you can see, the number in variable A requires every position in the field to the left of the decimal point. There is no room for the dollar sign, so it is not printed. The other two numbers are smaller, so they allow the dollar sign to print. Notice that the dollar sign moves to the position immediately in front of the first digit printed.

NOTE! If a floating dollar sign is used in a field that will print negative as well as positive numbers, then a minus sign must follow the last # symbol. Negative numbers will have their sign printed in that position. If you do not add this minus sign, then error number 116 (from Appendix 2) will occur when a negative number is printed with that format specification. For example, the format

"$$#,###.##-"

can be used to print both positive and negative numbers with a floating dollar sign. A negative number will be printed with a trailing minus. For example, −1234.56 will print as

```
0++++5+++10+++15+++20+++25+++30+++35+++40+++45+++50
 $1,234.56-
```

Asterisk Fill—**

In a number of commercial applications, for security reasons, it is undesirable to leave blanks in front of a number. Check writing is an example. When a numeric format field starts with two asterisks, then all spaces in the field before the first digit are filled with asterisks.

Example 11.11

```
10    DECLARE REAL A, B, C, STRING FORM
20    A = 528639 \ B = 37 \ C = 5287.1
30    FORM = '**#,###.##'
40    PRINT USING FORM, A
      PRINT USING FORM, B
      PRINT USING FORM, C
32767 END
```

prints this output:

```
0++++5+++10+++15+++20+++25+++30+++35+++40+++45+++50
528,639.00
*****37.00
**5,287.10
```

As with the floating dollar signs, since the first example requires all field positions for digits, no asterisks can appear. The other two numbers are sufficiently small so that leading asterisks are printed.

NOTE! If a field using asterisk fill is used to print negative numbers, then a minus sign must follow the last # symbol. Negative numbers will have their sign printed in that position. If you do not add this minus sign, then error number 116 (see Appendix 2) will occur when a negative number is printed with that format specification. For example, the format

```
"**#,###.##-"
```

can be used to print both positive and negative numbers with asterisk fill. A negative number will be printed with a trailing minus. For example, −1234.56 will print as

```
0++++5+++10+++15+++20+++25+++30+++35+++40+++45+++50
**1,234.56-
```

Other Editing Characters

Alphanumeric characters and spaces, as well as most special characters not mentioned in the previous sections, are printed exactly as they appear in the format string; they are not replaced by data. We can use these characters to identify our values.

Example 11.12

```
10    DECLARE REAL A, B, Sum, STRING Form
20    A = 56
      B = 72
      Sum = A + B
```

```
30   Form = "A = ###     B = ###      SUM = ####"
40   PRINT USING Form, A, B, Sum
32767 END
```

prints the following output:

```
0++++5+++10+++15+++20+++25+++30+++35+++40+++45+++50
A =  56     B =  72     SUM =  128
```

The characters A, B, and SUM and the equality symbol (=) are printed exactly as they appear in the format string. The # symbol is used to format the numeric variables.

11.3 MATCHING HEADINGS WITH DATA LINES

The PRINT USING statement greatly simplifies the process of creating professional-looking reports.

Assume that we have a number of column headings we want to print at the top of a report, above the columns of data. We can place the headings in a string variable that will be used to print the headings. The format-string that will be used to print the data is put into another string variable. If we physically line up the two format strings, we ensure that the data values will line up correctly under their proper headings. We will illustrate this method with an example.

Example 11.13 Assume that we have a file called SALES.DAT. Each record consists of a salesman's name and three sales. We want to read each record, print the name, the three sales, and the salesman's total sales. Furthermore, we want each of these data items to be printed directly under appropriate headings. The last record in the file is a sentinel record, consisting of END in the name field and three 0's for the data. If possible, an end-of-file trap should be used instead. Our pseudocode will be:

```
Print a report:
  Open the file
  Process the file
  Close the file
Stop

Process the file:
  Set up formats
  Print headings
  Read the first record
  While not sentinel record (or not eof)
    Find sum of sales
    Print name, sales, sum
    Read next record
  End of loop
Return
```

In the program that follows in Figure 11-1, note the physical alignment of the strings containing the headings with the PRINT USING format

Figure 11-1.
Program to Print a Report

```
10  ! Print a report
20      DECLARE STRING    HEADING_1, HEADING_2, DATA_FORMAT, &
                          NAME_, &
                DECIMAL(7,2) SALE1, SALE2, SALE3, SUM_SALES
30      OPEN 'SALES.DAT' FOR INPUT AS FILE #1
40      GOSUB Process_file            ! Process the file
50      CLOSE #1
60   EXIT PROGRAM

1000 Process_file:                    ! Process the file
1010    GOSUB Make_formats            ! Set up headings and formats
1020    GOSUB Print_headings          ! Print heading
1030    GOSUB Read_rec                ! Read first record
        WHILE NAME_ <> 'END'
          SUM_SALES = SALE1 + SALE2 + SALE3
          GOSUB Print_rec             ! Print a record
          GOSUB Read_rec              ! Read next record
        NEXT
1040 RETURN

1100 Make_formats:                    ! Set up headings and formats
1110    HEADING_1= "SALESMAN    SALE        SALE        SALE           TOTAL"
1120    HEADING_2= "  NAME       1           2           3             SALES"
1130    DATA_FORMAT="'LLLLLLL  $$##.##     $$##.##     $$##.##      $$#,##.##"
1140    RETURN

1200 Print_headings:                  ! Print the headings
1210   PRINT HEADING_1 \ PRINT HEADING_2 \ PRINT
1220 RETURN

1330 Read_rec:                        ! Read a record
1310    INPUT #1, NAME_, SALE1, SALE2, SALE3
1320 RETURN

1400 Print_rec:                       ! Print a record
1410   PRINT USING DATA_FORMAT, NAME_, SALE1, SALE2, SALE3, SUM_SALES
1420 RETURN

32767 END
```

strings (lines 1110 through 1130). The headings will be in the strings HEADING_1 and HEADING_2, and the format will be in the string DATA_FORMAT (FORMAT and FORMAT$ are reserved words).

Subroutine Make_formats illustrates the method of aligning the headings with the data format string. HEADING_1 and HEADING_2 will be printed exactly as shown and become the headings. DATA_FORMAT is the format that is used to print the data. The format specifications are lined up under the headings exactly as the corresponding data will be lined up. When used in this manner, the process is almost foolproof.

Incidentally, that last field in DATA_FORMAT has a comma after the first # symbol and is followed by two additional # symbols. The comma must be put after the first #, but, together with the two dollar signs, $$, this field allows numbers as large as $9,999.99.

Notice also that DATA_FORMAT in line 1130 used double quotes to enclose the format string. This is necessary because the string format itself contains a single quote.

The best way to learn to use the PRINT USING statement properly is to try these examples and then experiment with various other formats.

Other Formats

There are a number of other format specifications possible, but they will not be discussed here. They allow you to print numbers with leading zeros instead of blanks, or with the minus sign placed after the number, or with credit and debit symbols instead of + or − signs. If you are interested, refer to the VAX-BASIC manual or ask your teacher.

11.4 PRINT USING FOR TERMINAL-FORMAT FILES

You can use PRINT USING for terminal-format files; the output in the file will be exactly as it would be at the terminal. To write to the file, first open the file FOR OUTPUT on any desired channel. Then use the statement as follows:

PRINT #channel USING format, list

Examples are:

```
1030 PRINT #1 USING Format_string, A, B, C
1030 PRINT #2 USING "'LLLL   $$####.##", Name_, Price
```

SUMMARY

This chapter discussed a method of precisely controlling the appearance of output data. The keyword USING is added to the output instruction and a format string provides the necessary information. The format string includes certain special characters that have specific effects on the output. The format information can be included with the PRINT USING statement as a string constant in quotes, or it can be put into a string variable to which the PRINT USING statement refers. Here is a brief list of the items discussed in this chapter.

1. PRINT USING format-string, list
2. Numeric field—#
3. Character field—'
4. String field
    Left justified—'L
    Right justified—'R

Center justified—'C
Extended format—'E
5. Floating dollar sign—$$
6. Asterisk fill—**
7. Comma—,
8. Decimal point—.
9. Other characters: used for output identification.

REVIEW QUESTIONS

1. What are the advantages of using a PRINT USING statement rather than a PRINT statement with the TAB function?
2. Which symbol is used to designate a position in a numeric field?
3. What editing characters are permitted in a numeric field? How is a floating dollar sign handled? How are commas handled? How is the decimal point handled?
4. Which symbols are used to designate a string field? Explain the distinction between the different characters used.
5. Explain how it would be possible to write a program in which the output has a different appearance each time the program is run.
6. What special requirement is there if a floating dollar sign or asterisk fill is used in printing a negative number?

SYNTAX EXERCISES

Each statement below contains one or more errors. Find and correct them.

1. `1020 FORMAT = ' ### ###.##   'LLLL   $$###,.##'`
2. `1020 Format_string =`
   `'$$###.##   ,###.##   'RRRR  **####'`
3. `1020 PRINT USING ###.##, A`
4. `1020 PRINT USING 'LLLLLL   'L, Name_, Average`
5. `1020 Form = "$$#,###.##   $$#,###.##"`
   `     PRINT USING Form`
6. `1020 Format_ = "Hours = ##.#    Salary = $$##,.##"`
   `     PRINT USING Format_, Name_, Hours, Salary`
7. `1020 Format_ = "'EEEE   ###.##"`
   `     PRINT USING Format_, Hours, Salary`

PROGRAMMING EXERCISES

Write subroutines or programs to solve the following problems. Use PRINT USING statements for all output. Be sure all output is identified.

■
1. The built-in variable PI contains the value of pi (approximately 3.14159265359). Use the PRINT USING statement to print this value to two, then three, then four, then five decimal places.
2. A real estate agent sells eight houses in one month. The agent gets a 7% commission on each sale.
   a. Write a subroutine that prints the sale price and commission. The output must have floating dollar signs and a comma every third digit to the left of the decimal point.

b. The sales prices are in a file called HOUSE.SLS, or if you prefer, you may put them into DATA statements. Read the sales prices into an array. For each house, print the sale price and the commission. The amounts are to have a floating dollar sign and must also have a comma every third digit to the left of the decimal point. The amounts are to be identified as SALE PRICE and COMMISSION, respectively. Finally, print the total of all sales and the total commission, also using the aforementioned format, but identified as TOTAL SALES and TOTAL COMMISSION.

3a. Write a subroutine that prints a name and an average. The name is to be left-justified in a field of 20 columns. The average is to be printed to one decimal place.

3b. Enter a name and five grades. Find the average of the grades. Print the name in the first 20 columns of the line and the average (to one decimal place) in the next five columns. Repeat for more students until the end-of-file condition is met (or until the sentinel END is read for the name).

4. Repeat Exercises 3a and 3b, but also print the letter grade (A, B, C, D, or F) in the fourth column after the average.

5. You work for a baseball team. The manager wants you to write a program for him that will use as input each player's name, times at bat, number of singles, number of doubles, number of triples, and number of home runs. The output should be the name, batting average, and slugging percentage.

The batting average is calculated by taking the total number of hits (singles, doubles, triples, and home runs) and dividing by the number of at-bats. The slugging percentage is calculated by taking the number of singles, plus two times the number of doubles, plus three times the number of triples, plus four times the number of home runs, and dividing that total by the number of at-bats.

a. Write statements that will print the headings and data lines in the format shown below.

```
PLAYER    AT                              HOME    BAT.    SLUG.
NAME      BATS   SNGLES   DBLES   TRPLES  RUNS    AVG.    PCT.

'LLLLLL   ###    ###      ###     ###     ###     .###    #.###
```

b. Write a program that reads the player's statistics from a file called STATS.DAT (or from DATA statements). Use an end-of-file trap (or EOF as the end-of-data sentinel). When out of data, print the number of players, team batting average, and team slugging percentage, using the above format.

6. Read a first name, middle name, and last name into 3 string variables. Print the last name, using 15 columns, then the first name in 10 columns, and then the middle initial only, followed by a period. Do all output with a PRINT USING statement, and use no string functions.

7. Each of the DATA statements below has four numbers. The first DATA statement represents Republican responses to four questions, the second represents Democratic responses, and the third represents responses from independent voters. The four numbers in each DATA statement represent the numbers of voters who gave affirmative responses to each of four questions asked by a poll taker.

Figure 11-2.
Format of Output for Exercise 7

	Ques 1	Ques 2	Ques 3	Ques 4	Totals
Republicans	52	13	9	82	(sum)
Democrats	18	6	42	102	(sum)
Independents	163	45	79	12	(sum)
Totals	(sum)	(sum)	(sum)	(sum)	

You are to read the data and find the total number of positive Republican, Democrat, and Independent replies. Also, find the total number of people who answered "yes" to each question. The output is to be arranged in tabular form as shown in Figure 11-2. The DATA statements are:

DATA 52,13,9,82
DATA 18,6,42,102
DATA 163,45,79,12

HINT: Use a two-dimensional array.

8. Take any programs you have done previously whose output you felt was unsatisfactory in appearance and improve the output with PRINT USING statements. This will be accomplished easily if your output was handled with output subroutines.

12 Relative Files

Outline

12.1 Basic Concepts of Relative Files
12.2 Defining a Program Buffer—The MAP Statement
　　　Defining String Length
12.3 Opening a File—The OPEN Statement
12.4 Reading Relative Files—the GET statement
12.5 The PUT Statement
12.6 The UPDATE Statement
Summary
Review Questions
Syntax Exercises
Programming Exercises

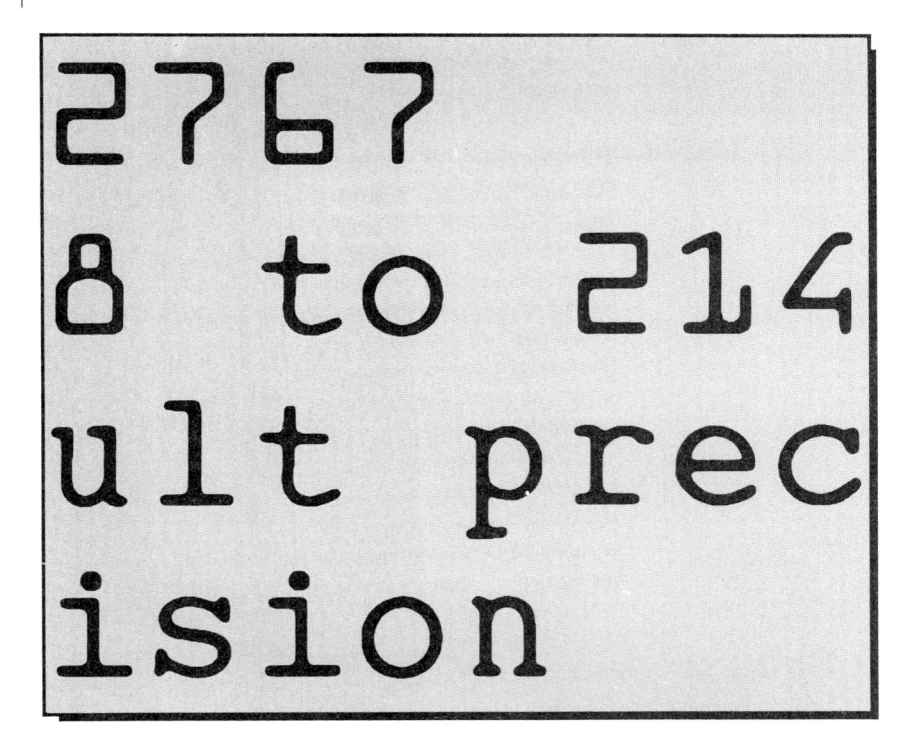

Introduction In chapter 8, we learned of the concept of files by studying terminal-format files. Such files are sequential—each record must be accessed in the order in which it was written.

In this chapter, we learn of a file organization, called **relative file,** that permits us to access the records of a file randomly, that is, in any order.

12.1 BASIC CONCEPTS OF RELATIVE FILES

In chapter 8, different types of file organizations were described. At that time, we considered only terminal format files because they were closest to the type of input/output you had been doing at the terminal. But one disadvantage of this type of file is that it must be accessed sequentially. In many cases, a sequentially organized file is inadequate, and a means of reading or writing any record in the file randomly—in any order—is necessary. VAX-BASIC has a type of file called a **relative file** that permits this type of random access.

In a relative file, as in a number of other types, data are read or written in groups of fields called **records.** Each input or output instruction reads or writes a complete record. The data pass from the program to the file, or from the file to the program, through an entity called the **program buffer.** Each item that is to be output to the file is assigned a specific place in the buffer. To be sent to the file, the value must first be put into the buffer in its assigned location. After all items of the record have been put into the buffer, the entire buffer is then output as a single unit with a single statement (refer to Figure 12-1).

12.2 DEFINING A PROGRAM BUFFER—THE MAP STATEMENT

The MAP statement is used to define a program buffer and give names to each of its fields. The names of the fields look and behave like ordinary variables as far as the program is concerned. The program can put data into the buffer, or read data from the buffer, by means of these field names.

Figure 12-1.
Buffer Usage in Relative File Access

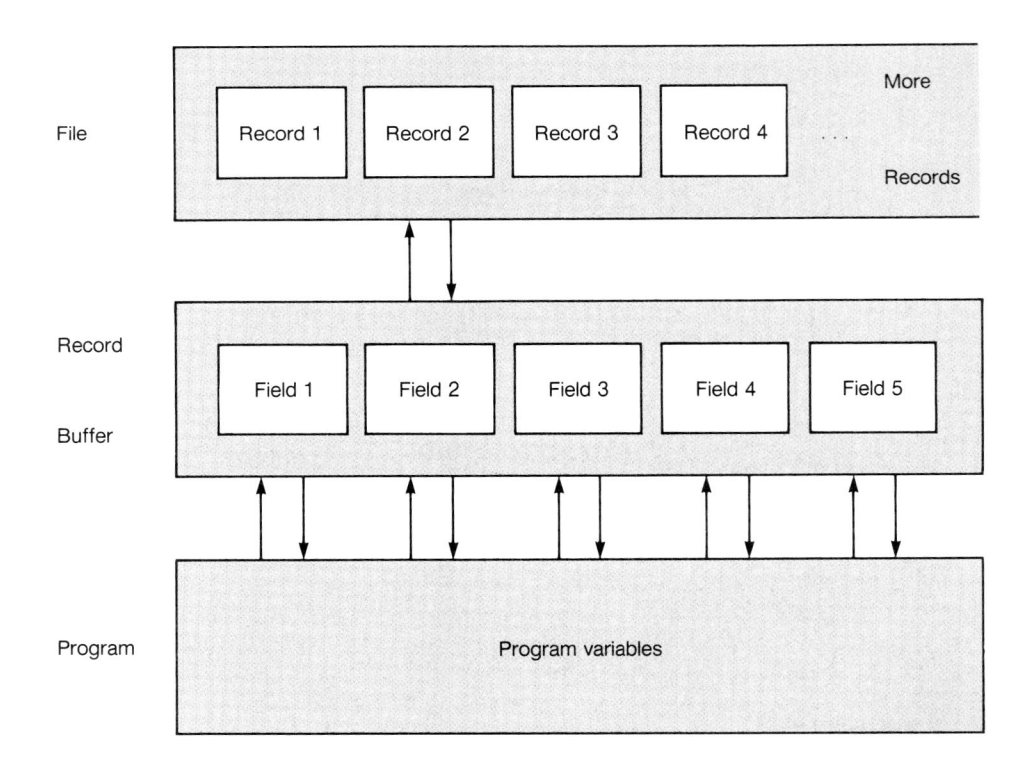

In other words, the MAP statement divides the buffer into fields and gives each field a name; the name of the field is then used as if it were an ordinary variable. When a value is assigned to a field variable, the value will be put into the buffer in the corresponding field. When that field variable is referred to, the corresponding value in the buffer is obtained.

The MAP statement will be associated with a file when the file is OPENed and causes the defined buffer to be used when reading or writing the file.

The syntax of the MAP statement is:

MAP (map-name) data-type field-name [, ...]

For example:

```
MAP (Payroll) STRING ID_no., Name_, &
              REAL Hrs_worked, &
              DECIMAL(6,2) Salary
```

The map-name, which must be in parentheses, is the name by which the OPEN statement (explained in section 12.3) can refer to this particular MAP and differentiate it from other MAPs the program may have. The rest of the statement is similar to a DECLARE statement. The various field-names are declared and typed here. The field-name may also be an array containing subscript information.

Defining String Length

A string variable in a MAP statement is always a **fixed-length** string variable. Fixed length means that if a short string is put into such a variable, blanks are added to pad it to the fixed length. This can be very wasteful if only short strings are needed because much of the file will contain only blanks. Such a file will take more disk space than is necessary, and you will usually be assigned a limited amount of space for your files. In addition, a larger buffer than necessary is required, using additional memory which may be limited.

The *default* length of a STRING in a MAP statement depends on the system used, but two common lengths are 80 and 255 characters. A field-name declared STRING will probably be designated as one of those two lengths. A string length different from the default length may be defined by following the string variable name with an equal sign and the length. Consider the following MAP:

```
MAP (DETAIL) STRING ID_no.=11, Name_=25, &
             DECIMAL(3,1) Hrs_worked
```

In this example, `ID_no.` is a string variable whose length is 11 characters (possibly a social security number), and `Name_` is a string variable whose length is 25 characters. These string variables will have the constant lengths stated regardless of the strings that are actually assigned to these variables.

(Remember that VAX-BASIC permits strings to be up to 65535 characters in length.)

Fixed-length strings can also be defined in a DECLARE statement. The format is exactly the same as shown above. For example,

DECLARE STRING Letter_grade = 2

defines `Letter_grade` to be a variable with a fixed length of 2 characters. For ordinary variables, there is usually no need to define such fixed-length variables. We will reserve their use primarily for buffer field-names.

12.3 OPENING A FILE—THE OPEN STATEMENT

The OPEN statement for a relative file is more complicated than that for a terminal-format file; more items must be specified. There are many options that may be selected, but, fortunately, most of them are optional. We will limit ourselves to the most important ones only. Refer to the BASIC manual and user's guide if you need more information.

For our purposes, we will use the following OPEN statement:

OPEN file $\begin{bmatrix} \text{FOR INPUT} \\ \text{FOR OUTPUT} \end{bmatrix}$ **AS FILE** #channel, **RELATIVE**, **MAP** map-name

The OPEN statement up to the first comma is the same as that used for terminal-format files. After that, we add the keyword RELATIVE to select the relative file organization. Finally, we add a MAP clause in which we supply the name of the MAP that will be used as the program buffer. As an example, we have the following OPEN statement:

```
1010 OPEN "PAYROL.DAT" FOR INPUT AS FILE #1, &
         RELATIVE, MAP Payroll
```

The file `PAYROL.DAT` is connected to channel #1 as a relative file. The program buffer will be the MAP whose name is `Payroll`. In this example, the file will be an input file. For output, we can change INPUT to OUTPUT in the OPEN statement.

12.4 READING RELATIVE FILES—THE GET STATEMENT

A relative file will most often be accessed randomly, but it may also be accessed sequentially if desired. In either case, a GET statement must be used. The GET statement transfers one record from the file into the record buffer. The associated MAP then permits access to the individual fields of the record. The format of the GET statement is:

GET #channel
GET #channel, **RECORD** record-number

The first format is used to access records sequentially. Each time it executes, the next record is obtained from the file and moved into the program buffer. The second form is used for random access. By specifying the record number, which may be a variable, that specific record will be obtained and read into the program buffer. As examples:

```
500 GET #1
600 GET #1, RECORD 20
```

The first example shows the GET statement used for sequential access. Each time the statement executes, it gets the next record from the file connected to channel #1, and places it in the program buffer.

The second example illustrates random access. The record that is to be read follows the keyword RECORD. Hence, in the example above, the twentieth record will be read from the file and placed into the program buffer. Records are numbered starting with record number 1. When the file is OPENed, the first record becomes available for input with a GET instruction.

The RECORD number can be a variable:

```
700 GET #3, RECORD I
```

where the value of I determines which record will be read.

Example 12.1

In this example, we will read the records from a relative file using the sequential access mode. Each record will then be printed at the terminal. A record will consist of an 11-character I.D. number, a 25-character name, the hours worked (for the week), and the salary. The program will end when we read the sentinel record whose I.D. number is 000-00-0000, a fictitious social security number.

The logic is very simple:

    Print relative file:
      Open file
      Get first record
      While I.D. number <> sentinel
        Print record
        Get next record
      End of loop
      Close file
    Stop

We are led to the program in Figure 12-2. The MAP statement uses the option of fixing the string length for the variables I.D. and NAME_. If we do not do so, then the file will be much larger than necessary.

You might take note of the way the PRINT USING statement has been used in this program. Two formats have been defined: one for the heading and one for printing each record. They have been physically aligned to ensure that the data will line up with the headings.

Figure 12-2.
Print Relative File Using Sequential Access

```
10   ! Print contents of a relative file using sequential access
20       MAP (Pay_rec) STRING I.D.=11, NAME_=25, &
                           DECIMAL(5,2) SALARY, DECIMAL(3,1) HOURS
30       DECLARE STRING IN_FILE, Out_form, Heading
40       GOSUB Open_file              ! Open the file
50       GOSUB Process_file           ! Read an print file
60       GOSUB Close_file             ! Close the file
70     EXIT PROGRAM

1000 Open_file:                        ! Open the file
1010   INPUT "Enter name of input file"; IN_FILE
1020   OPEN IN_FILE FOR INPUT AS FILE #1, RELATIVE, MAP Pay_rec
1030 RETURN

1500 Close_file:                       ! Close the file
1510   CLOSE #1
1520 RETURN

2000 Process_file:            ! Read and write the file
2010   Heading =   &
       "  I.D. no.          Name                      Hours       Salary"
2020   Out_form =  &
       "'LLLLLLLLLL   'LLLLLLLLLLLLLLLLLLLLLLLLL    ##.#     $$####.##"
2030 ! Print headings
       PRINT \ PRINT
       PRINT Heading
       PRINT
2040 ! Read and print the records
       GET #1                  ! Get the first record
       WHILE I.D. <> "000-00-0000"
         PRINT USING Out_form, I.D., NAME_, HOURS, SALARY
         GET #1                ! Get next record
       NEXT
2050   PRINT \ PRINT
2060 RETURN

32767 END
```

Instead of using a sentinel record, an end-of-file trap could be used instead. Line 2040 could be rewritten as follows:

```
2040 ! Read and print the records
       WHILE I.D. <> "000-00-0000"
         GET #1                ! Get record
         PRINT USING Out_form, I.D., NAME_, HOURS, SALARY
       NEXT
2050   PRINT \ PRINT
2060 RETURN
```

An error routine would have to be included. It might be written as follows:

```
19000 Error_routine:
19010    IF ERR = 11 AND ERL = 2040 THEN   ! End-of-file
            RESUME 2050
         ELSE
            ON ERROR GOTO 0
         END IF
19020 ! End of error routine
```

The program in Fig. 12-2 used sequential access for the relative file. That means that we read every record in sequence from the first to the last. If desired, though, we can also access any specific record if we know which one it is. For example, for the program mentioned, if we wanted to print the data in record number 5 only, we would replace line 2040 with

```
2040 ! Read and print record number 5
        GET #1, RECORD 5        ! Get record
        PRINT USING Out_form, I.D., NAME_, HOURS, SALARY
2050    PRINT \ PRINT
2060 RETURN
```

The RECORD clause in the GET statement causes a specific record to be read; in this case, it is the fifth record.

12.5 THE PUT STATEMENT

A relative file is written in either a sequential or random access manner. Both methods use the PUT statement, whose syntax is:

> **PUT #channel**
> **PUT #channel, RECORD record-number**

As was the case with GET, the first format is used for sequential access, while the second is used for random access. Examples of the PUT statement are:

```
100 PUT #1
200 PUT #1, RECORD 5
```

The first example writes the contents of the program buffer as the next sequential record of the file connected to channel #1. The second example writes the program buffer to the fifth record of the file connected to channel #1. In both cases, data must first be placed into the buffer for the file by assigning values to the field variables.

Example 12.2 In this second example, we will create a data entry program. We will enter data at the terminal, then print it to the file. Essentially, this program will be the reverse of Example 12.1. The file will be created sequentially. The logic this time is:

```
Create a file:
  Open output file
  While I.D. number <> sentinel
    Read data from terminal
    Print data to file
  End loop
  Close file
Stop
```

The input will involve interaction with the user. We will invoke a subroutine to perform the input function. As soon as the sentinel is entered, we will end the input, but still print the sentinel record to the file. Notice that there is no priming read. We have encountered this before, whenever we found it necessary to process the sentinel record. (The program could also be written so that the sentinel is not printed to the file. In that event, the program that reads the file will have to use an end-of-file trap.)

The program is shown in Figure 12-3. The PUT statement in line 2020 causes the entire record defined by the MAP to be output to the file on channel #1. Since no RECORD number is specified, the records are stored in the file sequentially. If you wanted to store the buffer in a specific record, record number 12, for instance, you would use a statement like:

```
PUT #1, RECORD 12
```

12.6 THE UPDATE STATEMENT

When a PUT statement is executed, the record that is being written to the file must not be one that already exists; it must be a new record. Otherwise, error number 153 from appendix 2, *Record already exists*, occurs.

However, we frequently have to read a record, modify it, then write it back to the same file from which it was read. This is called **updating** a record, and may be accomplished with the UPDATE statement. Normally, the UPDATE statement follows a GET instruction from the same file; and we will always use it that way. The syntax of this statement is:

UPDATE #channel

For example, to update the last record that was read from channel #3, we would use:

```
200 UPDATE #3
```

The UPDATE instruction is a very important one when random access file operations are used. It allows you to both read and write the records of one file.

Example 12.3 In this example, we will combine sequential and random access for relative files in a simple inventory control program. We assume that a master file exists. Each record corresponds to a part number; i.e., the first record is for part number 1, the second for part number 2, and so on. (This has been done

Figure 12-3.
Data Entry Program Using Sequential Access

```
10  ! Data entry program, store data in relative file
20      MAP (Out_data) STRING I.D.=11, NAME_=25, &
                       DECIMAL(5,2) SALARY, DECIMAL(3,1) HOURS
30      DECLARE STRING Out_file
40      GOSUB Open_file              ! Open the file
50      GOSUB Process_data           ! Enter data, output to file
60      GOSUB Close_file
70      EXIT PROGRAM

1000 Open_file:                      ! Open output relative file
1010    INPUT "Enter name of output file"; Out_file
        OPEN Out_file FOR OUTPUT AS FILE #1, RELATIVE, MAP Out_data
1020 RETURN

1200 Get_data:                       ! Get input data
1210    PRINT \ PRINT
1220    INPUT "Enter I.D. number, 000-00-0000 to end "; I.D.
        IF I.D. <> "000-00-0000"
        THEN
           INPUT "Enter name          "; NAME_
           INPUT "Enter hours worked  "; HOURS
           INPUT "Enter salary        "; SALARY
        END IF
1230 RETURN

1500 Close_file:                     ! Close the output file
1510    CLOSE #1
1520 RETURN

2000 Process_data:                   ! Enter data at terminal,
                                     ! Write to output file
2010    I.D. = ""                    ! Initialize for loop
2020    WHILE I.D. <> "000-00-0000"
           GOSUB Get_data            ! Get input data
           PUT #1
        NEXT
2030 RETURN

32767 END
```

for illustrative purposes only.) Each record contains the name of the part (20 characters), the price of the part, and the quantity of that part available in the warehouse.

A second file, called a **detail file,** exists. Each record in that file represents a single transaction, such as a sale to a customer or a receipt from a supplier. The detail record contains the part number involved in that transaction, the quantity of the item, and a character representing the type of transaction. If the type is S, then the transaction is a sale; the quantity must be subtracted from inventory. If it is an R, then a shipment was received; the quantity must be added to inventory. This file will be accessed sequentially until a sentinel record is read, which we will call type D (for Done).

We will have to both read from and write to the master file. Therefore, we will not open it either for input or for output—it will be an update file. When a detail record is read, we will use the part number to read the corresponding master record from the master file. (Remember that in this program, the part number is equal to the record number.) After we either add to or subtract from the quantity at hand, we will update the record in the master file.

The pseudocode for this program will be as shown below.

```
Inventory control:
    Open files
    Process files
    Close files
Stop

Process files:
    Get first detail record
    While not sentinel record
        Get master record
        Adjust quantity
        Update master record
        Get new detail record
    End While
Return

Adjust quantity:
    Case Type
        "S": Subtract quantity from master
        "R": Add quantity to master
        Else: Print error message
    End Case
Return
```

In the "Process files" routine, "Adjust quantity" means to calculate the new values for the record. The record itself will not be written to the file until the "Update master record" routine executes. The program is shown in Figure 12-4 below.

Line 2010 illustrates how the master file is updated. A record is read with the GET #1 statement which, incidentally, specifies the specific record to be read. After the appropriate field or fields of this record are modified, the record is written back to the file with the UPDATE #1 statement. An UPDATE after a GET will rewrite the same record that was read; no RECORD number is required.

The program uses the SELECT-CASE construct to check the type and perform the appropriate calculation. Provision is made for either upper or lower case type. A CASE-ELSE is provided as a rudimentary error check.

Example 12.4 | A bank has its depositor's accounts on a computer in a relative file called ACCOUNTS.DAT. Each account number is a five-digit number, with 10001

Figure 12-4.
Program Using the
UPDATE Statement and
Random Access

```
10  ! Inventory control program
20     DECLARE STRING Master_file, Detail_file
30     MAP (Master) STRING Part_desc=20, &
             DECIMAL(7,2) Price, INTEGER Quantity
40     MAP (Detail) INTEGER Part_no., Detail_qty, STRING Type_=1
50     GOSUB Open_files           ! Open master and detail files
60     GOSUB Process_files        ! Create new master file
70     GOSUB Close_files          ! Close master and detail files
80  EXIT PROGRAM

1000 Open_files:                  ! Open master and detail files

1010   ! Open master file
           INPUT "Enter master file name: "; Master_file
           OPEN Master_file FOR INPUT AS FILE #1, RELATIVE, MAP Master

1020   ! Open detail file
           INPUT "Enter detail file name: "; Detail_file
           OPEN Detail_file FOR INPUT AS FILE #2, &
                RELATIVE, MAP Detail

1030 RETURN

1500 Close_files:                 ! Close master and detail files
1510     CLOSE #1, #2
1520 RETURN

2000 Process_files:               ! Create new master file
2010     GET #2                   ! Part_no., Detail_qty, Type_
         WHILE SEG$(Type_,32)<>"D"  ! Convert to upper-case
            GET #1, RECORD Part_no. ! Get master record
            GOSUB Adjust_quantity   ! Update master buffer
            UPDATE #1               ! Write new master record
            GET #2                  ! Read new detail record
         NEXT
2020 RETURN

2100 Adjust_quantity:             ! Update the master record buffer
2110     SELECT Type_
            CASE "R","r"
                Quantity = Quantity + Detail_qty
            CASE "S","s"
                Quantity = Quantity - Detail_qty
            CASE ELSE
                PRINT "Error in detail record. Type = "; Type_
         END SELECT
2120 RETURN

32767 END
```

being the lowest. Each record number corresponding to an account is equal to the account number minus 10,000. In other words, the information for account number 15287 is in record number 5287 (15287 − 10000 = 5287). Account number 10001 corresponds to record number 1 in the file.

Each record in the account contains the name on the account, the previous month's balance, an array of 50 dates that holds the date of each of 50 transactions that may take place in a month, an associated array of 50 amounts that take place on those dates, and another associated array that contains the type of the transaction. Transactions can be deposits (D), withdrawals (W), or interest (I). Finally, there will be a field that stores the number of transactions that have already taken place that month.

Deposits, withdrawals, and interest are merely stored in the transaction array; they will not immediately affect the balance. The transactions entered with this program will be used to calculate the new balance when a subsequent program is run at the end of the month.

To calculate interest, we multiply the previous balance by the current interest rate, assumed to be 5.25%.

The MAP statement for this record will be:

```
MAP (Account)    STRING Acct_name=25, Dates(50)=8, &
                 DECIMAL(7,2) Transaction(50), &
                 STRING Type_(50)=1, &
                 INTEGER No.Transactions, &
                 DECIMAL(9,2) Prev_balance
```

Notice that the program buffer contains three 50-element arrays—one for the dates, one for the transactions, and one for the types. Also, `DATE` and `DATE$` are reserved words, so we used `Dates`.

We will write this as a menu-driven program. The pseudocode for the program will be as follows:

```
Process bank transactions:
  Enter today's date
  Open the account file
  Initialize selection
  While selection <> 0
    Print the menu
    Make the selection
    Execute appropriate routine
  End loop
  Close the updated account file
Stop

Execute appropriate routine:
  If end-of-program selection then
    Execute end-of-program routine
  Else
    Enter account number
    Read record from file
    Update the record (based on selection)
    Rewrite record to file
Return
```

Update the record:
   Determine new transaction number
   If transaction > 50 then
      Print error message
   Else
      If selection is I (interest) then
         Calculate and store interest, date, and type
      Else
         Enter amount
         Store amount, date, and type
      End if
Return

Perhaps a few words concerning the pseudocode are in order. First, all transactions require that the date be stored. But there is no need to enter this for each transaction because the date is entered once when the program is first executed and then stored into each record as the current transaction date.

Second, in the "Update the record" routine, the new transaction number is determined by reading the number of transactions that have already been stored and adding 1 to this value. The number of transactions stored in a record is stored in the record itself in the field reserved for the variable No.Transactions. Since each record has such a field, the number of transactions will be different for each account, as it should be.

Third, a simple error check is included to prevent storing more than 50 transactions. If this is attempted, an error message will be printed.

Fourth, when the program is to be terminated, an end-of-program routine will print a closing message to inform the user of successful completion of the program.

The program generated by this pseudocode is shown in Figure 12-5.

Figure 12-5.
Program to Update a Bank Transaction File

```
10  ! Bank transaction file update
20     MAP (Account)   STRING Acct_name=25, Dates(50)=8, &
                       DECIMAL(7,2) Transactions(50), &
                       STRING Type_(50)=1, &
                       INTEGER No.Transactions, &
                       DECIMAL(9,2) Prev_balance
30     DECLARE    STRING In_file, Todays_date,&
                  INTEGER Selection, Record_no., Acct_no.
40     GOSUB Enter_date              ! Enter today's date
50     GOSUB Open_file               ! Open transaction file
60     Selection = -1                ! Needed to get into loop
       WHILE Selection <> 0          ! 0 = end-of-program choice
          GOSUB Print_menu           ! Menu and selection
          GOSUB Select_routine       ! Invoke selected routine
       NEXT
70     CLOSE #1
80  EXIT PROGRAM

1000 Open_file:                      ! Open transaction file
1010    INPUT "Enter name of transaction file "; In_file
1020    OPEN In_file AS FILE #1, RELATIVE, MAP Account
1030 RETURN
```

Figure 12-5. (*Cont.*)

```
1200 Enter_date:                        ! Enter today's date
1210     PRINT
         INPUT "Enter today's date, MM/DD/YY "; Todays_date
1220 RETURN

1400 Print_menu:                        ! Print main menu
1410     PRINT \ PRINT \ PRINT
         PRINT TAB(20); "1. Deposit"
         PRINT TAB(20); "2. Withdrawal"
         PRINT TAB(20); "3. Interest"
         PRINT TAB(20); "0. End transactions"
1420     PRINT \ PRINT
1430     INPUT "Make selection: "; Selection
         WHILE Selection < 0 OR Selection > 3
            PRINT
            PRINT "Selection out of range"
            INPUT "Make selection: "; Selection
         NEXT
1440 RETURN

1600 Select_routine:                    ! Invoke selected routine
1610     IF Selection = 0
         THEN GOSUB Quit_rtn             ! End-of-program routine
         ELSE
            GOSUB Get_record             ! Read transaction record
            No.Transactions = No.Transactions + 1

            IF No.Transactions > 50
            THEN
               PRINT "Too many transactions, record ignored"
            ELSE
               SELECT Selection
                  CASE = 1               ! Deposit
                     GOSUB Make_deposit
                  CASE = 2               ! Withdrawal
                     GOSUB Make_withdrawal
                  CASE = 3               ! Interest
                     GOSUB Post_interest
               END SELECT
               UPDATE #1
            END IF
         END IF
1620 RETURN

2000 Quit_rtn:                          ! End-of-program routine
2010     PRINT \ PRINT
2020     PRINT "File closed. Program done."
2030     PRINT
2040 RETURN
```

Figure 12-5. (*Cont.*)

```
2200 Get_record:                  ! Get record from transaction file
2210   ! Enter Account number
         INPUT "Enter 5-digit account number: "; Acct_no.
2220   ! Calculate record number
         Record_no. = Acct_no. - 10000
2230   ! Get the record
         GET #1, RECORD Record_no.
2240 RETURN

2400 Make_deposit:                ! Transaction is a deposit
2410   ! Enter transaction amount
         INPUT "Enter deposit amount: "; &
                 Transactions(No.Transactions)
2420   ! Complete rest of record
         Dates(No.Transactions) = Todays_date
         Type_(No.Transactions) = "D"
2430 RETURN
2600 Make_Withdrawal:             ! Transaction is a withdrawal
2610   ! Enter transaction amount
         INPUT "Enter withdrawal amount: "; &
                 Transactions(No.Transactions)
2620   ! Complete rest of record
         Dates(No.Transactions) = Todays_date
         Type_(No.Transactions) = "W"
2630 RETURN

2800 Post_interest:               ! Calculate and post interest
2810   ! Calculate the interest, assume 5.25% rate
         Transactions(No.Transactions) = 0.525 * Prev_balance
         Dates(No.Transactions) = Todays_date
         Type_(No.Transactions) = "I"
2820 RETURN

32767 END
```

Line 1610 is one long nested IF-THEN-ELSE statement. If its length is disturbing, a section of it can be removed and made into a subroutine. Barring that, it is necessary to write it all as one logical line because any ELSE clause would normally end at the end of the logical line.

SUMMARY

This chapter dealt with files organized as relative files. In a relative file, each record is assigned a record number equal to its position in the file. As a result, records in a relative file may be accessed in either a random or sequential mode. The following is a list of the topics discussed in this chapter.

1. Before a record can be read from a relative file, a MAP statement must be used to describe the fields of the record:

MAP (Map-name) Type variable, . . . [, Type variable, . . .]

2. The OPEN statement has the syntax:

OPEN filename $\begin{bmatrix} \text{FOR INPUT} \\ \text{FOR OUTPUT} \end{bmatrix}$ AS FILE #channel, &
RELATIVE, MAP map-name

3. The CLOSE Statement is the same as that for terminal-format files:

CLOSE #channel

4. Input is done with the GET statement:

GET #channel
GET #channel, RECORD record-no.

The first is used for sequential access and always reads record by record. The second format is used for random access and lets you select the specific record to be read.

5. Output is accomplished with the PUT statement:

PUT #channel
PUT #channel, RECORD record-no.

The first is used with sequential access and always writes the record that is next in the file after the previous one. The second format is used for random access and allows you to specify the specific record to be written.

6. Updating a file is done with the UPDATE statement:

UPDATE #channel

This statement must always follow a GET statement that refers to the same file. The UPDATE statement is then used to rewrite the same record that was previously read with the GET statement.

REVIEW QUESTIONS

1. Define a field. Define a record. Define a file.
2. What is a relative file? How does it differ from a terminal-format file?
3. How is a relative file opened? How does the OPEN statement differ from that for a terminal-format file?
4. Which statements are used to read records from a relative file? What is the syntax of these statements?
5. How do you specify which record will be read from a relative file? How do you specify which record will be written?
6. What is the purpose of a MAP statement? What is its syntax?
7. How does a specific MAP get selected and associated with a specific file?
8. How is the length of a string specified in a MAP statement? What is the advantage of specifying the string length?

9. Which statements are used to write records to a file? What is their syntax?
10. What is meant by a file update?
11. How are records in a file updated? What is the syntax of the update statement? Can a record be updated without reading it?
12. How is a relative file closed? How does this differ from closing a terminal-format file?
13. Can an end-of-file trap be used for relative files?

SYNTAX EXERCISES

The following contain one or more errors. Find and correct them. Assume that all I/O is to RELATIVE files.

1. `1020 OPEN "DATA.DAT" FOR INPUT AS FILE #1, RELATIVE FILE, & MAP Data_map`
2. `1020 OPEN In_file FOR INPUT AS FILE #2, MAP "Data_record"`
3. `1020 OPEN "DATA.OUT" FOR OUTPUT AS FILE #3, RELATIVE`
4. `1020 OPEN Data_out FOR OUTPUT, RELATIVE, MAP Out_map`
5. `2020 INPUT #1`
6. `2020 INPUT #1, RECORD N`
7. `2020 PRINT #2`
8. `2020 PRINT #2, RECORD 10`
9. `2020 UPDATE #2, RECORD 12`
10. `3020 UPDATE #2, A, B, C`
11. `3020 GET #1, A, B, C`
12. `3020 PUT #2, A, B, C`

PROGRAMMING EXERCISES

Write statements, subroutines, or programs that will perform the requested activities. Wherever a field length is not stated, assume a name is 25 characters, an address is 50, a social security number is 11, and a telephone number is 20.

1a. Write a MAP statement to define a buffer that will have three fields. The first is a name (30 characters), the second is an address (50 characters), the third is a telephone number (25 characters).

1b. Write the OPEN statement that opens a relative file for output operations, using the MAP of part a.

1c. Write a program that will create a relative file to be accessed sequentially. Data will be entered from the terminal. Each record will contain a name, address, and telephone number. The last record entered will be a sentinel with a name field of XXXX and a telephone field of 000-0000. If you have not learned error trapping, output this sentinel record as the last record of the file. The address field of the sentinel may be arbitrarily assigned. Call the file PHONE.NOS. If you have learned error trapping, do not output the sentinel record.

2a. Write a subroutine that will search a relative file for a record that contains a specific name. If the record is found, the subroutine is to return the record number; if it is not, a 0 is to be returned.

2b. Write a program that will be used to look up addresses and telephone numbers from the file created in Exercise 1c. Input to the program will be a name. The program will do a sequential search of the file until it finds the required name; at which point, the program will print the name, address, and telephone number at the terminal for the user. If the name is not found, a message to that effect will be printed instead.

■ **3a.** Write a statement that outputs a specified record to a relative file.

3b. Write a program that will create a relative file to be accessed randomly. Each record in the file will contain a name, address, and telephone number. Input to the program will be the same (see exercise 1a. for lengths). The record number will be determined by the last four digits of the telephone number. Use string processing concepts to extract these digits from the telephone number string.

Each record entered at the terminal will be output to the file at its correct relative record position. Assume that each telephone number has a different last four digits so that no two records will contend for the same spot in the file.

4. Write a program that can be used to access the file created in Exercise 3. Input to the program will be a telephone number. The last four digits will be used to locate the appropriate record. Once found, the corresponding name and address will be printed at the terminal. (NOTE! This problem requires error trapping if there are missing records. If you have not learned error trapping, do not prepare the file with missing records—it must be complete.)

5. A relative file, `CLASS.REC`, contains student records, each with the name and five test grades of a student. Write a program that accesses the record of each student, reads his name and grades, finds his average, then prints a report about the entire class. The report has each student's name, five grades, and average on one line of the report. The report will, therefore, have as many lines as there are students in the class. The file will be accessed sequentially. Use error trapping or a sentinel record containing the name XXXX.

6. The file of Exercise 5 is to be used in the random access mode to look up the records of individual students. Input to the program will be the student number entered at the terminal. The program will find the corresponding record and print the student's name and five grades. It will also print his average. The program will allow examination of as many records as the instructor desires until student number 0 is entered; at which time, the program terminates.

7. A payroll program is needed by a large engineering company. You have been hired for the job. A relative file will be used to store the necessary information. The last four digits of a worker's social security number will be used to access the appropriate record. Each record will consist of the worker's name, social security number, regular hours worked, and overtime hours worked. The record will also include the hourly rate of pay.

NOTE! | **If a large number of students write this program, disk space may become a problem. In that case, it is suggested that a simpler problem be programmed, using only the last two digits of the social security number instead of the last four. This limits the number of records to 99, an adequate number for a student project.**

For this problem, you will write the file maintenance section of the program. It will be menu driven, and will allow for the following options:

1. A complete weekly initialization of the file. All records, from record 0001 to record 9999, will be read. Records whose social security number field contains 000-00-0000 are dummy records and do not correspond to an actual employee; these records may be ignored. The other records will have the hours worked set to 0, and be written back to the file. At the start of the initialization routine, the user will be warned that the file will be destroyed if he continues and be given the option of aborting this selection.

2. A backup of the complete file. The user will be prompted to enter a name for the backup file. This file is then to be opened, and each record is to be read from the original file and written to the backup file.

3. A new worker is to be added to the data base. The user is to be prompted for the new worker's social security number, name, and base hourly pay. The last four digits of the social security number are to be extracted and converted to a numeric value to be used as the record number. The hours worked are set to 0. The entire record is to be printed on the screen to be checked for accuracy, and the user is to be given the option of making corrections. If the record is not correct, the user will be permitted to reenter the data; if correct, the record is to be written to the file. You may assume that no two social security numbers vie for the same record.

4. A worker is to be deleted from the data base. The user will be prompted for the social security number of the worker. The last four digits will be extracted and converted to a numeric value to become the record number. The record will be read and printed so that it can be checked. If it is the correct record, it is to be deleted by replacing it with a record like that specified in item 1 above (000-00-0000). If it is not the correct record, the user is to be permitted to reenter the social security number to try again.

a. Write subroutines for each of the four design criteria specified above.
b. Write the menu-driven program.

8. Refer to the file described in Exercise 7. In this problem, you will write the weekly payroll portion. It is to be menu-driven and have the following options:

1. Enter hours worked for all employees. The computer will read each record sequentially, skipping those dummy records whose social security numbers are 000-00-0000. It will print the name and social security number of each worker after reading it, then prompt the user to enter the number of hours worked. If the number of hours is less than 40, this becomes the regular hours, and the overtime hours is set to 0. If the hours are greater than 40, then the regular hours becomes 40, and the excess becomes the overtime hours. The record in the file will now be updated.

2. Print a report of salaries. Each record will be read sequentially. If the record is a dummy, then it will be ignored. Otherwise, the salary will be calculated, with overtime paid at "time-and-a-half." The report will contain the social security number, name, regular hours, overtime hours, and salary for each worker.

3. Correct a single record. This option will allow the user to enter the hours worked for a single employee. The user will be prompted for the social security number of the worker. The last four digits will be used to access the record, which will be printed at the screen. If the record is correct, the user will be prompted to enter the hours worked, and the record will be rewritten to the file. If not, the user will be prompted to reenter the social security number.

4. Print a single record. This will do the same as item 2, except that it will be done for one record only. The user will be prompted to enter the social security number of the desired record. The salary will be calculated and the data printed as in item 2.

a. Write a subroutine for each design section specified above.

b. Write the menu-driven program.

9. Refer to Exercises 7 and 8. Write a program that will do all of the operations specified in those two problems. It should be menu-driven at two levels. The main menu should give the options of file maintenance, weekly payroll, and program exit. The file maintenance section will present a menu that gives the options of "weekly initialization," "program backup," "employee create," "employee delete," and "return to main menu." The weekly payroll menu will permit the user the choices of entering hours worked for all employees or for one employee, printing a report for all employees or for one employee, or returning to the main menu.

If Exercises 7 and 8 have already been done, Exercise 9 can use those programs as subroutines, which will considerably simplify this program.

10. Write a program that will create a relative file to be used by a teacher to keep student records. Each record will contain information for one student: the students name, social security number, grades for five regular tests, and a final exam. The teacher has five classes, with 30 students in a class. The record number will be determined using the following formula:

Record number = 30 * (class number − 1) + student number

For example, the fifth student in the third class will correspond to record number 65, calculated as follows:

Record number = 30 * (3 − 1) + 5
= 65

The program will be menu-driven. Options will include:

1. Initialize the file. All records will have their social security numbers set to 000-00-0000, names set to blanks, and all test grades to zero.

2. Enter name and social security number for a new student. Input will have to include the class and student number.

3. Enter grades for existing students. There will be prompts that allow the teacher to enter the class number (1 to 5) and test number (1 to 5, or 6 for the final). The class number and test number should be entered only once for a given class and given test.

4. Print a report of each class, with each student's name, five tests, final test, and average. The average is calculated by counting the final grade twice and adding it to the regular five test grades, then dividing by 7. Only those records whose social security number is not 000-00-0000 shall be included in the report.

11. A student runs a physics experiment twice. The results of the first run are stored in the file DATA.1; the results of the second are stored in the file DATA.2. Both are relative files.

In the experiment, the student rolls a steel ball down an inclined ramp and measures the time it takes the ball to reach the bottom of the ramp. The experiment is done for different ramp angles. Each record in each file contains the angle of the ramp and the time it takes the ball to reach the bottom. The ramp angles used are the same for both runs of the experiment, and corresponding records in the files contain data for the same angle. The last record in each file has an angle of 90 degrees.

Write a program that reads corresponding records of both files and creates a new file. Each record of the new file will contain the ramp angle, the average of the two times measured, and the relative difference between these times. The relative difference is found by subtracting the second time from the first, and dividing by the first. This new file may be named DATA.12.

12. Write a program that will print the file created in Exercise 11. The output should have column headings for angle, average time, and relative difference. The last record in the file has an angle of 90 degrees.

13a. For the inventory control program, Figure 12-4, rewrite the program so that the detail file is processed until an end-of-file condition is read instead of a sentinel.

13b. Modify the program of part 13a to protect against reading a nonexistent record from the master file. That is, if the part number from the detail record is 12, but there is no twelfth record in the master file, print a message that includes the part number, and then go on to the next detail record. HINT: First find the appropriate error number by running the program and letting it crash, then typing PRINT ERR in the immediate mode. Once this is known, provide an appropriate error trap.

13 BASIC Built-In Functions

Outline

13.1 Defining the Built-In Functions
13.2 Mathematical Functions
13.3 Print Function
13.4 String Functions
13.5 Matrix Functions
13.6 System Functions
13.7 Predefined Constants
Summary
Review Questions
Programming Exercises

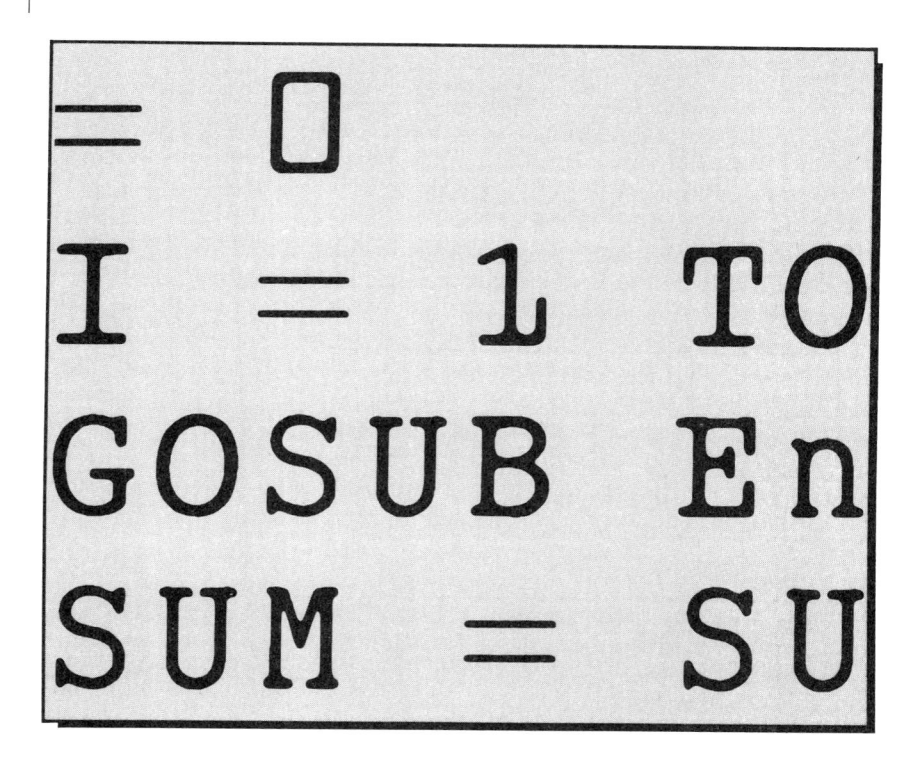

Introduction Many types of calculations are standard and are used repeatedly in many programs in various applications. Rather than write the code needed for these calculations each time it is needed, we can use the built-in functions provided by BASIC. Some of these functions were introduced previously, but others are new. This chapter presents a number of the BASIC built-in functions, provides their syntax, and explains how they can be used.

13.1 DEFINING THE BUILT-IN FUNCTIONS

VAX-BASIC provides a number of built-in functions that perform frequently used operations. In general, all of the built-in functions require that one or more arguments be sent to the function. The function then performs some calculations using the arguments and finally returns one calculated result.

Causing a function to be used is called **invoking** the function. The function is invoked by means of a function reference, which consists of the name of the function followed by an argument list. In the statement

```
100    A = SIN(X)
```

statement 100 invokes the sine function where SIN(X) is the function reference, and X is the argument—the angle sent to the function that is used to calculate the result.

Quick Reference

For quick reference, a list of the functions discussed in this chapter follows.

Mathematical functions:

ABS(X)	SQR(X)	PI	SIN(X)
COS(X)	TAN(X)	ATN(X)	EXP(X)
LOG(X)	LOG10(X)	RND[(X)}	RANDOM[IZE}
FIX(X)	INT(X)	SGN(X)	

Print functions:

TAB(X)

String functions: (Note: A$, B$ are strings; N is an integer)

SEG$(A$,N1,N2)	LEN(A$)	POS(A$,B$,N)	SPACE$(N)
CHR$(N)	ASCII(A$)	VAL(A$)	NUM$(N)
STR$(N)	EDIT$(A$,N)	TRM$(A$)	

Matrix functions: (Note: X is an array)

TRN(X)	INV(X)	DET	ZER
CON	IDN		

System functions:

DATE$(0)	TIME$(0)	TIME(0)	TIME(1)
TIME(2)			

Predefined constants:

BEL (bell)	BS (backspace)	HT (horizontal tab)
LF (line feed)	VT (vertical tab)	FF (form feed)
CR (carriage ret)	ESC (escape)	SP (space)
PI (value of pi)		

13.2 MATHEMATICAL FUNCTIONS

ABS(X) finds the absolute value of **X**. Examples:

```
X = -5
Y = ABS(X)   ! Y becomes 5

A = ABS(3)   ! A becomes 3
```

SQR(X) finds the square root of **X**. Examples:

```
X = 9
Y = SQR(X)   ! Y becomes 3

A = SQR(16)  ! A becomes 4
```

PI returns the value of π (3.14159265359). No arguments are required with this function.

SIN(X) finds the sine of the angle X.

> **NOTE!** The angle X must be in radians. To convert degrees to radians, use the formula
>
> **radians = degrees * π/180**

Example:

```
Y = SIN(2)   ! Y becomes the sine of 2 radians
```

COS(X) finds the cosine of the angle **X**. Again, the angle must be in radians. Example:

```
Y = COS(2)   ! Y becomes the cosine of 2 radians
```

TAN(X) finds the tangent of the angle **X**. Again, the angle must be in radians.

ATN(X) finds the arctangent of the number **X**. The result is an angle in radians whose tangent is **X**. To convert the result to degrees, use the formula

degrees = radians * 180/π

EXP(X) returns the value of **e** raised to the power **X**, where **e** is the base of natural logarithms: **e** = 2.718281828

LOG(X) returns the natural log of **X**; that is, the base **e** logarithm of **X**. In engineering, this function is referred to as ln(x).

LOG10(X) returns the common log of **X**; that is, the base 10 logarithm of **X**.

RND or **RND(X)** returns a random number between 0 and 1, carried to six decimal places. The argument is optional and has no effect. RND always generates the same sequence of numbers unless initialized with the RANDOMIZE statement. This is a useful feature when debugging a program. (Note: The random number generator was discussed in great detail in section 5.4.)

To get a random number in the range from LOW to HIGH, use

```
(HIGH + LOW) * RND + LOW
```

For example, a random number in the range 200 to 800 can be obtained using

```
600 * RND + 200
```

The number 200 is one of the numbers that can be generated when the above is used; the number 800 is not. In other words, the range of random numbers generated includes LOW but not HIGH.

To generate a random integer in the range LOW through HIGH inclusive, use the INT function (explained in section 5.4, and later in this section):

```
INT ((HIGH - LOW + 1) * RND + LOW)
```

For example, to generate a random integer in the range 200 through 800 inclusive, use

```
INT(601 * RND + 200)
```

Both 200 and 800 may be returned as randomly selected integers. If the statement

```
INT(600 * RND + 200)
```

were used instead, then 200 could be one of the generated integers but 800 could not be. The largest integer returned would be 799.

RANDOMIZE or **RANDOM** is used to initialize the RND function so that it generates a different sequence whenever the program is run. RANDOMIZE is not a function and returns no values. It should be executed only once in a program that uses the RND function. Care should be used to ensure that it is not placed in a loop. The best place for the RANDOM statement is at the very beginning of the program:

```
10 RANDOM
```

FIX(X) returns the truncated value of **X**. For example, FIX(5.6) returns 5, and FIX(-5.6) returns -5.

INT(X) returns the largest integer less than or equal to **X**. INT(5.6) returns 5, but INT(-5.6) returns -6. Note that for positive values of **X**, FIX and INT return the same result. For negative numbers, they do not.

SGN(X) is the signum, or sign, function (not to be confused with the sine function). It returns the values -1, 0, or +1 depending on whether **X** is negative, zero, or positive, respectively. Examples:

```
SGN(78) is 1
SGN(-15) is -1
SGN(0) is 0
```

The signum function can be used to take the sign of one number and assign it to another number, as follows:

```
Y = SGN(X) * ABS(Y)
```

This statement puts the sign of **X** in front of the number **Y**.

13.3 PRINT FUNCTION

TAB(X) moves the print head to column **X** (zero-based) of the current line. It is ignored if the print head is beyond column **X**. This function is used in a PRINT statement with packed format. For example, the statement

```
100 PRINT TAB(35); 200
```

prints the number 200, with a leading blank in the sign position, starting in column 36 (one-based) of the current print line. If the argument is not an integer, it will be converted to integer.

NOTE: The `TAB` function must be followed by a semicolon to work properly (as in statement 100 above).

13.4 STRING FUNCTIONS

Many of the functions described here have been discussed and illustrated extensively in chapter 9.

For convenience and quick identification, string variable arguments for the following functions have the $ symbol appended, as if they were implicitly declared. Programs using these functions should replace these arguments with explicitly declared variables of the STRING data-type.

SEG$(A$,N1,N2) returns the substring of **A$** consisting of all characters from position **N1** to position **N2** of **A$**. The first argument must be STRING type. The last two arguments should be INTEGER type, or they will be converted to INTEGER.

```
A$ = 'STEVENSON'
B$ = SEG$(A$,3,6)      ! B$ becomes 'EVEN'
C$ = SEG$(A$,1,6)      ! C$ becomes 'STEVEN'
D$ = SEG$(A$,7,9)      ! D$ becomes 'SON'
```

LEN(A$) returns the length, in characters, of **A$**. For example,

```
10  A$ = 'BASIC'
20  N = LEN(A$)        ! N will be 5
```

POS(A$,B$,N) return the position in **A$** where **B$** begins; **A$** and **B$** must be string constants or variables. The search starts at position **N** of **A$**. The number returned will be either 0 or it will be at least as large as **N**. A 0 is returned if **B$** is not contained in **A$** on or after position **N**. For example:

```
10 DECLARE STRING A, INTEGER N1, N2, N3
20 A = 'EVERYWHERE'
30 N1 = POS(A,'ER',1)    ! Find first ER, N1 is 3
40 N2 = POS(A,'ER',N1+1) ! Find second ER, N2 is 8
50 N3 = POS(A,'ER',N2+1) ! Find the third ER, N3 is 0
60 PRINT N1, N2, N3
```

The numbers 3, 8, and 0 are printed. Statement 30 looks for the substring ER starting at position 1 of **A**. Statement 40 looks for ER also, but the search begins at column 4. Statement 50 looks for ER starting in column 9 but does not find it, so the value of 0 is returned.

SPACE$(N) returns a string of **N** spaces. It is useful for inserting blanks in an output line with a PRINT statement. For example:

```
PRINT "ABC"; SPACE$(5); "DEF"
```

prints the following:

```
0++++5+++10+++15+++20
ABC     DEF
```

SPACE$ can also be used when concatenating strings:

```
RESULT$ = FIRST$ + SPACE$(10) + SECOND$
```

Ten spaces will be inserted between the strings contained in the variables FIRST$ and SECOND$.

CHR$(X) returns the character corresponding to the ASCII value **X**. The complete list of ASCII codes is given in appendix 3. For example, CHR$(65) is the letter A.

This function is useful for outputting certain unprintable characters. Some examples:

```
10  PRINT CHR$(7)  ! Ring terminal bell or buzzer
20  A = 7.2
    B = 19.3
    PRINT A, CHR$(13), CHR$(10), B
          ! Two lines with 1 print
          ! CHR(13) and CHR(10) are the carriage
          ! return and line feed, respectively
30  A = 7.2 \ B = 19.3
    PRINT CHR$(12), A, CHR$(12), B
```

In statement 20, CHR$(13) causes a carriage return and CHR$(10) causes a line feed. (These two characters are automatically sent to the computer when you press <Return>.) Therefore, 7.2, the value in A, is printed on one line, and 19.3, the value in B, is printed on the next line.

In statement 30, ASCII code 12 outputs a form feed. If a hard-copy printer is used as the output device, this code will cause the printer to roll the paper forward to a new page. Therefore, 7.2 is printed at the beginning of one page and 19.3 is printed at the top of the next page. (On the screen, the result will vary, depending on the characteristics of the terminal. Some terminals will clear the screen when this code is received, others will skip a number of lines.)

ASCII(A$) returns the decimal ASCII code corresponding to the first character of string variable **A$**. Example:

```
10 N = ASCII('A')
```

N will be 65, the ASCII code for the letter A. The ASCII function is the inverse of the CHR$ function. Example:

```
10 A$ = 'JOHN' \ N = ASCII(A$)
```

N will be 74, which is the ASCII code for the letter J, the first character of JOHN. Refer to appendix 3 for ASCII codes.

VAL(A$) returns the numerical value of the numerical string stored in **A$**. Example:

```
A$ = '76.24'
N  = VAL(A)
```

N will store the number 76.24 in a form in which it can be used for arithmetic operations. A more comprehensive example is given later in this chapter. Others were given in chapter 9, where many of these functions are discussed and illustrated extensively.

NUM$(N) returns a string containing the value of **N** exactly as it would be printed by a PRINT instruction. If **N** is positive, the first character of the returned string is a blank; if negative, it is a minus sign. The last character returned is always a blank. Example:

```
10 N = 17.6
   M = -254.70
20 A$ = NUM$(N)
   B$ = NUM$(M)
```

A$ will be " 17.6", and B$ will be "-254.7"—the values of M and N exactly as they would appear when printed.

STR$(N) is identical to NUM$ except that no leading or trailing spaces are returned. Example:

```
10 N = 17.6
   M = -254.70
20 A$ = STR$(N)
   B$ = STR$(M)
```

A$ will be "17.6" and B$ will be "-254.7".

EDIT$(A$,N) performs certain editing functions on string **A$**. The specific editing performed depends on the value of integer **N**. The following table gives a brief description relating the N to the function performed.

N	PURPOSE
1	Discard all parity bits
2	Discard all spaces and tabs
4	Discard all carriage returns, line feeds, form feeds, deletes, escapes, and nulls
8	Discard leading spaces and tabs
16	Convert multiple spaces and tabs to a single space
32	Converts lower case to upper case
64	Converts [to (and] to)
128	Discards trailing spaces and tabs
256	Suppresses all of the above for characters within quotation marks, i.e., no editing on literal strings

The individual values specified for **N** above may be added to obtain a single value for **N** that will perform more than one editing function. For example, suppose we are given the string "The quick brown fox jumped over the lazy dog". We would like to eliminate all the blanks in the string, and also convert all characters to upper case. Referring to the above table, we see that **N** must have the value of 2 to remove all spaces and tabs, and a value of 32 to convert lower case to upper case. Therefore, we will give **N** a value of 2 + 32 or 34. A program segment to perform this editing is as follows:

```
1000 Sentence = "The quick brown fox jumped over the lazy dog"
1010 Sentence = EDIT$(Sentence,34)
1020 PRINT Sentence
```

As a result of the above statements, the string:

THEQUICKBROWNFOXJUMPEDOVERTHELAZYDOG

is printed at the terminal, all in capital letters, and with no spaces.

TRM$(A$) removes trailing blanks and tabs from string **A$**. Therefore, `TRM$(A$)` is identical to `EDIT$(A$,128)`.

13.5 MATRIX FUNCTIONS

Most matrix operations are beyond the mathematical level of this text. The matrix built-in functions are included here for the benefit of those individuals who require them for advanced mathematical operations.

TRN(X) returns the transpose of matrix **X**. This means that the rows and columns of **X** are interchanged. Example:

```
10   DECLARE REAL X(10,5), Y(5,10)
20   MAT INPUT X    ! Enter 10 × 5
30   MAT Y = TRN(X) ! Form 5 × 10
```

The TRN function requires that a MAT assignment statement be used if the result is to be stored. To print the transpose of an array without first storing it, use PRINT TRN(X);.

INV(X) returns the inverse of matrix **X**. This function is useful in solving simultaneous equations. Example:

```
1000 MAT Y = INV(X)
```

Again, a MAT instruction is necessary if the result is to be stored.

DET returns the determinant of **X** after **X** has been inverted by INV(X). Example:

```
MAT A = INV(X) \ D = DET
```

D will contain the determinant of array X. There are no arguments for this function. It must be used after the INV function. Some knowledge of linear algebra is required to use the INV and DET functions productively.

ZER, CON, and **IDN** are used to initialize arrays to frequently used initial values where ZER sets all elements of an array to 0; CON sets all elements of an array to 1; and IDN sets all elements on the main diagonal of a square array to 1, and all other elements to 0 (a matrix known as the **identity matrix**). Examples:

```
100 MAT A = ZER   ! All elements of A set to 0
200 MAT B = CON   ! All elements of B set to 1
300 MAT C = IDN   ! C set to identity matrix
```

Array C would have to be a square array (two-dimensional, with the same number of rows as columns).

13.6 SYSTEM FUNCTIONS

DATE$(0) returns the current date in the format: DD-MMM-YY.

TIME$(0) returns the current time in the format HH:MM XX where XX is either AM or PM.

TIME(N) returns time usage information to the program: TIME(0) returns the number of seconds since midnight; TIME(1) returns the current job's CPU time in tenths of a second; and TIME(2) returns the current job's connect time in seconds.

As an example, suppose you wish to know exactly how long it takes to run your program and also how much CPU time it takes. (These will be different because you use CPU time only when the computer is actually working on your program. But your total run time includes that CPU time plus any time that elapses while the computer is servicing another user and while your program is waiting for I/O.) At the beginning of your program, you can put the statements:

```
30   Run_start = TIME(0)
     CPU_start = TIME(1)
```

At the end of the program, you can then put the statements;

```
3000 Run_end = TIME(0)
     CPU_end = TIME(1)
3010 Run_time = Run_end - Run_start
     CPU_time = CPU_end - CPU_start
3020 PRINT "Run time = "; Run_time
     PRINT "CPU time = "; CPU_time
```

The run time will be printed as the number of seconds from begin to end, and the CPU time will be in tenths of a second. If the CPU time is 46, then the program used 4.6 seconds of CPU time. (You could divide CPU_time by 10 before printing to convert it to seconds.)

13.7 PREDEFINED CONSTANTS

Technically, predefined constants are not functions. They are equivalent to specific non-printable characters, called **control characters.** These characters can be obtained using the CHR$ function mentioned in section 13.4. However, the predefined constants are more descriptive of their purpose and easier to write. The following table describes these constants.

Constant	ASCII	Equivalent	Meaning
BEL (bell)	7	CHR$(7)	Sound terminal bell
BS (backspace)	8	CHR$(8)	Backspace the cursor
HT (hor tab)	9	CHR$(9)	Cursor to next horizontal tab stop
LF (line feed)	10	CHR$(10)	Cursor to next line
VT (vert tab)	11	CHR$(11)	Cursor to next vertical tab stop
FF (form feed)	12	CHR$(12)	Cursor to start of next page
CR (carr ret)	13	CHR$(13)	Cursor to beginning of line
ESC (escape)	27	CHR$(27)	Start of escape sequence
SP (space)	32	CHR$(32)	Equivalent to " " (space)
PI (pi)	none	3.14159	Equal to value of pi

A large number of additional functions are available. The reader is invited to consult the language reference manual for his system for additional information regarding other functions.

Example 13.1 We will make a table of numbers from 1 to 100, their squares, and their square roots. The pseudocode is:

```
Make math table:
  Print headings
  Loop number = 1 to 100
    Find square of number
    Find square root of number
    Print number, square, square root
  Next number
Stop
```

The code appears in Figure 13-1.

Figure 13-1.
Program to Generate a Table of Squares and Square Roots

```
10  ! Make table of squares and roots

20     DECLARE INTEGER Number, Square, REAL Root

30     ! Print headings with underlines
       PRINT 'Number';TAB(21);'Square';TAB(41);'Sq. root'
       PRINT '------';TAB(21);'------';TAB(41);'--------'
       PRINT

40     ! Print the table
       FOR Number = 1 TO 100
          Square = Number * Number
          Root = SQR(Number)
          PRINT Number; TAB(21); Square; TAB(41); Root
       NEXT Number

50     END
```

The SQR function was used to find the square root of the loop counter, Number. We used the TAB function to illustrate its use, but PRINT USING could have been used effectively instead.

Example 13.2 In this example, we read a record from a file in which the data items in the record are separated by spaces, not commas. The entire record is read into a string variable. Then various string functions are used to separate the record into its component parts.

To keep things simple, we read only one record, and we assume that it contains five numbers separated by one or more blanks. The object of this exercise is to store each of the numbers in an element of an array. The array will, of course, consist of five elements. Here is the pseudocode:

```
Separate a string into five numbers:
    Dimension the array
    Open the file
    Read the record

    Loop I = 1 to 5
        Get number from record
        Convert number to arithmetic type, store it
    End of loop

    Close file
Stop

Get number from record:
    Remove leading blanks
    Find blank after number
    Copy number from record
    Remove number from record
Return
```

13 BASIC BUILT-IN FUNCTIONS

Figure 13-2.
Program to Separate String into Numbers

There is a small error in this logic: The last number may not be followed by a blank. This will create a problem in the statement "find blank after number." We will fix this problem by concatenating a blank onto the end of the record after reading it. With this small addition, the program is as shown in Figure 13-2.

```
10  ! Separate string into numbers
20      DECLARE REAL No.(5), &
                INTEGER I, Blank_posn, &
                STRING In_file, In_rec, Number
30      GOSUB Open_file        ! Open the file
40      GOSUB Get_record       ! Get the record
50      FOR I = 1 TO 5
            GOSUB Get_number   ! Get numeric string from record
            No.(I) = VAL(Number)
        NEXT I
60      CLOSE #1
70      GOSUB Print_numbers    ! Print array of numbers
80      EXIT PROGRAM

1000 Open_file:                ! Open the file
1010    INPUT ' Enter filename '; In_file
1020    OPEN In_file FOR INPUT AS FILE #1
1030 RETURN

1100 Get_record:               ! Get the record
1110    INPUT #1, In_rec
1120    In_rec = In_rec + ' '  ! Concatenate a blank to end
1130 RETURN

1200 Print_numbers:            ! Print array of numbers
1210    PRINT \ PRINT
        PRINT "The numbers are :";
        FOR I = 1 TO 5
            PRINT No.(I);
        NEXT I
        PRINT \ PRINT
1220 RETURN

1500 Get_number:               ! Get numeric string from record
1510 ! Remove leading blanks (and tabs)
        In_rec = EDIT$(In_rec,8)
1520 ! Find blank after number
        Blank_posn = POS(In_rec,' ',1)
1530 ! Get number from In_rec
        Number = SEG$(In_rec,1,Blank_posn)
1540 ! Remove number from In_rec
        In_rec = SEG$(In_rec,Blank_posn+1,LEN(In_rec))
1550 RETURN

32767 END
```

Once the numbers are in the array `No.`, they can be used for any arithmetic operations in the usual manner. This program can be extended to read additional records from the file, continuing until some sentinel record has been read.

This example used various string functions, which were explained in greater detail in chapter 9.

Example 13.3

In this example, we will make a graph of the sine function. The graph will be printed sideways: the *y* axis will be horizontal and the *x* axis will be vertical. The graph will include one complete cycle of the sine curve.

Angles will go from 0 to 360 degrees, in increments of 10 degrees. Each horizontal line represents one of these angles. For each angle, we will calculate the sine. Then we will print an asterisk at a column that corresponds to this value. Because the sine function has extreme values of +1 and −1, we will scale the *y* values. Zero will be plotted in column 40, and we will let the graph swing 30 columns on either side of that. The scaling will be done by multiplying the *y* value by 30 and then adding 40 to the result:

```
Column No. = 30 * Y value + 40
```

You can see that if the *Y* value is −1, this results in a column number of 10; if it is +1, the column number is 70. The result will be the column in which to print the asterisk. Here is the pseudocode:

```
Graph of sine function:
  Print a heading
  Loop for angle = 0 to 360 step 10
    Convert angle to radians
    Find y value from SIN function
    Scale y value to find column number
    Print asterisk in column
  End of loop
Stop
```

The code appears in Figure 13-3.

To find `Column`, we add 0.5 and then take the integer part of the result. This is the standard technique for rounding. For example, to round 17.8, we perform the following steps:

```
17.8 + 0.5 = 18.3
INT(18.3) = 18
```

Thus 17.8 has been rounded up to the next integer, 18. If we start with 17.2 instead, note that we round the result down:

```
17.2 + 0.5 = 17.7
INT(17.7) = 17
```

The same technique works for negative numbers. Here are the same two examples, but using −17.8 and −17.2 respectively. (Remember that the INT

Figure 13-3.
Program to Generate Sine Function

```
10  ! Graph of sine function
    ! Angles from 0 to 360 degrees
    ! Increment of 10 degrees

20      DECLARE INTEGER Degree, Column, &
                REAL Radian, Y

30  ! Print headings
        PRINT TAB(10); 'Graph of sine function'
        PRINT

40      FOR Degree = 0 TO 360 STEP 10

          ! Convert to radians
            Radian = Degree * PI / 180      ! Note use of PI

          ! Find y value
            Y = SIN(Radian)                 ! Note use of SIN

          ! Scale the y value and round it to nearest column
            Column = INT(Y * 30 + 40 + .5)  ! Note use of INT

          ! Plot an asterisk
            PRINT TAB(Column); '*'          ! Note use of TAB

        NEXT Degree

50      END
```

function does not truncate negative numbers, but instead returns the largest negative integer less than or equal to the argument.)

```
-17.8 + 0.5 = -17.3
INT(-17.3) = -18


-17.2 + 0.5 = -16.7
INT(-16.7) = -17
```

The graph produced by this program is shown in Figure 13-4.

Example 13.4 — We will take a string and convert every upper case letter to lower case. (Notice that to convert from lower case to upper case, the EDIT$ function can be used with the second argument set to 32.) All characters that are not letters will be left unchanged.

Figure 13-4.
Sine Function Generated
by Program of Figure 13-3

```
Graph of Sine Function
                                          *
                                         *
                                        *
                                       *
                                        *
                                         *
                                          *
                                           *
                                            *
                                            *
                                           *
                                          *
                                         *
                                       *
                                     *
                                   *
                                 *
                               *
                             *
                           *
                         *
                       *
                      *
                     *
                    *
                     *
                      *
                       *
                        *
                         *
                           *
                             *
```

Referring to appendix 3, ASCII Codes, we see that upper case letters have codes between 65 and 90 and lower case letters have codes between 97 and 122. Each lower case letter has an ASCII code that is exactly 32 units larger than the corresponding upper case code. To convert from upper to lower case, we have to find the ASCII code of the character, add 32 to the code if the code is between 65 and 90, and then convert the result back from ASCII to character. In pseudocode we have the following:

372 | 13 BASIC BUILT-IN FUNCTIONS

        Convert characters:
           For position = 1 to length of string
             Get one character from string
             Convert this character
           Next position
        Return

        Convert upper to lower case:
           Find ASCII code of character
           If code is between 65 and 90 then
             add 32 to code
             convert back to character
             replace original character with new character
           End if
        Return

As you can see, two subroutines are used here: one to get characters from the string one character at a time, the other to convert the character to lower case if necessary. The code that follows (Fig. 13-5) assumes that the string has already been read into the variable Letters.

Notice the use of the ASCII function to convert the character to its decimal code (line 1510), and the use of the CHR$ function to change the decimal code back to character (line 1520).

The last statement in the THEN clause concatenates the front of the string, the converted character, and the back of the string to form the new string. Each time this statement executes, one additional letter has been converted to lower case. This statement also uses an ampersand as a line continuation symbol because the statement is too long to fit on one physical line.

Figure 13-5.
Subroutine to Convert String to Lower case

```
20 DECLARE STRING Letters, Character, &
            INTEGER Position, ASCII_code, Length

1000 Convert_chars:              ! Convert a string to lower-case
1010     Length = LEN(Letters)
1010     FOR Position = 1 TO Length
            Character = SEG$(Letters,Position,Position)
            GOSUB Lower_case   ! Convert Character to lower-case
         NEXT Position
1020 RETURN

1500 Lower_case:                 ! Convert Character to lower-case
1510     ASCII_code = ASCII(Character)
1520     IF ASCII_code >= 65 AND ASCII_code <= 90
         THEN  ASCII_code = ASCII_code + 32
               Character = CHR$(ASCII_code)
               Letters = SEG$(Letters,1,Position-1) + Character &
                      + SEG$(Letters,Position+1,Length)
         END IF
1530 RETURN
```

The program required the length of the string in various places. It was found once and stored in the variable Length. This is good programming because the LEN function need only be invoked once, saving time. Of course, this only works because the length of the string remains constant.

Example 13.5

In this example, we will use some of the predefined constants to control the appearance of the output. If a PRINT statement contains the constant CR, the cursor returns to the beginning of the line. (On many terminals, it will also move down to the next line; on others, it will not. We will assume that it will not.)

If BS is used, the cursor will backspace. This lets you print another letter in the same position as the previous one. On CRT terminals, you will see only the second character, but on hard-copy output, both characters will be printed. Thus you can overprint a character for emphasis, or underline a character that has already been printed.

HT can be used to move the cursor to the next tab stop on the terminal. FF can be used to move the paper of a hard-copy terminal to the top of the next page. (On some CRT terminals, the cursor will move to the top left corner of the screen. On others, it may also clear the screen; and on some, the cursor will merely advance a few lines.)

We will write a subroutine that can be used to create a table on a hard-copy terminal. The table will consist of three columns: angle in degrees, the sine of the angle, and the cosine of the angle. There will be an underlined title and underlined column headings. Each column will be at a new horizontal tab stop. The subroutine is shown in Figure 13-6, and produces the output shown in Figure 13-7.

Figure 13-6.
Subroutine to Print Trigonometric Table

```
1000 Print_trig_table:              ! Make a trig table
1010 ! Print underlined title
     PRINT TAB(30); "Table of trig values";
     FOR I = 1 TO 20
        PRINT BS;                   ! Backspace the cursor
     NEXT I
     PRINT "_____  __  ____  _____" ! Do underlining
     PRINT
1020 ! Print column headings
     PRINT TAB (20); "Angle"; HT; "Sine"; HT; "Cosine";
     PRINT CR;                      ! Cursor to start of line
     PRINT TAB (20); "_____"; HT; "____"; HT; "_____"
                                    ! Do underlining
     PRINT
1030 ! Print values
     FOR Degree = 0 to 90
        Angle = Degree * PI / 180
        Sine = SIN(Angle)
        Cosine = COS(Angle)
        PRINT TAB(20); Degree; HT; Sine; HT; Cosine
     Next Degree
1040 RETURN
```

Figure 13-7.
Table of Trigonometric Values

```
            Table of trig values
   Angle    Sine            Cosine
   ─────    ────            ──────

     0       0                1
     1       .174524E-01      .999848
     2       .348995E-01      .999391
     3       .052336          .99863
     4       .697565E-01      .997564
     5       .871557E-01      .996195
     6       .104528          .994522
     7       .121869          .992546
     8       .139173          .990268
     9       .156434          .987688
    10       .173648          .984808
    11       .190809          .981627
    12       .207912          .978148
    13       .224951          .97437
    14       .241922          .970296
    15       .258819          .965926
    16       .275637          .961262
    17       .292372          .956305
    18       .309017          .951057
    19       .325568          .945519
    20       .34202           .939693
    21       .358368          .93358
    22       .374607          .927184
    23       .390731          .920505
    24       .406737          .913545
    25       .422618          .906308
    26       .438371          .898794
    27       .453991          .891007
    28       .469472          .882948
    29       .48481           .87462
    30       .5               .866025

    88       .999391          .348994E-01
    89       .999848          .174524E-01
    90       1               -.437114E-07
```

SUMMARY

This chapter presented a large number of built-in functions, which can be invoked by using a function reference: the function name followed by the arguments it needs to return a result. A function can return only one value each time it is invoked. (The three matrix initialization routines **ZER**, **CON**, and **IDN**, return more than one value, but technically they are not functions.)

For quick reference, here is a list of the functions described in this chapter.

Mathematical functions:

```
ABS(X)      SQR(X)       PI           SIN(X)
COS(X)      TAN(X)       ATN(X)       EXP(X)
LOG(X)      LOG10(X)     RND[(X)]     RANDOM[IZE]
FIX(X)      INT(X)       SGN(X)
```

Print functions:

```
TAB(X)
```

String functions: (Note: A$, B$ are strings; N is an integer)

```
SEG$(A$,N1,N2)   LEN(A$)       POS(A$,B$,N)   SPACE$(N)
CHR$(N)          ASCII(A$)     VAL(A$)        NUM$(N)
STR$(N)          EDIT$(A$,N)   TRM$(A$)
```

Matrix functions: (Note: X is an array)

| TRN(X) | INV(X) | DET | ZER |
| CON | IDN | | |

System functions:

| DATE$(0) | TIME$(0) | TIME(0) | TIME(1) |
| TIME(2) | | | |

Predefined constants:

BEL (bell)
LF (line feed)
CR (carriage ret)
PI (value of pi)

BS (backspace)
VT (vertical tab)
ESC (escape)

HT (horizontal tab)
FF (form feed)
SP (space)

REVIEW QUESTIONS

1. What is a function?
2. How many values does a function return?
3. What is the difference between the INT and FIX functions?
4. Which function finds the square root of a number?
5. Which function is used to find random numbers?
6. Explain the CHR$ function. Which function is the inverse (has the opposite effect) of the CHR$ function?
7. Which function allows you to print the date at the terminal? Which prints the time?
8. Which predefined constant corresponds to CHR$(8)? What does it do?
9. Which predefined constant can be used to ring the terminal bell or buzzer? Which ASCII code corresponds to it?
10. Which predefined constants can be used to cause the cursor to move to the start of a new line of output?

PROGRAMMING EXERCISES

Write subroutines or programs to solve the following problems. All output should include the date and time the program was run.

■ 1. Make a table of numbers from 1 to 50 and their square roots, using the SQR function. Print the square roots to four decimal places.

2. Make a table of sines and cosines of angles between 0 and 90 degrees in intervals of 5 degrees. (Remember to convert from degrees to radians.) Print sine and cosine values to four decimal places. Line up decimal points in the table by using the PRINT USING statement.

3a. Write a subroutine that stores integers into a 100-element array. The integers are to be in the range from 200 to 800, inclusive.

3b. Set up a 100-element array of random integers, each between 200 and 800. Find the average of all the numbers. Determine how many numbers are in each of the ranges 200–299, 300–399, 400–499, 500–599, 600–699, and 700–800. Print the information in a professional manner (make it look as if your job depended on it).

4. Write a program that will print a table of the ASCII codes 32 through 126, together with their ASCII character equivalents. (HINT: Use the CHR$ function.)

■ **5a.** Write a subroutine that can determine whether an integer is even or odd? HINT: What is the remainder when an even number is divided by 2?
5b. Write a subroutine that can determine whether an integer is divisible by 5.
5c. Write a program that reads 10 integers into an array, and then prints them followed by the words EVEN or ODD, depending on whether the number is even or odd. After printing EVEN or ODD, print DIVISIBLE BY 5 if the number is also divisible by 5.
6. Write a program that lets the user play a game of craps. The game is played by the following rules (a simplification):

1. Enter the amount to bet.
2. Roll a pair of dice.
3. If a 7 or 11 is rolled then you win
   else if 2, 3, or 12 is rolled then you lose
   else
      your first roll becomes your point and you must
      continue rolling until either you match your point
      and win, or you roll a 7 and lose.

Let the user enter the bet, and have the computer "roll" the dice. Keep track of the total amount won or lost. Play until the bet entered is 0. Then print the total amount won or lost.
7. Make a graph of the cosine function, using angles from 0 to 360 degrees and an increment of 5 degrees.
8. Make a graph of the following function:

$$y = e^{-x/4} \sin x$$

Scale the y axis as in Example 13.3. Let x vary from 0 to $4*(\pi)$ radians in steps of $(\pi)/15$ radians.

■ **9.** Write a program that finds all two-digit Fahrenheit temperatures having the property that, when the digits are reversed, the result is the equivalent temperature in degrees Celsius. The formula to convert from Fahrenheit to Celsius is:

$$C = 5 * (F - 32) / 9$$

The program requires that the Celsius temperature be rounded to the nearest integer.
10a. Modify the subroutines of Figure 13-5 so that all upper case letters are converted to lower case, *except* for the first letter of a sentence. HINT: Set a flag when a period is detected, reset it when the first character of the following sentence is detected.
10b. Write a program that reads a sentence from DATA statements. The sentence contains upper case letters only. Your program will convert this sentence to lower case, *except* for the first letter of the sentence, which will remain upper case. Your program will then print the converted sentence.
11. Same as Exercise 10b, except that the first letter of every word will remain capitalized.

14 | User-Defined Functions

Outline
14.1 One-Line Functions
14.2 Arguments and Parameters
14.3 Using Global Variables
14.4 Multi-Line Functions
    Defining Multi-line Functions
    The DECLARE FUNCTION Statement
    Returning a Result from a Multi-Line Function
14.5 Rules Governing Functions
    Function Name
    Parameters and Arguments
    Invoking a Function
14.6 Side Effects
14.7 Flow Charts
Summary
Review Questions
Syntax Exercises
Programming Exercises
Enrichment Topics
    Defining External Functions
    The EXTERNAL Statement
    Invoking an External Function
    The EXIT FUNCTION Statement
    Error-Trapping in External Functions

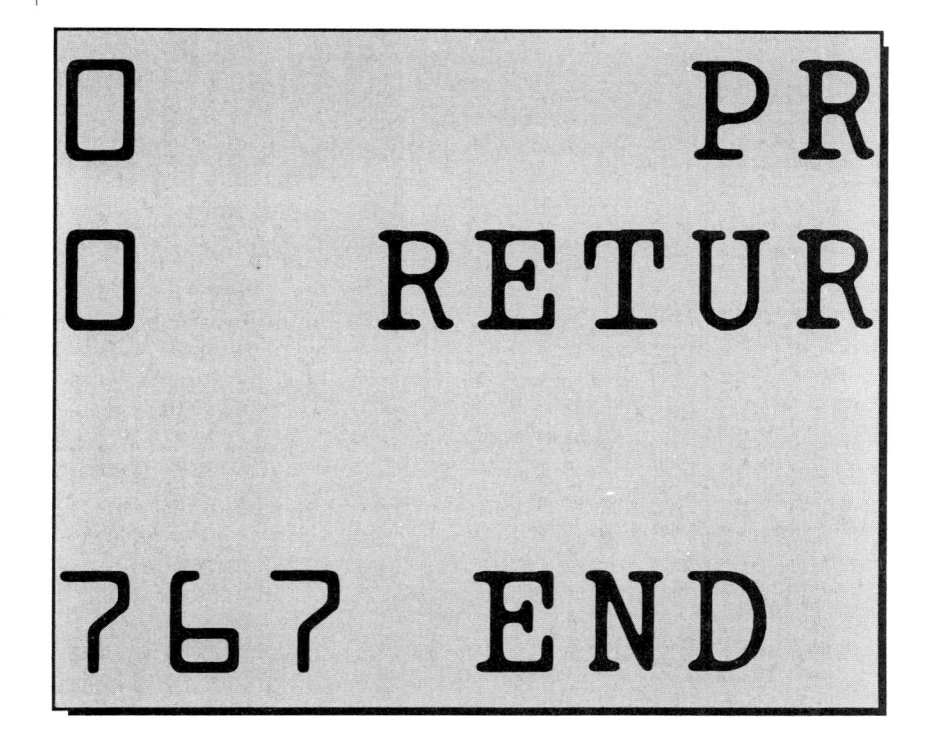

Introduction   In the previous chapter, you learned of a number of BASIC built-in functions. You learned that you could pass one or more arguments to a function, and that the function would return a result.

In this chapter, you will learn how to write your own functions. Once these functions are written, they are used in the same way as the built-in functions. You will be able to pass parameters to a user-defined function, invoke the function with a function reference, and have the function return a calculated value.

14.1 ONE-LINE FUNCTIONS

A function is a module to which you can send a number of arguments and it will calculate and return a single result. The built-in functions you have been using all have this property of returning exactly one answer.

A function that can be defined in only one line has the following syntax:

sn DEF [data-type] name [(parameters)] = expression

where

sn = the usual statement number.
data-type = one of the usual data-types described previously: REAL, INTEGER, and so on. The data-type following the keyword DEF determines what type of result is returned by the function.
name = the name of the function. It can consist of 1 to 28 alphanumeric characters, underscores, or periods, beginning with an alphabetic character.

A function is invoked by a function reference of the form:

name (arguments)

For example, the function defined by the statement

```
20 DEF REAL Find_sum (REAL X,REAL Y,REAL Z) = X+Y+Z
```

can be invoked with the statement

```
40    SUM = Find_sum (A,B,C)
```

The following additional rules apply to the naming of functions:

1. If the function is invoked in the program *before* the function is defined, then the function name must begin with the letters FN. For example,

```
1020 Answer = FN.Find_avg (87, 92,82)
5000 DEF REAL FN.Find_avg (REAL A,REAL B, REAL C) = (A + B + C) / 3
```

Line 1020 invokes function FN.Find_avg. Because the function itself is not defined until line 5000, the name of the function had to begin with FN. (The period after FN is optional; when used, as it is here, it becomes part of the function's name. FN.Find_avg and FNFind_avg would be the names of two different functions.)

The prefix FN is not required if the function is defined before it is used. If the function is defined in statement 100, and invoked in statement 1020, the above statements could then have been written as follows:

```
100 DEF REAL Find_avg (REAL A, REAL B, REAL C) = (A + B + C) / 3
1020 Answer = Find_avg (87, 92,82)
```

The prefix FN could still have been used, if desired.

2. If no data-type is supplied, then the suffix appended to the name of the function determines the type of the value returned by the function. These rules are the same as those for implicitly declared variables: If the suffix is a percent symbol (%), the function returns an INTEGER type value. If it is a dollar symbol ($), the value returned is of the STRING type. If there is no suffix, the value returned is REAL. The following examples explain this implicit typing.

```
DEF Sum%     (REAL A,REAL B,REAL C) = A + B + C       ! Integer returned
DEF Avg      (REAL A,REAL B,REAL C) = (A + B + C) / 3 ! Real returned
DEF Combine$ (STRING A,STRING B)    = A + B           ! String returned
```

If any of these functions are invoked before being declared, their names would require the FN prefix as explained above.

We will use explicitly typed functions only; this is in accordance with Digital Equipment Corporation's recommendation.

As an example of naming functions, here is a program that uses a function to find the sum of the three numbers 10, 20, and 30—not a useful program but good for illustrating how a one-line function is used!

```
10 DECLARE REAL A, B, C, SUM

20     DEF REAL Find_sum (REAL X,REAL Y,REAL Z) = X+Y+Z

30     A = 10 \ B = 20 \ C = 30
40     SUM = Find_sum (A,B,C)
50     PRINT "The sum = "; SUM
60 END
```

Output is: The sum =   60.

We now continue our explanation of the syntax of one-line functions, which we began above:

parameters = a list of variables that are local to the function. They serve as the receivers of the data that are sent to the function when the function is invoked.

arguments = a list of actual values or variables that are passed to the parameters of the function. Each argument must correspond to a parameter. Furthermore, the type of each argument must be the same as the type of its corresponding parameter. (It does not matter if implicit or explicit typing is used as long as the end result of the typing is identical.)

expression = the expression that calculates the result. This result will be given the data-type of the function, as explained earlier. The value of this expression is returned to the point of invocation.

14.2 ARGUMENTS AND PARAMETERS

Arguments and parameters are very important, so we will spend a little more time studying them.

To try to explain parameters, let us posit the following scenario. You have been given the job of finding the names of the directors of a number of companies. The name of each company is written on an index card. Your local library has a thick tome containing all sorts of information about American corporations, so you call the librarian, who says he will help you. You read the name of the first company from your index card. The librarian writes it down on an index card he has. He looks up the company in his book and tells you the director's name. You repeat this sequence for each of your index cards. The librarian writes each company on his own index card, then furnishes you with the name of the director.

The information on your index cards is comparable to the arguments of a function reference; they must exist before the function is invoked (or the librarian called). The information on the librarian's index cards is similar to the parameters of a function. For the parameter to have a value, it must receive it from an argument. Notice also that the parameters are local to the function. If the librarian decides to cross out the name on his index card, that will in no way affect the information on yours.[1]

The name of the director that the librarian gives you over the telephone is comparable to the result returned from a function. For each argument you send to the function, the function uses the parameter to calculate a result. It then returns the result to whatever invoked it.

A program supplies data to a function (or other subprogram) by using arguments and parameters. The **arguments** are variables that exist in the invoking procedure before the function is invoked. (They are sometimes called actual parameters, but we will not use this terminology.) The values of the arguments in the function reference are sent to the function to its corresponding parameters. The function then has access to these values.

The **parameters** are variables that are local to the function; they are not known elsewhere in the program. (Parameters are sometimes called dummy arguments; we will not use this terminology). The parameters are the memory locations that receive the values of the arguments that are sent to the invoked function. The names of the parameters need not be the same as those of the arguments, but they must be of the same type. The first parameter receives the value of the first argument, the second receives the second, and so on. Therefore, the number of parameters must equal the number of arguments.

There may be zero to eight parameters. The parameters may be either implicitly or explicitly typed, but explicit typing is preferred, as usual. Implicit typing is presented for completeness.

1. Implicit typing of parameters is the same as for other variables. A suffix of a percent symbol (%) declares an INTEGER variable. A dollar sign suffix ($) declares a STRING variable. No suffix declares the variable to be of the REAL type. Here is a function that uses implicit typing for its parameters. Its purpose is to concatenate the strings and return the resultant string.

---

[1]. Parameters in VAX-BASIC functions are entirely local to the function and changing them has no effect on the arguments. The passing mechanism is by value only. This is not true in all languages. It is also not true for VAX-BASIC subprograms or external functions. See the enrichment topics at the end of chapter 4 and at the end of this chapter.

```
30 DEF STRING Combine (A$, B$) = A$ + B$
```

2. A parameter is explicitly declared by stating a data-type before the parameter name in the parameter list. For example, the following function definition defines a function that has two string parameters. It has the same purpose as the previous function.

```
30 DEF STRING Combine (STRING A, STRING B) = A + B
```

The word STRING before each parameter declares each of them to be of type STRING.

To repeat: An argument is the entity that exists and has a value before the function is invoked. It is sent to the function and is received by a parameter. The parameter does not have a value of its own until it receives one from the argument.

As an example, consider the following program (again):

```
10 DECLARE REAL A, B, C, SUM

20     DEF REAL Find_sum (REAL X, REAL Y, REAL Z) = X + Y + Z

30     A = 10 \ B = 20 \ C = 30
40     SUM = Find_sum (A, B, C)
50     PRINT "The sum = "; SUM
60 END
```

The function is defined in line 20. Its parameters are X, Y, and Z. You may consider the function to be a rule that has not yet been applied. The function rule in this example is to add the three parameters, X + Y + Z. Line 40 invokes the function and sends the arguments A, B, and C to the parameters X, Y, and Z. This situation is illustrated in Figure 14-1. The function rule is now applied to the parameters with the result being 60. This result is returned to line 40 and replaces the function reference. The result is stored in SUM, which is printed by line 50.

Figure 14-1.
Passing Arguments to Parameters and Returning the Result

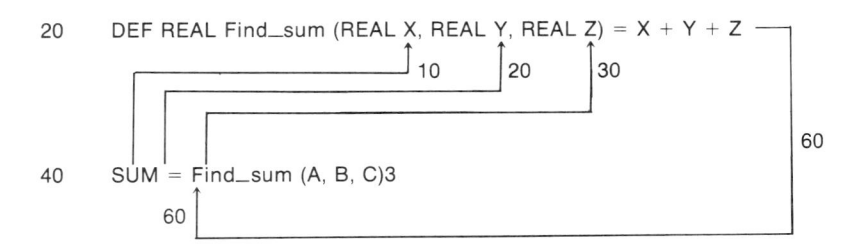

```
20     DEF REAL Find_sum (REAL X, REAL Y, REAL Z) = X + Y + Z
                                    10    20    30

                                                                60
40     SUM = Find_sum (A, B, C)3
           60
```

In the above example, the function was defined in line 20 before it was used in line 40. If the function had been defined after it had been invoked, in line 55 for instance, then we would have had to use the prefix FN for the function name:

```
55     DEF REAL FN.Find_sum (REAL X, REAL Y, REAL Z) = X + Y = Z
```

Line 40 would then be:

```
40      SUM = FN.Find_sum (A,B,C)
```

As mentioned, a parameter is a local variable that exists and has meaning *only* inside the function. It is unknown outside the function and we say it does not exist there. For a parameter to receive a value that the function can use, the value has to be passed to it from an argument in the argument list. The arguments are known in the program even outside the function.

To help clarify the concept of parameters, consider the following example:

```
10  DECLARE INTEGER A, X, Y

20      DEF INTEGER FNF(INTEGER X) = 10 * X
30      A = 100 \ X = 150
40      Y = FNF(A)
50      PRINT X,Y
60  END
```

The output from this program is shown below.

```
 150               1000
```

In line 20, the function is defined with the parameter X. This parameter does not yet have a value. At line 30, two actual variables are defined and given values. The variable A is set to 100 and the variable X is set to 150. Line 40 invokes the function. The variable A is sent as an argument, causing the function parameter, X, to assume the same value as A, 100. (Remember: An argument is the entity that exists and has a value and is sent to a function parameter. The parameter does not have a value of its own until it receives the value of an argument.)

You can see that we now have two X's: The actual variable X, whose value is 150, and the parameter X, which got its value from the argument A and is therefore 100. The function expression multiplies its parameter by 10. The parameter is 100, not 150, so the result is 1000. This value is returned to statement 40 and stored in variable Y.

Statement 50 then prints the values of X and Y. But which X is printed? The answer is simple: It is the actual variable X, not the parameter X, which is entirely local to the function and it is therefore ignored by the program outside the function itself.

In the preceding program, if we add the statement

```
35  Y2 = FNF(X)
```

then the parameter and argument will both be 150, and the function will return a value of 1500 to variable Y2. Even though both X's are 150 in this case, they are still conceptually separate items, and each is allocated its own storage in memory.

The point being made here is that the parameters of a function do not exist independently, as other variables do. They have no value until the function is invoked and arguments are passed to them. A program can have actual variables and parameters that look alike, as in this example, but conceptually they are different entities.

> **NOTE!** A function is executed only when invoked by a function reference. If the program reaches a function that has not been invoked, it ignores the entire function and control passes to the statement after the function. Consider the example we used above, repeated here for reference.
>
> ```
> 10 DECLARE INTEGER A, X, Y
>
> 20    DEF INTEGER FNF(INTEGER X) = 10*X
>
> 30    A = 100 \ X = 150
> 40    Y = FNF(A)
> 50    PRINT X,Y
> 60 END
> ```
>
> Execution of the program proceeds as follows. Statement 10 defines the variables. Statement 20 is then *skipped*. This statement *defines* a function, but the function has not been *invoked*. The program executes statement 30. Statement 40 then executes and invokes the function at line 20, causing the function to execute. The function returns its result back to the function reference at line 40, effectively replacing the function reference with the answer. Lines 50 and 60 then execute in turn.

Example 14.1

```
10 DEF FN.Root_sum_squares (REAL X, REAL Y) = SQR(X*X + Y*Y)
```

The function name is FN.Root_sum_squares. It receives two values into parameters X and Y. The function then calculates the square root of the sum of the squares of these two numbers. To find the square root of 3 squared plus 5 squared, we could use:

```
40 Result = FN.Root_sum_squares (3,5)
```

The numbers 3 and 5 are sent to the parameters X and Y. The square root of the sum of the squares is then calculated and returned to Result.

Example 14.2

```
100 DEF STRING Combine (STRING Str_1, STRING Str_2, &
                 INTEGER N1, INTEGER N2)      &
   = SEG$(Str_1, 1, N1) + SEG$(Str_2, N2, LEN(Str_2))
```

The function Combine combines the left-most N1 characters of Str_1 with the right-most characters of Str_2, starting at position N2 of Str_2, where N1, N2, Str_1, and Str_2 are local parameters and have meaning only to the function.

If, for instance, `Name_1` were `SAMUEL` and `Name_2` were `WILLIAMSON`, then the statements

```
100 New_name = Combine(Name_1, Name_2, 3, 8)
200 PRINT New_name
```

would print `SAMSON` at the terminal. `SAMSON` would be comprised of the first three characters of `SAMUEL`, and the characters of `WILLIAMSON` starting in position 8.

A one-line function can be invoked many times in a program, from many points in the program. That is one of the advantages of using a function. In general, one-line functions are used under the following conditions:

1. The calculation can be performed with one expression.
2. The same calculation is required at different places in the program.
3. It is necessary to perform the same calculations using more than one set of values.

Example 14.3

We will read three sides of a triangle and then determine whether it is a right triangle. An appropriate message will be printed.

A right triangle must satisfy the Pythagorean equation: The sum of the squares of two sides must equal the square of the third. Equivalently, the sum of the squares of two sides, minus the square of the third, must equal zero. Algebraically, we must either satisfy

$$a^2 + b^2 = c^2$$

or

$$a^2 + b^2 - c^2 = 0$$

The second relationship is easier to incorporate into a one-line function.

Because the sides can be read in any order, we cannot know if the hypotenuse will be the first side, the second, or the third. We will have to try all possibilities. If all three attempts fail to satisfy the Pythagorean relationship, then the triangle is not a right triangle. Figure 14-2 is a solution, written with a loop to permit the testing of any number of triangles. (Can you determine the exit condition?)

The function references are in the conditional statement of the print subroutine, line 1110. The function is invoked three times: once with side A as the third argument, once with side B as the third argument, and once with side C.

In statement 30, the function is defined, using A, B, and C as parameters. These receive values from the arguments each time the function is invoked. If every A in statement 30 were replaced with an X, every B with a Y, and every C with a Z, there would be no change in the operation of the program from the user's viewpoint.

The important point, as far as this function is concerned, is that the third parameter is used by the function as the hypotenuse. Each of the three function invocations passes a different argument to this third parameter. Thus, each of the sides typed in is tried as the hypotenuse of the triangle.

Figure 14-2.
Program to Identify Right Triangles

```
10  ! Find right triangles

20      DECLARE REAL A, B, C

30   ! Function to determine if a right triangle exists
        DEF REAL Triangle (A,B,C) = A^2 + B^2 - C^2

40      GOSUB Read_sides            ! Read sides of triangle
50      UNTIL A = 0 AND B = 0 AND C = 0
60        GOSUB Print_result        ! Print appropriate message
70        GOSUB Read_sides          ! Read sides of new triangle
80      NEXT

90      EXIT PROGRAM

1000 Read_sides:                    ! Read sides of triangle
1010    INPUT 'Enter 3 sides of triangle. 0,0,0 to quit'; A,B,C
1020 RETURN

1100 Print_result:                  ! Print appropriate message
1110    IF Triangle(A,B,C) = 0 &
           OR Triangle(B,C,A) = 0 &
           OR Triangle(C,A,B) = 0
        THEN PRINT TAB(20); 'Right triangle. Sides are     '; A; B; C
        ELSE PRINT TAB(20); 'Not a right triangle. Sides are '; A; B; C
        END IF
1120    PRINT \ PRINT
1130 RETURN

32767 END
```

Be aware that the function at line 30 is not executed until the program reaches line 1110. As was stated earlier, a function is not executed until it is invoked.

14.3 USING GLOBAL VARIABLES

So far, all data the function required was sent to it in the argument list. The corresponding parameter was then local to the function. This is the desired method of passing data.

Unfortunately, the preferred method is not always possible. For example, VAX-BASIC does not allow the passing of an array to a function.[2] If the function requires access to an array, another, albeit inferior, mechanism must be relied on. Specifically, the use of global variables is necessary.

---
2. However, see the enrichment topics section at the end of this chapter.

14 USER-DEFINED FUNCTIONS

Variables that are known everywhere in a program are called **global variables.** In BASIC, every variable in a program that is not a parameter is global and may be used in every function.[3] Since parameters are local to their functions and thus are not global variables, they can be used only in the functions in which they are defined.

Example 14.4 | In this example, we have two associated arrays—one containing names, the other social security numbers. The arrays will be read from a file called

Figure 14-3.
Program with Function
Using Global Arrays

```
10  ! Print selected names and social security numbers
    ! Global arrays are used by a function

20       DECLARE INTEGER Number, I, &
                  STRING Result, Names(100), Soc_sec_no.(100)

30       MAP (Id) STRING Name_in=25, SSN_in=11

40  ! Function to concatenate array elements
         DEF STRING Combine (INTEGER Number) &
                 = Soc_sec_no.(Number) + " " + Names(Number)

50       GOSUB Read_file            ! Read the arrays

60       INPUT "Enter integer (1-100), 0 to end "; Number
         WHILE Number <> 0
            Result = Combine(Number)    ! Concatenate name and SS#
            PRINT Result
            PRINT
            INPUT "Enter integer (1-100), 0 to end "; Number
         NEXT

70       EXIT PROGRAM

1000 Read_file:                     ! Read file into arrays
1010     OPEN "ID.DAT" FOR INPUT AS FILE #1, RELATIVE, MAP Id
1020     FOR I = 1 TO 100
            Get #1
            Names(I) = Name_in
            Soc_sec_no.(I) = SSN_in
         NEXT I
1030     CLOSE #1
1040 RETURN

32767 END
```

---

3. An exception: When a variable in the program has the same name as a parameter, the function can use only the parameter; the global variable will be unknown to it.

ID.DAT. When the program is run, we will enter an integer. A function will use this integer as a subscript in the array. It will then concatenate the social security number to the name, returning the resulting string to the point where the function was invoked. This result will be printed as a single string. In pseudocode we have the following program.

> Concatenate array elements:
>   Read arrays from file
>   Enter integer
>   While integer <> 0
>   Concatenate array elements
>   Print result
>   Read another integer
>   End loop
>   Stop

The program is shown in Figure 14-3.

The function is defined in line 40. It uses Number as a subscript, which is passed to the parameter list. It also uses the two arrays, Names and Soc_sec_no.. Because they are arrays, they may not be passed as parameters. Therefore, the function uses them as global arrays. Unlike parameters whose names are local, global references must use the same names as the main program. In other words, the function could have used another name for Number, but it had to use the array identifiers Names and Soc_sec_no.. For instance, the function could have been written as shown below:

```
40      ! Function to concatenate array elements
        DEF STRING Combine(INTEGER N) =   &
                    Soc_sec_no.(N) + " " + Names(N)
```

The parameter is now N, having gotten its value from the argument Number on the third line of statement 60. The array names must be as shown.

It is always best to avoid using global variables and arrays. Instead of passing the subscript, as we did in the example above, we could have passed the array elements themselves. Passing an array element is not the same as passing an array. An element contains but a single value, while an array contains many. Lines 40 and 60 of the above program could be rewritten as follows:

```
40      ! Function to concatenate array elements
        DEF STRING Combine(STRING SSN, STRING Name_)   &
                    = SSN + " " + Name_
60      INPUT "Enter integer (1-100), 0 to end "; Number
        WHILE Number <> 0
           Result = Combine(Soc_sec_no.(Number), Names(Number))
           PRINT Result
           PRINT
           INPUT "Enter integer (1-100), 0 to end "; Number
        NEXT
```

The parameters of the function are now local STRING variables SSN and Name_. The function reference in line 60 sends, as arguments, the two elements that are to be combined. Each element is a single value that will be received by the corresponding parameter. We have thus eliminated any global reference to the array from within the function.

14.4 MULTI-LINE FUNCTIONS

Defining Multi-Line Functions

Like the one-line function, the multi-line function[4] returns one result. However, the logic required to calculate this result may involve more than one statement. The syntax of a multi-line function is:

>   **sn DEF [data-type] [FN]name (parameters)**
>   **statements**
>   **[FN]name = expression**
>   **END DEF**

where

>   **[FN]name** = the function name
>   **parameters** = a parameter list

An example is:

```
100 ! Function to find letter grade
    DEF STRING Letter (REAL Mark)
110   ! Assign letter grade
      IF Mark >= 90 THEN Letter = "A"
      ELSE IF Mark >= 80 THEN Letter = "B"
      ELSE IF Mark >= 70 THEN Letter = "C"
      ELSE IF Mark >= 60 THEN Letter = "D"
      ELSE Letter = "F"
      END IF  END IF  END IF  END IF
120   END DEF                          ! End of function
```

This function is used later in an example. An explanation of it will be delayed until then. We have other things to learn first.

The DECLARE FUNCTION Statement

Before a multi-line function is defined, the function-type and parameter-types should be declared in a DECLARE FUNCTION statement.[5] The syntax of this statement is:

DECLARE function-type FUNCTION function-name [(parameter-type, . . .)],
. . .

---

4. Not all dialects of BASIC support multi-line functions.
5. Technically, declaring functions this way is not required. It is recommended by DEC as good programming practice and the author agrees.

For example:

```
30 DECLARE STRING FUNCTION Letter(REAL), ID_string(STRING,STRING)
```

This statement declares two functions that will be defined later in the program. Both will return STRING results. The first is a function named Letter. It has one parameter of type REAL. The second is a function named ID_string. It has two parameters, both of type STRING.

Notice that only the names of the functions are given above. The names of the parameters are *not* given; they will be defined when the functions are written.

The parameter types are optional in the DECLARE FUNCTION statement. If they are omitted, then each argument must agree in type with its corresponding parameter. If included, then each argument is converted to the type of the corresponding parameter when the function is invoked. In other words, the arguments and parameters do not have to be of the same type, initially. Notice that it is the argument that is converted to the type of the parameter.

Each DECLARE FUNCTION statement may be used to declare functions of only one type. In the example above, both functions—Letter and ID_string—were of type STRING (even though their parameters may not have been). Therefore, there will be as many such statements as there are function types. Even though a separate statement is required for each type, they may all be grouped together on one logical line, using one line number. Or, each may be given its own line number, if desired.

Functions that are not DECLAREd follow the same rules as their equivalents for the one-line functions as far as the FN prefix is concerned. The rules regarding implicit typing are also the same as for one-line functions. This applies both to the function name and to the parameters.

Returning a Result from a Multi-Line Function

The next-to-last statement, prior to the END DEF statement, assigns a value to a local variable **that is identical to the function name.** This variable is unique; it has the specific purpose of storing the result that the function calculates. When the function ends, the value stored in this variable will be returned to the statement that invoked the function (known as the **point of invocation**).

IMPORTANT! | **The only way a function can return its result is if you store the result in this special variable. Should you fail to do this, the function will return unpredictable garbage.**

To clarify a bit further: if the first line of the function is

```
1000 DEF REAL Calc (X,Y,Z)
```

then the function has been given the name Calc and it has three parameters. The function requires an assignment statement of the form

```
1100 Calc = any expression
```

Whatever value has been assigned by this statement will be returned by the function when END DEF is executed.

The function is invoked with a statement of the form

```
200 ANSWER = Calc (A,B,C)
```

Each of the statements within the function can have its own statement number if required by the logic.

NOTE! | **The entire function, including all of the statements between DEF and END DEF, is executed only when it is invoked via a function reference. If the computer encounters a function in its normal sequential flow, it passes over the entire function and execution continues with the first statement following END DEF. This is the same behavior we saw earlier when we studied one-line functions.**

Example 14.5 | We will write a program that uses a function to calculate the average of the elements of an array. The array consists of 250 random numbers in the range of 1000 to 2000 (more precisely, 1000.00 to 1999.99).

This function will have no parameters, and we will pass no arguments to it. Instead, the function will use data from a global array A. Here is the pseudocode for the main program:

    Average of array using function:
      Dimension the array
      Fill array with random numbers
      Invoke function to find average
      Print average
    Stop

The logic for finding an average has been shown before, so we will not repeat the pseudocode for it. The solution appears in Figure 14-4.

There are no arguments for the function Avg. The function uses array A in a global manner, sharing it with the main program.

Note the statement at line 130 of Figure 14-4. This statement assigns an expression to Avg. When END DEF is executed, the value of this variable will be returned to the statement that invoked the function.

(Reminder: If we had not used a DECLARE FUNCTION statement, the letters FN would have to be used as a prefix to the function name in this example—FN.Avg, for example—because line 40 would invoke the function before it is defined. A function name must begin with the letters FN in such a circumstance.)

Example 14.6 | In this example (Fig. 14-5), we will enter student averages one at a time and send them to a function. The function will calculate the letter grade each

Figure 14-4.
Program to Find the Average of Elements in an Array

```
10  ! Average of randomly generated array using a function
20      DECLARE REAL A(250), Sum_A, Average, INTEGER I
        DECLARE REAL FUNCTION Avg
30      GOSUB Set_up_array     ! Set up array of random numbers
40      Average = Avg          ! Invoke function to find average
50      PRINT "Average of array = "; Average \ PRINT
60   EXIT PROGRAM

100 ! Function to find average
110     DEF REAL Avg
120     ! Find sum of elements
        Sum_A = 0
        FOR I = 1 TO 250
          Sum_A = Sum_A + A(I)
        NEXT I
130     ! Assign answer to special variable Avg
        Avg = Sum_A / 250
140     END DEF

200     Set_up_array:          ! Set up array of random numbers
210       RANDOMIZE
220       FOR I = 1 TO 250
            A(I) = 1000 * RND + 1000
          NEXT I
230     RETURN

32767 END
```

student has earned. The program will end when a sentinel average of 0 is entered. The logic for this program has been explained earlier in this book (see chapter 6) and will not be repeated here.

The function is invoked in the WHILE loop of statement 40. Avg, the student's average, is passed to the function as the only argument. The function itself begins at line 100, and its parameter is Mark. When the function is invoked, Mark takes on the value of Avg. The function uses the value in Mark to calculate the letter grade, which it does with the nested IF-THEN-ELSE structure at line 110. The special variable Letter is assigned the letter grade that is returned when END DEF is executed.

In Example 14.6, the argument is Avg and the parameter is Mark. The two have different symbolic names. However, other alternatives exist. Both the argument and parameter could be the same—Avg, for instance. Every occurrence of Mark in the function would then be replaced with Avg. Or, as another possibility, no argument or parameter needs to be used at all. In this case, Avg would be a global variable, and the function would be able to use its value just as the rest of the program can. In general, the use of global variables should be minimized where possible to reduce side effects, as explained in section 14.6.

Figure 14-5.
Student Grading Program

```
10  ! Assign letter grade given average
20      DECLARE REAL Avg, STRING Grade
30      DECLARE STRING FUNCTION Letter (REAL)

40      INPUT "Enter average (0 to stop) "; Avg
        WHILE Avg <> 0                  ! 0 is sentinel
          Grade = Letter (Avg)          ! Calculate letter grade
          PRINT TAB (20); "Letter grade = "; Grade
          PRINT
          INPUT "Enter average (0 to stop) "; Avg
        NEXT
50  EXIT PROGRAM

100 ! Function to find letter grade
    DEF STRING Letter (REAL Mark)
110     ! Assign letter grade
        IF Mark >= 90 THEN Letter = "A"
        ELSE IF Mark >= 80 THEN Letter = "B"
        ELSE IF Mark >= 70 THEN Letter = "C"
        ELSE IF Mark >= 60 THEN Letter = "D"
        ELSE Letter = "F"
        END IF  END IF  END IF  END IF
120     END DEF                         ! End of function

32767 END                               ! End of program

runnh
Enter average (0 to stop)? 87
                    Letter grade = B

Enter average (0 to stop)? 90
                    Letter grade = A

Enter average (0 to stop)? 52
                    Letter grade = F

Enter average (0 to stop)? 77
                    Letter grade = C

Enter average (0 to stop)? 0
```

14.5 RULES GOVERNING FUNCTIONS

The following rules relate to function usage. They are a compendium of previously presented concepts.

Function Name

1. The name of the function must begin with a letter, and may be followed by an additional 27 letters, digits, periods, or underscores.

2. You should always declare your functions with a DECLARE FUNCTION statement. Thus various requirements regarding the name of your function, and the suffix it must have, will be void.

3. If the function has been typed in a DECLARE FUNCTION statement, then the type designator is not necessary in the DEF statement where the function is defined. It is permitted, however. For example:

20 DECLARE STRING FUNCTION Combine (STRING, STRING)

1000 DEF Combine (STRING First, STRING Second)

In line 1000, which starts the function definition, the function-type STRING has been omitted. Because of the typing in line 20, it was optional in line 1000. Line 1000 could also have been written:

1000 DEF STRING Combine (STRING First, STRING Second)

NOTE! **The DEFINE FUNCTION statement does not define parameters; their type designators are for reference only. Parameters must be typed separately, either explicitly as shown above (line 1000), or implicitly.**

Parameters and Arguments

1. A function may have zero to eight parameters in VAX-BASIC. Parameters must be scalars; arrays cannot be sent to DEF functions. (However, see the enrichment topics at the end of this chapter.)

2. The number of parameters must be equal to the number of arguments passed to these parameters.

3. The type of each parameter may be stated in the DECLARE FUNCTION statement. This will cause the corresponding argument to be converted to that type, if necessary, and if possible. If the parameter type is not given in the DECLARE FUNCTION statement, then the arguments must be of the same type as the parameters. Only the parameter type is used in the DECLARE FUNCTION statement, not the parameter name.

4. Each parameter should have its own type specifier to declare the parameter's type. (Without it, the rules for implicit declarations apply.) The type keyword immediately precedes the parameter in the parameter list.

5. The parameters of a function are local variables, known only to the function. The rest of the program is unaware of their existence.

6. Changing a parameter in a function will have no effect on the corresponding argument in the invoking procedure.

7. The argument of a function reference can be any legal expression, not necessarily only a simple variable.

8. Global variables: All variables used in a function are global, except those mentioned in the parameter list. That is, they refer to the same items in the function as in the rest of the program. In general, it is not good practice to use global variables unless such use is unavoidable.

Invoking a Function

1. A function is executed only when it is invoked by means of a function reference. If a function is encountered in the normal program flow, it is skipped, and execution continues with the statement following END DEF for a multi-line function, or the function definition for a one-line function.

2. A function is invoked by giving the name of the function followed by an argument list, if any. This may be used anywhere a variable may be used. The value returned by the function then replaces the function reference.

Example 14.7 This example illustrates how a parameter is a local variable that has no effect outside the function. The function will change the value of the parameter during its calculations, but this change will not be felt after the function ends. This program's sole purpose is to illustrate this point.

```
10    DECLARE INTEGER X, A
      DECLARE INTEGER FUNCTION FNQ (INTEGER)
20    X = 10
30    A = FNQ (X)
40    PRINT X, A

50    DEF INTEGER FNQ (INTEGER X)
60        X = 5 * X
70        FNQ = X
80    END DEF

100   END
```

The output from this program is:

```
10              50
```

Statement 30 passes the argument X, whose value is 10, to the function. The corresponding parameter is also called X. The function multiplies this parameter by 5 and stores the answer, 50, in X.

Even though X becomes 50 in the function, the X in the main program remains 10. When the function returns the value of FNQ, which is 50, statement 30 stores it in A. The PRINT statement causes the two numbers 10 and 50 to be printed.

Example 14.8 In this example, we invoke a function, using an expression for the argument. The program uses a one-line function that multiplies its parameter by 10.

```
10    DECLARE REAL X, Y, A
      DECLARE REAL FUNCTION B (REAL)
20    DEF REAL B (REAL Z) = 10 * Z
30    X = 3 \ Y = 4
40    A = B (X^2 + Y^2)
50    PRINT A
60    END
```

This program will print the number 250 at the terminal. When the function is invoked at line 40, the argument is evaluated (3 squared plus 4 squared), and the result, 25, is passed to the parameter Z of the function in line 20. The parameter is then multiplied by 10 and returned to line 40, replacing the function reference. Line 50 prints the result, 250.

14.6 SIDE EFFECTS

A function has access to the values of its parameters, and also to all global variables and arrays of the program. The function is supposed to use these values without changing them, calculate the result, and then return this result to the statement that invoked it.

Notice this clause in the previous paragraph: "The function is supposed to *use* these values without changing them. . . ." A function *can* change the value of a global variable or array element. Such a change is called a **side effect** and is undesirable from a programming standpoint.

A person reading a program expects that, when a function is invoked, the only purpose of the function is to return its one result to the point of invocation. The person does not expect any other changes to take place. If such changes occur, they are unanticipated and obscure the logic of the program. They also make debugging very difficult. Even the programmer may have forgotten about the side effects after writing the program.

CAUTION! **Never allow functions to produce side effects!**

One of the best ways to avoid side effects is to pass all needed values to the function in the argument list. Any attempt by the function to assign a new value to the corresponding parameter will have no effect on the argument.

Example 14.9

We will write a program that reads a value of N, then uses a function to calculate N factorial, N!, which is the product of all integers from 1 to N. For example, 4! is 24 (4 × 3 × 2 × 1). 0! is defined 1.

To calculate a factorial, we consider two possibilities: If N is 0 or 1, then the answer to N! is 1. If N is greater than 1, then we initialize a product to 1 (not 0) and proceed to multiply this product by all integers from 1 to N.

The solution is shown in Figure 14-6, which includes output for two sample runs.

In this program, the first statement executed is line 40. The function, line 30, is executed only when it is invoked by the second instruction in line 40.

You may be wondering why we made the factoral function and the variable Answer of type REAL. The reason is simple: the maximum value that can be stored in an integer variable is 32,767. This is less than 7 factorial. By using REAL-type varaibles, much higher factorials are possible.

In this example, the argument and parameter are the same variable, N. Since the parameter is local to the function, it could have been changed to any other name, as long as it was of type INTEGER.

Example 14.10

A teacher has 35 students, each of whom takes five tests. The tests are stored in a 35 × 5 array (35 rows, 5 columns). The teacher would like to enter a student number (row number) and have the computer calculate the

Figure 14-6.
Program to Calculate N!

```
10 ! Program to calculate N!
20     DECLARE INTEGER I, N, REAL Product, Answer
       DECLARE REAL FUNCTION Factorial (INTEGER)

30     ! The N Factorial function
       DEF REAL Factorial(INTEGER N)
         IF N = 0 OR N = 1 THEN Factorial = 1
         ELSE
             Product = 1
             FOR I = 1 TO N
               Product = Product * I
             NEXT I
             Factorial = Product
         END IF
       END DEF

40 ! Now the main program
       INPUT "Enter N "; N
       Answer = Factorial(N)        ! Invoke the function
       PRINT N; "! = "; Answer      ! Print factorial

32767 END

runnh
Enter N? 5
 5 ! = 120

Ready

runnh
Enter N? 8
 8 ! = 40320

Ready
```

average and letter grade for that student. Two functions will be used: one for the average and one for the letter grade (see Fig. 14-7).

Notice one item: The main program uses the variable Student as a loop counter in line 110. The function Find_avg uses the parameter Student as the row number of the Std_Grades array. Because the parameter is entirely local to the function, there is no interference between the function and the main program even though they use the same identifiers—conceptually, they are not the same.

The program of Fig.14-7 is self-explanatory and should not require further elaboration. The two functions are executed only when they are invoked, in statements 60 and 70.

The program would also work if the EXIT PROGRAM instruction were removed, but the program would not be as clear because it would not be obvious where the program ended.

Figure 14-7.
Student Grading Program

```
10  ! Selected student average and grade

20        DECLARE INTEGER Std_Grades(35,5), Student, Test, I, &
                          Std_sum, Std_number, &
                  REAL    Std_average, &
                  STRING  Letter_grade

30        DECLARE REAL FUNCTION Find_avg(INTEGER)
          DECLARE STRING FUNCTION Find_grade(REAL)

40        GOSUB Enter_grades                    ! Enter class grades
50        INPUT "Enter student number ", Std_number
60        Std_average = Find_avg (Std_number)
70        Letter_grade = Find_grade (Std_average)
80        PRINT Std_number, Std_average, Letter_grade
90     EXIT PROGRAM

100 Enter_grades:                               ! Enter class grades
110      FOR Student = 1 TO 35
             PRINT "Enter 5 grades for student" ; Student
             FOR Test = 1 TO 5
                INPUT Std_Grades(Student ,Test)
             NEXT Test
         NEXT Student
120 RETURN

1000 ! Function to calculate student average
     DEF REAL Find_avg(INTEGER Student)
1010    ! Average of selected row
        Std_sum = 0
        FOR I = 1 TO 5
            Std_sum = Std_sum + Std_Grades(Student, I)
        NEXT I

1020    Find_avg = Std_sum / 5
1030  END DEF

1100 ! Function to calculate letter grade
     DEF Find_grade(REAL Average)
1110     IF Average < 60 THEN Find_grade = "F"
         ELSE IF Average < 70 THEN Find_grade = "D"
         ELSE IF Average < 80 THEN Find_grade = "C"
         ELSE IF Average < 90 THEN Find_grade = "B"
         ELSE Find_grade = "A"
1120   END DEF

32767 END
```

Figure 14-8.
Function Flow Chart Symbol

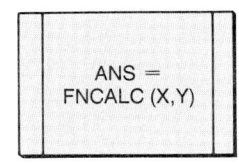

14.7 FLOW CHARTS

User-defined functions are flow charted as separate modules, similar to the manner in which subroutines are handled.

The terminator at the top of the flowchart contains the name of the function, followed by its parameters in parentheses. The terminator at the end contains the word END DEF. The function reference itself appears in a double-barred rectangle, just as is done with the GOSUB statement, which invokes a subroutine. For example, the function reference ANS = FNCALC (X,Y) would appear as in Figure 14-8.

Figure 14-9.
Flow Charts for Program to Calculate N Factorial

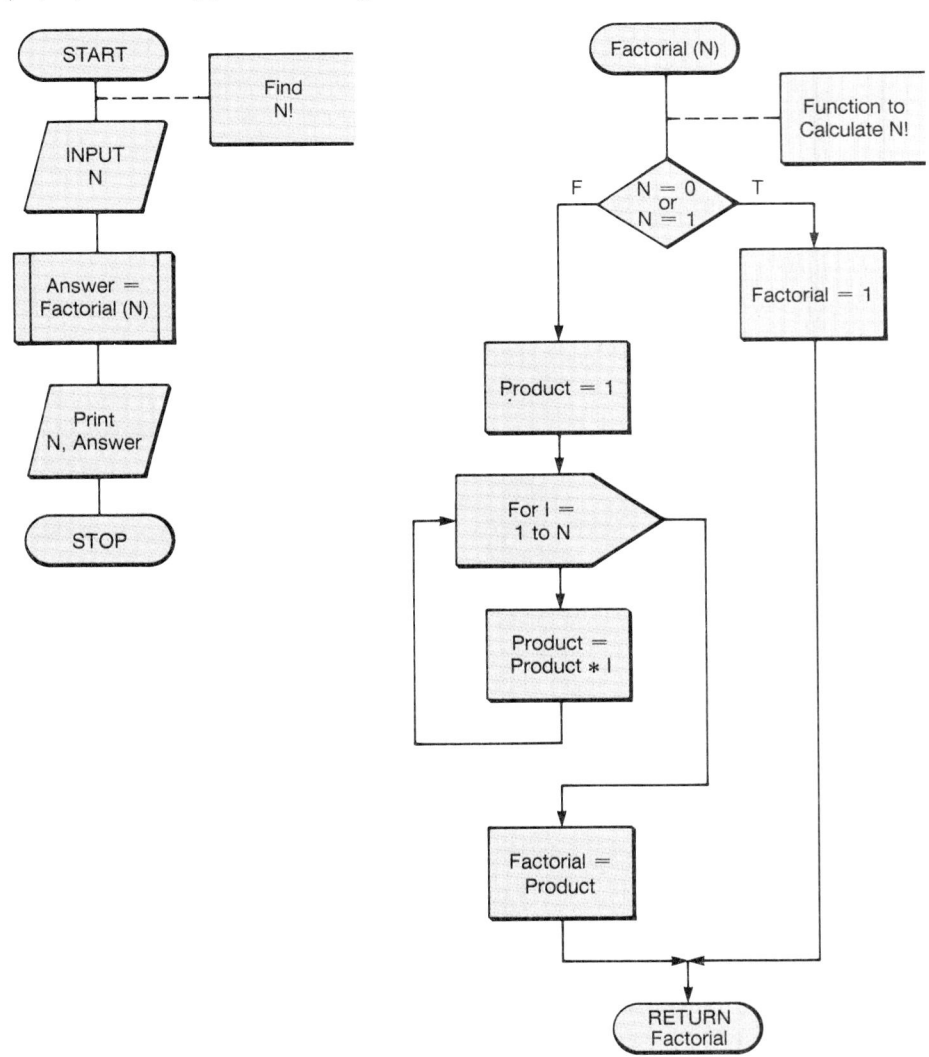

The following programs have been done previously, so their logic is not explained here.

Example 14.11 Figure 14-9 is the flow chart for the program presented in Example 14.9 and shown in Fig. 14.6.

Example 14.12 The flow chart shown in Figure 14-10 refers to the student grading program presented in Example 14.10 and shown in Fig. 14-7.

SUMMARY

1. A user-defined function is a module to which arguments can be sent and which can return one result to the point of invocation. (This is also true of built-in functions.)

2. Besides using its parameters, the user-defined function can also use any global variables for its calculations. Such use is avoided wherever possible, but it is unavoidable for arrays.

3. A multi-line function can change the values of global variables in addition to calculating its result. These inadvertent changes are called side effects. Side effects are to be avoided, lest the program become unmanageably obscure.

4. A one-line function has the format

DEF [data-type] [FN]name [([data-type] parameter [, . . .])] = expression

5. A multi-line function begins with the line

DEF [data-type] [FN]name [([data-type] parameter [, . . .])]

contains the line

[FN]name = expression

and ends with the line

END DEF

6. There may be zero to eight parameters in VAX-BASIC user-defined functions.

7. The number of arguments in the function reference must equal the number of parameters in the function definition. The type of each argument (real, integer, or string) must agree with the type of its corresponding parameter unless a DECLARE FUNCTION statement specifies the parameter-type.

8. A function, particularly a multi-line function, should be declared in a DECLARE FUNCTION statement. This statement defines the type of result returned by the function and the type of each parameter. Functions that are DECLAREd may be defined later, either before or after the statements that invoke them. A separate DECLARE FUNCTION statement is required for each function type, but several functions that return the same

400 14 USER-DEFINED FUNCTIONS

Figure 14-10.
Flow Charts for Student Grading Program

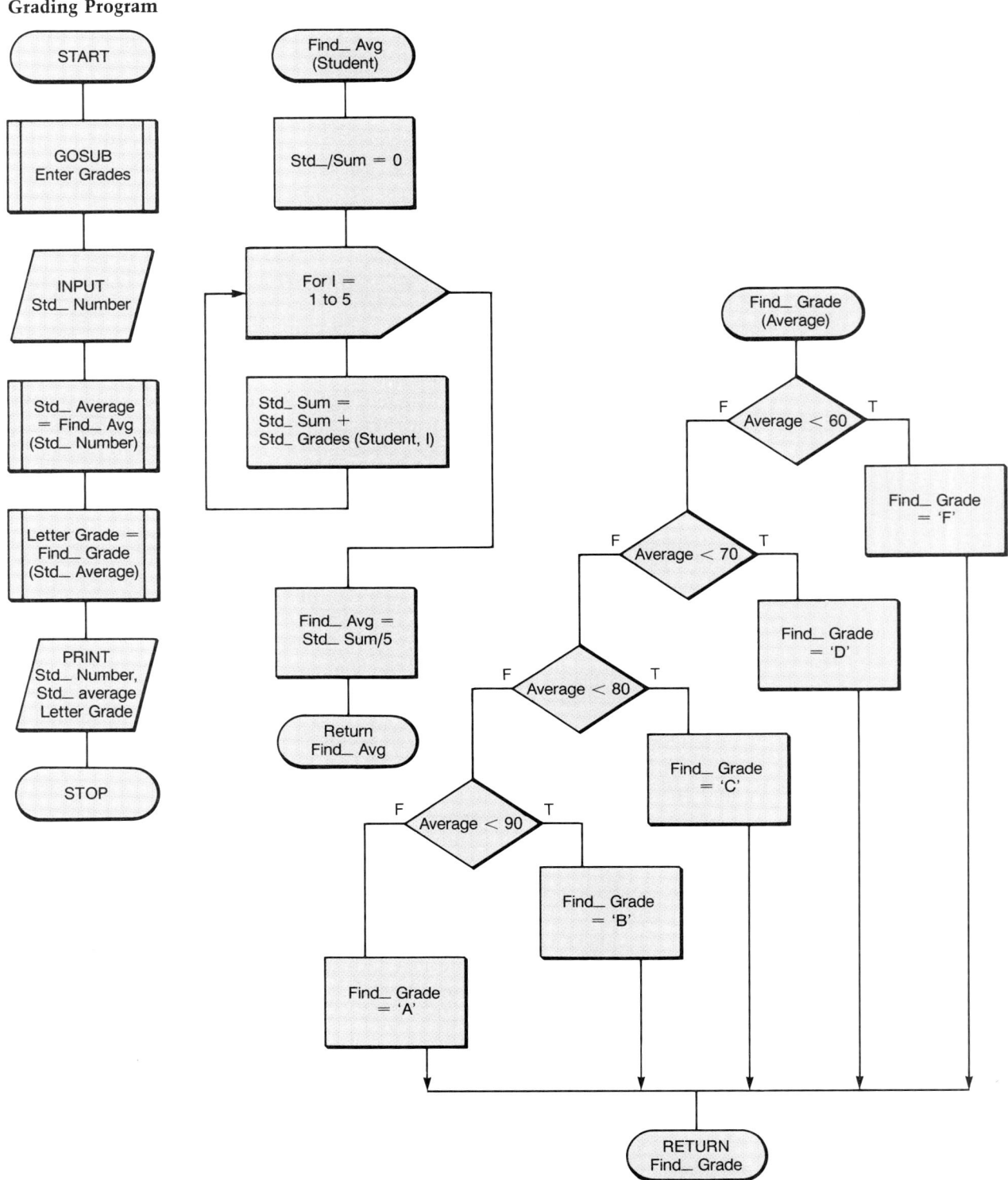

type may be declared with one such statement. The syntax of the DECLARE FUNCTION statement is:

DECLARE type FUNCTION name [(type, . . .)], . . .

REVIEW QUESTIONS

1. What is a user-defined function?
2. What is the distinction between an argument and a parameter?
3. What are the restrictions governing the argument and parameter lists? Discuss restrictions on the number of parameters and the types of parameters.
4. How many results can a user-defined function return? What are side effects? How many results *should* a user-defined function return?
5. What is the difference between a one-line function and a multi-line function? What is the difference in the DEF statements for these two types of functions?
6. When should you use a user-defined function instead of a subroutine?
7. How is a function invoked?
8. Can a function invoke a subroutine? Can a subroutine invoke a function?
9. What is the purpose of the DECLARE FUNCTION statement? What information does it provide? What is its syntax?

SYNTAX EXERCISES

The following all contain one or more syntax errors. Find and correct them.

1. ```
30 DEF Average REAL (A, B, C) = A + B + C) / 3
```
2. ```
30 DEF STRING FUNCTION Add (A, B, C) = A + B + C
```
3. ```
20 DECLARE FUNCTION REAL Hypotenuse (REAL A, REAL B) &
       = SQR (A^2 + B^2)
```
4. ```
20 DECLARE FUNCTION STRING (STRING A, STRING B)
```
5. ```
2000 DEF INTERGER Flag (REAL Number)
        IF Number > 90 THEN Flag = 1
        ELSE IF Number < 50 THEN Flag = -1
        ELSE Flag = 0
        END IF
     END DEF
```
6. ```
2000 DEF STRING Words(STRING Str_1, Str_2)
        IF Str_1 > Str_2 THEN
           Words = Str_1 + Str_2
        ELSE
           Words = Str_2 + Str_1
        END IF
     END DEF
```
7. ```
2000 DEF STRING Grade (REAL Average)
        SELECT Average
           CASE >= 90
              Result = "A"
           CASE >= 80
              Result = "B"
```
```

```
              CASE >= 70
                 Result = "C"
              CASE >= 60
                 Result = "D"
              CASE ELSE
                 Result = "F"
           END SELECT
        END DEF
8. 20 DECLARE INTEGER Rand (INTEGER Code)
        IF Code = 1 THEN Result = 100*RND
        ELSE IF Code = 2 THEN Result = 100*RND + 100
        ELSE Result = 100*RND + 200
        END IF
     END DEF
```

PROGRAMMING EXERCISES

Write programs to solve the following problems.

■ **1a.** Write a one-line function that calculates a salesman's salary equal to $200.00 plus 10% of total sales. The sales are calculated from a global 10-element array.

1b. Read a salesman's name, employee number, and ten sales from a file SALES.ACT or from DATA statements. Using a function, add the sales and calculate the salesman's salary as $200.00 plus 10% of the total sales exceeding $1000.00. Print the salesman's name, employee number, total sales, and salary. Repeat for additional salesmen in the file until the sentinel name END is read.

2. Read a student's five test grades. Use a function to find the student's average. Then use another function to calculate the student's letter grade based on his average. Print the average, the letter grade, and the student's name. Repeat for additional students until a sentinel is entered.

■ **3a.** Write a function that receives an INTEGER argument whose value is between 1 and 4. It will return the STRING value CLUBS, DIAMONDS, HEARTS, or SPADES depending on the value of this integer.

3b. Use the random number generator to get two random numbers: the first between 1 and 4, and the second between 1 and 13. Send the first number to a string function that will return CLUBS, DIAMONDS, HEARTS, or SPADES, depending on the value of the number sent to it. Send the second number to another function that returns ACE, DEUCE, TREY, 4, 5, 6, 7, 8, 9, 10, JACK, QUEEN, or KING, depending on the value sent to it. Print the selected card—QUEEN OF SPADES, for example.

4. Refer to Exercise 3b. Select 100 cards in the random manner specified. Count the number of aces produced and the number of spades produced. Print both these numbers. All calculations should be performed by user-defined functions. (Theoretically, you should get approximately 8 aces and 25 spades.)

5a. Write a function that simulates the rolling of a pair of dice. The function should return the sum of the spots on the two dice.

5b. Another function is to receive the value from the function of part a. If the value passed to this second function is 7 or 11, then the second function is to return the string WIN. If the value passed is 2, 3, or 12, then the second function is to return LOSE. In all other cases, the value rolled is called the "point" and the function is to return POINT.

5c. If the function of part b returns POINT, then a third function is invoked that receives the POINT. This function continues to roll the dice, using the first function, until either a 7 or the point is rolled. If 7, then the function is to return LOSE; if the point is rolled, then the function is to return WIN.

5d. Write a complete program that incorporates the above functions and plays craps 20 times. Print the result of each game. To interest the user, print the result of each roll so that he can follow the game.

6. Read data from a file into a 10 x 5 array called A. A number between 1 and 5 will be read from the terminal into variable COL. Write three functions that will:

    a. Sum the elements in column COL of array A. If, for example, 2 is read into variable COL, then the numbers in column 2 of the array will be summed.

    b. Find the largest number in column COL.

    c. Find the smallest numbers in column COL.

Now incorporate these three functions into a program. The main program should read the array with a subroutine, prompt for the input of variable COL, and then invoke the functions to find the sum of the numbers in the column and the largest and smallest numbers in the column. Use a subroutine for output.

7a. Write a function that converts a date into the number of days since January 1. For example, if the date sent to the function is March 3, 1988, then the function should return the number 63: 31 days for January, plus 29 days for February (1988 is a leap year), plus 3 days in March totals 63. (Do not use the variable DATE in your program; it is a reserved word.)

7b. Write a main program that can be used to test the accuracy of the function in Exercise 7a. It should allow you to enter various dates from the terminal and then print those dates and the number returned by the function. A sentinel of your choice can be used to end the program.

8. Write a program with a function that can do the reverse of the function of Exercise 7. This function will accept two arguments: the number of days since January 1 and the year. The function will return a string containing the correct date.

9a. Write a function that can do modulo arithmetic. A modulo function is sometimes called a remainder function, because it returns the remainder of a division. For example, 85 modulo 5 is 0, because the remainder of 85 divided by 5 is 0; 19 modulo 4 (also written 19 mod 4) is 3, because 19 divided by 4 leaves a remainder of three.

9b. Write a program using the function of part a. The program should let you enter two integers, then print the integers and the modulo result.

10. The mod function, as described in Exercise 9a, can be used to convert numbers from one base to another. To convert the number 28 into base 4, for instance, we would proceed as follows:

> 28 divided by 4 is 7, remainder is 0
> 7 divided by 4 is 1, remainder is 3
> 1 divided by 4 is 0, remainder is 1

As you can see, we kept dividing the integer quotients by 4. If we reverse the remainders, we get the value we seek: 130 is the base 4 equivalent of 28 in base 10. We stop the divisions when the dividend becomes 0. To get the number 130 from the digits 0, 3, and 1, we would add 0, 10 times 3, and 100 times 1. With more digits, the process would continue with higher powers of ten.

In your program, use the main program to enter the number that is to be converted and the base to which it is to be converted. Use a function to perform the conversion. This function can make use of the mod function of Exercise 9 to get the remainders.

11. We will calculate the cost per mile to operate various automobiles and their average miles per gallon. The input to the program will consist of the following items:
   a. Automobile model
   b. Insurance premium
   c. Monthly loan payment
   d. Amount spent on repairs for the year
   e. Number of gallons of gasoline used for the year
   f. Average price per gallon of gasoline
   g. Total miles driven during the year

The average cost per mile driven is the total cost for all expenses during the year, divided by the number of miles driven. Average miles per gallon is total number of miles driven divided by total gallons used. Output will consist of the following:
   a. Automobile model
   b. Total expenses
   c. Total number of miles
   d. Total number of gallons
   e. Cost per mile
   f. Miles per gallon

The program is to perform its calculations for all automobile data available until the end-of-file condition is raised (or until the car model DONE is entered as a sentinel).

You should use a subroutine to enter the data, functions to perform the calculations, and a subroutine to produce the output. For added variety, the program can be written to permit a choice of entry devices. The user would be prompted to select the terminal, a file, or DATA statements as the input medium.

Output should be in tabular form with appropriate headings.

12. We will make and print an amortization table. Input will be the size of the loan, the yearly interest rate, and the number of years to repay the loan. The monthly payment is determined from the formula:

$$\text{PAYMENT} = \text{LOAN} * \frac{I}{1 - (1 + I)^{-N}}$$

where

> **I** = the monthly interest rate. (Example: If the yearly rate is 12%, then the monthly rate is 1%, and I is .01, the decimal equivalent of 1%.)
> **N** = the term of the loan in months (12 times the number of years to repay the loan).

■ **a.** Write a function that receives the values of LOAN, I, and N, and calculates the monthly payment.

b. Each monthly payment consists of two parts: the interest due on the loan and the rest of the payment (called the amortization), which is used to reduce the outstanding balance. Use a subroutine to make a table that lists the interest, the amortization, and the new balance for each month of the loan. The last payment may be different from the others because the remaining balance may be too small to make up a full payment. For this last month, print only the required amount needed to reduce the loan to zero. The interest and amortization calculations should be performed by functions, either one-line or multi-line.

ENRICHMENT TOPICS 14

External Functions

VAX-BASIC allows you to write function subprograms. These are functions that are external to your program and are compiled separately from your main program. In that respect, they are the equivalent of the SUB subprograms discussed in the enrichment topics section of chapter 4. They may be defined after the main program, or they may be written as stand-alone functions and stored on disk in their own disk files. We will treat only the first case here. Refer to the VAX-BASIC programmer's guide for information on linking separate files into one task.

An external function is useful for any of the following reasons:

1. You want to use the function in many programs but do not wish to write the code more than once.
2. You need more than 8 parameters. External functions allow you to use up to 255 parameters in VAX-BASIC.
3. You want to pass arrays to your functions as parameters. Internal DEF functions do not permit this.

DEFINING EXTERNAL FUNCTIONS

The syntax for an external function is:

> **FUNCTION data-type function-name [(parameter, . . .)]**
> ...
> body of function
> ...
> function-name = expression
> **END FUNCTION**

where

> **data-type** = the data-type of the value that will be returned by the function
> **function-name** = the name of the function
> **parameter** = a parameter—as many as 255 of them. Each parameter may include a data type and subscript information. For example, a parameter list may appear as follows:

```
                    (INTEGER Size, REAL Avgs(,), STRING Grades())
```

In the above example, `Size` is of type INTEGER, `Avgs` is a two-dimensional array of type REAL; and `Grades` is a one-dimensional array of type STRING. As you can see, the parameter that corresponds to an array has parentheses following the name of the parameter. If the array is one-dimensional, then only parentheses are used. If it is two-dimensional, then a comma is included in the parentheses. Only arrays of one or two dimensions may be passed to an external function; higher order arrays may not be passed.

The body of the function may contain any statements required to produce the result. **All** variables are local to the function, not only the parameters. No variables used in the function have any effect on the invoking program, even though they have the same name. An external function will usually have its own DECLARE statement to declare variables used in the function.

> **NOTE!** **If an external function changes the value of one of its parameters, and if the corresponding argument is a variable (not a constant), the value of the argument may be changed as well. This practice should be avoided to prevent side effects. If a function must change the value of a parameter, declare a local variable, store the parameter in the local variable, and change only the local variable. (There is a mechanism that can determine whether an argument is passed by value and cannot be changed, or by reference, in which case it can be. This will not be discussed here; passing by reference to a function is to be discouraged.)**

Example 14.13 We will write an external function to which we send a two-dimensional array of test marks and a row number. We will also send the number of columns as an additional argument. The function will find the average of the tests in the given row, returning this average to the point of invocation. The function is as follows:

```
10000 FUNCTION REAL Find_row_avg (INTEGER Grades(,), &
                                  INTEGER Row, INTEGER No.cols.)

10010 ! Function to find average of specified row of 2-D array

10020    DECLARE INTEGER Sum, Column

11130    Sum = 0
         FOR Column = 1 TO No.cols.
            Sum = Sum + Grades(Row,Column)
         NEXT Column

10040    Find_row_avg = Sum / No.cols.

10050 END FUNCTION
```

This function would be placed after the main program or it could instead be stored in a file on your disk, usually with the extension .BAS. In that event, line numbers could have begun with line 10, the same as the main program.

THE EXTERNAL STATEMENT

When you want your program to use an external function, you must let the program know that an external function will be invoked, the type of value that will be returned by the function, and the type and number of arguments that must be sent to the function. You do this with the EXTERNAL FUNCTION statement. It is similar to the DECLARE FUNCTION statement that is used for internal function declaration. Its syntax is as follows:

> **EXTERNAL data-type FUNCTION function-name [(argument-type, . . .)]**

where

> **data-type** = the data-type of the value that will be returned by the function
> **function-name** = the name of the function (up to 30 characters)
> **argument-type** consists of a data type followed by dimension information if the argument is an array. It will be of the form:
>
> > [data-type] [DIM([,]. . .)]
>
> For example, STRING is the argument-type you use to declare that an argument is a string scalar. REAL DIM (,) would be the argument-type you would use to declare that an argument is a REAL, two-dimensional array.

To use the function of Example 14.13, we would use the following EXTERNAL statement in the invoking procedure:

```
EXTERNAL REAL FUNCTION Find_row_avg (INTEGER DIM (,), INTEGER, INTEGER)
```

Types are given for three arguments. The first is a two-dimensional INTEGER array, the second and third are both INTEGER scalars. Notice that no actual argument names are used; only the types are given.

Invoking an External Function

An external function subprogram is invoked the same way any other function is invoked—with a function reference. When an argument is an array, the name of the array is used followed by parentheses for a one-dimensional array or parentheses enclosing a comma for a two-dimensional array.

Assume that a two-dimensional array Tests has 35 rows and 5 columns, and that we want the average of column 10, using the function of example 14.13. The following statement would be used:

```
Row_avg = Find_row_avg (Tests( , ), 10, 5)
```

The first argument is the array, the second is the row whose average is required, the third is the number of columns. Before this function can be invoked, the appropriate EXTERNAL statement is required.

Example 14.14 We will use the function of example 14.13 in a complete program. The main program will read a two-dimensional array and then ask the user to enter a row number. The external function will be invoked to find the average of the numbers in that row. The main program will print the average. The program is shown in Figure 14-11.

Figure 14-11.
Program Using External Function

```
10  ! Program using external function
20      DECLARE INTEGER Grades(50,10), Row, Column, &
            REAL Average
30      EXTERNAL REAL FUNCTION Find_row_avg (INTEGER DIM( , ), INTEGER, &
                                             INTEGER)
40      GOSUB Read_grades
50  ! Enter row number whose average is desired
        INPUT "Enter row number (1 to 50)"; Row
60      Average = Find_row_avg (Grades( , ), Row, 10)
70      PRINT \ PRINT "Average of row"; Row; "is"; Average
        PRINT
80  EXIT PROGRAM

1000 Read_grades:
1010    OPEN "ARRAY.DAT" FOR INPUT AS FILE #1
1020    FOR Row = 1 TO 50
            FOR Column = 1 TO 10
                INPUT #1, Grades(Row,Column)
            NEXT Column
        NEXT Row
1030    CLOSE #1
1040 RETURN

9999 END

10000 FUNCTION REAL Find_row_avg (INTEGER Grades(,), INTEGER Row, &
                                  INTEGER No.cols.)

10010 ! Function to find average of specified row of 2-D array

10020   DECLARE INTEGER Sum, Column

10030   Sum = 0
        FOR Column = 1 TO No.cols.
            Sum = Sum + Grades(Row,Column)
        NEXT Column

10040   Find_row_avg = Sum / No.cols.

10050 END FUNCTION
```

Since all identifiers in the external function are local, the parameters do not have to be given the same names as the arguments. The `Read_array` routine could be changed easily so that a relative file could be used. The MAP for this file could define a buffer that includes the entire array:

```
MAP (Array_buffer) INTEGER Grades(50,5)
```

The file would be opened with:

```
OPEN "GRADES.DAT" FOR INPUT AS FILE #1, &
        RELATIVE, MAP Array_buffer
```

The array would be read with the single statement:

```
GET #1
```

THE EXIT FUNCTION STATEMENT

An external function may include internal functions and GOSUB subroutines. These must all be defined in the external function before the END FUNCTION statement. Just as the EXIT SUB statement was placed at the end of the "main program" of an external subprogram, the EXIT FUNCTION is placed at the end of the "main program" of an external function. This will return the function result, and program control, back to the statement that invoked the function. An example of such an external function is shown below.

```
10000 FUNCTION REAL Find_row_avg (INTEGER Grades(,), INTEGER Row, &
         INTEGER No.cols.)

10010 ! Function to find average of specified row of 2-D array

10020    DECLARE INTEGER Sum, Column, Row_sum
         DECLARE INTEGER FUNCTION Find_row_sum (INTEGER, INTEGER)

10030    Row_Sum = Find_row_sum (Row, No.cols.)

10040    Find_row_avg = Row_Sum / No.cols.

10050 EXIT FUNCTION

10100 DEF INTEGER FUNCTION Find_row_sum (INTEGER Row, INTEGER No.cols.)

10110    Sum = 0
         FOR Column = 1 TO No.cols.
            Sum = Sum + Grades(Row,Column)
         NEXT Column

10120 END DEF

10999 END FUNCTION
```

Only one DEF function was included above. There is no restriction on the number of modules the external function may contain.

Error-Trapping in External Functions

Error traps can be used in external functions the same way they are used in external subprograms. See the enrichment section at the end of chapter 4.

C

Programming Tool: The GOTO

Outline

C.1 Unconditional GOTO
C.2 Conditional GOTO
C.3 Argument Against GOTOS

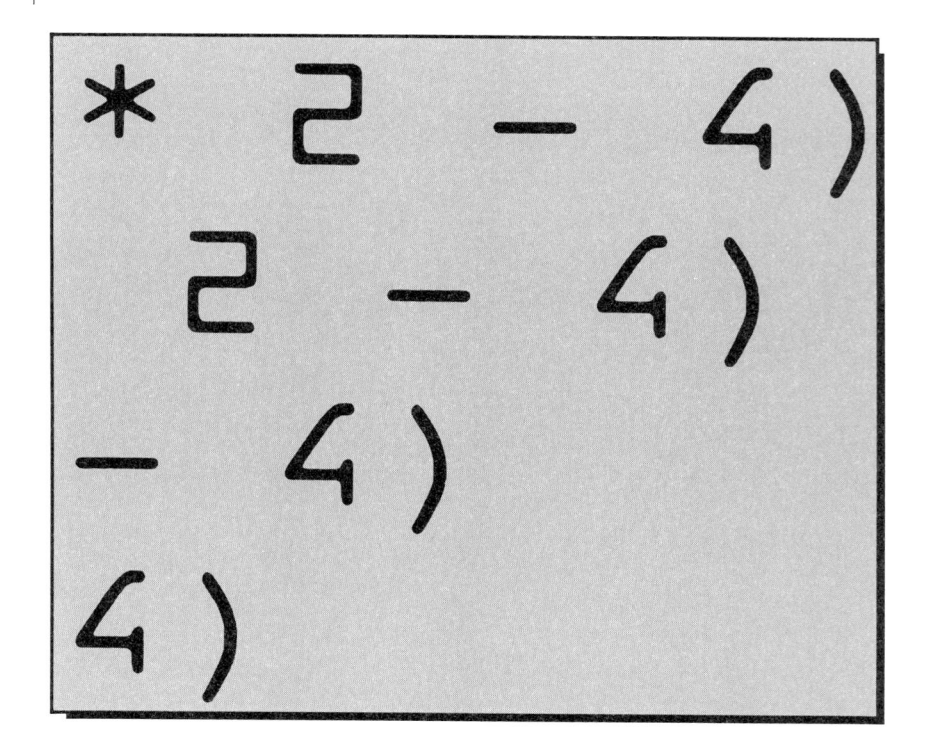

Introduction Well, we finally made it. For all those who were wondering where the GOTO went, here it is. For all those who have gotten this far and have never heard of a GOTO—good for you!

The GOTO is an instruction that lets you jump from one section of your program to another. Thus it is often called a **jump instruction.** It can be either unconditional or conditional, and its use should generally be avoided in favor of other structures we have discussed in previous chapters.

C.1 UNCONDITIONAL GOTO

The syntax of the unconditional jump instruction is:

sn1 GOTO sn2

or

sn1 GOTO label

For example:

```
100 GOTO 150
200 GOTO Error_routine
```

When the GOTO executes, it causes control to pass to the statement number or statement label specified. The statement GOTO 150 will cause the computer to jump to statement 150 and continue execution from that point on. It can cause the computer to jump either forward to some later statement or backward to some previous one.

You have used such a GOTO in your error routines where you had the statement ON ERROR GOTO 0. There was no line number 0; it was a special case that BASIC understood to mean to go to the system error handler.

Similarly, GOTO Error_routine causes the computer to jump to the statement whose label is Error_routine. We have used such a statement in our error traps. It was unavoidable in that situation.

In a BASIC dialect that has a WHILE or UNTIL loop, there is no reason to use an unconditional GOTO instruction, but there are many reasons not to (see chapter 4 and section C.3 below).

C.2 CONDITIONAL GOTO

The syntax of the conditional jump is:

sn1 IF condition THEN GOTO sn2

or

sn1 IF condition THEN GOTO label

For example:

```
100 IF X = 0 THEN GOTO 32767
200 IF A > B THEN GOTO Read_routine
```

In the first example, if X is zero, control transfers to statement 32767 which, presumably, is an END statement. In the second, if A is greater than B, control transfers to the statement whose label is Read_routine.

If your BASIC has a WHILE or UNTIL loop, there should not be many conditional jumps in your program. The main use of a conditional jump should be to get out of a subroutine if an abnormal condition is detected during execution. For example, suppose you are in a subroutine that calculates an average. Division by zero is not permitted, so you check the value of the denominator before you divide. If the denominator is zero, you print an error message and then skip the rest of the subroutine with a conditional jump:

```
1000 ! Subroutine
1010    ! Various calculations
           . . .
           . . .
           . . .
1060    ! Check for abnormal condition
          IF N = 0 THEN
              PRINT 'ERROR! Denominator is 0'
              GOTO 1080
1070    ! Find average
          AVG = SUM / N
1080    RETURN
```

Line 1060 checks the value of the denominator to be used in line 1070. Normally, this should not be zero. If it is, an error message is printed, and control is passed to the RETURN statement so that processing can continue.

A much better way to handle the above is with an error trap, trapping the division-by-0 error (see the Programming Tool B).

> **NOTE!** After the condition, either THEN alone, GOTO alone (as one word or two), or THEN GOTO can be used before the line number or label. Thus the following are all equivalent:
>
> IF condition THEN 1080
> IF condition GOTO 1080
> IF condition GO TO 1080
> IF condition THEN GOTO 1080
> IF condition THEN GO TO 1080

C.3 ARGUMENT AGAINST GOTOS

In this chapter, we learned of a statement that should be used only rarely in a structured program. The nature of a structured program is to have only one way to reach a given statement. A jump violates this precept. If a program contains the statement

```
200 GOTO 50
```

then line 50 can be reached both from line 40 and from line 200. If we later eliminate line 50 because of some program modification, then the program will crash when it reaches line 200, because there is no longer a line 50 to transfer to. The situation is only slightly improved if a label is used.

If the program contains many jumps, then any change to one statement may have an effect on other parts of the program. If the jumps are totally unrestrained, and tend to cross each other in what is frequently referred to as **spaghetti code,** then any attempt to modify the program will involve such a plethora of side effects as to make the attempt futile. Such programs are more often discarded and started over than successfully modified.

SUMMARY | In this chapter you learned about the unconditional and conditional GOTO statements. Unconditional GOTOs should be avoided, and conditional GOTOs should be restricted to a few specific uses.

Appendix 1 | Reserved Words

The following keywords are reserved in VAX-BASIC. They may not be used as variables, labels, or subroutine and function names. Adding a period or underscore will change them sufficiently so that the identifier is no longer a reserved word.

Reserved Keyword List[*]

ABORT	BUFFERSIZE	CVT%$
ABS	BUFSIZ	CVTF$
ABS%	BY	DAT
ACCESS	CALL	DAT$
ACCESS%	CALLR	DATA
ALIGNED	CCPOS	DATE$
ALL	CHAIN	DECLARE
ALLOW	CHANGE	DEF
ALTERNATE	CHANGES	DEF*
AND	CHR$	DEFAULTNAME
ANY	CLK$	DEL
APPEND	CLOSE	DELETE
AS	CLUSTERSIZE	DELIMIT
ASC	COM	DENSITY
ASCII	COMMON	DESC
ATN	COMP%	DET
ATN2	CON	DIF$
BACK	CONNECT	DIM
BEL	CONSTANT	DIMENSION
BIN$	CONTIGUOUS	DOUBLE
BINARY	COS	DOUBLEBUF
BIT	COT	DUPLICATES
BLOCK	COUNT	ECHO
BLOCKSIZE	CR	EDIT$
BROADCAST	CTRLC	ELSE
BS	CVT$$	END
BUCKETSIZE	CVT$%	ENDIF
BUFFER	CVT$F	EQ

---

[*] Copyright, Digital Equipment Corporation, (1981). All rights reserved. Reprinted by pemission.

EQV	INSTR	NOT
ERL	INT	NOTAPE
ERN$	INTEGER	NUL$
ERR	INV	NUM
ERROR	INVALID	NUM$
ERT$	JSB	NUM1$
ESC	KEY	NUM2
EXP	KILL	OCT$
EXTEND	LEFT	ON
EXTENDSIZE	LEFT$	ONECHR
EXTERNAL	LEN	ONENDFILE
FF	LET	ONERROR
FIELD	LF	OPEN
FILE	LINE	OR
FILESIZE	LINO	ORGANIZATION
FILL	LINPUT	OUTPUT
FILL$	LIST	PAGE
FILL%	LOC	PEEK
FIND	LOCK	PI
FIX	LOF	PLACE$
FIXED	LOG	POKE
FLUSH	LOG10	POS
FNEND	LONG	POS%
FNEXIT	LSA	PPS%
FOR	LSET	PRIMAY
FORCEIN	MAGTAPE	PRIN
FORMAT$	MAP	PRN
FORTRAN	MAR	PROD$
FREE	MAR%	PUT
FROM	MARGIN	QUO$
FSP$	MAT	QUOTE
FSS$	MAX	RAD%
FUNCTION	MID	RAD$
FUNCTIONEND	MID$	RANDOM
FUNCTIONEXIT	MIN	RANDOMIZE
GE	MOD	RCTRLC
GET	MOD%	RCTRLO
GO	MODE	READ
GOSUB	MODIFY	REAL
GOTO	MOVE	RECORD
GT	MSGMAP	RECORDATTR
HANGUP	NAME	RECORDSIZE
HEX	NEXT	RECORDTYPE
HEX$	NOCHANGES	RECOUNT
HT	NODATA	REF
IDN	NODUPLICATES	RELATIVE
IF	NOECHO	REM
IFEND	NOEXTEND	RESET
IFMORE	NOMARGIN	RESTORE
IMAGE	NONE	RESUME
IMP	NOPAGE	RETURN
INDEXED	NOQUOTE	RIGHT
INIMAGE	NOREWIND	RIGHT$
INPUT	NOSPAN	RND

APPENDIX 1: RESERVED WORDS

RSET	SUBROUTINE	UPDATE
SCRATCH	SUM$	USEAGE
SEG$	SWAP%	USEAGE$
SEQUENTIAL	SYS	USEROPEN
SGN	TAB	USING
SHIFT	TAN	USR
SI	TAPE	USR$
SIN	TASK	VAL
SINGLE	TEMPORARY	VAL%
SLEEP	TERMINAL	VALUE
SO	THEN	VARIABLE
SP	TIM	VFC
SPACE$	TIME	VIRTUAL
SPAN	TIME$	VPS%
SPEC%	TO	VT
SQR	TRM$	WAIT
SQRT	TRN	WHILE
STATUS	TST	WINDOWSIZE
STEP	TSTEND	WITH
STOP	TYP	WORD
STR$	TYPE	WRITE
STREAM	TYPE$	WRKMAP
STRING	UNALIGNED	XLATE
STRING$	UNDEFINED	XOR
SUB	UNLESS	ZER
SUBEND	UNLOCK	
SUBEXIT	UNTIL	

Appendix 2 | Error Messages

The following is a table of error numbers and their corresponding messages for VAX-BASIC 3.0. It was produced with the following program. If you are not using the 3.0 version of BASIC, use the program below to print all the errors for your system. Error 0 contains the version number.

```
10 ! Print BASIC error messages
20   DECLARE INTEGER I
30   OPEN "ERROR.TXT" FOR OUTPUT AS FILE #1
40   FOR I = 0 TO 255
         PRINT I, ERT$(I)
     NEXT I
50   CLOSE #1
60 END
```

Errors whose text begins with a % symbol are fatal. Those that begin with a ? symbol are trappable in a user-defined error trap. Those that start with neither are merely warnings and also are not trappable (see the Intermezzo chapter).

Not all of the listed errors can occur in VAX-BASIC. Those that can are listed in bold face. The others are listed only because they exist and may be available for other versions of VAX-BASIC.

0	**VAX-11 BASIC**	16	?Name or account now exists
1	?Bad directory for device	17	?Too many open files on unit
2	?Illegal file name	18	?Illegal SYS() usage
3	?Account or device in use	19	?Disk block is interlocked
4	?No room for user on device	20	?Pack IDs don't match
5	**?Can't find file or account**	21	?Disk pack is not mounted
6	?Not a valid device	22	?Disk pack is locked out
7	**?I/O channel already open**	23	?Illegal cluster size
8	?Device not available	24	?Disk pack is private
9	**?I/O channel not open**	25	?Disk pack needs 'CLEANing'
10	**?Protection violation**	26	**?Fatal disk pack mount error**
11	**?End of file on device**	27	?I/O to detached keyboard
12	**?Fatal system I/O failure**	28	**?Programmable ^C trap**
13	?User data error on device	29	**?Corrupted file structure**
14	**?Device hung or write locked**	30	?Device not file-structured
15	?Wait exhausted	31	?Illegal byte count for I/O

APPENDIX 2: ERROR MESSAGES

32	**?No buffer space available**	81	?Illegal function name
33	?Odd address trap	82	?Illegal dummy variable
34	?Reserved instruction trap	83	?Illegal FN redefinition
35	**?Memory management violation**	84	?Illegal line number(s)
36	?SP stack Overflow	85	?Modifier error
37	?Disk error during swap	86	?Can't compile statement
38	?Memory parity (or ECC) failure	87	?Expression too complicated
		88	**?Arguments don't match**
39	?Magtape select error	89	**?Too many arguments**
40	?Magtape record length error	90	%Inconsistent function usage
41	?Non-res run-time system	91	?Illegal DEF nesting
42	**?Virtual buffer too large**	92	?FOR without NEXT
43	**?Virtual array not on disk**	93	?NEXT without FOR
44	?Matrix or array too big	94	?DEF without FNEND
45	**?Virtual array not yet open**	95	?FNEND without DEF
46	?Illegal I/O channel	96	?Literal string needed
47	?Line too long	97	**?Too few arguments**
48	**?Floating point error or overflow**	98	?Syntax error
		99	?String is needed
49	**?Argument too large in EXP**	100	?Number is needed
50	%Data format error	101	**?Data type error**
51	?Integer error or overflow	102	**?One or two dimensions only**
52	?Illegal number	103	**?Program lost-Sorry**
53	?Illegal argument in LOG	104	**?RESUME and no error**
54	?Imaginary square roots	105	**?Redimensioned array**
55	?Subscript out of range	106	%Inconsistent subscript use
56	**?Can't invert matrix**	107	?ON statement needs GOTO
57	**?Out of data**	108	?End of statement not seen
58	?ON statement out of range	109	**?What**
59	?Not enough data in record	110	?Bad line number pair
60	?Integer overflow, FOR loop	111	?Not enough available memory
61	**?Division by 0**		
62	?No run-time system	112	?Execute only file
63	?FIELD overflows buffer	113	?Please use the RUN command
64	?Not a random access device		
65	**?Illegal MAGTAPE() usage**	114	?Can't CONTinue
66	**?Missing special feature**	115	?File exists-RENAME/REPLACE
67	**?Illegal switch usage**	116	?PRINT-USING format error
68	?Unused	117	?Matrix or array without DIM
69	?Unused	118	?Bad number in PRINT-USING
70	?Unused		
71	?Statement not found	119	?Illegal in immediate mode
72	**?RETURN without GOSUB**	120	?PRINT-USING buffer overflow
73	**?FNEND without function call**		
		121	?Illegal statement
74	**?Undefined function called**	122	**?Illegal FIELD variable**
75	?Illegal symbol	123	**Stop**
76	?Illegal verb	124	**?Matrix dimension error**
77	?Illegal expression	125	?Wrong math package
78	?Illegal mode mixing	126	**?Maximum memory exceeded**
79	?Illegal IF statement	127	**?SCALE factor interlock**
80	?Illegal conditional clause	128	**?Tape records not ANSI**

APPENDIX 2: ERROR MESSAGES

129	?Tape BOT detected	178	?System memory for file sharing exhausted
130	?Key not changeable	179	?Unexpired file date
131	?No current record	180	?No support for operation in task
132	?Record has been deleted		
133	?Illegal usage for device	181	?Decimal error or overflow
134	?Duplicate key detected	182	?Network operation rejected
135	?Illegal usage	183	?REMAP overflows buffer
136	?Illegal or illogical access	184	?Unaligned REMAP variable
137	?Illegal key attributes	185	?RECORDSIZE overflows MAP buffer
138	?File is locked		
139	?Invalid file options	186	?Improper error handling
140	?Index not initialized	187	?Illegal record locking clause
141	?Illegal operation	188	?UNLOCK EXPLICIT requires RECORDSIZE 512
142	?Illegal record on file		
143	?Bad record identifier	189	%Too little data in record
144	?Invalid key of reference	190	?Illegal network operation
145	?Key size too large	191	?Illegal terminal-format file operation
146	?Tape not ANSI labelled		
147	?RECORD number exceeds maximum	192	?Illegal wait value
		193	?Detected deadlock while waiting for GET or FIND
148	?Bad RECORDSIZE value on OPEN		
		194	?Not a BASIC error
149	?Not at end of file	195	?Dimension number out of range
150	?No primary key specified		
151	?Key field beyond end of record	196	?REMAP string is not static
		197	?Array too small
152	?Illogical record accessing	198 to 225	?Unused
153	?Record already exists	226	?VAX GKS is not installed
154	?Record/bucket locked	227	?String too long
155	?Record not found	228	?Record attributes not matched
156	?Size of record invalid		
157	?Record on file too big	229	?Differing use of LONG/WORD or SINGLE/DOUBLE qualifiers
158	?Primary key out of sequence		
159	?Key larger than record		
160	?File attributes not matched	230	?No fields in image
161	?Move overflows buffer	231	?Illegal string image
162	?Cannot open file	232	?Null image
163	?No file name	233	?Illegal numeric image
164	?Terminal format file required	234	?Numeric image for string
165	?Cannot position to EOF	235	?String image for numeric
166	?Negative fill or string length	236	?TIME limit exceeded
167	?Illegal record format	237	?First arg to SEG$ greater than second
168	?Illegal ALLOW clause		
169	?Unused	238	?Arrays must be same dimension
170	?Index not fully optimized		
171	?RRV not fully updated	239	?Arrays must be square
172	?Record lock failed	240	?Cannot change array dimensions
173	?Invalid RFA field		
174	?File expiration date not yet reached	241	?Floating overflow
		242	?Floating underflow
175	?Node name error	243	?CHAIN to non-existent line number
176	%Negative or zero TAB		
177	%Too much data in record		

244	?Exponentiation error	250	**?Not implemented**
245	**?Illegal exit from DEF***	251	?Recursive subroutine call
246	**?ERROR trap needs RESUME**	**252**	**?FILE ACP failure**
247	**?Illegal RESUME to subroutine**	**253**	**?Directive error**
248	?Illegal return from subroutine	254	?Unused
249	?Argument out of bounds	255	?Unused

Appendix 3 ASCII Codes

The following is a list of ASCII codes and their character equivalents.

DEC	CHAR	KEY
0	NULL	CTRL-@
1	SOH	CTRL-A
2	STX	CTRL-B
3	ETX	CTRL-C (Break)
4	ET	CTRL-D
5	ENQ	CTRL-E
6	ACK	CTRL-F
7	BEL	CTRL-G
8	BS	CTRL-H
9	HT	CTRL-I
10	LF	CTRL-J
11	VT	CTRL-K
12	FF	CTRL-L
13	CR	CTRL-M
14	SO	CTRL-N
15	SI	CTRL-O
16	DLE	CTRL-P
17	DC1	CTRL-Q (Scroll)
18	DC2	CTRL-R (Refresh)
19	DC3	CTRL-S (No scroll)
20	DC4	CTRL-T
21	NAK	CTRL-U (Delete)
22	SYN	CTRL-V
23	ETB	CTRL-W
24	CAN	CTRL-X
25	EM	CTRL-Y
26	SUB	CTRL-Z (EOF)
27	ESC	Escape
28	FS	n/a
29	GS	n/a
30	RS	n/a
31	US	n/a
32	SPACE	space
33	!	!
34	"	"
35	#	#
36	$	$

APPENDIX 3: ASCII CODES

DEC	CHAR	KEY
37	%	%
38	&	&
39	'	'
40	(	(
41	)	)
42	*	*
43	+	+
44	,	,
45	-	-
46	.	.
47	/	/
48	0	0
49	1	1
50	2	2
51	3	3
52	4	4
53	5	5
54	6	6
55	7	7
56	8	8
57	9	9
58	:	:
59	;	;
60	<	<
61	=	=
62	>	>
63	?	?
64	@	@
65	A	A
66	B	B
67	C	C
68	D	D
69	E	E
70	F	F
71	G	G
72	H	H
73	I	I
74	J	J
75	K	K
76	L	L
77	M	M
78	N	N
79	O	O
80	P	P
81	Q	Q
82	R	R
83	S	S
84	T	T
85	U	U
86	V	V
87	W	W
88	X	X
89	Y	Y
90	Z	Z
91	[	[

DEC	CHAR	KEY
92	\	\
93	]	]
94	^	^
95	_	_ (underscore)
96	`	`
97	a	a
98	b	b
99	c	c
100	d	d
101	e	e
102	f	f
103	g	g
104	h	h
105	i	i
106	j	j
107	k	k
108	l	l
109	m	m
110	n	n
111	o	o
112	p	p
113	q	q
114	r	r
115	s	s
116	t	t
117	u	u
118	v	v
119	w	w
120	x	x
121	y	y
122	z	z
123	{	{
124				
125	}	}
126	~	~
127	DEL	(Delete)

The first 32 of these characters are known as **control characters.** Most can be obtained by holding the CTRL key and pressing the accompanying key at the same time. Some of them have a separate key as well. For example, CTRL-M is the same as the <Return> key; CTRL-H is the same as the BACKSPACE key; CTRL-I is the same as the TAB key; and CTRL-G rings the terminal bell or buzzer.

Some of the control characters are not standard, and different manufacturers assign them different meanings. The DEC machines define CTRL-C as a <Break> character, which can be used to interrupt a program (useful if you are stuck in a loop). CTRL-U has been defined as an "erase line" character (if you type a line that you want to delete, type CTRL-U before pressing <Return>). CTRL-Z is defined as an end-of-file. CTRL-R is used as a line "refresh." This is particularly useful when you are using a printing terminal. If you type a line and use the delete key to correct some errors, it will be difficult to read the printed line with all of its corrections. Type CTRL-R to see the line with all the corrections made.

Appendix 4 Solutions to Selected Exercises

Chapter 2

```
1. 10  ! Read and print three numbers
   20      DECLARE REAL No.1, No.2, No.3
   30      INPUT "Enter three numbers"; No.1, No.2, No.3
   40      PRINT "Numbers in reverse order are"; No.3; No.2; No.1
   50  END

4. 10  ! Print customer purchase
   20      DECLARE DECIMAL(6,2) Price, STRING Name_
   30      INPUT "Enter customer name"; Name_
   40      INPUT "Enter purchase price"; price
   50      PRINT "Name  :"; TAB(9); Name_
   60      PRINT "Price :"; TAB(29); Price
   70  END

7. 10  ! Names and averages
   20      DECLARE STRING Name_, REAL No.1, No.2, No.3, Average
   30      PRINT "Name"; TAB(25); "Numbers"; TAB(50); "Average"
   40      READ Name_, No.1, No.2, No.3
   50      PRINT Name_; TAB(20); No.1;No.2;No.3; TAB(50); Average
   60      PRINT TAB(50); (No.1 + No.2 + No.3) / 3
   70      READ Name_, No.1, No.2, No.3
   80      PRINT Name_; TAB(20); No.1;No.2;No.3; TAB(50); average
   90      PRINT TAB(50); (No.1 + No.2 + No.3) / 3
   100     READ Name_, No.1, No.2, No.3
   110     PRINT Name_; TAB(20); No.1;No.2;No.3;
   120     PRINT TAB(50); (No.1 + No.2 + No.3) / 3
   130     DATA "John Smith", 78, 87, 83
   140     DATA "Jane Doe", 92, 88, 92
   150     DATA "Tom Jones", 84,82,89
   160 END

10. 10 ! Print the alphabet
    20     DECLARE STRING Alphabet
    30     READ Alphabet
    40     PRINT Alphabet
    50     DATA "ABCDEFGHIJKLMNOPQRSTUVWXYZ"
    60 END
```

430 APPENDIX 4: SOLUTIONS TO SELECTED EXERCISES

Chapter 3

```
1. 10   ! Perimeter of triangle
   20       DECLARE REAL Side_1, Side_2, Side_3, Perimeter
   30       INPUT "Enter 3 sides of triangle"; Side_1, Side_2, Side_3
   40       Perimeter = Side_1 + Side_2 + Side_3
   50       PRINT
   60       PRINT "Sides of triangle are"; Side_1; Side_2; Side_3
   70       PRINT "Perimeter is"; Perimeter
   80   END

4. 10   ! Various Averages
   20       DECLARE REAL No.1, No.2, No.3, No.4, No.5, &
                           Avg_first_2, Avg_last_2, Avg_all_4
   30       INPUT "Enter four numbers"; No.1, No.2, No.3, No.4
   40       Avg_first_2 = (No.1 + No.2 / 2
             Avg_last_2  = (No.3 + No.4) / 2
             Avg_all_4   = (No.1 + No.2) + No.3 + No.4) / 4
   50       PRINT
             PRINT "First two numbers are"; No.1; No.2, &
                  "Average is"; Avg_first_2
             PRINT "Last two numbers are "; No.3; No.4, &
                  "Average is"; Avg_last_2
             PRINT TAB(30); "Average of all four is"; Avg_all_4
   60   END

7. 10   ! Evaluate quadratic polynomial
   20       DECLARE REAL A, B, C, X, Y
   30       INPUT "Enter coefficients a, b, c"; A, B, C
             INPUT "Enter value for x"; X
   40       Y = A * X^2 + B * X + C
   50       PRINT "x ="; X, "y ="; Y
   60   END

9a. 50  ! Determine amount left to each child and to wife
         First_child = .25 * Estate
            Remainder = Estate - First_child
         Second_child = .25 * Remainder
            Remainder = Remainder - Second_child
         Third_child = .25 * Remainder
            Remainder = Remainder - Third_child
         Wife = Remainder

12a. 50 ! Calculate interest and new balance
         Total_withdrawals = Withdraw_1 + Withdraw_2 + Withdraw_3
         Total_deposits = Deposit_1 + Deposit_2 + Deposit_3 &
                          + Deposit_4
         Balance = Old_balance + Total_deposits - Total_withdrawals
         Interest = .01625 * Balance
         New_balance = Balance + Interest

14a. 50 ! Convert ml/hr to drops/minute
         ML_per_min = ML_per_hr / 60
         Drops_per_min = ML_per_min / .065
```

APPENDIX 4: SOLUTIONS TO SELECTED EXERCISES | 431

Chapter 4

1.
```
10  ! Perimeter of triangle
20      DECLARE REAL Side_1, Side_2, Side_3, Perimeter
30      GOSUB Read_sides       ! Read sides of triangle
40      GOSUB Find_perimeter
50      GOSUB Output_routine   ! Print sides and perimeter
60   EXIT PROGRAM

1000 Read_sides:                ! Read sides of triangle
1010    INPUT "Enter sides of triangle"; Side_1,Side_2,Side_3
1020 RETURN

1200 Find_perimeter:
1210    Perimeter = Side_1 + Side_2 + Side_3
1220 RETURN

1400 Output_routine:            ! Print sides and perimeter
1410    PRINT
        PRINT "Sides of triangle are"; Side_1; Side_2; Side_3
        PRINT "Perimeter of triangle "; Perimeter
1420 RETURN

32767 END
```

4a.
```
1500 Find_averages:             ! Find various averages
1510    Avg_first_two = (No.1 + No.2) / 2
        Avg_last_two  = (No.3 + No.4) / 2
        Avg_all_four  = (No.1 + No.2 + No. + No.3 + No.4) / 4
1520 RETURN
```

7.
```
10  ! Evaluate quadratic polynomial
20      DECLARE REAL A, B, C, X, Y
30      GOSUB Input_routine    ! Enter a, b, c, x
40      GOSUB Calculate_y      ! Evaluate polynomial
50      GOSUB Output_routine   ! Print x and y
60   EXIT PROGRAM

1000 Input_routine:             ! Enter a, b, c, x
1010    INPUT "Enter coefficients of equation, a, b, c"; A,B,C
1020    INPUT "Enter value for x"; X
1030 RETURN

1200 Calculate_y:               ! Evaluate polynomial
1210    Y = A*X^2 + B*X + C
1220 RETURN

1400 Output_routine:            ! Print x and y
1410    PRINT
        PRINT "x ="; X, "y ="; Y
1420 RETURN

32767 END
```

9a.
```
1200 Estate_probate:            ! Apportion estate
1210    First_child_share = .25 * Estate
        Remainder = Estate - First_child_share
```

432 | APPENDIX 4: SOLUTIONS TO SELECTED EXERCISES

```
     1220    Second_child_share = .25 * Remainder
             Remainder = Remainder - Second_child_share
     1230    Third_child_share = .25 * Remainder
             Remainder = Remainder - Third_child_share
     1240    Wife = Remainder
     1250 RETURN
12a.
     1200 Find_new_balance:          ! Find interest new balance
     1210    Total_deposits = Deposit_1 + Deposit_2 &
                              + Deposit_3 + Deposit_4
     1220    Total_withdrawals = Withdrawal_1 + Withdrawal_2 &
                                 + Withdrawal_3
     1230    Balance = Old_balance + Total_deposits &
                        - Total_withdrawals
             Interest = Interest_rate * Balance
             New_balance = New_balance + Interest
     1240 RETURN
```

Chapter 5

```
1.  10  ! Table of squares and cubes
    20       DECLARE INTEGER I, Square, Cube
    30  ! Print heading
             PRINT TAB(10); "Number"; TAB(30); "Square"; TAB(50); "Cube"
    40  ! Print values
             FOR I = 1 TO 10
                Square = I * I
                Cube = Square * I
                Print TAB(11); I; TAB(31); Square; TAB(50); Cube
             NEXT I
    50  END

4a.
    50       GOSUB Read_data
             WHILE No.1 <> 0 AND No.2 <> 0 AND No.3 <> 0 AND &
                No.4 <> 0 AND No.5 <> 0
                Sum = No.1 + No.2 + No.3 + No.4 + No.5
                PRINT "Sum of numbers ="; Sum
                GOSUB Read_data
             NEXT

7.  10  ! Sum of successive integers between end points
    20       DECLARE INTEGER First, Last, Sum, I
    30       GOSUB Enter_endpoints
    40       GOSUB Find_sum          ! Find sum, First to Last
    50       GOSUB Print_menu
    60  EXIT PROGRAM

    1000 Enter_endpoints:
    1010    INPUT "Enter first and last values for sum"; &
                   First, Last
    1020 RETURN
```

```
      1100 Find_sum:                    ! Find sum, First to Last
      1110   Sum = 0
             FOR I = First TO Last
                Sum = Sum + I
             NEXT I
      1120 RETURN

      1200 Print_sum:
      1210   PRINT
             PRINT "Sum of integers from"; First; "to"; Last; &
                   "is; Sum
      1220 RETURN

      32767 END
```

11.
```
      10 ! Sum of numbers until sum exceeds 250
      20     DECLARE INTEGER Sum, Number
      30     Sum = 0 \ Number= 0
             WHILE Sum < 250
                Number = Number + 1
                Sum = Sum + Number
             NEXT
      40     PRINT "Number of successive integers until sum "; &
                   "exceeds 100 is"; Sum
      50 END
```

13a.
```
      1000 Roll_dice:         ! Simulate rolling a pair of dice
      1010   Die_1 = INT(6*RND + 1)
             Die_2 = INT(6*RND + 1)
      1020   Dice = Die_1 + Die_2
      1030 RETURN
```

13b.
```
      1100 Roll_dice_until_7:
      1110   GOSUB Roll_dice
             Number_of_rolls = 1
             WHILE Dice <> 7
               GOSUB Roll_dice
               Number_of_rolls = Number_of_rolls + 1
             NEXT
      1120 RETURN
```

16a.
```
      1200 Grow_rabbits:
           ! Note: All variables are type REAL because of size
      1210   No.rabbits = 2
             No.years = 0
      1220   WHILE No.rabbits < 100000
                No.females = No.rabbits / 2
                New_rabbits = 8 * No.females
                No.rabbits = No.rabbits + New_rabbits
                No.years = No.years + .5
             NEXT
      1230 RETURN
```

Chapter 6

```
1. 10  ! Number guessing game
   20      DECLARE INTEGER Number, Count_, Guess
   30      RANDOMIZE
   40      Number = INT(101*RND)    ! Integer from 0 to 100
   50      GOSUB Accept_guesses     ! Guess until correct
   60      GOSUB Final_message
   70  EXIT PROGRAM

   1000 Accept_guesses:             ! Guess until correct
   1010    PRINT "I have a number between 0 and 100."
            INPUT "Can you guess what it is"; Guess
            Count_ = 1
   1020    WHILE Guess <> Number
               PRINT
               IF Guess > No. THEN
                  PRINT "Too High Guess Again"
               ELSE
                  PRINT "Too Low Guess Again"
               AND IF
               INPUT Guess
               Count_ = Count_ + 1
            NEXT
   1030 RETURN

   1200 Final_message:
   1210    PRINT
            PRINT "Congratulations! That is the number."
            PRINT "You required"; Count_; "guesses."
   1220 RETURN

   32767 END
```

4a.
```
   1200 Find_lowest:                ! Find lowest of five grades
   1210    Lowest = Grade_1
            IF Grade_2 > Lowest THEN Lowest = Grade_2   END IF
            IF Grade_3 > Lowest THEN Lowest = Grade_3   END IF
            IF Grade_4 > Lowest THEN Lowest = Grade_4   END IF
            IF Grade_5 > Lowest THEN Lowest = Grade_5   END IF
   1220 RETURN
```

7a.
```
   1600 Find_new_balance:           ! Find finance charge and new
                                    ! balance
   1610    Unpaid_balance = Old_balance - payment
            Finance_charge = .015 * Unpaid_balance
   1620    New_balance = Unpaid_balance + Finance_charge &
                       + Total_purchases
   1630 RETURN
```

```
11. 10  ! Solve linear equation
    20      DECLARE REAL A, B, X
    30      INPUT "Enter coefficients a,b"; A, B
    40      GOSUB Solve_equation
    50      GOSUB Output_routine
    60   EXIT PROGRAM
```

APPENDIX 4: SOLUTIONS TO SELECTED EXERCISES

```
1000 Solve_equation:
1010    IF A <> 0 THEN
            X = -B / A
        END IF
1020 RETURN

1100 Output_routine:
1110    PRINT "a ="; A, "b ="; B,
1120    IF A = 0 THEN PRINT "No solution for x"
        ELSE PRINT "x ="; X
        END IF
1130 RETURN

32767 END
```

14a.
```
1600 Find_new_balance:     ! Find interest and new balance
1610    IF amount_owed <= 100.00 THEN
            Interest = .02 * Amount_owed
        ELSE IF Amount_owed <= 1000.00 THEN
            Interest = 2.00 + .015 * (Amount_owed - 100.00)
        ELSE
            Interest = 15.50 + .01 * (Amount_owed - 1000.00)
        END IF
1620    New_balance = Amount_owed + Interest
1630 RETURN
```

16b.
```
1500 Throw_100_darts:
1510    No.in_circle = 0
1520    FOR Throw = 1 TO 100
            GOSUB Throw_a_dart
            IF (X^2 + Y^2) < 1 THEN
                No.in_circle = No.in_circle + 1
            END IF
        NEXT Throw
1530 RETURN
```

Programming Tool A

1.
```
10 ! Immediate assignments
20    DECLARE INTEGER A, B, Product
30    PRINT "Assign two values in the form"
      PRINT "    A=value <RETURN>"
      PRINT "    B=value <RETURN>"
      PRINT "Then type CONT"
      STOP
40    Product = A*B
50    PRINT "Product ="; Product
60 END
```

Chapter 7

1a.
```
1200 Avg_alternate_elements:    ! Find average of even- &
                                ! numbered elements
1210    Sum = 0
        FOR I = 2 TO 100 STEP 2
            Sum = Sum + A(I)
        NEXT I
```

APPENDIX 4: SOLUTIONS TO SELECTED EXERCISES

```
1220    Average = Sum / 50
1230 RETURN
```

3a.
```
1200 Find_smallest:           ! Find smallest of 31 elements
1210    Smallest = A(1)
        FOR I = 2 TO 31
            IF A(I) < Smallest THEN
                Smallest = A(I)
            END IF
        NEXT I
1220 RETURN
```

7a.
```
1500 Bubble_sort:
1510    No.comparisons = No.elements - 1
        Interchange = "yes"
1520    WHILE No.comparisons >= 1 AND Interchange = "yes"
            Interchange = "no"
            GOSUB Do_comparisons
            No.comparisons = No.comparisons - 1
        NEXT
1530 RETURN

1600 Do_comparisons:
1610    FOR I = 1 TO No.comparisons
            IF A(I) > A(I+1) THEN
                Temp = A(I)
                A(I) = A(I+1)
                A(I+1) = Temp
                Interchange = "yes"
            END IF
        NEXT I
1620 RETURN
```

12a.
```
1600 Find_mode:               ! Find mode of sorted array
1610 ! Initialize
        Max_count = 0
        I = 1                 ! Subscript into array
1620    WHILE I <= No.elements
1630      ! Start counting new number
            Number = A(I)
            Count_ = 0
1640      ! Find frequency of this number
            WHILE A(I) = Number AND I <= No.elements
                Count_ = Count_ + 1
                I = I + 1
            NEXT
1650      ! Save this number if it has highest frequency
            IF Count_ > Max_count THEN
                Max_count = Count_
                Mode_ = Number
            END IF
1660    NEXT                  ! Continue with next number
1670 RETURN
```

APPENDIX 4: SOLUTIONS TO SELECTED EXERCISES | 437

17a.
```
1500 Reverse_doors:         ! For every fifth door --
                            ! Open closed door, close open door
1510 ! Open door = +1, closed door = -1
1520    FOR Door = 5 TO 100 STEP 5
            Cell(door) = - Cell(door)
        Next Door
1530 RETURN
```

Chapter 8

1a.
```
1000 Open_files:           ! Open input and output files
1010    OPEN "STORY.DOC" FOR INPUT AS FILE #1
        OPEN "FILE.OUT" FOR OUTPUT AS FILE #2
1020 RETURN
```

4a.
```
1200 Find_smallest:        ! Find smallest number in file
1210    INPUT #1, Number
        Smallest = Number
1220    WHILE Number <> -999
            IF Number < Smallest THEN Smallest = Number   END IF
            INPUT #1, Number
        NEXT
1230 RETURN
```

5b.
```
1300 Find_largest:         ! Find largest number in file
1310    INPUT #1, Number
        Largest = Number
1320    FOR I = 2 TO 100
            IF Number > Largest THEN Largest = Number   END IF
            INPUT #1, Number
        NEXT I
1330 RETURN
```

9a.
```
1600 Count_numbers:        ! Find frequency numbers 1 to 10
1610    FOR Number = 1 TO 10
            GOSUB Count_number    ! Frequency of one number
            PRINT "Number ="; Number, "Frequency ="; Count_
        NEXT Number
1620 RETURN

1700 Count_number:         ! Find frequency of one number
1710    IF Number = 1 THEN INPUT #1, Number_in   END IF
1720    Count_ = 0
1730    WHILE Number_in = Number
            Count = Count + 1
            INPUT #1, Number_in
        NEXT
1740 RETURN
```

438 APPENDIX 4: SOLUTIONS TO SELECTED EXERCISES

Chapter 9

1a.
```
1200 Reverse_name:        ! Change order of name
1210    Name_ = EDIT$(Name_, 152)
                          ! Discard excess spaces
1220 ! Get first and last names
        Blank_posn = POS(Name_, " ", 1)
        First_name = SEG$(Name_, 1, Blank_posn-1)
        Last_name = SEG$(Name_, Blank_posn+1, LEN(Name_))
1230 ! Reassemble name
        Name_ = Last_name + ", " + First_name
1340 RETURN
```

4a.
```
1300 Check_numeric:       ! See if string is numeric
1310    Flag = "numeric"
1320    FOR I = 1 TO LEN(String_)
           Character = SEG$(String_, I, I)
           IF (Character < "0" OR Character > "9") AND &
                            Character <> "." THEN
              Flag = "non-numeric"
           END IF
        NEXT I
1330 RETURN
```

7.
```
10 ! Program to find number of names in file whose first
   ! name is John
20      DECLARE STRING In_file, Name_, First_name, &
                INTEGER Blank_posn, EOF, Count_
30      ON ERROR GOTO Error_handler
40      GOSUB Open_file    ! Open input file
50      GOSUB Count_Johns  ! Count names with first name John
60      GOSUB Print_count  ! Print number of names
70      CLOSE #1
80   EXIT PROGRAM

1000 Open_file:            ! Open input file
1010    INPUT "Enter input file name"; In_file
1020    OPEN In_file FOR INPUT AS FILE #1
1030 RETURN

1200 Count_Johns:          ! Count names with first name John
1210    Count_ = 0
1220    EOF = 0            ! Set to 1 by error handler
        WHILE EOF = 0
           INPUT #1, Name_
           GOSUB Get_first_name
           IF First_name = "JOHN" THEN
              Count_ = Count_ + 1
           END IF
        NEXT
1230 RETURN

1400 Get_first_name:
     ! Names are last name first
1410    Name_ = EDIT$(Name_, 152) ! Remove excess blanks
```

```
1420    Blank_posn = POS(Name_, " ", 1)
1430    First_name = SEG$(Name_, Blank_posn+1, LEN(Name_))
1440 RETURN

1600 Print_count:             ! Print number of names
1610    PRINT
        PRINT "Number of names with first name John is"; Count_
1620 RETURN

19000 Error handler:
19010    IF ERR = 5 THEN        ! Bad file name
            PRINT "Incorrect file name. Please reenter."
            RESUME
         ELSE IF ERR = 11 THEN   ! End of file
            RESUME 1230
         ELSE
            ON ERROR GOTO 0
         END IF
19020 ! End of error handler

32767 END
```

11a.
```
1500 Decode_message:
1510 ! Coded_message is a string containing integers.
     !       The last integer is the sentinel 99
     ! Decoded_message is the character string message
     ! TRANSL_STRING is the translation string
1520 ! Remove all blanks from the coded string
        Coded_message = EDIT$(Coded_message, 2)
1530    Decoded_message = ""
1540    WHILE Coded_message <> "99"
           GOSUB Get_number
           Character = SEG$(TRANSL_STRING, Number, Number)
           Decoded_message = Decoded_message + Character
        NEXT
1550 RETURN

1600 Get_number:       ! Get a number from the coded_string
1610    Comma_posn = POS(Coded_message, ",", 1)
        Number_string = SEG$(Coded_message, 1, Comma_posn)
        Coded_message = SEG$(Coded_message, Comma_posn+1, &
                                     LEN(Coded_message))
1620    Number = VAL(Number_string)
1630 RETURN
```

15a.
```
1300 Create_record:      ! Create a fixed format record
1310    NEW_record = Name_
        FOR I = LEN(New_record) TO 20
           NEW_record = New_record + " "
        NEXT I
1320    New_record = New_record + Soc_sec_no.
        FOR I = LEN(New_record) TO 31
           New_record = New_record + " "
        NEXT I
```

```
1330      GOSUB Make_number_string ! Make string of 5 numbers
          New_record = New_record + Number_string
1340 RETURN

1400 Make_number_string:           ! Make string of 5 numbers
1410     No. = No.1
         GOSUB Convert_number    ! Convert to string
         Number_string = Number
1420     No. = No.2
         GOSUB Convert_number    ! Convert to string
         Number_string = Number_string + Number
1430     No. = No.3
         GOSUB Convert_number    ! Convert to string
         Number_string = Number_string + Number
1440     No. = No.4
         GOSUB Convert_number    ! Convert to string
         Number_string = Number_string + Number
1450     No. = No.5
         GOSUB Convert_number    ! Convert to string
         Number_string = Number_string + Number
1460 RETURN

1500 Convert_number:               ! Convert number to string of
                                   ! length 5
1510    Number = NUM$(No.)
1520    FOR I = LEN(Number) TO 5
            Number = Number + " "
        NEXT I
1530 RETURN
```

Chapter 10

1a.
```
1300 Find_row_average:
1310    FOR Row = 1 TO 10
            Sum = 0
            FOR Column = 1 TO 6
               Sum = Sum + A(Row, Column)
            NEXT Column
            ROW_Avg(Row) = SUM
        NEXT Row
1320 RETURN
```

4a.
```
1400 Divide_rows:          ! Divide row by first element
1410    FOR Column = 1 TO 10
            First_element = A(Row, 1)
            FOR Column = 1 TO 20
                A(Row, Column) = A(Row, Column) / First_element
            NEXT Column
        NEXT Row
1420 RETURN
```

9a.
```
1700 Bubble_sort:          ! Sort 2-D Array by column 1
1710    FOR No.Comparisons = No.Elements-1 TO 1 STEP -1
           FOR I = 1 TO No.Comparisons
              IF A(I,1) > A(I+1,1) THEN
                 GOSUB Interchange
              END IF
           NEXT I
        NEXT No.Comparisons
1720 RETURN

1800 Interchange:           ! Interchange two rows of 2-D array
1810    FOR Column = 1 TO 3
           Temp = A(I, Column)
           A(I, Column) = A(I+1, Column)
           A(I+1, Column) = Temp
        NEXT Column
1820 RETURN
```

13.
```
   10 ! Two rook problem
      ! Place two rooks on chessboard
      ! Determine if they are attacking each other
   20    DECLARE STRING Board(8,8), Result, &
                 INTEGER Row, Column, Count_
   30    GOSUB Board_setup   ! Place rooks on board
   40    GOSUB Check_rooks   ! See if rooks are attacking
   50    GOSUB Print_result
   60  EXIT PROGRAM

 1000 Board_setup:           ! Place rooks on board
 1010 ! Clear the board
         FOR Row = 1 TO 8
            FOR Column = 1 TO 8
               Board(Row, Column) = " "
            NEXT Column
         NEXT Row
 1020    Board(4,4) = "ROOK"     ! Place first rook
 1030 ! Place second rook, not on same square as first rook
         GOSUB Pick_square  ! Find square for rook
         WHILE Row = 4 AND Column = 4
            GOSUB Pick_square   ! Find another square
         NEXT
 1040    Board(Row, Column) = "ROOK"
 1050 RETURN

 1100 Find_square:           ! Find square to place rook
 1110    Row = INT(8*RND + 1)
         Column = INT(8*RND + 1)
 1120 RETURN

 1200 Check_rooks:           ! See if rooks are attacking
 1210    Result = "Pieces not attacking"
```

```
1220 ! Count number of rooks in each row
     FOR Row = 1 TO 8
        GOSUB Check_row      ! Count rooks in one row
        IF Count_ > 1 THEN
           Result = "Pieces attacking"
        END IF
     NEXT Row
1230 ! Count number of rooks in each column
     FOR Column = 1 TO 8
        GOSUB Check_column   ! Count rooks in one column
        IF Count_ > 1 THEN
           Result = "Pieces attacking"
     NEXT Column
1240 RETURN

1300 Check_row:              ! Count rooks in one row
1310    Count_ = 0
        FOR Column = 1 TO 8
           IF Board(Row, Column) = "ROOK" THEN
              Count_ = Count_ + 1
           END IF
        NEXT Column
1320 RETURN

1400 Check_column:           ! Count rooks in one column
1410    Count_ = 0
        FOR Row = 1 TO 8
           IF Board(Row, Column) = "ROOK" THEN
              Count_ = Count_ + 1
           END IF
        NEXT Row
1420 RETURN

2000 Print_result:
2010 ! Print the board
     FOR Row = 1 TO 8
        FOR Column = 1 TO 8
           IF Board(Row, Column) = "ROOK" THEN
              PRINT "R ";
           ELSE
              PRINT "- ";
           END IF
        NEXT Column
        PRINT                ! End of row
     NEXT Row
2010 ! Print result
     PRINT
     PRINT Result
2020 RETURN

32767 END
```

Chapter 11

1.
```
10 ! PI to various decimal places
20    DECLARE STRING Format_1, Format_2, Format_3
```

```
            30   ! Formats
                 Format_1 = "#.##"
                 Format_2 = "#.###"
                 Format_3 = "#.####"
            40   PRINT USING Format_1, PI
                 PRINT USING Format_2, PI
                 PRINT USING Format_3, PI
            50   END
```

5a.
```
          1000 Make_headings_and_formats:
          1010    Heading_1 = &
            "PLAYER        AT                         HOME    BAT   SLUG."
                  Heading_2 = &
            "  NAME       BATS    SNGLES   DBLES   TRPLES   RUNS    AVG.   PCT."
                  Format_ = &
            "'LLLLLLLL     ###      ###     ###     ###     .###   #.###"
          1020    PRINT Heading_1
                  PRINT Heading_2
          1030 RETURN
```

Chapter 12

1a.
```
            30   MAP (Rec) STRING Name_=30, Address=50, Telephone=25
```
1b.
```
          1030 OPEN In_file FOR INPUT AS FILE #1, RELATIVE, MAP Rec
```
3a.
```
          2030 PUT #1, RECORD N
```
7a.
```
          3000 Backup:                        ! Make backup file
          3010    ON ERROR GOTO Error_routine
                                              ! To trap end-of-file error
          3020    INPUT "Enter name of backup file", In_file
                  OPEN In_file FOR OUTPUT AS FILE #2, RELATIVE, &
                      MAP Map_rec
          3030    EOF = 0
                  WHILE EOF = 0
                     GET #1
                     PUT #2
                  NEXT
          3040 RETURN
```

Chapter 13

1.
```
            10   ! Table of square roots
            20       DECLARE INTEGER Number, REAL Root, &
                         STRING Heading, Outform
            30       Heading = "      Number         Root"
                     Outform = "        ##         #.####"
            40       PRINT Heading
                     PRINT
```

```
   50    FOR Number = 1 TO 50
             Root = SQR(Number)
             PRINT USING Outform, Number, Root
         NEXT Number
   60    END
```

5a.
```
   1100  Even_odd:         ! Determine if number is even or odd
   1110     Quotient = Number / 2
             Remainder = Quotient - INT(Quotient)
   1120     IF Remainder = 0 THEN Result = "EVEN"
             ELSE Result = "ODD"
             END IF
   1130  RETURN
```

9.
```
   10    ! Reverse temperature digits
   20        DECLARE INTEGER Farenheit, Celsius, Units, Tens, &
                            Reverse_farenheit
   30        FOR Farenheit = 10 to 90
                GOSUB Reverse_digits
                GOSUB Find_celsius
                IF Celsius = Reverse_farenheit THEN
                   PRINT "Temperature ="; Farenheit
                END IF
             NEXT Farenheit
   40     EXIT PROGRAM

   1000  Reverse digits:       ! Reverse digits of number
   1010     Tens = INT (Farenheit / 10)
             Units = Farenheit - 10*Tens
   1020     Reverse_farenheit = 10*Units + Tens
   1030  RETURN

   1100  Find_celsius:         ! Convert Farenheit to Celsius
   1110     Celsius = 5 * (Farenheit - 32) / 9
             Celsius = INT(Celsius)  ! Keep integer part only
   1120  RETURN

   32767 END
```

Chapter 14

1a.
```
   30    DEF REAL Find_salary (REAL Total_sales) &
                     = 200 + .10 * Total_sales
```

3a.
```
   1000  DEF STRING Find_suit (INTEGER Number)
   1010     SELECT Number
                CASE 1
                   Find_suit = "CLUBS"
                CASE 2
                   Find_suit = "DIAMONDS"
```

```
              CASE 3
                Find_suit = "HEARTS"
              CASE 4
                Find_suit = "SPADES"
           END SELECT
1020   END DEF
```

7a.
```
1500 DEF INTEGER Find_day (STRING Date)
1510    Date = EDIT$(Date, 184) ! Remove excess blanks
                                ! Make upper case
1520 ! Find first three letters of month
        Month = SEG$(Date, 1, 3)
1530 ! Find days
        Blank_posn = POS(Date, " ", 1)
        Comma_posn = POS(Date, ",", Blank_posn+1)
        String_days = SEG$(Date, Blank_posn+1, Comma_posn-1)
        Days = VAL(String_days)
1540 ! Find year
        String_year = SEG$(Date, Comma_posn+1, Comma_Posn+4)
        Year = VAL(String_year)
1550 ! Determine if leap year
        Quotient = Year / 4
        Remainder = Quotient - INT(Quotient)
        IF Remainder = 0 THEN Leap_year = "TRUE"
        ELSE Leap_year = "FALSE"
        END IF
1560 ! Accumulate days to date
        Find_day = Count_days(Month, Day, Leap_year)
1570 RETURN

1600 DEF INTEGER Count_days (STRING Month, INTEGER Day, &
                             STRING Leap_year)
     ! Accumulate days to date
1610    IF Month = "JAN" THEN Count_days = Day
        ELSE IF Month = "FEB" THEN Count_days = 31 + DAY
        ELSE IF Month = "MAR" THEN Count_days = 59 + DAY
        ELSE IF Month = "APR" THEN Count_days = 90 + DAY
        ELSE IF Month = "MAY" THEN Count_days = 120 + DAY
        ELSE IF Month = "JUN" THEN Count_days = 151 + DAY
        ELSE IF Month = "JUL" THEN Count_days = 181 + DAY
        ELSE IF Month = "AUG" THEN Count_days = 212 + DAY
        ELSE IF Month = "SEP" THEN Count_days = 243 + DAY
        ELSE IF Month = "OCT" THEN Count_days = 273 + DAY
        ELSE IF Month = "NOV" THEN Count_days = 304 + DAY
        ELSE IF Month = "DEC" THEN Count_days = 334 + DAY
        END IF
1620    IF Month <> "JAN" AND Month <> "FEB" &
               AND Leap_year = "TRUE"
        THEN Count_days = Count_days + 1
        END IF
1630 RETURN
```

12a.
```
1000 DEF REAL Monthly (REAL Loan, REAL I, INTEGER N)
     ! I = Interest rate per month
     ! N = Term of loan, in months
1010   Numerator = Loan * I
       Denominator = 1 - (1 + I)^(-N)
1020   Monthly = Numerator / Denominator
1030 RETURN
```

Index

ABS function, 359
Accumulator, 99
Active loop, 96
Addition, 46, 131–133
Address, 22–27
ALU (arithmetic/logic unit), 22
Ampersand, 51–52, 54
Annotation symbol, 83–84
Arguments, 89, 90, 380–385, 393
Arithmetic drill program, 113–115
Arithmetic/logic unit (ALU), 22
Arithmetic operators, 46
Array(s), 185–209; as arguments, 222–224; assignment statements and, 188; associated, 201–209; binary search and, 206–209; calculating with, 299–306; cross-section of, 296; defined, 185; dimensioning, 187–188, 216–224, 296–297, 312–318; loops and, 189–195, 297–298; one-based, 187, 296; printing, 191, 298–299; reading values into, 189–191, 194, 297–298; sequential search and, 201–204; sorting, 195–201, 204–206; string, 200–201; subscripts and, 186–187; three-dimensional, 186; zero-based, 187, 296. *See also* One-dimensional arrays; Two-dimensional arrays
Array name, 186
Arrow keys, 15
Ascending sort, 195
ASCII (American Standard Code for Information Interchange) codes, 201, 423–425
ASCII function, 363
Assignment operator, 47–48
Assignment statements, 45–60, 188; arithmetic operators, 46; flow charts, 57–59; hierarchy of operators, 46; multi-line statements, 51–57; multi-statement lines, 50–51; parentheses, 46–47; sequences, 48–49

Associated arrays, 201–209
Asterisk (*), 6–7, 46
Asterisk fill, 327
ATN function, 359
Averages, 133–135, 139–140, 391

Backslash, 107
BAS extension, 6
BASIC, 8–14; changing to, .8; creating programs, 9; deleting lines, 12; editing lines, 13–14; files, 226; help in, 13; inserting lines, 12–13; listing programs, 11–12; renaming programs, 10–11; retrieving old programs, 10; returning to VMS, 8–9; running programs, 11; saving programs, 10
BASIC built-in functions. *See* Built-in functions
BASIC files, 226
Billing program, 117–120
Binary search, 206–209
Block I/O files, 227
Boolean operators, 103–104
Break key, 178
Bubble sort, 196–200
Buffer, 226, 336–338
Bugs, 168–179
Built-in constants, see predefined constants
Built-in functions, 357–375; defining, 358; invoking, 358; mathematical, 359–361; matrix, 364–365; predefined constants, 366–373; print, 361; string, 361–364; system, 365–366
Built-in variables: ERL, 178, 179, 253; ERN$, 259–260; ERR, 253; ERT$, 253; NUM, 316–317; NUM2, 316

C command, 15
CALL statement, 90, 92
Card punches, 21
Card readers, 20

CASE clause, 150–152
Cathode-ray tube (CRT), 21
Center justify, 323
Central processing unit (CPU), 22–23
Change mode, 14, 15–16
Channel, 227–228
Character: deleting, 15–16; inserting, 16
Character string, 23, 25–26
Charge account program, 77–78
CHR$ function, 362–363, 366
CLOSE statement, 232
Colon, 70, 71, 72
Column(s): printing, 36–37; in two-dimensional array, 296
Column-order, 298
Comma, 35–36, 325–326
Commands, upper vs. lower case for, 3
Comments, 38–40
Comparison operators, 102–103
Computers, 20–28; arithmetic/logic unit of, 22; block diagram of, 20; control unit of, 22; input devices of, 20–21; memory of, 22–23; output devices of, 21; symbolic addresses in, 23–27
CON function, 365
Concatenation, 264–265
Conditional statements, 129–160; flow charts and, 156–160; IF-THEN-ELSE-END IF, 137–149; IF-THEN-END IF, 130–137; menus and, 152–156; SELECT-CASE, 150–152
Constants, 34; predefined, 366–373
CONT statement, 171–172, 179
Control characters, 366, 425
Control key, 178–179
Control unit, 22
Controlled loops, 102–108; arrays and, 189–191; counting and, 105–108; defined, 95; logical expressions and, 102–104; UNTIL, 108; WHILE, 104–105
COS function, 359

447

448 INDEX

Counting, 105–108
CPU (central processing unit), 22–23
Crap shooting program, 143–145, 146
Cross-section, of array, 296
CRT (cathode-ray tube), 21
CRTL/Z command, 9, 15
Cursor movement, 15

DAT file type, 6
Data abstraction, 82
Data files, 226. *See also* File(s)
Data flag, 116–119
Data lines, matching headings with, 328–330
DATA statement, 40–42
Data-type, 32
DATE$ function, 365
Debugging, 168–179. *See also* Error trapping
Decimal point, 325
DECIMAL variable, 26–27
DECLARE statement, 338; dimensioning arrays with, 187–188, 296; fixed-length strings and, 338; format of, 32; statement numbers and, 30; symbolic addresses and, 23–26
DECLARE FUNCTION statement, 388–389, 393
Deferred execution statement, 171
DEL command, 6–7
Delete key, 15–16
Descending sort, 196
DET function, 365
Detail file, 343
DIM statement, 187n, 216, 296
Dimensioning: with DECLARE statement, 187–188, 296; with DIM statement, 187n, 216; variable, 216–224, 312–318
DIR command, 6
Directory listing, 5–6
Disk drives, 20, 21
Disk packs, 20
Division, 46
DOC file type, 6

EDIT command, 13–14
EDIT$ function, 273–275, 364
Editing: lines, 13–14; strings, 273–275
Editor: change mode of, 15–16; leaving, 14–15
Editor environment, 14–15
Elements, 185, 186; zero'th, 186
END statement, 37–38, 89
END IF statement, 130–149
Endless loop, 178–179
End-of-file errors, 255–258

Enumerative loops, 96–102; arrays and, 189; defined, 95; summing and, 98–102
Environments, 2–5; BASIC, 8–14; editor, 14–15; programming, 3; VMS, 3–5, 8
ERL built-in variable, 178, 179, 253
ERN$ built-in variable, 259–260
ERR built-in variable, 253
Error(s): debugging and, 168–179; returning to system, 255; severity of, 253–254
Error messages, 419–422
Error trapping, 251–261; built-in variables and, 252–253, 259–260; criteria for error handlers, 258; defined, 251; examples of, 255–258, 260–261; in external functions, 411; ON ERROR statements and, 252, 259; RESUME statement and, 254–255, 258; in subprograms, 259–261
ERT$ built-in function, 253
EX command, 14
EXIT command, 8–9, 14
EXIT FUNCTION statement, 410–411
EXIT PROGRAM statement, 73–74
EXP function, 359
Explicit declarations, 23–26
Exponentiation, 46
Expression, 47, 380
Extended field format, 323–324
EXTERNAL FUNCTION statement, 408
External functions, 406–411; defining, 406–408; error trapping in, 411; invoking, 408–410
External modules, 89

Field, 35
File(s): BASIC, 226; block I/O, 227; closing, 232; data, 226; defined, 226; deleting, 6–7; detail, 343; directory listing for, 5–6; end-of-file errors and, 255–258; indexed, 227; input/output with, 231–232; MAT statements and, 250; opening, 227–231; purging, 7–8; random access, 227; record-oriented, 226–227; renaming, 7; sequential, 227; virtual array, 227. *See also* Relative files; Terminal-format files
File management, 5–8
File name, 5
File type, 5–6
File version number, 6
Final value, 96

FIX function, 360
Fixed-length string, 337–338
Flag, 208
Floating dollar sign, 326
Floating point numbers, 24
Floating point variable, 24
Floppy disks, 20
Flow charts, 57–59; conditional statements and, 156–160; loops and, 121–122; modules and, 82–84; user-defined functions and, 398–399, 400
FOR file type, 6
FORTRAN files, 6
FTN file type, 6
Full directory listing, 5
Functions, 69; built-in, 357–375; external, 406–411; invoking, 358, 383, 394–395, 408–410; mathematical, 359–361; matrix, 364–365; multi-line, 388–392; name of, 392–393; one-line, 378–380; print, 361; rules governing, 392–395; string, 361–364; system, 365–366; user-defined, 377–401. *See also* names of specific functions

Garbage in, garbage out, 99
GET statement, 338–341
GIGO (garbage in, garbage out), 99
Global variables, 385–388
GOSUB statement, 70–73
GOTO instruction, 412–415; conditional, 413–414; unconditional, 413
Grading programs, 52–53, 135–137, 143, 241–243, 300–306, 392, 397, 400

Hard-copy terminal, 21
Headings, matching with data lines, 328–330
Help: in BASIC, 13; in change mode, 16; in editor environment, 15; in VMS, 8
Hierarchy of operations, 46
High-speed printers, 21
Hypotenuse, formula for, 56

Identity matrix, 365
IDN function, 365
IF-THEN-ELSE-END IF structure, 137–149, 157–158
IF-THEN-END IF structure, 130–137, 157–158
Implicit declarations, 23–26
Increment, 96
Indexed file, 227

Initial value, 96
Initialization, 99
Input: using MAT INPUT instruction, 217–219; using MAT READ instruction, 219–220
Input devices, 20–21
INPUT statement, 32–34
INPUT LINE instructions, 264
Input/output (I/O), 31–43; comments, 38–40; DATA statement, 40–42; DECLARE statement, 32; END statement, 37–38; with files, 231–232; INPUT statement, 32–34; PRINT statement, 34–37; READ statement, 40–42; REM statement, 38
Insertion sort, 204–206
INSTR function, 266n
INT function, 360
INT reserved word, 108
Integer variables, 25, 30
Interactive system, 21
Interest rate program, 54–55
Intermediate mode, 171
Interpreter, 37
INV function, 365
Invoking functions, 358, 383, 394–395, 408–410
I/O. *See* Input/output

Jump instruction, 412
Justification, 321–323

Key, 227
Keyboard, 21
Keyboard keys, 16
Keypad keys, 15, 16

Labels, 70, 71
LEFT$ function, 265n
Left-justified characters, 321–322
LEN function, 265, 361
Levels of parentheses, 47
Line(s): deleting, 12; editing, 13–14; inserting, 12–13; logical, 50; multi-statement, 50–51; range of, 12
Line feed suppression, 37, 39–40
Line mode, 14
LINPUT instruction, 264. *See also* MAT LINPUT instruction
List, 33
LIST command, 11–12
LOG command, 5
LOG function, 359
LOG10 function, 359
Logging out, 5

Logical expressions, 102–104
Logical line, 50
Logical operators, 103–104
Login procedure, 3–4
Loop(s), 95–123; active, 96; arrays and, 189–195, 297–298, 299; controlled, 95, 102–108, 189–191; counting and, 105–108; endless, 178–179; enumerative, 95, 96–102, 189; flow charts and, 121–122; initialization and, 99; nested, 200, 297–298, 299; priming read and, 116–120; random number generation and, 109–116; sorting and, 197–200; summing and, 98–102; UNTIL, 108
Loop variable, 96, 97

Main program, 73
Mainframe, 22
MAP statement, 336–338
MARGIN statement, 233
MAT assignment statements, 221–222
MAT INPUT instruction, 217–219, 250, 313–315
MAT LINPUT instruction, 313–314, 315–316
MAT PRINT instruction, 220–221, 250, 317–318
MAT READ instruction, 219–220, 313–314, 316
MAT statements: files and, 250; one-dimensional arrays and, 216–221; two-dimensional arrays and, 313–318
Mathematical functions, 359–361
Matrix, 296; identity, 365. *See also* Two-dimensional arrays
Matrix functions, 364–365
Memory, 9, 22–23
Menus, 152–156
MID$ function, 265n
Modules, 66, 69–70; external, 89
Multi-line functions, 388–392
Multi-line statements, 51–57
Multiplication, 46
Multi-statement lines, 50–51

Nested loop, 200, 297–298, 299
Nesting, of IF-THEN-ELSE, 141–149
NEW command, 9
NEXT statement, 104, 108
NOMARGIN statement, 233
Null input, 201
NUM variables, 217–219, 316–317
NUM$ function, 363
NUM2 variable, 316

Number(s): floating dollar sign with, 326; floating point, 24; real, 24, 30
Numeric field, 324

OLD command, 9, 10
ON ERROR GO BACK statement, 259
ON ERROR GOTO statement, 252
One-based array, 187, 296
One-dimensional arrays, 185–209; assignment statements and, 188; binary search and, 206–209; dimensioning, 187–188, 216–224; loops and, 189–195; printing, 191; reading values into, 189–191, 194; sequential search and, 201–204; sorting, 195–201, 204–206; subscripts and, 186–187
One-line functions, 378–380
OPEN statement, 227–231, 338
Operators: arithmetic, 46; Boolean, 103–104; comparison, 102–103; hierarchy of, 46, 103–104; logical, 103–104; relational, 102–103
Output, using MAT PRINT instruction, 220–221
Output devices, 21

Packed format, 35, 220
Palindrome program, 283–288
Panic exit, 14–15
Parameters, 89, 90–93, 379–385, 393
Parentheses, 46–47
Partial directory listing, 6
Pass/fail program, 145, 147–149
Password: changing, 4–5; in login procedure, 3–4
Payroll program, 234–236
PI pre-defined constant, 359
Point of invocation, 389
Population growth program, 172–178
POS function, 266–273, 362
Predefined constants, 366–373
Priming read, 116–120
Print formatting, 35–37, 320–328
Print function, 361
PRINT statement, 34–37; arrays and, 191, 298–299; temporary, 169–170. *See also* MAT PRINT instruction
PRINT USING statement, 319–331; asterisk fill with, 327; center justify with, 323; comma with, 325–326; decimal point with, 325; extended field format with, 323–324; floating dollar sign

PRINT USING statement (Continued) with, 326; left justify with, 321–322; matching headings with data lines, 328–330; numeric field with, 324; quotation mark with, 321; for relative files, 339; right justify with, 322–323; for terminal-format files, 330
Printers, 21
Program: creating, 9; listing, 11–12; main, 73; renaming, 10–11; retrieving, 10; running, 11; saving, 10; structured, 66
Program buffer, 336–338
Programming environments, 3–16; BASIC, 9–14; editor, 14–16; VMS, 3–9
Prompt, 32–34
Pseudocode, 66
Punched cards, 21
PURGE command, 7–8
PUT statement, 341–342

Question mark, 33, 34
QUIT command, 15
Quotation marks, 33, 34, 320, 321

Random access, 345
Random access files, 227
Random integers, 111–113
Random number generator, 109–116
Random numbers, shifting range of, 110–111
RANDOMIZE statement, 109–110, 116, 360
Range of lines, 12
READ statement, 40–42
Real numbers, 24, 30
Record, 336
Record-oriented files, 226–227. See also File(s)
Relational operators, 102–103
Relative files, 335–350; defined, 227; GET statement and, 338–341; MAP statement and, 336–338; OPEN statement and, 338; PUT statement and, 341–342; UPDATE statement and, 342–349
REM statement, 38
RENAME command, 7, 11
REPLACE command, 9, 10, 11, 14
Report printing program, 328–330
Reserved words, 25, 417
RESUME statement, 254–255, 258
RETURN statement, 71–72
Right triangle, program to identify, 384–385
RIGHT$ function, 265n
Right-justified characters, 322–323

RND function, 109–113, 359–360
Row, in two-dimensional array, 296
Row-order, 298
RUN command, 11
RUNNH command, 11

Salary program, 79–81
SAVE command, 10
Scalars, 185
Scaling, 110
Search: binary, 206–209; sequential, 201–204
SEG$ function, 265–266, 361
SELECT-CASE statement, 150–152, 159
Semicolon, 35–36
Sentinel, 116–119, 189–190
Separators, 13–14
Sequence, 48–49
Sequential access, 339–341, 343
Sequential file, 227
Sequential search, 201–204
SET PASS command, 4
SGN function, 360–361
Side effects, 395
Simple variables, 185
SIN function, 359
Sine function, 359, 370, 371
Slash (/), 13, 46
Sorting: ascending, 195; bubble, 196–200; descending, 196; insertion, 204–206; of one-dimensional arrays, 195–201, 204–206; of string arrays, 200–201
SPACE$ function, 362
Spaghetti code, 415
SQR function, 359
Square root, 56, 367
Step, 96
Stepwise decomposition, 66–69
STOP statement, 170–178
STR$ function, 363
String(s): combining, 264–265; comparing, 277–288; defined, 264; editing, 273–275; fixed-length, 337–338; searching for substring, 266–273
String arrays, sorting of, 200–201
String constant, 34
String functions, 361–364
String length, defining, 337–338
String literal, 320
String processing, 263–289; concatenation, 264–265; defined, 263; EDIT$ function, 273–275; INPUT LINE instruction, 264; LEN function, 265; LINPUT instruction, 264; POS function, 266–273; SEG$ function, 265–266; VAL function, 275–277

String variables, 25–26, 269, 320
Structured programming, 66–85; exit program statement in, 73–74; flow charts in, 82–84; modules in, 66, 69–70; subroutines in, 70–73; top-down analysis in, 66–69
Subprograms, 89–93; arguments and, 89, 90; error trapping in, 259–261; parameters and, 89, 90–93
Subroutines, 69, 70–73; GOSUB, 70–73; labels and, 70, 71
Subscripts, 186–187
Substring, searching for, 266–273
Subtraction, 46
Summing, 98–102
Symbol(s): annotation, 83–84; for Boolean operators, 104; for conditional statements, 156–160; flow chart, 57–59; for loops, 121–122; for relational operators, 102, 104
Symbolic addresses, 23–27
Symbolic names, 23
System functions, 365–366

TAB function, 36–37, 361
TAN function, 359
Tape drives, 20, 21
Temporary PRINT statements, 169–170
Temporary variable, 199
Terminal, 20–21
Terminal-format files, 225–245; closing, 232; defined, 227; examples of, 233–244; input/output with, 231–232; opening, 227–231; PRINT USING for, 330
Terminators, 57
THEN GOTO, 414
Three-dimensional array, 186
TIME function, 365–366
TIME$ function, 365
Time-sharing system, 21
Top-down analysis, 66–69
TRM$ function, 364
TRN function, 364–365
Two-dimensional arrays, 295–318; calculating with, 299–306; defined, 186, 296; dimensioning, 296–297, 312–318; loops and, 297–298, 299; printing, 298–299; reading, 297–298

UNTIL loop, 108
UPDATE statement, 342–349
User ID, 3
User-defined functions, 377–401; multi-line, 388–392; one-line,

378–380; rules governing, 392–395

VAL function, 275–277, 363
Value(s): final, 96; initial, 96; reading into arrays, 189–191, 194
Variable(s), 23; built-in, 178, 179, 252–253, 259–260; DECIMAL, 26–27; floating point, 24; global, 385–388; integer, 25, 30; loop, 96; NUM, 217–219; simple, 185; string, 25–26, 269, 320; temporary, 199
Variable dimensioning: one-dimensional arrays, 216–224; two-dimensional arrays, 312–318
Version, 6
Virtual array files, 227
VMS: changing to BASIC, 8; environment, 3–9; file management in, 5–8; HELP in, 8; returning to from BASIC, 8–9

WHILE loop, 104–108
Wild card, 6, 7

ZER function, 365
Zero-based array, 187, 296
Zero'th element, 186

VAX-BASIC REFERENCE CARD

Below are examples of VAX-BASIC statements.
All examples are given without line numbers.

Arrays

```
DECLARE INTEGER Counts(100), &
        REAL    Sales(50,12), &
        STRING  ID(20,2)
MAT READ Counts
MAT INPUT Sales
MAT PRINT ID
MAT INPUT #1, Counts
MAT PRINT #2, Sales
```

Assignment Statements

```
Result = (A + B + C - SMALLEST) / 2
```

Conditional Statements

```
IF A>B THEN ... END IF
IF A>B THEN ... ELSE ... END IF
SELECT A+B
     CASE 1, 2, 7 TO 10    \ ...
     CASE >30              \ ...
     CASE ELSE             \ ...
END SELECT
```

Declare Statement

```
DECLARE INTEGER I, J, K, &
        REAL    X, Y, &
        STRING  Name_, Address, &
        DECIMAL(8,2) Salary, Tax
```

Debugging

```
STOP
CONT
```

End of main program

```
EXIT PROGRAM
```

End of program

```
END
```

Error Trapping

```
ON ERROR GOTO Error_routine
ON ERROR GOTO 0
ON ERROR GO BACK
RESUME
RESUME 2550
ERR   (Error number)
ERL   (Error line)
ERT$  (Error text)
ERN$  (Error module name)
```

External Functions

```
EXTERNAL REAL Avg (INTEGER DIM ())
FUNCTION REAL Avg (INTEGER DIM ())
EXIT FUNCTION
END FUNCTION
```

Loops

```
FOR I = 1 TO 100 STEP 2       \ ... \ NEXT I
FOR J = 100 TO 1 STEP -2      \ ... \ NEXT J
WHILE A > B AND C < 0         \ ... \ NEXT
UNTIL A+B>10 OR Name_="XXXX"  \ ... \ NEXT
```

Predefined Constants

```
BEL   7    Bell
BS    8    Backspace
HT    9    Horizontal Tab
LF    10   Line Feed
VT    11   Vertical Tab
FF    12   Form Feed
CR    13   Carriage Return
ESC   27   Escape
SP    32   Space
PI         Pi = 3.14159
```

Print Using

```
PRINT USING String_, A, B, C
PRINT #2 USING "##.##", X
    '     Single character
    'L    left justify
    'R    Right justify
    'C    Center justify
    'E    Extended field
    #     Digit
    .     Place decimal point
    ,     Comma every third digit
    $$    Floating dollar sign
    **    Asterisk fill
```

(continued on back)

Random number generator

```
RANDOM
Number = RND
Card = INT (13 * RND + 1)
```

READ and DATA

```
READ A, B, C
DATA 10, 20, 30
```

Relational and Logical Operators

```
<, <=, >, >=, =, <>
NOT, AND, OR
```

Relative Files

```
MAP (Fields) INTEGER A, B, REAL
 Avgs (100)
OPEN "FILE.IN" FOR INPUT AS FILE
 #1, RELATIVE, MAP Fields
GET #1
GET #1, RECORD 10
UPDATE #1
PUT #2
PUT #2, RECORD 10
CLOSE #1, #2
```

String Processing

```
LINPUT "Enter data", STR_1, STR_2
String_1 + String_2
LEN (String_)
POS (String_, "and", 5)
SEG$ (String_, 5, 10)
EDIT$ (String_, 32)
       1 Clear bit 0
       2 Discard spaces and tabs
       4 Discard CR, LF, FF, nulls
       8 Discard leading spaces
         and tabs
      16 Convert multiple spaces
         to single
      32 Convert lower to upper
         case
      64 Convert brackets to
         parentheses
     128 Discard trailing spaces
         and tabs
     256 Suppress editing on
         literal strings
```

Subprograms

```
CALL Routine (A, B, C)
SUB Routine (REAL X, REAL Y, REAL Z)
EXIT SUB
END SUB
```

Subroutines

```
GOSUB Calculate
RETURN
```

Terminal I/O

```
INPUT "Enter numbers"; A, B, C
PRINT "The numbers are:"; A, B, C
MARGIN 80
MARGIN 0
```

Terminal-Format Files

```
OPEN "DATA.IN" FOR INPUT AS FILE #1
OPEN Out_file FOR OUTPUT AS FILE #2
INPUT #1, A, B, C
PRINT #2, A, B, C
LINPUT #1, Str_1, Str_2
CLOSE #1, #2
MARGIN #1, #2
MARGIN #1, 132
MARGIN #1, 0
```

User-Defined Functions

```
DECLARE STRING Grade (INTEGER)
DEF REAL Hypotenuse (REAL A, REAL
 B) = SQR (A^2 +^B2)
DEF STRING Grade (INTEGER Avg)
END DEF
```

SUMMARY OF COMMANDS

Here is a summary of commands used in the VMS environment.

SET PASS	Change the password
LOG	Logoff command
DIR	Directory listing of files in account
DEL	Delete file from account
RENAME	Rename a file in account
PURGE	Delete old versions of files from account
BASIC	Enter BASIC environment

Here is a summary of commands used in the BASIC environment.

EXIT	Return to VMS
NEW	Create new program
OLD	Retrieve old program from account
REPLACE	Save a program to account
RENAME	Rename program in memory
RUN, RUNNH	Run a program
LIST	List program in memory
EDIT	Edit a line, or enter editor environment

Copyright © 1988 West Publishing Company